CASTLE
ON A HILL

CASTLE ON A HILL

THE VISEGRAD GROUP, REGIONALISM, AND THE REMAKING OF EUROPE

RICK FAWN

GEORGETOWN UNIVERSITY PRESS / WASHINGTON, DC

The publisher is not responsible for third-party websites or their content. URL links were active at time of publication.

Library of Congress Cataloging-in-Publication Data

Names: Fawn, Rick, author.
Title: Castle on a hill : the Visegrad Group, regionalism, and the remaking of Europe / Rick Fawn.
Description: Washington, DC : Georgetown University Press, 2024. | Includes bibliographical references and index.
Identifiers: LCCN 2024011597 (print) | LCCN 2024011598 (ebook) | ISBN 9781647125059 (hardcover) | ISBN 9781647125066 (paperback) | ISBN 9781647125073 (ebook)
Subjects: LCSH: Visegrád Group. | Regionalism—Europe, Central. | Security, International—Europe, Central. | Security, International—European Union countries. | Europe, Central—Relations—European Union countries. | European Union countries—Relations—Europe, Central.
Classification: LCC JN96.A38 R4333 2024 (print) | LCC JN96.A38 (ebook) | DDC 320.540943—dc23/eng/20240408
LC record available at https://lccn.loc.gov/2024011597
LC ebook record available at https://lccn.loc.gov/2024011598

25 24   9 8 7 6 5 4 3 2 First printing

Cover design by Pamela Pease
Cover image courtesy of Airpixel Drone Imagery / Shutterstock.com
Interior design by BookComp, Inc.

CONTENTS

ILLUSTRATIONS

TABLES

FIGURES

INTRODUCTION

A current search for "Visegrad" among publications produces results as variegated as the following examples:

- quality of life in patients with diabetic foot ulcer in Visegrad countries
- parental leave in Visegrad countries
- the elderly's subjective well-being in the Visegrad group
- physical activity and body-mass-index relation in students of the Visegrad region
- indoor radon in Visegrad countries
- spatial price transmission of milk prices in Visegrad countries
- board-level employee representation in Visegrad countries

The "Visegrad" that now appears ubiquitously did not exist in 1989, the year in which communist regimes toppled. Barely a year later, from February 1991 onward, Visegrad materialized as the name for the new interstate cooperation of Czechoslovakia, Hungary, and Poland and from 1993 as four countries, with the Czech Republic and Slovakia. Visegrad became shorthand for an official yet flexible format for diplomatic interactions among these states and allowed them to pursue together core foreign policy aims in European and international forums. More than that, as the publications above suggest, Visegrad has also become a recognizable name for diverse communities—including those working on foot ulcers, indoor radon, milk prices, body-mass indexes—and for much more. In a surprising marketing success, a region that possessed no definition acquired one in the minds of a broad international public.

True, when spelled "Visegrád," it exists as a place-name north of Budapest. But even as that, Hungary's smallest town was familiar probably only to determined medievalists and a few, fortunate tourists.[1] True, there is also "Višegrad," with a different diacritic but pronounced similarly. The first Visegrád, in Hungary, became the site in 1991 for launching a project to transcend histories of hatred; only a year later, and but 550 kilometers, or 350 miles, south, Višegrad, in Bosnia, became the site at which the International Criminal Tribunal for the former Yugoslavia determined that 1,600 Bosnian-Muslim civilians, half of them women and children, were massacred.

"Visegrád" versus "Višegrad" are two inflections of the same name, pointing glaringly to two contrasting histories: one of humanist diplomacy, the other of systematized mass murder. These differences say much of the disjunctures and possibilities for framing cooperation among peoples and states. The anglicized version of the first "Visegrad," as the four-state cooperation officially spells itself, became in months not just a new interstate diplomatic formation but a contributor to the refashioning of regional identity. That identity was intended to recast its neighborhood's history from one of distrust and open conflict to that, at a minimum, of mutual tolerance and understanding. It did so for its own sake. It did so for the West's sake, in order to renovate Western thinking about these post-communist countries and ultimately to lever open for membership the shut doors of North Atlantic Treaty Organization (NATO) and the European Union (EU) and fulfill an existential belief that these Visegrad countries were returning after decades of Soviet-enforced captivity to where they geoculturally belong. In that process Visegrad also helped fundamentally to change the post–Cold War European and even international order. After all, nothing has transformed the political and security dynamics of the northern hemisphere more than the enlargement eastward of those two colossal intergovernmental organizations.

Once all Visegrad countries had achieved Euro-Atlantic memberships by 2004, few expected Visegrad to continue. Few, that is, other than the far-sighted drivers of Visegrad itself. For Visegrad reinvented itself within the EU and helped to shape both its internal and its external agendas. And Visegrad resourcefully found ways to lead other countries, both post-communist and older established market economies, to undertake newer agenda items. But by 2015 Visegrad had soared to unprecedented European and international fame—for successfully countering the European Commission, supported especially by France and Germany, in demanding mandatory settlement in its countries of some of the hundreds of thousands of migrants that swelled into the EU that year. And still after that Visegrad has found other roles, including collaborative defense initiatives and being a military-political bridge between NATO and the EU.

This book asks how and why Visegrad arose, determines what it achieved, and accounts for its limitations and failures. Chapter 1 shows the unlikelihood of this interstate cooperation and the many obstacles with which it contended. The second chapter determines how Visegrad arose when it did, in February

1991, and demonstrates that it massaged and manipulated, albeit positively, selective pieces of history to generate a convincing story of itself. Historical recasting served both itself and its would-be new partners in the West. That chapter, too, identifies how quickly Visegrad became a known entity and with such success that it provoked envy from those excluded. Lessons from state cooperation are richer when not all goes well. Chapter 3 concerns Visegrad's collapse and not just with the reasons for that breakdown but also that determining exactly when and how we know it died is complex.

Chapter 4 accounts for the Group's resurrection in late 1998 and early 1999, and the robust program this rejuvenated interstate cooperation proclaimed. Among its aims was to ensure that Slovakia, which for internal political reasons had exited the Group, would join the three in NATO. All four sought EU membership. Chapter 5 therefore branches out into the debates on EU and NATO enlargement and determines the roles that Visegrad had in making those accessions possible. The chapter also tackles some otherwise significant literature that, wrongly, ignored Visegrad in these major processes. Chapter 6 shows how Visegrad disproved detractors who expected nothing of the Group once the paramount aims of Euro-Atlantic accession were achieved. Far from losing purpose, Visegrad progressed to find roles especially in the EU. Chapter 7, however, analyzes how and at what costs Visegrad became to be perceived as trouble making in the EU, when in 2015 and 2016 the Group stopped the mandatory settlement of migrants in member states. In that process, however, Visegrad gained its greatest notoriety, and seemed to replace its carefully constructed early history as a liberal-humanist project with the advocacy of intolerance and exclusion.

Chapter 8 illustrates more of Visegrad's ambitions. It assesses how Visegrad dealt with Ukraine, already an important partner since 1991, when both emerged into the new post–Cold War order and how Ukraine gave Visegrad added importance after Russian aggression started in 2014. Chapter 8 also investigates Visegrad's diplomatic efforts beyond Europe and in military cooperation, finding in both cases, however, that Visegrad has unnecessarily overstretched itself. Chapter 9 concludes with thirteen wider lessons from Visegrad's experiences for understanding the worldwide phenomenon of regional cooperation and of making regions.

A few words on the genesis of this work may give context to its aims. The book grew from a related but distinct work undertaken, alas, far back but auspiciously in the early 1990s. That study addressed how those, especially in then Czechoslovakia, who had resisted and suffered communist rule for years, were suddenly catapulted to power in late 1989 and how they then sought to make new, transformative foreign policies. What became Visegrad was part of a series of those foreign policy experiments. By the time that study was concluded, in the mid-1990s, Czechoslovakia had disappeared, and Visegrad was effectively dead, too. Or so one might have thought.

What that timing in the early and mid-1990s provided was, first, the opportunity to observe foreign policy activities and to engage with former dissidents, new policymakers, and domestic and foreign analysts and practitioners through observation and also interviewing. None of that is of course replicable. The second was the opportunity for continued observation of Visegrad, from its inception and initial growth, and its subsequent growth, early demise, and from thereafter, and through what is now a multidecade history. From that early observation came the thought that the Visegrad cooperation retained some quiet but essential support—support that would reignite it a few years later, allow it to institutionalize (though it officially claims otherwise) and sustain itself thereafter, even and especially in the face of later, different challenges. One person or perspective is unlikely to capture a totality of any process, not least one involving many people and institutions but hopefully some benefits are reflected here from a view spanning Visegrad's now-considerable lifespan.

That said, important too is to demarcate what this present work is not: a history of the region's *non*-cooperation or of the forced cooperation—and each of those exceeded genuine, organic cooperation. Some may expect that here. But voluminous literature already exists on how these countries before 1945 often failed to cooperate, even and especially when such fulfilled their interests and, worse, some aligned with extraregional powers to harm others. Still more literature exists on the Moscow-run "regional" institutions that followed from 1949 and 1955 and that both lasted to 1991, when Visegrad pushed to end them: the Council for Mutual Economic Assistance (CMEA) and the Warsaw Treaty Organization. Little more need here be said, other than the former might have generated some gains but was overwhelmingly categorized as the antithesis of a genuine common market, instead spreading inefficiency and misery. The latter, known better in the West as the Warsaw Pact, authenticated its coercive nature by becoming history's only military alliance to attack itself, when in August 1968 five members—the Soviet Union, Bulgaria, East Germany, Hungary, and Poland—assaulted a sixth, Czechoslovakia.

Nor is this a survey of past hopes for a positive, inclusive regional order. Of those, there were certainly some. This is a region where aspirations of not just amicable but genuinely mutual, nonthreatening, and productive relations failed to transcend the aspirational. Recounting those unanswered efforts brings us little further in our understanding of the region, in addition to, importantly, reiterating the considerable legacies of negative experience that Visegrad faced in attempting a new era of regional diplomacy.

What gains our focus hereafter stems from the time before 1989 under communist rule in Eastern Europe, when aspirational thinking developed but was taken even less seriously than its many stillborn predecessors. Those were the ideas developed, amid arduous political and physical circumstances before 1989, by the handful of free-thinking intellectuals, or dissidents, a term they tended not to use, or even disliked, but by which they nevertheless came to be called, especially internationally.

Those ideas and inspirations underpin the first chapter. Before that, a note on language is appropriate for approaches to the subject of Visegrad. Visegrad's working language is English, even if its founding Declaration was not written in that language but rather, in each of Czech (but not Slovak), Hungarian, and Polish. On one level, using only English might now be legitimate, and perchance adequate, when assessing Visegrad. And the Visegrad region enjoys a rich, robust scholarly and research / think tank community, dare one say, that not only is dynamically conversant in regional matters but also in international scholarship and approaches. The expanse of regional publications on Visegrad prevents citation of all. A celebratory bibliography published for Visegrad's twentieth anniversary in 2011 included more than a thousand titles.[2] Many major events, policy and scholarly, regarding Visegrad are conducted and published in English, even when primary contributors and consumers are from the Visegrad countries.

To focus, however, only on resources available in English is to miss the rich strata of material in the regional languages. Visegrad grew out of domestic interests in these countries, and those interests have fluctuated from being supportive of the Group to redirecting its activities, and even to its derailment. Those factors become evident through knowledge of languages and countries, which generate differences in information, understanding, and ultimately in conclusions. Understanding Visegrad requires four regional languages, and more, if those of its major interlocutors are added. A personal admission is that the greatest language ability and accessibility for dealing with this study has been Czech, imperfect Slovak, and some Polish, and two extraregional languages (French and Russian). To those the author admits the lack of Hungarian. That omission was compensated by conducting, beyond Czechoslovakia, both the earliest and the most frequent of considerable interviews with Hungarian policymakers. Those people are the first to receive acknowledgment in the substantial list of them, at the end of the book. First, we proceed to how the Visegrad project came to exist.

NOTES

1. "Welcome of the Major of Visegrad!," August 20, 2009, printout retained.
2. International Visegrad Fund.

1

VISEGRAD'S REAL BUT TENTATIVE FOUNDATIONS

THE EARLY 1990S

What became Visegrad in the early 1990s was, in the 1980s, nascent already in the minds of some intellectuals and activists who thought outside the strait-jacket of official communist ideology. The discussions and writings of those independent thinkers, or dissidents, were understandably foremost about domestic political matters—analyzing the power structures of socialist regimes and offering truth against the regimes' deceit.

Nevertheless, dissidents in especially Czechoslovakia and Poland also labored in arduous circumstances to establish and retain contact with each other and to offer solidarity in the face of persecution. Czechoslovakia's Václav Havel's tract "The Power of the Powerless," which in a few pages metaphorically grasped communist control better than some scholarly works, was dedicated to clandestine cooperation between activists in his country and Poland.[1]

Dissidents occasionally addressed both regional and international matters of foreign policy and security. Havel's close friend Jiří Dienstbier composed essays before 1989 on such topics, translated indicatively as *Dreaming about Europe*. He could not get the typescript published in the West before 1989, because of lack of interest in such seeming fantasies, nor after 1989, when those validated contents were superseded by events.[2] Nevertheless, and better still, his and other communist-era covert thinking and activism had gained unimaginable salience.

After the 1989 revolutions several dissidents were thrust into high office, becoming foreign policy architects. Others developed into, or continued to be, significant public figures. They would expressly refer to and tangibly build upon their dissident-era cooperation and discussions in what became the final years of communist rule. Part of those pre-1989 deliberations concerned the meaning and the geocultural place of their region in the challenging confines of the dangerous, adversarial, and highly armed Cold War international system, one that also denied these countries the ability to craft their own foreign policy.

As peaceful and even poetic were the negotiated revolutions in Warsaw, Budapest, and Prague in 1989, revolutions themselves create no new policy, let alone regional cooperation. Never had all of these countries willingly cooperated; the legacies were of distrust and animosity. Post-1989 Central Europe also faced extraordinary superstructures of Muscovite regional control through the institutions of the misleadingly named Council for Mutual Economic Assistance, and the Warsaw Treaty Organization.

Against overwhelming circumstances, four conditions were necessary to galvanize the thoughts and sentiments of those who had never held public office, these in times of unprecedented and uncertain international reordering into what became Visegrad:

1. a driving dissident intellectual imagination;
2. further political leadership changes that could allow those imaginations to work;
3. shocks external to the region, emanating from the Soviet Union; and
4. a hegemonic vacuum from the indifference of NATO and the European Communities[3] / European Union (EU).

Each of these factors are considered in turn.

DRIVING DISSIDENT INTELLECTUAL IMAGINATIONS

December 29, 1989. Dissident-playwright Václav Havel, who had spent over four years in communist prisons, looked at a television. He wore a tie and perhaps an ironed white shirt, certainly one that was uncreased. And he smoked. He watched Czechoslovakia's communist-controlled federal parliament—the same institution responsible for "laws" that had had him imprisoned—elect him the country's president.

Though called the "reluctant president,"[4] Havel embraced the duties of office. He dedicated his first presidential foreign visits to neighbors. He broke with bipolar Cold War thinking by postponing trips to Washington, DC, or Moscow, though those came soon too. Rather, he made his first presidential diplomatic overtures to Germany, Poland, and Hungary, demonstrating his commitment to reshaping the emergent post–Cold War regional dynamics.[5]

In January 1990 Havel addressed the Polish and Hungarian Parliaments, calling for his and their countries to work together to achieve a transformative foreign policy goal: returning their region to the West. He expressly referred to communist-era mutual support of these populations. He meant politically independent intellectuals and activists like himself. In Warsaw, he reminded those gathered, who included communists who had persecuted dissidents under the previous regimes, that Czechoslovaks and Poles had met secretly in the later 1970s in the mountains bordering their countries. He called on them to translate that spirit into action in their new postrevolution political circumstances.[6] Havel announced, "Very soon, I would like to invite various representatives of the state and the public from Poland and Hungary, perhaps with observers from other Central European countries, to a meeting in the Bratislava Castle."[7]

Within weeks Czechoslovak, Polish, and Hungarian delegations assembled in that castle. The foreign ministers of Austria, Italy, and Yugoslavia attended also, even if only as observers. Havel had said in January 1990 that he imagined such a meeting to be a day when regional leaders could "quietly" talk "about current matters." Doing so, he thought, might "again make us somewhat wiser."[8] An era of atypical regional cooperation began. Not out of obligation or compulsion and without intentions of aligning themselves against others, these countries assembled willingly.

Havel's appeal to being "somewhat wiser" was laudable; necessary too were practical measures to convene such an event and by people who were not only new to high office but also lacked any diplomatic experience. Enacting new foreign policy is challenging; after the revolutions, this was even more so. The foreign ministries of all three countries were fully staffed by communist-era appointees. In multiple interviews, particularly regarding Czechoslovakia, former dissidents who became foreign policy policymakers after 1989 lamented the difficulties of working with communist-era appointees, who, if no longer in senior-most positions, still crowded the ministries. Returning émigré Petr Skalník wrote, "Practically all Czechoslovak diplomats and support personnel were members of the Communist party, many were known to be agents or informants" and that they could even still be "subservient to the Soviet secret services."[9] Irrespective of staffing issues, Dienstbier came abruptly into office only in December 1989, while his Polish counterparts had benefitted from a running start of a few months since the exchange of power that June.[10]

The difficulties of initiating new foreign policy in the testing period of regime change, with its unknown future, must not be overlooked. At many points basic protocol and even information sharing disrupted the conduct of diplomacy. So too did even physically arranging meetings. That said, preparations for the regional meeting gained momentum, involving a series of "working visits with very intensive debates" through which common foreign policy interests among the three countries were determined; Havel considered Bratislava the logical next phase for their advancement.[11]

Once convened in April, the Bratislava Process, as it was sometimes called, generated no outcomes. True, Havel set low expectations in January, saying that he wanted his invitees only "to spend a day quietly talking about these matters" arising from Europe's seismic political changes. But even that much proved too much. Political change and organization determined why.

Progress at Havel's Bratislava meeting was hampered by the types of representatives sent in what was still a transformative political time. Havel knew this, astutely saying that he wanted not only officials but others to attend. "Others" included, of all people, communist general Wojciech Jaruzelski, the head of Poland's delegation. Jaruzelski had overseen the imposition of martial law to crush the Polish Solidarity movement in 1980–81. Lech Wałęsa, hero of the Gdánsk shipyard strikes that ignited Solidarity, was elected president only after a second round of voting in December 1990.

Communists also led the Hungarian delegation, though they might have been the most reform-minded of the Soviet bloc. They had just been defeated in that country's first free elections. So unmemorable were some of these envoys that former Czech dissident and post-1989 foreign policy adviser Alexandr Vondra wrote that a Hungarian communist in attendance had quite simply vanished from his mind.[12] Rudolf Tőkés called Hungarian foreign minister Gyula Horn the "born-again democrat" who said less than his Italian and Austrian counterparts.[13] That aside, the Hungarian delegation arrived intent on addressing bilateral matters—foremost and predominantly the status of Hungarian minorities in Slovakia. The Czechoslovaks refused to discuss that, saying the meeting was concerned with regional, that is, multilateral matters. The Hungarians, perhaps still too communist and less mindful of international human rights than was Havel, objected that the Czechoslovak president raised Tibet's treatment in China as one of his opening questions. Quite apart from disagreement on contents, Horn also contributed nothing at the final press conference, he and his delegation having already departed.[14] And that early departure was unrelated to their objection that the Czechoslovak hosts had tried to get a communiqué agreed on for that press conference.

Horn had become known in the West in an iconic photograph of him cutting the barbed wire along the Austrian-Hungarian border in 1989 with his Austrian counterpart,[15] Alois Mock, who was also in attendance at Bratislava. Horn was nevertheless a transitional figure at this point. His career history was similar to Jaruzelski's, in forcibly ending dissent, when he had aided the Hungarian militia in crushing Hungary's 1956 uprising. A later US ambassador to Budapest, Donald Blinken, branded the episode "a black mark against him."[16] Such history put Horn at odds with a gathering of dissidents, even though he became foreign minister on May 10, 1989, amid unprecedented change in the communist bloc. Under a year later, he was no longer in that office. His departure was indicative of the need for further leadership change in the region. And change continued: Horn would return in July 1994 and for four years serve as Hungarian prime minister. In that period, and accustomed now to democratic politics, he would oversee policies that intended to ease some tensions between Slovakia and his country.[17]

The observer states of Austria, Italy, and Yugoslavia had their own interests in encouraging regional cooperation. At Bratislava, however, they duly remained quiet. Italy especially had already launched an initiative, on November 11, 1989, just two days after the Berlin Wall and other East German border crossings had been opened. Rome's enterprising foreign minister Gianni De Michelis assembled representatives of Austria, Hungary, and Yugoslavia to build upon what had previously only been meetings of substate, not national, governments.

The mixed pedigrees of political leadership—of old communists and their dissident-democratic detractors—and their varying interests and ambitions did not make the April 1990 meeting fundamentally difficult. One might think that both non-communist Poles who had suffered directly under Jaruzelski's military crackdown and the Czechoslovaks who could remember that he had also commanded Polish troops that contributed to the liquidation of Czechoslovakia's 1968 reformist experiment could have created a challenging environment for the region's very first attempt at genuine multilateral discussions. But humanist Havel stated in January 1990 that that legacy "did not prevent my very frank and intensive talks with him." That was surely partly because, even as Havel noted, Jaruzelski acknowledged frequently the 1968 intervention and apologized for his actions. Havel, characteristic of his ethos of apology and forgiveness and one that he would apply even to his foreign policy,[18] in turn replied that "it is the future rather than the past with which we have to be concerned."[19] And for his part, Jaruzelski had hosted Havel in Warsaw in January 1990, even if having done so "stone-faced."[20] Thereafter Jaruzelski made comments in support of regional and pan-European cooperation that could easily have come from Havel: "We have to contribute to the creation of a new Europe and not to create the syndrome of late-comers." Indeed, Jaruzelski rhetorically encouraged the region's return to Europe and urged the countries not to compete against each other in that process. These were entirely apposite words.[21] Nevertheless, observers asserted that Jaruzelski's background complicated matters. Vondra stated that from "sour smiles" on faces of the former Polish dissidents it appeared they wished for him not to represent them.[22] Ironically, personality tensions seemed greatest between former dissidents, notably between Havel and Wałęsa, the latter known to have resented the fact that after all of his struggles, he was not Poland's president.

Issues of political backgrounds and personalities aside, merely organizing the event proved trying, as key Czechs later conceded.[23] When Havel announced the idea for the Bratislava Summit, he called it "symbolic," presumably of a new regional beginning and of the ability to sit and to discuss freely. And so the meeting was to be, but as a hastily arranged affair. Fellow former Czech dissident Jan Urban, surely supportive of Havel, called the meeting the worst organized that he had seen. Vondra, who as a Czechoslovak dissident advanced the Prague Appeal of 1985 that prophetically called for German unification, confessed that his fellow Czechoslovak organizers did "less than a stellar job."[24] Jaroslav Šedivý, another former Czech dissident who contributed to postrevolution Czechoslovak foreign policy, called the meeting unsuccessful and recalled the embarrassment expressed by all parties.[25] Region-based secondary accounts recorded that the meeting "ended in bewilderment."[26] Before that, Havel commenced his address to the assembled dignitaries of six states by acknowledging "how complicated it was for you to arrange to meet here."[27] He also conceded months after, in advance of the Visegrad meeting in February 1991, that its Bratislava prequel "was marked by improvisation. It was characterized by speedy preparation," and he acknowledged, "We did not really have enough experience in the organization of such a meeting."[28]

Over two decades later, Havel explained that the meeting was convened partly because many of those present were unknown to each other and had come to power through varying paths. The organizers, Havel confessed, did not know what kind of relationship they might have with one another.[29]

External assessors critiqued the meeting harshly. Tőkés lamented that "the host country did not have much of an agenda."[30] But we must not lose sight that Bratislava was the first attempt at new entries on a blank page of diplomatic record. The communist states were run by functionaries who had previously, and strictly, operated under Moscow-devised regional agendas. The new heads of the Czechoslovak Foreign Ministry held preparatory meetings in advance of Bratislava but indeed did not generate a formal agenda. And Havel and his foreign minister had advised in advance that they wanted that meeting to encourage open discussion and free thinking. Consequently, Havel opened the gathering not with even an informal program but with ten largely philosophical questions. That style was perhaps more typical of him, and certainly in his first few months he took an unconventional approach to foreign policy and to public events generally.[31]

Not all present took well to the unconventional Czechoslovak approach. Czechoslovak media reported of Hungary's interim president Mátyás Szűrös that he considered the meeting to have had an "ample menu of issues [that] was a little too much"—a stinging if unstated reference to Havel's opening questions. Worse still, Szűrös "harped on" about the absence of time for bilateral issues, demonstrating again that the transitional Hungarian figures had not grasped the essence of this particular type of meeting.[32]

Even before the pathbreaking Bratislava meeting was convened, Dienstbier, perhaps anticipating criticism, called it a "brainstorming session." It was, he said, a summit intentionally without specific ideas and at which "everyone should be able to say what he wants behind closed doors." The emphasis was on fomenting new ideas, some of which he thought could be readily actionable.[33] Lack of agendas were corrigible, and Dienstbier later wrote that the founding Visegrad meeting, convened only seven months after Bratislava, was specifically designed to resolve concrete matters.[34]

And brainstorming has a place in extemporized diplomacy—in this case an essential one, despite the many criticisms. Other diplomatic practitioners affirmed that what the Bratislava organizers undertook was hardly an everyday initiative and was even remarkable. Dienstbier gave appropriate recognition retrospectively of the 1990 meeting (just as it was renewing itself nearly a decade later) when he recorded that "Havel launched an official dialogue of the Central European countries."[35] Czechoslovakia's Michal Žantovský, a former dissident and close friend of Havel who served as his presidential spokesman, went further: he credited the April 1990 meeting with having "conceived" the Visegrad idea, which was "delivered on the Hungarian banks of the Danube River nine months later."[36] Havel's Bratislava meeting, in Žantovský's metaphoric thinking, gestated Visegrad. Historical claims to the genesis and later importance of Bratislava are not simply a particular Czechoslovak/Czech/Slovak matter. The first Czech Visegrad presidency report (i.e., both the first Visegrad presidency report and consequently also the first by the Czechs), which was issued in 2000, expressly stated, "Four summits were held in the V3 format: in April 1990 (Bratislava), February 1991 (Visegrad), October 1991 (Cracow) and in May 1992 (Prague)."[37] Better yet, the Declaration that launched Visegrad in February 1991 also referred back to the Bratislava meeting in April 1990. Bratislava then was being deemed a "Visegrad Summit" before Visegrad even existed and was being credited officially as this regional cooperation's commencement. These initiatives were both a historical break from the region's turbulent history, one riddled with mistrust and betrayals, and also the only case across Europe where post-communist countries initiated and drove cooperation themselves.[38] Elsewhere, for example, Germans and Danes teamed up to launch the Council of the Baltic Sea States, Italy led what became the Central European Initiative (CEI), and Turkey steered the Black Sea Economic Cooperation.

The achievement of Bratislava deserves elaboration and credit to the Czechoslovaks. The summit was organized with their Foreign Ministry still in confusion.[39] Considering the region's postrevolution situation, the fact of the meeting was a significant achievement. Poland's dissident-era newspaper editor and activist Adam Michnik, for decades a towering figure among regional intelligentsias, recognized the gathering's "improvisation and stop-gaps, poorly prepared discussions, and misunderstandings." He acknowledged that "nothing actually happened" but similarly displayed realism, calling the meeting "what any beginning of a long road looks like." That such a meeting finally happened, he concluded, was important in itself and portended that "something new and significant was being born."[40] For a note of historical context that also signals the region's discordant relations, Slovak premier Milan Čič's opening remarks stated that no significant regional meeting had occurred in Bratislava since the signing of the Treaty of Pressburg (the then Germanic name for Bratislava), by Napoleon and Holy Roman Emperor Francis II, in 1805, following French defeat of the Russian and Austrian empires.[41]

Central European states had limited experience engaging in cooperation genuinely of their own initiative and making, and certainly not on an inclusive basis. Slovak representatives continue to recognize the importance of the April 1990 meeting in Bratislava, particularly as Visegrad's inception. Slovak diplomats remind that the Bratislava meeting three months earlier was the start of the whole cooperation and affirm that the formative dates of Visegrad's foundation should include the 1900 Bratislava meeting, even and perhaps especially, as Bratislava, again in 2011, is otherwise taken as the twentieth anniversary of the cooperation.[42] Visegrad would also be relaunched in 1999 and once more, intentionally for the symbolism, in Bratislava.[43]

The Slovak-specific presence in and contributions to the April 1990 assembly are also overlooked. The plenary session of the April 1990 meeting was opened not by Havel, who spoke second, but by Slovak premier Čič.[44] This diplomatic representation of Slovakia within the Czech and Slovak Federation, however, remains overlooked, even as its advocates assert this distinct Slovak contribution to Visegrad. If confirmation of Bratislava's rightful place in Visegrad's history were needed, no better a source is the Group's founding Declaration, which refers to it in its third and fourth opening words.

However the Bratislava meeting may be judged, it unquestionably achieved what its hosts intended: acquainting new regional political actors with each other and establishing the familiarity and networks for subsequent consultations. Trilateral meetings of military, economic, and political officials in 1990 and 1991 testified to that. Those meetings also created channels for a later meeting, in February 1991, and one with an agenda. The three presidents and other senior officials from each country convened for what was formally called a summit and which produced its original Declaration. This would be the birth of Visegrad. But for Visegrad to be born, much else had to occur. That included a more thorough change in leaderships across the region, a transformative process that can be called foreign policy "refolution."

FOREIGN POLICY REFOLUTION
AND REGIONAL COOPERATION

The importance of former dissidents to regional cooperation can be seen in the failure of the first initiative at Bratislava to produce concrete results.[45] An adaptation is helpful here of Timothy Garton Ash's term "refolution," devised from observations of the political transformations particularly in late-communist Poland and Hungary.[46] Those changes came as the result of reform from above—the "ref" of refolution—and revolutionary pressure from below.

Refolution accounts for the indeterminacy, even contrarianism, in the earliest Central European foreign policy after the 1989 revolutions. The communists in attendance at Bratislava in April 1990 still retained important posts in Poland and Hungary, and many had limited interest, and perhaps little ideological capacity, to contemplate foreign policy cooperation with ex-dissidents. Such activities were numbed until that old guard was replaced by more ex-dissidents, as happened in the course of 1990. As seen above, Havel, already in the role of statesman, welcomed Jaruzelski warmly to Bratislava in April 1990. Havel had spoken of politics and diplomacy being foremost a matter of etiquette, even of good taste, and perhaps out of such values acted graciously to a nemesis.

That graciousness was not shared even by some of his fellow former dissidents, who wished not to be represented by communists. And while the titans of dissident, Wałęsa and Havel, interacted poorly on a personal level,[47] the former's replacement of Jaruzelski as Poland's president was important for progress.

April 1990 was also an atypical diplomatic meeting for its inclusion of non-officials, a measure on the part of the Czechoslovak organizers to ensure inclusion of those in civil society who were essential to their countries but held no public office. Havel explained this hybrid arrangement: "Some of us here, public servants in Poland, Hungary, and Czechoslovakia, hold high state office; others will perhaps hold them after us. Because we are interested in the future of our nations and states and not in personal political prospects, this brutal assault on the usual diplomatic protocol will not bother us."[48]

With dry understatement, Dienstbier elaborated that Havel additionally invited "some citizens from Poland and Hungary, active in public life."[49] In that regard the meeting was even more notable. Vondra reminisced that "almost everyone who meant something in the Central European discourse was there."[50] "Some citizens" included intellectual luminaries like Michnik (who, while immensely influential, did not seek public office after 1989), and of course Lech Wałęsa.[51]

The inclusion of so many different officeholders, political pedigrees, and personalities, however, also caused friction.[52] The worst was between Havel and Wałęsa, rather than between the dissident-absurdist-playwright-Havel and the martial law–instigating communist Jaruzelski. Ironically, friction was between the former dissidents. Already apparent during Havel's January 1990 visit to Poland, Wałęsa's jealousy emerged that Havel had so easily secured his country's presidency.[53] The Nobel Peace Prize laureate refused to travel to Warsaw to meet the new Czechoslovak president. The president, thought Wałęsa, should travel to him in Gdánsk.[54] Wałęsa also claimed that an important meeting in the ship-building city kept him from traveling; this was simply untrue.[55] Czechoslovak officials said that they had tried unsuccessfully to arrange a meeting. Relations at the meeting three months later seemed little improved, although at least the two men met. The only person in the records surveyed to suggest that relations among would-be leaders of Visegrad were good, both in April 1990 and thereafter, was Hungary's Géza Jeszenszky (and some accounts of others that will also be debated later in this book).[56]

Refolution had run more of its course in Hungary. Already by May 2, 1990, but weeks too late for the Bratislava summit, Arpád Göncz was installed as the country's new president. This writer and translator had been jailed for six years following participation in Hungary's 1956 anti-communist uprising. His priorities unsurprisingly differed from the Hungarian communists who had attempted regional cooperation. Göncz's like-mindedness toward other dissident-intellectuals involved in the nascent regional cooperation was apparent from his work with people like Bronisław Geremek and Havel who sought to create a regional and cosmopolitan-spirited university. This work also helped to create the intellectual foundations for the Central European University, which was founded in 1991 and initially based in Prague.[57] But despite his dissident pedigree, Göncz was among the most unhopeful of those associated with Visegrad's early life. While he wrote later that Visegrad could help its member countries, nevertheless he thought (and rather counterfactually) that "the Visegrad summits had no tangible diplomatic or historical consequences."[58]

Nor was political leadership change an absolute guarantee for regional cooperation. The Visegrad Summit of February 1991, which began not in Visegrád but in the Hungarian Parliament in Budapest, continued to suffer from personality issues. This happened to the point that the three presidents had not met together in the same place while in Budapest. Czechoslovak diplomat Rudolf Chmel, who was part of Havel's presidential delegation, recorded that the atmosphere of the eventual summit was "quite stiff" and dynamics between Havel and Wałęsa were insincere.[59] British journalist Michael Simmons, an early biographer of Havel, who characterized Havel and Wałęsa as "very different" from each other, even "irreconcilably," doubted that the two by themselves would be capable of achieving bilateral agreements.[60]

Visegrad's historiography attributes cooperation particularly to certain individual leaders who had a dissident pedigree. Surely, as we have seen, the

cooperation had to be created, and some retrospective commentaries are perhaps accepting what became the cooperation as given. Despite some interpersonal differences, and despite different accounts of the president's own
"dissident" experiences, the dissident-era legacies have come to be seen as
essential to the cooperation. As an example, Jaroslav Daniška wrote: "Havel,
Walesa and [József] Antall valued mutual cooperation and were mindful not
only of the cultural and intellectual legacy of anti-Communist solidarity among
dissidents, but also of the cross-border political declarations and inspirations,
and the legacy of persecution under Communism prior to 1989."[61] Of fundamental importance in this dissident heritage was the concept of "Central
Europe," which was introduced into unofficial, even clandestine, discussions in
the region in the mid-1980s. The value-laden term's usage was partly intended
to reinforce that the peoples of Czechoslovakia, Hungary, and Poland shared
among themselves and with Western Europe common historical development
and culture. To differing degrees, that appellation also served to differentiate
Central Europe from the backward East, the occupying colonizer in the form
of the USSR, as émigré Moravian novelist Milan Kundera argued in his seminal essay of 1983 that ignited debate.[62] Havel, Wałęsa, and Antall were seen to
have "revived the once derided idea of central Europe, ridiculed or ignored by
too many in the first half of the twentieth century."[63] Visegrad would become
the operational embodiment of Central Europe.[64]

    This dissident pedigree, of common thinking and experience and also per-
sonal bonds built in adversity, contributed subtly but substantively to Visegrad's
functionality. These connections have been marked in subsequent regional foreign policy activity and in Visegrad commemorations. Twenty-five years later,
the Czech foreign minister Vondra, himself a communist-era dissident and
present at the earlier post-communist regional cooperation initiatives, made
Poland an early priority for a foreign visit (not as early as Havel in 1990—Poland
was his third destination, after the United States and Germany). But on October 7, 2006, he attended a conference in Wrocław commemorating the twenty-
fifth anniversary of Polish-Czechoslovak solidarity.[65] Visegrad prime ministers,
themselves unconnected to that communist-era dissident solidarity, chose to
meet on June 3, 2009—on the eve of the twentieth anniversary of the ground-
breaking semifree elections in Poland that brought Solidarity into power and
which in turn encouraged further unimagined change in the Soviet bloc.

    Official Visegrad statements referring to the common dissident experience
hardly mean that the dissidents-cum-presidents shared identical outlooks. We
have already seen the ongoing issues between Havel and Wałęsa. Because the
latter, the dockyard electrician, had limited education (so too did Havel, but
that was because the regime disallowed him university education because of
his family's propertied status), Wałęsa's staff tried to compensate by prepping

him for a later meeting with Havel so that Wałęsa came briefed on philosophical treatises and intent on discussing them with Havel.[66] In contrast again, Hungary's new president, Antall, a historian, described himself as having "very different political roots from those in the samizdat [writings that were deemed subversive and illegal by communist regimes]. That group is made up of former Marxists and Maoists,"[67] and more than in Poland or Czechoslovakia, many of Hungary's prominent intellectual "dissidents" coalesced around revisionist Marxism.[68]

Irrespective of how important political leadership change was to starting Visegrad, and then the roles of dissidents to it, the irony of Hungary's evolutionary process of change in the late 1980s meant that its Foreign Ministry was nevertheless the best able of three ministries to organize the Visegrad meeting in 1991. Unlike for the Czechoslovak-convened meeting of April 1990, the Hungarians produced an agenda for February 1991.[69] Credit to the host country for having an agenda is one of many factors that confuse the determination of who began Visegrad. Hungary evidently organized and hosted the founding meeting. But that event would not have occurred without prior interactions by the regional leaders.

Before assessing the aims of the Visegrad Summit of February 1991, we should ask what brought these countries three together, and why not others, and why specifically in February 1991. Raising these questions helps to inform the fast-changing circumstances in this postrevolution region and of post–Cold War Europe. The answers are further found in four other factors: the convergence of the three countries' foreign policies, changes in the Soviet Union, and the relative indifference of both NATO and the EC/EU.

CONVERGENCE OF FOREIGN POLICIES

The year 1990 was a seismic time, and Central Europe remained a focus of this systemic reordering period—both as a subject of it and, as Visegrad intended, also as an empowered actor in it. The NATO and EU enlargements to the Baltic and Black Seas may, in retrospect, seem inevitable, but such perspective masks what was at the time a great deal of uncertainty and required foreign policy ingenuity.

Visegrad states now celebrate together successive anniversaries of their entry into the EU and NATO. It may thus be even harder to fathom that those countries started their post-communist existences with diverging foreign policies. These would have to be aligned before Visegrad could start. Table 1.1 summarizes the three countries' conflicting priorities and aims in 1990.

Poland began the momentous year of 1990 in fear. Of Germany. Of what quickly became a great-power momentum to allow German unification. Poland

TABLE 1.1. Starting positions of post-communist foreign policies

State	Position on German unification and post–World War borders	Position on Soviet-led regional institutions and Soviet troops
Poland	Severe fear of German intentions; heightened by Bonn's refusal to acknowledge the postwar (East) German-Polish border	Retention of Warsaw Pact and of Soviet forces in Poland, to 1993, and ratification of Polish-German border treaty
Hungary	Possession of innovative foreign policy experience before 1989; first communist state to have signed agreement with EC, in 1988, and a victory for reformers;* no historical territorial or populations issues with Germany	Immediate withdrawal of Soviet military forces; negotiations begun and concluded in early 1990
Czechoslovakia	Havel on Polish fears: Czechoslovakia "does not have such a problem." Havel and Dienstbier were highly supportive of German unification.	Immediate withdrawal of Soviet forces; negotiations begun and concluded in early 1990

*Germuska, "Balancing," 401–20.

was not even privy to those talks, even though its postwar borders were intentionally shifted to incorporate German lands. And many of the Germans who did not flee advancing Soviet forces were expelled. Would new Germany seek its old territories? The West German government initially refused even to confirm that a united Germany would retain the post–World War II border created between East Germany and Poland. The need for international agreement on those borders both contributed to the Helsinki process and was then reaffirmed as part of its Accords. The border was reguaranteed in 1976. It was meant to be rock-solid. Until concrete shards were hacked off the Berlin Wall on the night of November 9, 1989.

In the unforeseen prospects of German unification, and in view of decades of Soviet occupation, Poland's government initially sought the antithetical: to retain Soviet troops on its soil and to preserve the Warsaw Pact as counterweights to any new Germany.[70] The irony of the situation caused US State Department analyses to note that the Solidarity Poles rediscovered "the virtue

Position on NATO	General view of European security	How and when foreign policy convergence achieved
Later, last of these countries to apply for NATO membership; Wałęsa even mooted "NATO 2" for region	Nascent thinking on European integration but heavy concentration on risks from German unification and border issues	Border reassurances from Germany and peaceable German unification, October 1990; resurgent fears of Soviet Union, especially January 1991
Clearest interest of the Three in Euro-Atlantic memberships	Support for Conference on Security and Co-operation in Europe (CSCE) but also earliest of three on end to Moscow-based organization and to seek NATO membership	Initially individualistic foreign policy converges with those of the other two countries
NATO, along with Warsaw Pact, first to evolve from military organizations to political ones, then dissolved in a revamped "Helsinki II" pan-European security system, as per April 1990 European Security Memorandum	Highly experimental, with broadest thinking of all Three	Pressure from West, especially US, to reconsider NATO's role; Helsinki II unable to secure wide support; recognition of renewed dangers from Soviet Union

of Soviet troops" because of this legacy of Stalin's rearrangement of Poland's postwar borders.[71] Warsaw's concerns were unshared by the other countries.[72] Czechoslovakia's Havel, on the one hand, recognized Warsaw's dilemma, telling Germany's *Die Welt*, "I absolutely understand Poland's anxiety concerning the security of its western border." On the other, Havel underscored the differences in foreign policy concerns by saying that his country "fortunately . . . does not have such a problem,"[73] even if in so saying he discounted demands by postwar German expellees and their descendants against Czechoslovakia. Instead, Havel actively supported German unification, with the proviso that any new Germany had to be democratic. Hungary held still another perspective on European security: it sought the immediate dismantling of Soviet-era structures, a position made easier by its geographic position of bordering only neutral Austria. It was a non-NATO country and its reform-minded Hungarian communists who dismantled in summer 1989 some of the barbed wire that had physically divided Europe in two.

Soviet leader Mikhail Gorbachev had recognized and commended the reformist intentions of Hungarian communists. Those same Hungarian communists could and did think very much more radically about changes in their region.

In addition to wanting the immediate withdrawal of Soviet troops, Hungary's leadership sought in 1990 termination of the two Soviet-run regional organizations: the Warsaw Pact and the Council for Mutual Economic Assistance. In fact, others tried to talk the Hungarians out of these intentions! A character whom we could presume from his own personal and national experience to be ill disposed to the Warsaw Pact later recalled how, at the Warsaw Pact meeting in Moscow in 1990, "the Poles, East Germans and Czechs [sic] sat long into the night trying to persuade the Hungarians to change their minds, until they finally relented." Those recollections, and efforts at dissuading the Hungarians, were from none other than Havel.[74]

His Czechoslovakia had not merely another view but another blueprint for European security. And that partly explains why Havel tried, initially, to dissuade his Hungarian counterparts from terminating the Warsaw Pact. In a burst of revolutionary idealism, Havel and his fellow former dissident and new foreign minister, Jiří Dienstbier, thought big. Despite the painful history of Czechoslovakia's invasion by the Warsaw Pact, the two men envisaged a big new, harmonious pan-European and Euro-Atlantic space in which both the Soviet armed alliance and NATO would evolve from being military formations into political ones.[75] Then the political NATO and Warsaw Pact, having served as negotiating platforms for disarmament, would melt into a revamped Helsinki II—the process that in 1975 finally brought diplomatic, economic, and human rights understandings between East and West. To that end, Dienstbier sent his "Memorandum on European Security" to all embassies in Prague of the thirty-four states that had signed Helsinki and also isolationist Marxist Albania, which in 1975, uniquely among all European states, did not participate. Dienstbier took these steps in the week before the Bratislava meeting. And so supportive was Havel of this plan that in May 1990 he called on NATO to change both its role and its name.[76]

The United States in particular, while admiring the men, worked firmly to disabuse them of these lofty ideals. In turn, as chapter 5 shows, Havel could also revise his views and then become a compelling advocate to the American foreign policy establishment for encouraging the admission of his and neighboring countries into NATO—and the Alliance by that name. By early 1991, Prague continued to support Helsinki (as did all signatory governments), but it too wanted an end to the Warsaw Pact and began working determinedly for NATO membership.

In short, Visegrad could not have happened, let alone with its founding Declaration that called for the countries' integration into the EC/EU and NATO, until the three countries' postrevolution foreign policies became aligned. But what accounts for this foreign policy convergence, which itself was essential for Visegrad to become possible? And then why in February 1991? We start with developments in the Soviet Union and their implications for Central Europe.

SHOCKS EXTERNAL TO THE REGION:
FEARS FROM THE SOVIET UNION

Certainly by the start of 1991, the three divergent Central Europe foreign policies had united. Each country in that year had a relatively benign, even supportive attitude toward the Soviet Union. After all, Gorbachev had not ordered any of the over 500,000 combat troops already in the region to prevent regime change. He thereby ensured that these momentous events were peaceable. He also supported the Polish roundtable talks, which led to the installation of a non-communist prime minister, and that in turn had knock-on effects, giving impetus for unprecedented negotiations and power-sharing arrangements elsewhere.

With some initial hesitation, and still outstanding issues, such as the costs of environmental damage, Moscow had fairly quickly agreed and finalized its troops' withdrawal from Czechoslovakia and Hungary.[77] The Central European states advocated, perhaps counterintuitively because of their histories of Soviet occupation, that the Soviet Union be fully included in whatever pan-European security system emerged. Central European–Soviet relations started to look positive.

Then came January 1991. Peaceful demonstrators in the Baltic republics in the USSR who advocated for the restoration of their independence were killed by internal Soviet forces. Images of Soviet tanks rolling over unarmed protestors in Vilnius filled Western media, a continuation of violent repression arising in the physical extremities of the Soviet Union. In April 1989 in Tbilisi, and in January 1990 in Baku, the Georgian and Azerbaijani republics inside the USSR, unarmed protestors were similarly killed, including with sharpened shovels and poison gas.

The Baltic states were physically and culturally close, especially to the Poles, and their spokespeople would also invoke "Central Europe" as part of their heritage.[78] The Lithuanian Soviet Socialist Republic within the Soviet Union shared a long border with Poland, as well as having shared much history, including their two-century joint commonwealth.

The Baltic crackdown shocked the newly liberated Czechoslovaks, Hungarians, and Poles and helped to cement what was underway: the convergence of their foreign policies to pursue their full and final extraction from Soviet regional systems and to seek membership of Western institutions. Meetings among the three governments, including not only of diplomatic staffs but also of their militaries, having started slowly in later 1990, quickened immediately in 1991. The foreign ministers of Czechoslovakia, Hungary, and Poland then convened on January 21 in Warsaw, and what became Visegrad in February 1991 was meant also to have been convened already in that month. Cooperation urgently intensified.

Still, the Central Europeans were neither unified in how they read the threats emanating from Soviet actions in the Baltic, nor exactly in how they responded. But the influence of those events nevertheless contributed to the creation of Visegrad. A few strands of Central European reaction are therefore relevant. In any case, the events came as a shock and international actors ignored the violent Soviet crackdown against unarmed protestors. Jennone Walker summarized this with "nobody . . . used agreed CSCE [Conference on Security and Cooperation in Europe] procedures for questioning 'unusual military activities' by the Soviets in the Baltic republics."[79] Additionally, the Baltic states were excluded from the CSCE Paris Summit in November 1990. Central European sympathy was such that Havel tried physically to get the three Baltic delegations into the meeting, and he raised the ire of the French hosts in so attempting. He also reportedly angered Gorbachev enough from his engagement with Baltic representation that the Soviet leader cancelled a meeting with him. Other states including the United States, which never accepted the Baltic annexation into the USSR, did not assist these republics at Paris.[80]

By contrast Central European concern and activism were recorded in the summit's press conference as having "endorsed the efforts of Lithuania, Latvia and Estonia to break with the Kremlin." Czechoslovakia went further than Hungary and Poland, recognizing the new non-communist governments in each republic, and Havel said that it would open an "office of representation," a diplomatic existence short of a full embassy, in the Lithuanian capital.[81]

The Soviet-conducted January violence in the Baltic and the Central European policy coordination in light of them were contributing factors to the establishment of Visegrad. Nevertheless, as much as Soviet-Baltic events contributed to the start of Visegrad, its framers were intent from the outset not to create panic or indeed to alarm Moscow through their actions. Dienstbier categorically contradicted assertions that the Soviet Union was going to "overrun the Baltic states" and then attack former socialist bloc countries. He also rejected linkage of the Central European meeting with the Baltic events and stated that Central European discussions of ending the Warsaw Pact had preceded the Soviet violence in the Baltic republics. Dienstbier further explained that the Central European governments were regardless moving toward the abolition of the Warsaw Pact. But Soviet forces did kill unarmed protestors in Vilnius and Riga, and in spite of Dienstbier's seeming hesitancies, after the

Baltic events of January 1991, Czechoslovak-Hungarian-Polish cooperation intensified, including militarily.

The few contemporary observers of emerging Central European cooperation also indicated that the Baltic crackdown was a motivator.[82] Hungary's Foreign minister Géza Jeszenszky wrote retrospectively that "if the 19 August [1991] coup in Moscow had succeeded—which could have been the case—1989 would have been in vain, and Central Europe might have been returned to Soviet dependence." As further evidence of Visegrad's alarm, Jeszenszky points to the fact that the Three immediately convened after the coup and formulated joint reactions.[83]

Even after the Soviet Union's formal termination on December 25, 1991, Visegrad continued to anticipate Moscow's pernicious influences. At the May 1992 Visegrad Summit, held in Prague, Hungary's Antall spoke of both new and continuing dangers facing Visegrad from the former Soviet Union: "It would be a colossal mistake on our part to believe that there aren't dangers. Despite our best wishes the danger always remains that forces, be they among the politician or in the army, may make attempts in the coming years or decades to disrupt these developments. It is imperative that we work together to block any such attempts as we will be [the] first ones affected by any negative tendencies cropping up in the region."[84] The Group, however, was already and would remain careful of provoking Moscow, even through its mere existence. The limited cooperation that occurred among the three countries between the April 1990 Bratislava meeting and the Visegrad Summit, as we saw, included military agreements. But these were deliberately and strictly signed bilaterally, precisely to avoid alarming Moscow that a new, multilateral alliance was being formed on its Western frontiers. The 1991 Declaration, detailed in the next chapter, specified that the cooperation "will not be directed against the interests of any other party." What became Visegrad was in no way an alliance, let alone a bloc, nor a military one, despite some contemporary and subsequent misstatements.[85] Despite organizers stating otherwise, some press unhelpfully called the meeting an "East bloc summit" (and Visegrad would later also be called a "bloc").[86] Indeed, even later, key figures in Visegrad's foundation, including Jeszenszky, have used such terms as "pact" to describe the Group.[87] Fortunately, other external observers concluded that Visegrad was "taking care not to annoy their giant eastern neighbour," commenting that "they meant no offense."[88] Avoiding the appearance from Visegrad of threat to Moscow was an understated yet carefully crafted essential aim.

That avoidance even meant that other new partners tried to limit Visegrad's activities. One account contended, "Germany attempted to dissuade the Central European states from forming the Višegrad [sic] group because it might offend Moscow." The Polish government, particularly fearing Russian-German hegemony over the region, "had to turn to Washington before Bonn withdrew its objections."[89] The historical record may disagree with such an interpretation, but it indicates the perception that Visegrad had to be contained.

And Visegrad also had utility in achieving aims toward Moscow. Once Warsaw wanted the Warsaw Pact's dissolution, Visegrad gave Poland, as a middle power and thus with relatively limited capacity, a "perfect strategy to disband the Warsaw Pact."[90]

Even so, and perhaps especially because of such language, nascent Visegrad continued its approach toward Moscow. Without expressing such, Visegrad may well have astutely responded at that point to the Soviet and Russian mindsets of recalling the repeated historical threats to them from Mongols in the East and, more recently, from the West, and across contemporary Poland by Napoleonic and Imperial German (and Austro-Hungarian) and then Nazi German forces. And, so too did Polish and Czechoslovak soldiers partake in the Allied Intervention that sought to reverse Bolshevik conquests of former imperial Russian power and territories.

It was very conceivable then that a new military coalition, even of smaller powers, could appear threatening to Moscow.[91] Visegrad held 65 million people, all of whom could harbor resentment from recent history permeated by Muscovite violence and occupation, and physically centered on that most sensitive geopolitical territory in the Soviet-Russian strategic mindset: Poland. The prominent, Warsaw-born, US political scientist and policy practitioner Zbigniew Brzezinski advocated in January 1990 that Poland and Czechoslovakia should even create a confederation that would be "a stronger unit in the vulnerable area between Germany and Russia." The new Czechoslovak government rejected the idea outright. Brzezinski nevertheless lamented that something similar after 1945 could have prevented the region's communist takeover.[92] Eleven years later Brzezinski adjusted his view to say that Visegrad worked suitably instead.[93]

Visegrad's potential potency was noted by Hungary's Jeszenszky, citing Germany's *Frankfurter Allgemeine Zeitung*: "Separately, the Central European countries are weak; united they are indomitable, and Gorbachev was the first to note that."[94] That was precisely the sentiment that Visegrad sought to avoid sending to an insecure and unpredictable Moscow, and one retaining combat troops across Central Europe.[95] Poland's post-communist foreign minister Krzysztof Skubiszewski was summarized as perhaps more moderate and more accurate on Visegrad's intentions toward Moscow: "Regional cooperation aided all three states to coordinate more effectively toward the East."[96]

Visegrad's Eastern apprehensions proved correct. Further alarm for Visegrad came in August 1991 with the anti-Gorbachev coup. Some records suggest that despite Visegrad's "scrupulous" efforts to dissuade that they were creating any type of military formation, their responses to the coup "indicated that there might have been a greater depth to their military cooperation than they might have been willing to make public."[97]

Of Soviet influence on Visegrad's inception, Andrzej Korbonski contended that "it became clear that the Visegrad Agreement turned out to be a kind of knee-jerk reaction to events in the former Soviet Union and that once the situation there got under control, there was no longer any persuasive rationale for the treaty."[98] How does that now concur with the historical record? The Soviet Union de facto fragmented throughout the course of 1991, and Central European security perceptions of the East consequently changed. The Three saw far more purpose in Visegrad than merely dealing with Moscow, and their input into the cooperation increased. Additionally, the Atlantic Alliance still made no overtures to Visegrad for what the Group enunciated in and after February 1991, as a primary objective: NATO membership. Absence of NATO guarantees coincided with insufficient offers from the EC. Rather, those institutions pursued policies that seemed to keep Central Europe afar. NATO and the EC partly inspired Visegrad because of what they did *not* offer the Central European. In that way they were absent, or indifferent, hegemons, and they indirectly encouraged Visegrad's cooperation. It is to these absent hegemons to which we turn to establish why Visegrad arose when it did.

VISEGRAD COOPERATION
IN A HEGEMONIC VACUUM

Regional integration is often explained by the presence of a hegemon who is willing politically to support such a project and also to provide the public goods—usually the finances but also other material means—to achieve it.[99] As Visegrad coalesced in the early 1990s, Western institutions were not even supporting Central European regional cooperation, let alone underwriting its costs, as a hegemon typically does. However, the West exerted an atypical and invisible hegemonic characteristic: an ideational one, of encouraging the Central European region to develop and project itself in a particular way. The absence of conventional hegemonic influence and the ideational self-expressions explain this important dimension of Visegrad's emergence.

Visegrad became Visegrad in part because benevolent hegemons were *not* in place in or active enough toward Central Europe. That said, the new Central European leaderships understood that the West wanted reassurances that their region was conflict free. That was not a condition taken for granted. Brzezinski warned of the region's "historical immaturity" that manifested expressions of nationalism that were "more volatile, more emotional and more intense than those in the West."[100] Other government-related researchers mapped dozens of ethnonational flashpoints arising from disputed borders and territorial and demographic claims against each other.[101]

Projecting a positive "Western" image back to the West was a natural, even innate project for the Central Europeans, and also a necessary one. Because for them, they as individuals and their region had always been part of the West. As novelist Kundera had graphically written in 1983, Central Europe was a part of the West that had been kidnapped and forcibly dragged East.[102]

While Central Europeans may have felt, understandably, a historical right to rejoin the West, and by that also institutional memberships, already in 1990 some Central European figures had asked enough to know that any entry process would be far longer and more complex than they had hoped, if it were to happen at all. In those circumstances, Visegrad was cooperation when and where alternative, even more desirable cooperation was not available.

The Central Europeans also understood enough of the need and the benefit of signaling to an anxious West that they were not merely suitable partners but that they were real contributors to Europe and the Euro-Atlantic community. Visegrad became an extremely important device for exhibiting what can rightly be called civilizational values. First we detail that it is worth considering the absence of sufficient overtures from NATO and the EC/EU that contributed to Visegrad's foundation. The story of how Visegrad contributed to the formal accession processes of those organizations and how Visegrad functioned inside of them is addressed in later chapters.[103]

Even in the mid-1990s, the post-communist states would, as J. F. Brown wrote, "never be taken seriously by the West or by each other until they themselves make some real effort at regional and subregional cooperation. They all need help and must get it. But, in the end, they must pull their own chestnuts out of the fire."[104] They salvaged some of those chestnuts rather creatively with Visegrad. In turn they also provide an intriguing case in the study of international relations when small, neighboring states could band together to increase their collective punch through fortuitous leadership and circumstances.

NATO AND ITS EARLY INSUFFICIENCIES AS A MOTIVATION FOR VISEGRAD

Despite initial foreign policy differences among the leaderships of Czechoslovakia, Hungary, and Poland, by 1991 the three governments understood that NATO was not offering them Alliance membership. Visegrad would serve as their platform to express three interrelated geopolitical sentiments: dismay at NATO's unsatisfactory offerings; the Central European need for a security guarantee; and a mode to express their Europeanness and, on that basis, their eligibility for membership, despite NATO's established resistance.

On one hand, NATO quickly recognized that Czechoslovakia, Hungary, and Poland, even before they became the Visegrad states, stood out among post-communist states. On the other hand, NATOs actions and offerings fell far short of what the three countries' leaderships came to seek.

At the Turnberry Summit in Scotland, in June 1990, NATO secretary general Manfred Wörner referred to the inclusion of representatives from Czechoslovakia, Hungary, and Poland as historic and as examples of NATO's post–Cold War "broadened dialogue." Far from discussing a security guarantee, the NATO head said, "We look to further such opportunities in the future."[105] Wörner did also say, after the aborted August Coup in Moscow that spelled the end of the Soviet Union, that the West's "security [was] inseparably linked to all other states in Europe, particularly eastern Europe." For a later observer, that comment was taken by the Visegrad Three as an "important breakthrough in [NATO] member states' perceptions of regional security needs."[106]

Organizationally and operationally, however, the Visegrad countries ensured that their military cooperation would always be insufficient for NATO to be able to claim that the region's own (noble) initiatives obviated the need for a security guarantee from, let alone membership in, NATO. Consequently, the three countries avoided establishing formal military structures among themselves that could relieve NATO of a sense of responsibility to the region and its desire for the meaningful security guarantee that only full Alliance membership would provide. Although the Three avoided trilateral military agreements to acknowledge Moscow's sensitivities, various defense officials, including deputy defense ministers, held trilateral meetings, even before Visegrad's formal launch, particularly at Zakopane, Poland, in September 1990. These were also meetings that have rarely featured in the records of Visegrad or of others, but to its participants they were when "we began to realize that [our] three independent neighboring states can constitute some type of" emerging community.[107]

In military matters, twice over then, Visegrad could not appear to be too successful. As a contemporary analyst put it, perhaps with unintended yet graphic reference to historical horrors in the region, too successful cooperation among the Three could seem to risk consigning them to "an eastern ghetto."[108] Though the EU acted more tangibly than NATO, its actions, too, made Visegrad feel the risk of ghettoization.

VISEGRAD AND THE EU

Regarding NATO, Visegrad cooperation was inspired by the need simultaneously to effect a certain level of cooperation while not being too good at it to obviate achieving the real and final aim of membership. Western media observed that the EC might seek not only to keep the Central European states away from the community but more bound to each other, and instead "support closer cooperation among the east Europeans."[109]

The EC Copenhagen Summit of 1993 gave general guidelines for accession, including features that the Central Europeans had already achieved or knew were needed—democracy for the former and further market reforms for the latter. Polish premier Hanna Suchocka, the region's first-ever female government leader, called Copenhagen's outcome "too little for our needs."[110] Central European analysts worried as late as 1994 that far from welcoming Visegrad's regional cooperation, the EU "would probably do everything in its power to weaken regional solidarity if the four countries developed a common external economic policy" toward it.[111]

Some calls were made not to prioritize Central European free trade as part of the region's overtures to the EU: "to accelerate the integration process the Visegrád countries do not need regional co-operation but first and foremost growth of their domestic economies."[112] But Visegrad read the EC as wanting not just domestic political-economic transformation but also those countries' willingness and indeed tangible capacity to cooperate with each other. And in the economic realm, an important initiative—and lasting achievement—of Visegrad was the creation of their own free trade area. This is analyzed in the next chapter.

Visegrad was already negotiating with the EC, and not merely as quiet guests. In March 1991 Visegrad "refused to accept the EC's offers on a range of issues."[113] European Community organs themselves recognized "already a process has begun between the Community and the three Visegrad countries which points towards a multilateralisation of relations between the parties involved. This could provide a valuable model for other countries in the future."[114] Contemporary analyses of the Europe Agreements between the EC and the Visegrad countries, albeit with each separately, saw those three countries as "a unity."[115]

That Visegrad could hold negotiations with the EC in 1991 and 1992 was a remarkable achievement. However, those negotiations also showed Visegrad that EU membership was at best a distant prospect. Visegrad had to exist to convince the EC/EU that its countries were making the monumental conversion to a market economy and that domestic laws and practices could converge with European Community law. Visegrad was in part created in anticipation of what the EC wanted of the Central Europeans and in part because the EC's overtures were insufficient, not least because the Central European starting point was membership. The obstacles and delays being created, at least from the Central European perspective, may now be forgotten. For perspective, take the year in which this is being read. Add to it fifteen years. That date, a long and uncertain time in the future, would be the equivalent time of working and then waiting for membership from today.

Like it did for NATO, Visegrad came into existence to send fundamental messages about a positive political identity and reliability as partners and eventual members to the EC/EU and because those Visegrad countries realized that they had no other opportunities, or substitutes, for cooperation.[116] No hegemon in Visegrad's early life was present to directly aid cooperation; but two distant hegemons contributed to setting the existential need of generating a cooperative regional environment.

Having considered when, how, by whom, and why Visegrad came to life, the next chapters will assess its establishment and early achievements.

NOTES

1. Probably the most common English publication version in the pre-1989 era was as "Power of the Powerless," in the collection of dissident and other supporting writings, in Vladislav (ed.), *Living*.
2. As per interviews with the author in August 1995. The dissident writings were published only in Czech, after the 1989 revolution, as Dienstbier, *Snění o Evropě*. Other statements and commentaries on and by Dienstbier feature later. He wrote a later book, also only in Czech, on the experience of changing ideas into practice: *Od snění k realitě*. Dienstbier also kindly met with the author in the early 1990s.
3. The European Union (EU) was founded on November 1, 1993, as a result of the Treaty of the European Union, or the Maastricht Treaty, which was signed February 7, 1992. The Visegrad states were engaging with the European Communities until the treaty went into effect and obviously the EU thereafter. When engagements spanned only one period, either the EC or EU will be used, and the more cumbersome formulation of EC/EU will be used for both periods.
4. Simmons. By contrast, in a later and prominent biography, John Keane asserts that Havel was determined to secure the presidency.
5. Non-communist Polish prime minister Tadeusz Mazowiecki and Havel were criticized by Zbigniew Brzezinski for not making their first international trips to each other's capital. Cited in "Brzezinski Urges Poles, Czechoslovaks to Unite," UPI, January 3, 1990.
6. Non–political scientists and security scholars note the potency of these speeches, e.g., Havel "claiming" that Central Europe has been reawakened.
7. "Speech by Vaclav Havel to the Polish Sejm and Senate (Warsaw, January 25, 1990)." Office of the Czech President, http://old.hrad.cz/president/Havel/speeches/index_uk.html.
8. "Speech by Vaclav Havel to the Polish Sejm."
9. Skalník, 29.
10. Dienstbier, appointed December 10, 1989, had more than two weeks over Havel. See *Od*.
11. "Havel Responds to Questions," Prague Domestic Service, January 29, 1990, in *Foreign Broadcast Information Service—Eastern Europe* (hereafter, *FBIS*), January 30, 1990, 11.

12. Vondra, 80. Vondra was another of the many former dissidents in foreign policy who graciously granted an interview that also informed of the atmosphere in which these early regional policy initiatives were made.
13. Tökés, 103.
14. MTI (Hungarian broadcasting), as reported in BBC Monitoring, "Czechoslovak, Polish and Hungarian Leaders meet in Bratislava," April 11, 1990.
15. E.g., "He is credited with having set the stage for the fall of the Berlin Wall by opening Hungary's border with Austria in 1989 so that East Germans could flee." David B. Ottaway, "Hungary May Seek Detente with Neighbors," *Washington* Post, May 29, 1994.
16. Blinken and Blinken, 170.
17. Resumed in chapter 3.
18. Fawn, "Symbolism."
19. Prague Domestic Service, January 29, 1990, as "Havel Responds to Questions," *FBIS*, January 30, 1990, 11.
20. Patricia Koza, "Havel Meets Grim-Faced Jaruzelski, Snubbed by Walesa," UPI, January 15, 1990.
21. As broadcast on ČTK (Czech News Agency), April 9, 1990, as "Leaders Meet on Role in Europe," *FBIS*, April 10, 1990, 2.
22. Vondra, 80. Jaruzelski's legacy is complicated. He was given a state funeral and veteran, communist-era dissident Adam Michnik even "began canonizing" him. Chenoweth, 58.
23. "Czech" is used when an individual is Czech, as in the case of the two people here; "Czechoslovak" is used when individuals represented the country of Czechoslovakia. Similarly, those being Slovak are referred to as "Slovaks," and when holding federal positions as "Czechoslovak."
24. Vondra, 79–80.
25. Šedivý, *Čzernínský*.
26. Kopecek, 5.
27. "A Meeting of Leaders from Three Neighboring Countries. Bratislava Castle, April 9, 1990," https://archive.vaclavhavel-library.org/Archive/Detail/62749?q=A%20Meeting%20of%20Leaders%20from%20Three%20Neighboring%20Countries.%20Bratislava%20Castle,%20April%209,%201990.
28. *Népszabadság*, February 13, 1991, as "CSFR's Havel Previews Visegrad Summit," *FBIS*, February 19, 1991, 1.
29. Havel, *To the Castle*.
30. Tökés, 103; *Lidové Noviny*, April 10, 1990.
31. These are identified in Fawn, "Symbolism."
32. Prague Domestic Service, April 9, 1990, as "Further on Havel's 10 Summit Questions," *FBIS*, April 10, 1990, 5.
33. *Die Presse*, March 8, 1990, as "Dienstbier Queried on German Unity, Austria," *FBIS*, March 9, 1990, 26.
34. Dienstbier, *Od*, 143.
35. Dienstbier, "Visegrad—The First Phase," 16.
36. Žantovský, "Visegrad," 84.
37. *1999/2000 Czech Presidency* (no pagination), https://www.visegradgroup.eu/documents/annual-reports/1999-2000-czech-110412. These summits are detailed and analyzed in the next chapter.

38. Comparison of cooperation initiatives in and involving post-communist countries appear in Fawn, "Regional Relations" and "International."
39. Former-dissident, postrevolution Czechoslovak foreign policymakers spoke extensively in interviews of the difficulties of getting even routine matters done and of the obstruction or simply the indifference and the inefficiency of existing communist-era staff.
40. Cited in Matynia, 16.
41. Also commented on by Spero, *Bridging*, 93.
42. One now-senior Slovak diplomat, then a junior official in the Czechoslovak Foreign Ministry, was both surprised and delighted that I even knew of this meeting. Interview, July 9, 2009. Slovakia's Visegrad national coordinator ambassador Ivan Pavol also stressed that Visegrad began in Bratislava in April 1990. Interview, February 9, 2011. See also Figel, "Foreword," 7, for a formal Slovak view that Bratislava/1990 was Visegrad's start. Others have asserted the same.
43. See chapter 4.
44. Čič had joined the Communist Party in 1961 and remained a member until 1990, although he did not hold state office during communist rule. He was appointed premier of the still-socialist Slovak Republic within the Socialist Czechoslovak Federation on December 10, 1989. He therefore could be said to be another "refolution" figure present at Bratislava, and who left that post in the course of 1990.
45. See again Tökés, 100–114.
46. Garton Ash, *We*.
47. Ex-dissidents brought into foreign policy immediately after the 1989 revolutions have informed me quite graphically of the differences between Havel and Wałęsa and how they tried desperately to get the latter to meet with the former on his visit to Poland. An account of early wrong-footing by Wałęsa with Hungarians and its effect on regional cooperation is in Engelmayer.
48. "A Meeting of Leaders from Three Neighboring Countries. Bratislava Castle, April 9, 1990."
49. Dienstbier, "Visegrad," 15.
50. Vondra. Vondra was also referring to the meeting of intellectuals.
51. A conference entitled "Ethics and Politics" was also organized in the castle and ran immediately before the diplomatic meeting.
52. Tökés.
53. Some of cited literature makes this point, as did interviews in the 1990s conducted with those who sought to facilitate these talks.
54. Aspects of the efforts made to convince Wałęsa to travel from Gdánsk to Warsaw to meet Havel were also conveyed to me in interviews conducted in the early 1990s. Czechoslovak diplomats also ultimately said that "timing" did not allow for the meeting to occur.
55. Boyes, 232.
56. Biographies of Havel and Wałęsa are clear about the discord between them, principally of the latter toward the former. Simmons; Boyes.
57. As mentioned positively in Jařab, 160.
58. Göncz, 49. His contribution to this enormous book on Visegrad uncharacteristically includes a photograph unconnected to the Group and its history, of him attending a state dinner at Oslo's Royal Palace.
59. Quoted in Grabiński.

60. Simmons, 206.
61. Daniška, 43.
62. Milan Kundera, "Un occident kidnappé, ou la tragédie de L'Europe Central," *Le Débat*, November 27, 1983, 2–24. Published with greater attention in English in 1984: Kundera, "The Tragedy of Central Europe," *New York Review of Books*, April 26, 1984.
63. Daniška, 44.
64. This is not to say that only Visegrad countries possessed and produced "Central European" culture. Whatever might be taken to define "Central Europe"—even the most daily if also consequential characteristics, like styles of baking—extends beyond the political boundaries of the Visegrad states because of the region's shifting borders. Politically and diplomatically, however, a strong argument can be made that Visegrad became the operational representation of Central Europe. Some of this is debated in Fawn, "Elusive Defined," and further examples of how Visegrad became Central Europe for other countries appear in the next chapter.
65. "Czech Foreign Minister to Visit Poland 6–7 October," PAP, October 4, 2006.
66. I am grateful to a number of people directly involved in Czechoslovak-Polish dissident circles and/or post-1989 diplomacy for detailing many of the efforts made.
67. Quoted in Blaine Harden, "'Hungarian-ness' Back in Fashion," *Washington Post*, April 11, 1990.
68. The literature on Central European dissent and on independent intellectual activity before 1989 is now considerable. This briefest discussion is in no way meaning to reduce these complexities to a few words. As but one qualification, Czechoslovak dissidents also comprised a significant number of former Communist Party members and (not always being the same) Marxist-inclined intellectuals. None of them, however, were either in the Czechoslovak Communist Party or remained in it once "normalization" began in 1969 as part of the crackdown following liberalization in 1968. See, esp. Falk, and Bolton. On illegal literature, see Skilling, *"Samizdat."*
69. Vondra. Dienstbier, however, as noted earlier in this chapter, stated that the agenda arose from three-way consultations before the February 1991 Summit.
70. This is not to say that *all* of Polish foreign and security policy uniformly saw threat and responded with efforts at counterweights. Poland's post-communist foreign minister Krzysztof Skubiszewski elaborated on April 25, 1990, a "Polish-German Community of Interests," though that still has been interpreted in terms of fulfilling Polish security needs. For example, Wiatr, 52. Polish executives changed frequently in the early 1990s, but the foreign-policy specialist Skubiszewski was consistently retained in this vital period of September 1989 to October 1993.
71. Cited in Sarotte, *1989*, 139.
72. That is not to say that other countries lacked concern over a united Germany. Initially, both Britain and France were apprehensive.
73. *Die Welt*, March 10, 1990, as "Havel Discusses European Political Future," *FBIS*, March 12, 1990, 13.
74. Havel, *To the Castle*, 294.
75. They and all of their administration, however, sought immediate negotiations for the withdrawal of the Soviet armed forces stationed in Czechoslovakia since the crushing of the 1968 Prague Spring reform movement.
76. Havel urged this of NATO in his address to the Parliamentary Assembly of the Council of Europe: NATO "must definitely change. Above all, in the face of today's reality, it should transform its military doctrine. It should also—in view of its

changing role—change its name without delay." Archived as "Václav Havel President of the Czech and Slovak Federal Republic. Speech made to the Assembly.
Thursday, 10 May 1990," http://www.assembly.coe.int/nw/xml/Speeches/Speech
-XML2HTML-EN.asp?SpeechID=88.
77. See, e.g., Šedivý, "Pull-out," and Savranskaya.
78. Estonian foreign minister Lennart Meri insisted in November 1990 that his country, the most northern of Estonia, Latvia, and Lithuanian, and facing Finland, was
"Central European." Meri, esp. 108.
79. Walker, 65.
80. The Havel-Gorbachev matter and non-Western support are recorded in
Maresca, 134.
81. AP, "Czechoslovaks to Set Up Office in Lithuania," *New York Times*, February 17,
1991. See also Jan Obrman, "Czechoslovakia Reacts to Crackdown in the Baltic
Republics," RFE/RL *Report on Eastern Europe*, February 8, 1991, 25–28.
82. Tökés.
83. Jeszenszky, "Visegrád: Past and Future."
84. Antall, "Ties that Bind," in Jeszenszky, *Antall*, 278.
85. E.g., that Visegrad established "a system of defence coordination." Sperling and
Kirchner, 38.
86. See, e.g., George Jahn, "Czechoslovakia Moves toward Diplomatic Ties with Lithuania," Associated Press, February 15, 1991.
87. Jeszenszky, "Origins," 61.
88. Wedel, 20; Stephen Engelberg, "Three Eastern European Leaders Confer, Gin-
gerly," *New York Times*, February 17, 1991.
89. Prizel, 120.
90. Spero, *Bridging*, 6.
91. Moscow's discourse before and especially after its own full-scale attack on Ukraine
in February 2022 generated official narratives that Poland was planning to attack
and annex western Ukraine. Stanislav Kuvaldin, "Why Russia Keeps Insisting That
Poland Is Preparing to Partition Ukraine," Carnegie Endowment for International
Peace, December 7, 2022, https://carnegieendowment.org/politika/88585.
92. Brzezinski, 18; "Brzezinski Urges Poles, Czechoslovaks to Unite," UPI, January 3,
1990.
93. Brzezinski, "Slovenko sa zlepšuje," *Sme*, April 30, 2001.
94. Jeszenszky, "Visegrád: Past and Future."
95. Negotiations by the Czechoslovak and Hungarian governments to have Soviet
forces, numbering roughly 75,000 in each of those countries, were successfully
concluded at that point, but troops still remained until summer 1991. Soviet forces
remained in Poland, and approximately 350,000 Soviet troops remained in former
East Germany—a force sizeable enough to overwhelm any European military. The
Soviet military only left Germany completely in 1994. From the perspective of
early 1991, and the bloodshed in the Baltic, Central European apprehensions over
possible Soviet intentions are understandable.
96. Spero, *Bridging*, 68.
97. Cited in Terry, "Beyond," 237.
98. Korbonski, "Facing," 48.
99. The immense literature on regionalism contain arguments that "post-hegemonic"
regional cooperation is possible, but already that implies previous hegemonic contributions. E.g., Riggirozzi and Tussie.

100. Brzezinski, "Post-communist," 4.
101. Dick, Dunne, and Lough.
102. Kundera, "Un occident kidnappé" and "Tragedy."
103. See chapters 5 and 6.
104. Brown, "Introduction: A Year of Productive Discontent," 8.
105. "Final Communiqué, North Atlantic Council, Turnberry, United Kingdom, 7–8 June 1990," updated October 27, 2000, http://www.nato.int/docu/comm/49-95/c900608a .htm.
106. Lašas, 68.
107. Wagrowska, 35.
108. Treverton, 169.
109. John Palmer, "More Countries Clamour to Join the Community," *Guardian*, March 15, 1991.
110. Cited in ČTK, June 24, 1993, as "Suchocka, Klaus, to Sign Treaties," *FBIS*, June 25, 1993, 17.
111. Inotai and Sass, *Economic*, 6.
112. Gärtner and Sens, 192.
113. Papadimitriou, 119.
114. "Speech of Mr Frans Andriessen at the UK Presidency Conference 'Europe and the World after 1992'—London, 7 September 1992: Central And Eastern Europe," http://europa.eu/rapid/press-release_SPEECH-92-80_en.htm (neither that cite nor the extract provides the original date).
115. Dauderstädt, 11.
116. Vachudova, "Visegrad."

2

GETTING TO VISEGRAD
AND ITS EARLY ACHIEVEMENTS

Visegrad was born on February 15, 1991. Conventional history of that day and of that location leading to Visegrad's creation are, simply, incorrect. Not to be mistaken: these misrepresentations are positive misuses of history and of place-names. Misrepresentations, nevertheless, they are.

How the Visegrad meeting arose and what it sought initially to achieve constitute this chapter. The chapter also determines Visegrad's immediate accomplishments in its foundational years, which included creating internal group practices and its establishment as a European and to an extent even an international actor. From nowhere, Visegrad became a formation that engaged by that name with NATO and the European Community / European Union and with others. Visegrad also devised and implemented the first and leading regional free trade agreement. A final section shows another dimension of Visegrad's rapid and remarkable success—the degree to which other states envied that cooperation and also used it as a benchmark for their own post-communist transformations.

HOW DID VISEGRÁD BECOME VISEGRAD?

A first "Visegrad"[1] meeting—of foreign ministers, not heads of state—was supposed to have occurred in January 1991—not in February, and in Budapest, not in Visegrád. Then that Hungarian-hosted meeting was delayed to February 1991. The actual February meeting also started with a meeting of the three leaders not initially in Visegrád but instead in the Hungarian Parliament in Budapest.[2] Nor did the three leaders initially meet together. Even that aside, more important at that point were the committees they brought to formalize details of their cooperation. The successive meeting, at which the three leaders appeared together, convened twenty-five miles north from the

Hungarian capital, in the biggest bend in the Danube River, where fourteenth-century Hungarian king Charles I of Anjou had relocated his royal seat in 1323: Visegrád.[3]

The 1991 meeting was still neither in the location, nor even in the castle, with which it is now associated. For in the town of Visegrád, there were and remain not one but two royal venues, and even the remains of a third. And that ruined one first bore the name "Visegrád."[4] The first venue is atop a hill, overlooking that great Central European river, as in figure 2.1. The second is at ground level, sometimes also called the Visegrád Castle, or more often the Lower or Royal Palace, depicted in figure 2.2. Visegrad's inaugural meeting had no plan to be called "Visegrad" nor had any cooperation that ensued. No name was formally fashioned in advance for the meeting, even if some officials referred to "Visegrad" before February 15, as a name for the gathering.[5] Pegging suitable meeting names, not least when they germinate perennial initiatives, was an oversight of this early if innovative diplomacy.

Missed branding opportunities in 1991 paralleled the original and very functional name for Havel's first regional summit, in Bratislava in April 1990, which was simply "Meeting '90." That lackluster, generic tag never gained circulation; even Czechoslovaks came to refer to the meeting as the Bratislava Summit and the coordination that followed as the "Bratislava Process."[6]

It was unintended continuity that the February 1991 gathering was also labeled not by its initiators but by nonparticipants, which gave it the international recognition that the Visegrad cooperation enjoyed thereafter. Havel's memoires highlight that in no document signed, nor in any verbal expression at the Visegrad meeting, did the group refer to itself as "Visegrad." Havel records that "it was the Hungarian journalists who began calling us the Visegrad Group. . . . I would add that in no document from that period did we officially call ourselves the Visegrad Group."[7] Nor was the cooperation's founding Declaration originally called "the Visegrad Declaration," and it did not contain "Visegrad" anywhere in its lengthy title. Instead and only it was "Declaration on Cooperation. . . . " The official site now calls the Declaration "Visegrad Declaration 1991," and that became its adopted name.[8] Havel's assertion of the absence of any name conflicts with a Polish foreign ministry spokesperson's comments to Hungarian media on February 7, a week before the summit: "Contrary to rumours, the document—which will later be known as the *Visegrad Declaration*—is ready to be signed."[9] That Polish officials offered such confirmation, the Hungarians were the summit's physical hosts, and the Czechoslovaks were predominantly the intellectual originators speaks also to trilateral cooperation behind the summit—and in favorable contradistinction to the disordered unilateralism behind its April 1990 predecessor.

That Bratislava Summit of 1990 was both a "hastily arranged" affair, one in which the Hungarians castigated the Czechoslovaks for presenting, without prior discussion, a communiqué intended for signing on the spot. The meeting at Visegrád had an agenda that derived from substantial prior preparations, arising partly from the many trilateral meetings that the April 1990 Summit stimulated. Czechoslovak foreign minister Jiří Dienstbier even recalled that the contents of what became the Declaration signed in February 1991 were agreed upon at a trilateral meeting in late December 1990. A delaying issue was the degree to which the cooperation would be institutionalized; Poland sought a standing committee of deputy foreign ministers, Hungary was opposed, and Czechoslovakia thought the issue irrelevant. Ultimately, cooperation remained ad hoc, until 1999, when a relaunch of Visegrad included the establishment of regularized meetings.[10] Even a week before the summit, a Hungarian newspaper quizzed Dienstbier as to whether the date was certain. To that he replied emphatically in the affirmative. He added that Poland and Hungary had agreed, making him confident of the timing.[11]

Provenance aside, and with its timetabling finally agreed upon, the Visegrad cooperation still could have benefited from popularization. Fortuitously, the name "Visegrad" stuck and went into circulation, probably better than had politicians and diplomats so attempted themselves.

Better still, while likely unintended, the name was certainly providential for two reasons. First, Visegrád functions in Czech, Polish, and Slovak but is readily said and understood in all four countries' languages—a feat among Hungarian palace-names, the region's Finno-Ugric linguistic outlier that is unconnected to those three Western Slavic languages. Few other locations in the region could have worked so well. That remains true even if Visegrád and Visegrad continue to be confused and misspelled, even by member governments, and mispronounced by others.[12] So shared is the term that a mythical birthplace of the city of Prague is also called Vyšehrad—having the same pronunciation, though a different spelling. That Vyšehrad is also the burial site for many Czech cultural figures and was later appropriated by anti-Visegrad Czech politician Václav Klaus to ridicule Visegrad cooperation.[13]

Second, "Visegrad" coincidentally also had accidental but ideal resonance in the United States. Slovakia's ambassador to the United States Martin Bútora recounted from a meeting of Visegrad officials with the members of the newly installed second George W. Bush presidential administration that "when the former American Ambassador to NATO, Robert Hunter, had the term 'Visegrad' translated, he discovered that it meant 'the city on the hill', a phrase which occupies a unique and irreplaceable spot in American national mythology, the place where the 'American dream' of freedom, equality and prosperity was lived out. The noble idea of Central European cooperation thus became fused with American idealism."[14]

The Visegrád site was chosen to evoke a historical parallel with an occasion, really the only time, when Central European leaders might be said to

FIGURE 2.1: Visegrád Castle atop Visegrád hill in Hungary, overlooking the Danube River, and symbol of Visegrad cooperation.

have cooperated together. This was a meeting on November 19, 1335, of the Central European monarchs: king Robert of Anjou, Polish king Kazimierz, and Jan of Luxembourg.[15] The analogy proved valuable for conjuring a historical background for this novel cooperation, the enchantment of which the chapter returns to shortly.

With the 1991 summit date definite, and an agenda established as early as December 1990, securing the venue would, presumably, be elementary. But with not one but two "Visegrád" venues available, the summit still lacked a suitable room. A further aim in using this unique historical setting was to re-create the setting of the three 1335 monarchical predecessors, and more staging was needed.

To do that, archaeologists and art historians were recruited. They succeeded in re-creating at "record speed" (though presumably no comparative record existed) a facsimile of the fourteenth-century venue.[16] The upper Visegrád Castle today houses wax re-creations of a feast of three kings, as shown in figures 2.3 and 2.4. Unlike their late-twentieth-century would-be successors who met but for hours, the kings and their expansive entourages encamped for a month. The wax re-creations cannot convey the tons of supplies needed for the accompanying men and their 5,000 horses.[17] Ahistoricism continues: within

FIGURE 2.2: A ground-level Visegrád venue, the second castle or Visegrád Royal Palace.

FIGURES 2.3 and 2.4: A wax sculpture re-creation of the 1335 monarchical "Visegrad" summit.

that medieval chamber today are the flags, as in figures 2.5 and 2.6, of all four Visegrad countries, though Slovaks or Slovakia had no direct part in 1335. The 1991 efforts at historical re-creation did not address the real and contemporary impracticalities of the intended medieval setting: the summit was being convened in an unheated venue made of stone, in February.

Consequently, Visegrád mayor Sándor Hadházy later lamented "the mismatch of expectations between the top-level diplomats" and what was available.

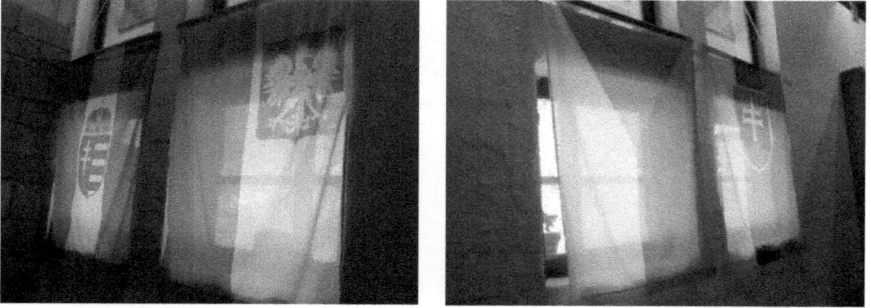

FIGURES 2.5 and 2.6: The current national flags displayed at the 1335 re-creation of the Czech, Hungarian, and Polish monarchs' meeting, and also including the flag of Slovakia.

FIGURE 2.7: The plaque and commemorative wreaths from four Visegrad foreign ministers but at the second- and ground-level of the Visegrád venue. Written only in Hungarian, it commemorates the meeting of the three countries under the leadership of Hungary's József Antall.

He revealed that the organizing diplomats "were very surprised because we couldn't find a site which met the safety and security requirements and additionally could be heated." The venue became the Royal Palace's cellar. Its previous purpose was housing a collection of stones. The mayor recalled that on the morning of the Declaration's signing, the royal grounds were freshly covered in heavy snow, and the temperature *inside* was minus-ten degrees Celsius, or fourteen degrees Fahrenheit. Some gas heaters were found and placed in the room to give a modicum of heat.[18] Photographs of the event, though, belie no cold and only pride, as the three national figures and their sizeable entourages assembled around the available tables for the Declaration's signature. For added posterity, the signing occurred in front of a plaque commemorating the 1335 meeting. The 1991 summit was marked by a larger group picture of leaders and dignitaries of the three countries (all being men), with a background of a wall-sized mural of medieval depictions.

Visegrad's launch was fine theater, employing a unique historical parallel for positive purposes. The castle atop Visegrád is taken as the symbol of the cooperation—a similar photograph to figure 2.1 has featured for years on the official Visegrad website's opening page.

Historical re-creation and theatrical parallels made, and the documents signed in each of the three languages—Czech, Hungarian, and Polish—but with no English counterpart even though that language would become the cooperation's working tongue, Visegrad's intentions deserve attention.

VISEGRAD'S INTENTIONS

Visegrad was performance: Czechoslovakia, Hungary, and Poland were theatrically demonstrating their ability to transcend historical differences and to achieve, summarily, their exit from the unnatural legacy of communist rule. The cooperation further communicated that three countries were the most advanced polities and economies of the entire post-communist world. They wanted, finally, to signal to and impress especially upon the EC, NATO, and the United States that they were both deserving of and prepared for membership. Visegrad was powerful theater, with a cast of the region's presidents, prime ministers, foreign ministers, and many parliamentarians. The Visegrad performance wanted to capture and enchant distant, potentially aloof, and indifferent audiences: Visegrad acted to make international actors think differently about their own role conceptions and their duties and responsibilities toward this newly democratized region of Europe.

How did Visegrad introduce itself to the world, and what did it intend? Entitled "Declaration on Cooperation between the Czech and Slovak Federal Republic, the Republic of Poland and the Republic of Hungary in Striving for European Integration," the document has since, as mentioned, become the "Visegrad Declaration 1991." The Declaration contained two parts. One could be called the character and aims of the cooperation but also contained extended references to historical and cultural determinants of these countries' place in Europe. The second part, bullet-pointed, established the cooperation's operational format. Seven observations arise from the Declaration's first section.

The first consideration is an absence from this otherwise ambitious document of references to hard security. Later in it, and only once, does the Declaration mention the Group's aims of "full involvement in the European . . . system of security." It forewent any allusion to developing security or military cooperation among the Three.

This telling omission speaks to the concerns observed earlier that the Group neither wanted to alarm Moscow nor permit a standoffish NATO to say that the Central Europeans were providing sufficient security for themselves.[19] Though by February 1991 all three states wanted NATO membership (but would only begin to enunciate that at their second summit, in October 1991, and then as a clear Group objective at their third summit, in May 1992), this omission was astute. The Declaration's wording also demonstrates the care with which these post-communist countries implicitly treated Moscow, and potentially other countries, many of whom became envious of Visegrad, and as this chapter soon recounts. The Declaration stated that this new cooperation would not exclude other relations and that it was "not directed against the interests of any other party." With Soviet troops still in eastern Germany, Poland, Hungary, Czechoslovakia, and the Baltic republics, and the Warsaw Pact moribund but not dismembered, this statement was calculated reassurance to Visegrad's neighbors that its existence and its intentions were benign.

The Declaration's second thrust was to communicate that these three countries belonged together, for several mutually reinforcing reasons. The Declaration pronounced that the three states possessed "convergent" policies to achieve their extraction from Soviet-era controls, without using such terminology. The three states were regaining their full sovereignty; building parliamentary democracy; implementing the rule of law and respect for human rights and a market economy; and returning to full involvement in European political, economic, and security systems.

A third dimension of the Declaration again concerns omissions that accentuated the validity of the second point: that these three countries, but not neighboring former fellow-socialist ones, were undertaking and excelling at the unprecedented process of their transformation from socialist authoritarianism and command economies. The Visegrad states implied through Visegrad their claim of being best placed among the entire post-socialist region because of their earlier historical legacies that would make their transition after 1989 easier and more fruitful. The language and the promises of democracy, market economy, human rights, and the rule of law in the Declaration were to reassure the West and to differentiate the Three from all others. This claim the Three made in the Declaration without specificity, but Visegrad leaders would detail these attributes later and as a justification for the Group's exclusive membership. Antall elaborated in October 1991 that the three countries' "rapid rapprochement" resulted from "the fact that parliamentary traditions in them are stronger than in the remaining postcommunist countries."[20]

Such differentiation among those countries was required because Visegrad's wider region contained new dangers and competing state interests. Yugoslavia was fragmenting, with Slovenia and Croatia having declared their independence from that socialist federation in June 1991. They shared some commonalities with the Visegrad Three—including having been in the Austro-Hungarian empire; being predominantly Western Christian; and using, unlike the other Slavic speakers of this multiethnic country, the Latin alphabet. As discussed later, Slovenia and Croatia sought close relations with Visegrad, and Slovenia was a country that entertained real prospects of joining the Group.[21]

Of the six communist-run states in the Moscow-run Warsaw Pact and CMEA, East Germany was already gone, having been absorbed into West Germany with unification in October 1990. Unlike the exception of East Germany, which cartographically disappeared in that month, Bulgaria and Romania remained as states, and as former socialist systems in Moscow's regional structures. Even the Baltic states, whose annexation into the USSR for over four decades still made their experience upon post-Soviet independence similar to those of the Visegrad Three, could have been included. The previous chapter indicated the Visegrad states' affinity toward the Baltic states and how Baltic representatives spoke of themselves also as "Central European."

By reiterating their commonality, the Declaration made Czechoslovakia, Hungary, and Poland stand out, and away from, all other former socialist regimes. Visegrad was advancing a tautological assertion regarding the relationship between developmental progress and cooperation: because the Three already had "a favorable basis" for its cooperation, its members also already shared a "similar character" from the wholesale domestic changes they were undertaking to return them to the West.[22] No other country, by implication, enjoyed those traits and therefore could not be included with them. The process of exclusion of countries from Visegrad at its outset began a permanent trend of nonexpansion of its membership. Unlike Visegrad, other contemporary regional formations were enlarged—such as the Council of the Baltic Sea States (CBSS), the Black Sea Economic Cooperation, the Pentagonale / Hexagonale / Central European Initiative (CEI), and the Central European Free Trade Agreement (CEFTA).[23] Visegrad's uniquely static yet secure group identity originated from the subtle choice of words in the 1991 founding Declaration that enunciated the Group's common and exclusive characteristics.

A fourth facet was the Declaration's repeated reference to the three countries having come historically from, and returning to, European values. These claims added to Visegrad's status of exceptionality, now stated in cultural-historical terms, and again for the benefit of their cautious Western partners. The Declaration asserted that the three members intrinsically had values that were part of "European thought" and that they were themselves upholding all that was fundamentally "European." This contention furnished a vital dimension for particularly Havel to advocate for the region's acceptance by NATO and the EC/EU. He would argue that those institutions needed, first, to recognize their own founding and common values and, second, recognize the same among the Central Europeans.[24] Through that recognition and that argument of common identity, Havel and other Central European leaders could impress additionally on the Euro-Atlantic community to reintegrate the Central European into these institutional hallmarks of being "Western."

Fifth, the Declaration asserted that despite past antagonisms, the Three had overcome animosities (questions over Hungarian minorities being set aside) and that these societies already re-adhered to European values in their everyday life and politics. The Declaration referred to "universal human values as the most important element of the European heritage." From those the Visegrad Group was expressly "developing a society of people cooperating with each other in a harmonious way, tolerant to each other" and which would extend from even "individual families" through to "local, regional and national communities," creating a transnational environment "free of hatred, nationalism, xenophobia, and local strife."[25] From the most elemental units of the family to the highest level of national governance and regional interactions, the Visegrad states would exude the tolerance and understanding that had become the norm of—and also requirement for—membership in the Euro-Atlantic community.

Those expressions of values yielded a sixth feature: that the three countries would not only "tolerate" each other (as "good" Europeans did) but also cooperate intensively and in the spirit of Western Europe's own history of successful integration. Better still: the Declaration was also articulating that the three Visegrad states were naturally "European" and ready to be not merely integrated into but returned to that geocultural fold.

A seventh aspect of the Declaration concerns two keywords, or rather one word with a specific qualifier: "Central Europe." This may seem semantic—but usage in the Declaration of "Central Europe" was, and remains, of paramount if symbolic substance.[26] For "Central Europe" also underlined the historicocultural belonging of the three signatory countries to Western Europe and, also, at least implicitly, contributed to the exclusion of others.

Visegrad mobilized the value-laden term "Central Europe" for its purposes. This is not to say that the framers of Visegrad thought that whatever "made" Central Europe into Central Europe was exclusively found there; they knew too well that the formative historical experiences that allowed them to claim a "Central European," and thus a European, identity were shared with and even inseparable from other geographic areas and populations. As much as such a regional identity was shaped by membership in the Austro-Hungarian empire, those legacies, as but starting points, extended also to the northwestern parts of Romania, the top of Yugoslavia/Serbia, and even western Ukraine and Belarus. Only some of Poland had had that experience, while it shared a deep history also with eastern neighbors, particularly Lithuania.

What precisely "Central Europe" might be—and unanswerable questions regarding that identity may themselves form some of the identity—the Declaration's enlistment twice of that term, and the nonuse anywhere of the passé and even pejorative "Eastern Europe," must be seen as intentional and momentous. And it planted seeds for early germination. For some in Central Europe, Visegrad's greatest early achievement was this "reintroduction of the term 'Central Europe' to the geopolitical dictionary."[27] The practical effects both for and on the foreign policy objectives and achievements of the Three demonstrate the Group's vitality.

The second part of the Declaration promises regularized, although still unspecified, meetings and activities, including advocacy of the Three's common interests. What Visegrad sought in practice and what it achieved in its early life now deserve consideration.

VISEGRAD COOPERATION AFTER THE "VISEGRAD DECLARATION"

Visegrad quickly made a name for itself and achieved significant foreign policy goals. Considering how crowded European and international politics are, and the myriad actors on the diplomatic stage, that a new group of countries could attract any attention, let alone secure objectives from a range of partners, speaks to Visegrad's early and noteworthy life.

The first essential feature of Visegrad was that it continued as a forum for cooperation. This should not be taken lightly, particularly in view of other regional experiments, including ones with the resources of established, wealthy Western democracies, which did not accelerate its activities and achievements comparably to Visegrad.[28] Political scientist Valerie Bunce attested that the Visegrad cooperation "proceeded very quickly" and that its Declaration was produced "a mere two years" after the Polish roundtable talks of 1989, which broke communism's forty-year monopolistic rule.[29] And it is important to record such testament to both the intensity and speed of Visegrad's early achievements. Within a couple of years, some analysts claimed that Visegrad had never worked.[30]

To achieve its European reputation, Visegrad had also to be able to function internally. This outsider assessment of the Group's early coherence is apposite: Visegrad had "acquired valuable habits of regular political consultation and a schooling in the challenges of multilateral cooperation."[31] Considering the diplomatic fumbling of 1990, and the limitations of foreign policy experience and of resources, such commentary is laudable. The Declaration's second section pledged that the Visegrad states would commence meetings, primarily of government entities, and to a lesser extent of society (which would begin in 1999), and also two further summits of heads of state, in Kraków in October 1991,[32] and in Prague in May 1992. In these first two years Visegrad intensified expressions of its unity and purpose. Dienstbier noted later that the three countries' ambassadors were instructed "to carry a common [Visegrad] message to the governments in whose countries they were accredited."[33] The natural differences of opinion among the Three in this early formative period were thoroughly gone by the Prague Summit of 1992. Instead, the three countries felt the readiness and urgency now to advance unambiguously a common position not only on their intentions regarding Euro-Atlantic integration but also on regional economic reforms and even on wider, world issues.[34]

A second set of achievements arose from Visegrad's aim to differentiate its three states from all other post-socialist ones, in name and in policy. Preeminent analyses already recognized Visegrad for being an attempt by its countries "to escape from eastern Europe" and to avoid association with, even before war, the "infinitely less attractive developments in the Balkans."[35] Policies extended first to these three countries included the removal of visa requirements by many Western countries. Similarly, Cold War–era arms embargos were lifted. US democratization support recognized the region's political distinctiveness. A Congressional Special Task Force on the Development of Parliamentary Institutions in Eastern Europe was created in April 1990, and got applied—despite the outdated and broad geopolitical reference—to only Czechoslovakia, Hungary, and Poland. Congressional support for the three countries' parliaments became "unique" among the region.[36]

The Three also coordinated on innovative policy initiatives, ones attempting to make the Group not a bridge but one side of a triangle, between the West and the Soviet Union and its successor states, whereby the Central Europeans supplied goods to the former Soviet Union, financed by the West.[37] In April 1992 the three countries' ambassadors to Washington jointly called on the United States to finance medications from their countries to then be sold in the former Soviet Union. They noted, by way of added argument, that the European Commission had already committed US$500,000,000 for that.[38]

Although some of these foreign responses were to the three countries, but bilaterally and initiated before Visegrad was created, a specific region within the former socialist world now existed among Western policymakers. Many of their foreign ministries also even reorganized themselves accordingly. The transformative effect of Visegrad's use of "Central Europe" is illustrated by leading US diplomat Richard Holbrooke:

> We abolished the outdated Office of Eastern European Affairs on our first day in office in September 1994, and created in its place three new offices that reflected the post–Cold War realities of Europe. One combined the Nordic countries and the three newly independent Baltic states. We also *banished the phrase "Eastern Europe"* from official vocabulary, *replacing it with the historically and geographically more accurate "Central Europe."* Unfortunately, most people, including the media, still use the outmoded phrase.[39]

Others, though, also sought to highlight Visegrad's efforts to transform thinking. A former American national security adviser, Poland-born Zbigniew Brzezinski, spoke in February 1992 of three Europes: a Europe of the established Western European democracies; a second, of Visegrad (with which he included Slovenia); and a third, comprising the other former socialist entities. Historian Norman Davies summarized that their "European aspirations would have to await the twenty-first century."[40] For regional-based analysts, "At the beginning of the 1990s, the word 'Visegrád' became an indispensable part of the political vocabulary in Central Europe and elsewhere."[41]

Although each of the three national leaders and other members of their governments had had bilateral engagements with other states and international institutions, following Visegrad they intensified their own efforts to coordinate their approaches especially to NATO and the EC. These endeavors receive focus in chapter 5; so important, if also debatable, is Visegrad's history in achieving Euro-Atlantic accession.

Some of Visegrad's recognition as a new international actor within months illustrate its success. British foreign secretary Douglas Hurd noted that the British presidency of the European Communities had invited the foreign ministers of the three Visegrad countries to take part in a meeting on October 4, 1991. The Council Presidency-in-Office also confirmed its intention to organize a "summit" of heads of state and government with these three countries on October 28, 1991. That these three counties already stood out among socialist countries was reinforced by failed efforts of some EC leaders to include other post-communist countries, particularly Bulgaria and Romania.[42] The Visegrad Three became a diplomatic performer that outpaced other post-communist countries.

By the end of 1992, then, Visegrad firmly existed in international official circles. Its activities were wide ranging, including statements on international affairs and a program of extensive trade liberalization. Documents such as the Kraków Declaration from the Visegrad Summit in October 1991 referred to the "Central European Three"; officials of the three countries used the terms "Triangle" or Visegrad in mutual reference;[43] and major international actors treated the three countries in common fashion. Kraków also reinforced the Three's united determination to seek NATO membership. Thus Poland used a CSCE meeting in October 1991, just after the Kraków Summit, to state that the three countries had requested their inclusion in NATO. United Germany too saw Visegrad early along "as a coherent grouping,"[44] and it would also be German defense minister Volker Rühe in March and October 1993 who first called for Visegrad's membership in NATO.

Additionally, Visegrad was experimenting with interregionalism, a theme that gained importance and formalization in the Group's later existence. In this initial period, interaction was primarily with Benelux, the Belgian-Dutch-Luxembourgish cooperation founded in 1944. By 1992 the two groups had begun meetings and had plans for more, including one to "define specific, practical means of co-operation." These included meetings on free trade and establishment of a unified customs system, lessons from Benelux's experience of joint policy on visas and migration, and transfrontier cooperation.[45]

Three further dimensions of Visegrad's early success merit consideration. The first derives from the enduring set of contrasting claims to the creation of Visegrad. The second is the early testament to Visegrad's success from the reactions it produced among its neighbors. The third was a partial answer to the limited response of the EC but also an achievement in its own right—Visegrad's creation of its own free trade area.

VISEGRAD: MULTIPLE PARENTAL CLAIMS

With issues of heating attended to for the summit, and the founding Declaration assessed, the matter of who deserves credit for the full creation of Visegrad now deserves attention. This is an important item, not least because it remains contested. To invert US president John F. Kennedy's statement on the failed invasion of Cuba at the Bay of Pigs: "There's an old saying that victory has a hundred fathers and defeat is an orphan."[46] By contrast, the intense (and contradictory) contestation over birth reconfirms Visegrad's value and importance.

A starting point for claims on Visegrad begin, perhaps naturally, with the host country. Hungarian claims need to be noted, but they also face contestation. Knowing that, Hungary's first post-communist foreign minister, Géza Jeszenszky, expressly counters "the many versions in circulation" regarding Visegrad's origins. He writes that "as probably the closest witness, I can testify that it was at the Paris summit of the CSCE in November 1990 that the Prime

Minister of Hungary, József Antall, invited the leaders of Poland and Czechoslovakia to Visegrad."[47] True, the three countries met as a "troika" during that CSCE Summit (further evidence itself of growing cooperation), to coordinate their approaches to Western institutions. In referring to the founding Visegrad declaration, Jeszenszky also retrospectively wrote of "the signing of Antall's initiative."[48] Czechoslovakia's Jiří Dienstbier recounts that it was at the same meeting and, from Antall, that the invitation to Visegrád was made. That is important credit to Hungary, although Dienstbier also said that Antall issued the invitation in order "to follow up the meeting in Bratislava."[49] Some Hungarian scholars, decades later and without reference to November 1990, similarly assert that Visegrad was a "Hungarian invention," and others have said, "Visegrad was held in Hungary, and therefore it is Hungarian."[50]

Such ex post facto associations with locality instinctively credit such Hungarian claims of initiation. Apart from the questions that those assumptions generate, they also neglect to answer when Visegrad was started. Hungary's Jeszenszky uniquely maintains that it was Antall's initiative, as mentioned, and at the Paris CSCE Summit of November 1990 that was, effectively, the place of Visegrad's inception.[51] That assertion, in turn, may have prompted further retrospective commentary, such as that "as for activities behind the scenes of the Visegrád summit, it was clear who would be the host and who would, therefore, invite the other parties," namely Hungary.[52] The edification of Hungary's role is also shown by the inscription at the ground-level Visegrád site, in figure 2.7 above, which credits by name only Antall for Visegrad, under his leadership, and with no stated reference to other leaders.

In asserting Hungarian parentage, practitioners and analysts of Hungary generated conflicting timelines. One of the first analysts of post-communist regional cooperation, Rudolf Tökés, also backs the Hungarian claim to Visegrad but then uniquely credits the birth of Visegrad to yet another, and entirely separate, meeting from the one to which Jeszenszky referred. Specifically rebuffing Bratislava's role, Tökés contends that the impetus for Visegrad occurred at the Warsaw Treaty Organization meeting in Moscow on June 7, 1990. There Hungary unilaterally declared that it would exit the Warsaw Pact and that that statement incentivized the others to contemplate joint achievements.[53] These Hungarian (and mutually exclusive) claims remain in the minority.

Even though Visegrád exists in Hungary, others make a claim for specifically Polish contributions. An early and insightful chronicler of Visegrad, and of Polish foreign policy broadly, Joshua B. Spero wrote that Polish "Foreign Minister [Krzysztof] Skubiszewski initiated and fortified a formalized Visegrad process."[54] Similarly, Bunce credits Polish prime minister Tadeusz Mazowiecki's contributions toward creating Visegrad, naming him as one of two people principally responsible for Visegrad, and elaborates his role, before naming the second person: Havel. In this account Havel is said in February 1990 to have "responded with enthusiastic support" to Mazowiecki's proposals; there are no references to Havel's January 1990 speeches, including in Warsaw.[55] Mazowiecki, however, records not his own input, let alone ownership, but instead ambiguity over its prospects: "From the very beginning I viewed the 'Visegrad process' with great expectations but, I must admit, a certain scepticism as well."[56]

Solidarity leader Lech Wałęsa credited Visegrad exclusively to Polish communist-era resistance, pronouncing it "the fruit of the idea of the Polish Solidarity movement, launched ten years before the start of Visegrad."[57] Mass Polish dissidence remains unquestionably fundamental to political change in Eastern Europe. Wałęsa's statement alone, however, gives no pedigree to Visegrad and does not refer to the Czechoslovak-Polish dissident meetings held *before* the Solidarity movement arose. Later perceptions of Polish initiation may also arise from confusion over CEFTA rather than Visegrad—some Western media took Poland to be the free trade instigator, something that Hungary accepted in principle (at the Hungarian Ministry of Economic Relations in April 1991) and about which Czechoslovakia seemed hesitant.[58] Unilateral Polish initiation of Visegrad seems, frankly, implausible.

Polish contributions more realistically to Visegrad are those that speak to its origins as a joint initiative and then mostly spiritually and ideationally, from the pre-1989 era of political dissent. Zbigniew Janas provides another claim to Polish-specific initiatives for Visegrad in *The Visegrad Group* commemorative book. He recounts dissident intellectual contributions in the 1970s and 1980s, especially also efforts in 1990—ones that he literally says he began on a Polish friend's kitchen table. Janas adds that he and Michnik took the initial ideas to Polish foreign minister Skubiszewski and then onward to Czechs and Slovaks, including Dienstbier and Havel.[59]

Even Janas, however, ultimately confirms joint Polish-Czechoslovak contributions, including those in thought and in action that derive from their interactions before 1989. That view also affirms the contents of interviews conducted with Czechoslovak/Czech activists in the early 1990s and more recent ones (i.e., diplomats who have come to the Visegrad portfolio without early-1990s experience), all of which see Visegrad as a Polish-Czechoslovak initiative and connected to their communist-era dissidents. Regional cooperation as an offshoot of communist-era Polish and Czechoslovak dissident contacts and mutual support certainly provided some inspiration. That is especially so with communist-era dissidents catapulted to office in or immediately after 1989 and who were extending personal experience to their new capacities to construct foreign policy. In those early days, when Havel talked already of regional cooperation, Polish dissidents had not fully grasped control of the making of foreign policy as their Czechoslovak counterparts had. But in terms of spirit and values, the communist-era Czechoslovak-Polish dissident cooperation certainly was significant, perhaps even imperative, for building interpersonal bonds (and compensating for others, especially perhaps those lacking between Havel and Wałęsa) and as a later inspiration for Visegrad.

Still other claims exist from Slovak, as opposed to Czechoslovak, accounts of the significance of the April 1990 meeting. While the Bratislava Summit is often forgotten, and the Visegrad cooperation is habitually (but not always) formally marked as having commenced in 1991, Slovak diplomats emphasize that the 1990 Bratislava meeting started the whole cooperation. Furthermore, they refer to "Bratislava to Bratislava." That assertion connects Bratislava 1990 to Bratislava 2011, the latter taken as the twentieth anniversary of cooperation.[60] The Slovak website Terez.sk has featured since 2015 the publication of "unique photos" of that April 1990 meeting, regularly referring to the trilateral meeting as "historic," although the page does not name the event as the precursor to Visegrad.[61]

By contrast, the strongest claim remains that Visegrad originated as a Czechoslovak initiative, particularly one from Václav Havel. To be sure, many asserting that entitlement were Czech or Czechoslovak. Former dissident and post-communist deputy prime minister of Czechoslovakia Ján Čarnogurský, himself a Slovak, states that inspiration for post-communist cooperation came from those advising Havel, and he unambiguously credits Havel for specifically initiating it. So too does post-communist Czechoslovak ambassador to Hungary Rudolf Chmel.[62] Some contemporary analysts, and not necessarily Czech(oslovak), also outright, and exclusively, recognize Havel: "The main initiator and author of the project of the founding documents was the then president of Czechoslovakia, Václav Havel, who—as befits an author of theatre plays—knew how to assign new political roles to particular states in the region."[63] Similarly, Libor Rouček, a Czechoslovak/Czech analyst, and later member of European Parliament (MEP), wrote in a near-contemporary work, "The idea of developing close relations between the three Central European states was first proposed by Czechoslovakia." He, too, cites Havel's visits to Warsaw and Budapest and the calls there for the three states to coordinate their return to Europe, along with proposals for what became the Bratislava Summit.[64] And further worth noting amid the many parental claims to Visegrad, the absurdist playwright Havel did not direct the opening of the Visegrad play, but he had a director's hand in its ultimate choice of stage. Better yet: he penned and redrafted the draft of what became Visegrad's founding Declaration, as figure 2.8 depicts.[65] The image is included, although not prominently, on the official Visegrad website and would, one might expect, help to dent some myths regarding Visegrad's genesis.

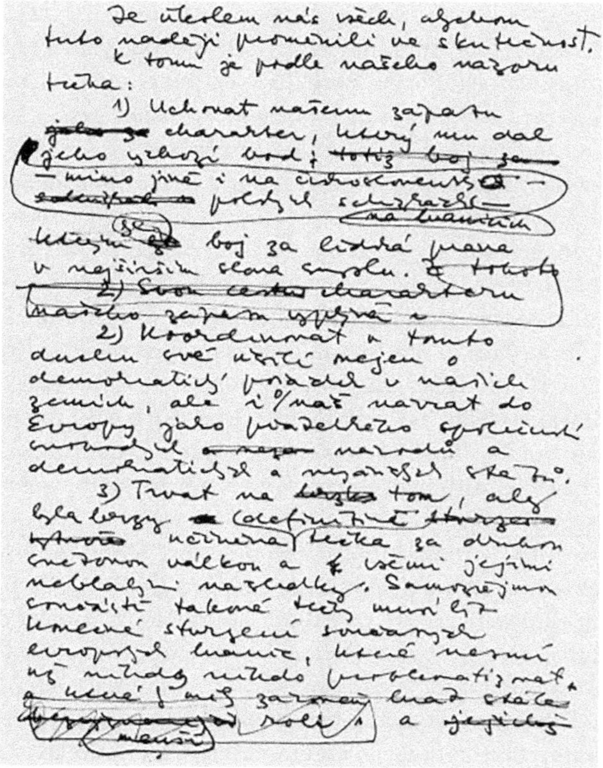

FIGURE 2.8: Vaclav Havel's handwritten draft of the founding Declaration of the Visegrad Group. *Visegrad Group.*

Occasionally some Hungarian sources, which otherwise assert ownership claims, also recognize contributions from Czechoslovakia and Havel, including that neighboring states "followed the unusually active foreign policy of Prague with astonishment."[66] One official Hungarian source even acknowledged the impetus behind Visegrad to be the Czechoslovak meeting in Bratislava the year before, even if it got the date wrong.[67] Hungarian foreign policy analyst László Andor wrote that the Czechoslovak president "initiated" Visegrad and attributed its origins to Havel's speeches in Poland and Hungary, as well as to the Bratislava meeting.[68] That assessment returns us to where we began: with Havel's pronouncement of the foundational idea in January 1990, in speeches in Poland and Hungary, and his appeal for regional solidarity to pursue their primary foreign policy goals.

Indeed on the whole, the Czechoslovak/Czech perception remains that the initiative was very heavily, even exclusively, Czechoslovak, and particularly originating with Havel. Havel's friend and presidential spokesperson Michael Žantovský avows: "The Visegrad idea [was] conceived by Havel at Bratislava."[69]

Apart from any achievements, Visegrad itself has gained multiple claims to its conception. What additionally attested to Visegrad's worthiness was the number of countries and the intensity by which they sought membership or even merely association.

VISEGRAD'S EXCLUSIVITY
AS A MARKER OF SUCCESS

Visegrad had established itself quickly. It did so to the point of fueling jealousy and fears of exclusion among neighboring states. These perceptions and concerns arose from Visegrad's early use and even monopolization of the potent geocultural term referred to earlier, "Central Europe," in place of the old, socialist-affiliated and even pejorative "Eastern Europe."[70] Doing so added to the abilities of the three countries, and Visegrad as a group, to distinguish themselves from the rest of the post-communist region, from the north, to the east, and to the south.

Two region-based analysts reflected common sentiments that the Visegrad countries were "constantly looking for evidence that they are distinct and separate from the rest of the former Soviet bloc."[71] They need not have looked; it was there. Visegrad's swift success in differentiating the three countries from the rest of the post-communist world at times brought admiration; at others, envy. Considered next are how Romania, Bulgaria, and Ukraine viewed Visegrad's emergence, and how it became a mirror that these countries held up to scrutinize their own progress.

Objective differences existed in the starting points of post-communist countries in the massive undertaking to become liberal-market democracies. Romania in 1990, for example, had less than half of Czechoslovakia's per capita GDP.[72] That did not stop Romania from reacting and may also have provoked Romania to react to Visegrad even before it existed. Aware of the Hungarian meeting, Romanian prime minister Petre Roman wrote to Antall four days before it convened to ask, even plead, for Romania's inclusion. Roman's letter anticipated the contents of the Declaration and tried to make Romania's case for inclusion: that it shared the same values and that its history and culture were intertwined with those of the others. Romania too, he claimed, was embarking on the same transformative processes. Considering that the northwest of Romania had belonged to the Austro-Hungarian empire and therefore shared some legal, administrative, and even culinary commonalities, not to mention some Catholic-Hungarian population, Romanian claims to Visegrad were made robustly and, to some degree, appropriately.[73]

The Czechoslovak, Hungarian, and Polish leaders, however, accepted none of that. As perhaps an early act of cooperation, the three leaders of the soon-to-be Visegrad Group promptly agreed that Antall should deliver the refusal to Romania. Nevertheless at the Visegrad Summit, on one hand Havel reiterated that the Group was not formed against anyone, but on the other, according to his foreign minister, Havel said that the Group should only have bilateral relations with Romania and with Bulgaria.[74]

Denial heightened attraction. Romania's Roman said that his country's inclusion in quadrilateral cooperation would improve the region's external impressions. Unswayed, Antall's written reply included that all three leaders agreed to discount the cooperation's expansion to Romania, or to any other country.[75] Poland's foreign minister recounted that during the Visegrad meeting, Bucharest's apprehensions manifested themselves as "strong criticisms" against even the fact of the summit and then as the presentation of it as "a kind of anti-Romanian bloc, [an] anti-Romanian conspiracy." The Romanian government was bothered enough about this exclusivist cooperation that its foreign minister sought Dienstbier at a CSCE meeting. The Czechoslovak foreign minister claimed later that he succeeded in diffusing Bucharest's fears of Visegrad "conspiracies" against Romania by merely joking about them.[76]

Romanian concerns about exclusion from Visegrad continued, despite comic reassurances. Asked if Poland, Hungary, and Czechoslovakia were seeking regional integration into Romania's marginalization, Romanian president Ion Iliescu's chief security and foreign policy adviser Ion Pancu replied in April 1991 by giving the proverbial brave face to reality: "In the wake of the disintegration of the Warsaw Pact and Council for Mutual Economic Assistance, the intention to create new structures is natural. Poland, Czechoslovakia, and Hungary rightly wish to strengthen the traditional ties that link them, and in the meantime, all three also want to be part of the large[r] European integration, too."[77] The *Economist*, however, was forthright: Romania felt "hurt to be left out" of the trilateral Central European cooperation.[78] Timothy Garton Ash was blunter about Visegrad's rejection of Romania: "The door was shut in its face." Domestically, Romania remained politically repressive, and the view was that Visegrad could turn westward more easily without it.[79] Bucharest's foreign policy ambitions came to include "a consistent attempt to eliminate the distinction between the Visegrad states and Romania."[80] After the Visegrad Summit Romania also unsuccessfully attempted to create an alternative "Central and Eastern European Union."[81]

Bulgarian political fears of and envy toward Visegrad echoed Romania's, and the country received similar rebuffs. When NATO introduced the Partnership for Peace (PfP), which was offered to almost all twenty-seven post-communist countries and thus could not serve as a security guarantee, Romania and Bulgaria consequently "greeted PFP with enthusiasm and relief because it closed off [they believed] the immediate entry of the Visegrad states into NATO."[82]

Bulgarian leaders acknowledged that post-communist political developments in their country lagged behind those of Poland, Hungary, or Czechoslovakia and that they provided standards against which to measure Bulgaria's progress. Bulgarian president Zhelu Zhelev and foreign minister Viktor Valkov visited Budapest in April 1991. Their Hungarian counterparts gave detailed updates on Budapest's involvement in regional initiatives, including both the Pentagonale (as the CEI remained at that point) and Visegrad. Bulgarian media reported that at the presidential meeting Zhelev "stressed that the Republic of Hungary, Czechoslovakia and Poland should not view Bulgaria as 'something different' from them." In his presidential toast at the Budapest gala dinner, Zhelev said that the countries shared the same strategic goals of "democratic legislation, democratization of the institutional system, market economies, civilized society, full respect of human rights, and cultural pluralism." The response, again, was clear: the Visegrad Three "had no intention of opening up to other countries of the former socialist camp."[83]

Two months later, and with no prospect of Visegrad engagement for Bulgaria, Zhelev told his political party conference that a measuring stick for the country's transition from communism was "whether Bulgaria will no longer be apart from *the three central European* countries—Poland, Hungary, and Czechoslovakia."[84] In turn, this exclusion made Bulgaria (and Romania) "wary of the [Visegrad] group because it implicitly excluded them as primary candidates for integration with the West."[85] When the EC detailed some of its expectations of relations with post-communist countries at its Copenhagen Summit in 1993, Visegrad apprehensions over its association with these Southeast European states materialized in statements of Polish premier Hanna Suchocka. She said that "we" (presumably Klaus, with whom she gave a press conference) "do not agree" with their countries being placed with Bulgaria and Romania.[86] Even the unpredictable leader of independent Slovakia, Vladimír Mečiar,[87] stressed in 1993 that mere talks with Bulgaria and Romania did not imply that Visegrad would expand.[88] Undeterred, Zhelev continued using Visegrad as a benchmark, stating in 1995: "Bulgaria is lagging farther and farther behind the Visegrad Four in the integration process."[89]

That Visegrad differentiated its members from the rest of the post-socialist world was quickly noted and disseminated in Western press. Thus, for example, while stating that Visegrad had achieved "little in concrete terms" at its founding meeting, as geographically remote a newspaper as the *Los Angeles Times* deemed Visegrad "an example of the emerging north-south divide that has opened up in Eastern Europe. . . . A constant state of crisis in Romania and Bulgaria has slowed reform and recovery, prompting their neighbors to the north to leave them behind in the quest for integration with Western Europe."[90] Years later Central European leaders returned to how Visegrad differentiated parts of the post-communist world. Polish president Aleksander Kwaśniewski wrote in 2006 that the "Visegrad Group has been regarded as the positive antithesis of the Balkan region."[91]

Visegrad's attractiveness extended eastward. Newly independent Ukraine saw association with Visegrad as a means to reject a Soviet identity and reassert a Central European, and thereby European, identity. As early as 1992, Ukrainian officials sought Polish support in advance of a presidential visit to Warsaw to help secure their country's admission.[92] Instead, Visegrad came to be known in Ukraine as a "discriminating mechanism" that separated it from the countries with which it wanted to be associated.[93] Ukrainian interest in Visegrad, including full membership, continued under presidencies and governments regardless of whether they were deemed to lean toward Moscow or the West.[94]

At its launch in February 1991 and at various points in its history, Visegrad often inferred or acknowledged that it was tantamount to an elite grouping. Such exclusivity is remembered by Visegrad. The 2012–13 Polish Visegrad Report reflected back more than two decades to say that Group's "first success was to make our countries stand out from the whole post-communist region."[95] That it most certainly did. But Visegrad did still more by liberalizing trade among its national economies, and through that demonstrated regional leadership as well as creating another cooperation platform which outsiders also desired. The Central European Free Trade Agreement would make sense for membership expansion.

VISEGRAD'S ADDITIONAL EARLY ACHIEVEMENT: THE CENTRAL EUROPEAN FREE TRADE AGREEMENT

Visegrad was about showing cooperation and using that cooperation to secure early and valuable engagement with NATO and the EC. Of course these countries were saddled with forty years of socialist economic planning or, rather, market distortions. The Visegrad Three was triply disadvantaged. Its member states faced all of the crippling legacies of socialist economic planning, which would make both a domestic and an international transition to market economics arduous. Additionally, while the socialist economies were, in principle, meant to be rationally planned, the three economies faced intense competition from each other because of socialist-era planning, which instead had these economies duplicate one another, problematic in itself. Compounding the problem was that the EC saw itself in competition with the Visegrad states' same economic sectors: textiles, agriculture, and steel. Third, in a coincidence of bad timing, Central European governments sought to make this unprecedented change in a worldwide recession, one heightened by soaring oil prices caused by the 1990–91 Gulf War by the fact that the Soviet Union had begun to demand hard currency payment for energy deliveries.

In short, each Visegrad state became the others' competitors. Consider the limited comparative advantage the region had toward the EC—they had relatively well-trained and cheap labor, industrial-labor salaries at the outset of the post-communist period being between one-tenth and one-fifteenth of German wages. These economies had also just entered the grand race to attract foreign investment to their capital-starved economies, to jettison aged industrial plants, and retool to produce to Western standards.

Between the poor state of their economies, and a natural competition between them in their most viable sectors, a free trade agreement would seem outlandish, even irresponsible. Many doubted that such could ever be concluded, or that "no amount of co-operation" would resolve their difficulties;[96] Hungary's Antall said in October 1991 that barrier-free trade was "impossible."[97]

It is all the more commendable that these three countries started to liberalize trade among themselves. Improving trade relations was already a starting aim of Visegrad in February 1991. By November 1991 the three countries' finance ministers had established the basis for what would become CEFTA, and it was formally announced at Visegrad's third summit, in Prague on May 6, 1992. CEFTA itself was signed on December 21, 1992, and went into effect on March 1, 1993. Although CEFTA initially did not significantly increase the three countries' trade, it importantly signaled to the West their willingness to expand cooperation and thereby also provided tangible evidence of their willingness to emulate Western practices in trade. Ironically, CEFTA had an inherent limitation: Visegrad's own goal of integration into and then membership in the EC/EU. As important as CEFTA became, a Visegrad champion like Dienstbier warned early along, "If it's possible, it could be useful. But we cannot do anything which would postpone a free trade agreement with the European Community."[98] The rhetorically free-market Klaus government could applaud CEFTA (and other times attack it). Czech foreign minister Josef Zieleniec proudly, if without substantiation, called CEFTA the world's most dynamic free-trade area.[99] For Hungary's doubting Antall, results spoke: in CEFTA's first year, 1994, Hungarian trade with its members jumped 30 percent.[100]

Although Visegrad refused to enlarge, CEFTA did open to other countries and thereby gave added testimony to being the ones to model and to join. Unlike the sacrosanct membership that was Visegrad, CEFTA, as one regional commentator wrote in the late 1990s, came "to include alongside the Central European states their embarrassing Eastern counterparts."[101] This phrase starkly reiterates the perception of distinctions between core Central Europe members and others, presumably even Slovenia, let alone Romania and Bulgaria.

Nevertheless, just as Visegrad became a marker of success for other social-ist countries, so too was membership of CEFTA seen not only as domestic political-economic progress but also as a country's ability to get closer to West-ern institutions, foremost the EU. By the late 1990s, Bulgaria's acceptance into CEFTA provided public testimonial to its domestic stabilization.[102]

Even so, Romania and Bulgaria remained into the 2000s relative outsiders of Central Europe. One observer contrasted Visegrad's impact on its members versus Southeastern Europe: "The Visegrad Group is particularly indicative of regional integrative efforts resonating positively with the wider process of Euro-pean integration. On the contrary, the region of the Balkans stands out as one where endeavours of state cooperation are effectively cancelled by the uneven distribution of progress towards the [European] Union."[103]

Even those who suggested that CEFTA might have been, in the early 1990s, the world's least-known and least-advertised trade grouping—and in contrast to Czech glorification—nevertheless noted the EU's recognition of CEFTA's utility in the region's accession preparations.[104] Although Czech prime minister Klaus later proactively and gravely disrupted Visegrad cooperation, as outlined in the next chapter, he routinely defended CEFTA. At its September 1996 summit in Jasná, Slovakia, he declared that CEFTA was not losing its breath and ratio-nalized that "it's easier to make large strides at the beginning. Once you get to the more sensitive stages, it becomes more difficult." Any seeming slowdown was "simply a logical development."[105] That supportive comment, too, should be put in the context of CEFTA having become operational in less than two years of Visegrad's existence. CEFTA would earn, and accept, the membership interests of Slovenia, Romania, Bulgaria, and Croatia, and with strong, if unre-ciprocated interest from Ukraine. And while the original CEFTA was appro-priated by the EU to help the Western Balkans by 2006, that project and that emulation continued, to the further point that the Western Balkan 6 Common Regional Market would expressly model itself on both Visegrad and the origi-nal CEFTA's lessons.[106]

CONCLUSION

At the end of 1992 Visegrad had achieved the inconceivable. It was an estab-lished European entity, able to demand not only the recognition of major actors but also concessions from them. Outside observers saw Visegrad—that is, as a cohesive diplomatic group of the four states—successfully engaging with and even exerting demands on the EC in 1992. Better still, the EC's own *The Con-clusions of the Presidency*, issued at the Edinburgh European Council of Decem-ber 1992, not only recognized Visegrad cooperation but also applauded the "intensified" high-level meetings that it and the Group were convening. And it called for more.[107] Visegrad had a clear identity; the name Visegrad was in international political vocabulary and drew the awe and envy of its neighbors. Visegrad also launched regional trade liberalization, setting the grounds for a free trade area, one that others clamored to join.

All those achievements aside, what greater accomplishment for a formation less than two years old, with dilapidated economies, to have become a lauded negotiating partner of the European Communities? Extraordinarily, this was the moment when Visegrad began to die. The next chapter explains this ironic turn of events.

NOTES

1. The spelling "Visegrád" is used here for locations—both for the Hungarian town and for its two historical royal venues. "Visegrad," as became the diplomatic convention, is the spelling of the cooperation.
2. Hungary was represented by its prime minister because of Hungarian constitutional powers that invest foreign policy powers comparable to those of presidents elsewhere, and certainly to those of Poland and Czechoslovakia. Hence "presidents" cannot be used to describe the three national leaders collectively. The extent to which constitutionally the Hungarian president or prime minister was to deal most with foreign policy also was an issue in Hungarian politics in the early 1990s. See Kim.
3. See Rácz, *Visegrád*.
4. Rácz, "Congress," 262.
5. *Népszabadság*, February 7, 1991, as "Dienstbier Comments on Cooperation, Prospects," *FBIS*, February 14, 1991, 20–21.
6. See chapter 1.
7. Havel, *To the Castle and Back*, 156.
8. The official site reference to the Declaration as "Visegrad Declaration 1991," is, e.g., at https://www.visegradgroup.eu/documents/visegrad-declarations/visegrad -declaration-110412-2.
9. *Népszabadság*, February 15, 1991, *FBIS*, as "Foreign Ministry Views Eastern European Prospects," February 21, 1991, 21.
10. See chapter 4.
11. *Népszabadság*, February 7, 1991, as "Dienstbier Comments on Cooperation, Prospects," *FBIS*, February 14, 1991, 20–21.
12. The Hungarian government routinely tends to use the geographic spelling in reference to the Group's activities in official statements. E.g., on the prime minister's official website: "Our Visegrád partners are ready to help with Hungary's border protection efforts," October 17, 2019; accessed October 26, 2019; or the Ministry of Agriculture: "Agricultural ministers of Visegrád Cooperation had talks in Prague," October 5, 2019, accessed October 26, 2019. At the height of the migrant crisis, the subject of chapter 7, Visegrad was routinely mispronounced, including by region-based veteran journalists.
    The Polish-language equivalent of "Visegrád," "Wyszehrad," may appear a different spelling but is pronounced similarly.

13. Chapter 3 refers to later antagonist of Visegrad, Czech prime minister Václav Klaus, who plays a mocking double entendre on this Czech place-name to deride Visegrad cooperation.

14. Bútora, "Spirit of Visegrad," 91–92. From various later informal discussions, Hunter's comments and Bútora's reference to them seem, however, otherwise not to have generated familiarity in wider American policy circles.

15. The monarchical names, spellings, and titles appear here in keeping with references by the Visegrad cooperation.

16. Klaniczay, 256; Michaud.

17. This tangential historical feature is mapped wonderfully in Rácz, "Congress," esp. 262–63, and contains further Hungarian sources.

18. Adapted from Grabiński.

19. NATO (and EC/EU) "standoffishness" is elaborated in chapter 5.

20. Życie Warszawy, October 8, 1991, as "Antall Interviewed on Central European Issues," FBIS, October 15, 1991, 18.

21. As noted elsewhere, Slovenia is the only country that some Visegrad politicians seriously considered for membership. Slovak foreign minister Jozef Moravčík said in May 1993 that Visegrad's format should be retained, and "at most, it is worth seriously considering the inclusion of Slovenia." Népszabadság, May 27, 1993, FBIS, June 1, 1993, 15.

22. Quotation from the English-language version of the now-named "Visegrad Declaration 1991," February 15, 1991, https://www.visegradgroup.eu/documents /visegrad-declarations/visegrad-declaration-110412-2.

23. Comparative histories and expansions of membership appear in Fawn, "Regional Relations," and are returned to in chapter 9.

24. A particularly strong statement of that, and then run in the US policy journal Foreign Affairs, was Havel's "A Call for Sacrifice," exhorting that "the West must open itself up to the states that Communism cleaved from Europe. Otherwise it risks undermining the values of its civilization."

25. "Visegrad Declaration 1991."

26. The journal Central European History states that it "perennially engages anew the old question, 'what and where is central Europe?,'" accessed December 22, 2023, https://www.cambridge.org/core/journals/central-european-history/information /about-this-journal/.

27. Bajda, "Visegrad Group," 30.

28. These would, again, be the CBSS and the CEI, and we reference the same comparative studies demonstrating their relative lack of success compared to Visegrad.

29. Bunce, 253.

30. Zbigniew Lewicki of the Institute of East-West Studies, quoted in Timea Spitkova, "Visegrad's Usefulness in Doubt," Prague Post, June 13, 1995.

31. Whitehall Papers, 29.

32. The English-language rendition of the southwestern Polish city of Kraków is "Cracow."

33. Dienstbier, "Visegrad—The First Phase."

34. Dunay, "Hungary," 152–53.

35. Strategic Survey, 159. Todorova remains a major work on conceptualizations of the Balkans.

36. Robinson, 32.

37. See Dienstbier's "Visegrad—The First Phase."

38. In her contribution, Czechoslovak ambassador Rita Klímová called for US law that prevented such transfers through third countries to be amended. *A-Wire*, April 9, 1992.

39. Holbrooke, 8 [emphasis added].

40. Davies, 1128.

41. Kopecek, 1.

42. Agence Europe, "U.K. Presidency Outlines Procedure for Managing Dossier on Enlargement," July 21, 1992, wrote for example: "[French minister for European affairs] Elisabeth Guigou also made a speech in which she said one should 'not forget Bulgaria and Romania.' The French Minister for European Affairs, backed mainly by the Spanish, Italian and Greek delegations, as well as by Vice President Andriessen, stated: 'If the aim is to strengthen political dialogue, it is very important for these two countries to be associated.'" Bulgaria and Romania did sign Association Agreements and were included with the then-four Visegrad countries in the 1993 EC/EU Copenhagen Summit, which began tentative terms for accession. In these senses Romania and Bulgaria could be said to have caught up with Visegrad. Chapter 5 addresses accession competition among postcommunist states.

43. Confirmation of usage and commentary in Clarke, 42; Thomas for contemporary analysis of the summit.

44. Handl, Longhurst, and Zaborowski, 55.

45. See the synopsis in *Annuaire Européen 1992 / European Yearbook 1992*, vol. 40, section 15.

46. Presidential press conference given on April 21, 1961, often misquoted as "a thousand fathers," written records at John F. Kennedy Library and Museum, https://www.jfklibrary.org/archives/other-resources/john-f-kennedy-press-conferences/news-conference-10.

47. Jeszenszky, "Origins," 60.

48. Jeszenszky, "Hungary's," 48.

49. Dienstbier, "Visegrad—The First Phase," 41–42.

50. E.g., Arató and Koller, unpaginated online version. This has also been said to me by other Hungarian scholars.

51. Jeszenszky, "Origins."

52. *Sharing the Experiences of Visegrad Cooperation in the Western Balkans and the Eastern Neighbourhood Countries Project Preparatory Study*, 15, last accessed January 23, 2024, https://s3.eu-central-1.amazonaws.com/uploads.mangoweb.org/shared-prod/visegradfund.org/uploads/2020/09/V4_WB_Online-4.pdf.

53. Tőkés, 103; supported by Dunay, "Security," 123, drawing from Hungarian-language sourcing.

54. Spero, *Bridging*, 226.

55. Bunce, 247–48.

56. Mazowiecki, 70. Mazowiecki was in attendance at the CSCE meeting in November 1990, at which some of the ideas for what became Visegrad were discussed.

57. Wałęsa, 81.

58. Francis Harris, "East European [sic] States to Hold Talks on Free Trade," *Daily Telegraph*, April 9, 1991.

59. Janas, 58–59.

60. Interview with Slovakia's Visegrad national coordinator, Ambassador Ivan Pavol, Bratislava, February 9, 2011.

61. "UNIKÁTNE FOTKY: Míting´90: Štátnici sa stretli na Bratislavskom hrade" [UNIQUE PHOTOS: Meeting '90: National leaders met at Bratislava Castle], accessed June 23, 2019, https://www.teraz.sk/slovensko/unikatne-fotografie-miting 90-bratislava/128744-clanok.html.

62. See Čarnogurský; and Chmel, "Visegrad."

63. Bajda, "Security."

64. Rouček, 20.

65. See http://www.visegradgroup.eu/documents/visegrad-declarations; it is copyright free.

66. Dunay, "Security," 122.

67. "The three countries met for the first time in Bratislava in *May 1990.*" [Emphasis added.] For debate in the Standing Committee, see Rule 47, Doc. 8163, July 9, 1998, Central European Free Trade Agreement (CEFTA) Report, Committee on Economic Affairs and Development; Rapporteur: Mr. András Bársony, Hungary, Socialist Group, http://www.assembly.coe.int/nw/xml/XRef/X2H-Xref -ViewHTML.asp?FileID=8604&lang=en.

68. Andor, 117. Less region-focused major studies have linked Havel's January 1990 speeches calling for the coordinated return to Europe as having "led to the Visegrad Joint Declaration." Barnes and Barnes, 399.

69. Žantovský, *Havel*, 440.

70. A claim that Visegrad had associated itself with "Central Europe" is made in, e.g., Fawn, "Elusive." Among the substantial literature on this contentious term are esp. Schöpflin and Wood; Graubard. For mapping and conceptions of the region, see Seegel; and Dhand.

71. Inotai and Sass, "Economic Integration," 8.

72. According to World Bank figures, Czechoslovak per capita GDP per annum in 1990 was US$3,941; Romania's was US$1,680. World Bank, last accessed October 31, 2023, https://data.worldbank.org/indicator/NY.GDP.PCAP.CD?locations= CZ and, https://data.worldbank.org/indicator/NY.GDP.PCAP.CD?locations=RO.

73. Austria in later years would express some interest in Visegrad, partake in a particular format with it on issues of common interest, and also start limited regional cooperation initiatives of its own. My experience with Austrian diplomats was that they were very much intent on *not* making reference to the Austro-Hungarian empire as grounds for commonality, let alone cooperation. Nevertheless, some observers have asserted that legacies of the empire, and often ones left undefined, account for the cooperation.

74. Dienstbier, *Od*, 144.

75. MTI, February 22, 1991, as "Romania's Roman Writes Antall on Cooperation," *FBIS*, February 25, 1991, 25.

76. Dienstbier's response was recounted by Hungarian foreign minister Jeszenszky, as in Budapest Domestic Service, February 24, 1991, *FBIS*, February 25, 1991, 25.

77. Budapest Domestic Service, 8 Apr. 1991, as "Policy Conference Delegates Interviewed," *FBIS*, April 15, 1991, 1–2.

78. *Economist*, July 13, 1991.

79. Timothy Garton Ash, "Puzzle of Central Europe," *New York Review of Books*, March 18, 1999.

80. Barany, *Future*, 145.
81. Romprest, May 2, 1991, as "Further on Chebeleu Statements," *FBIS*, May 3, 1991.
82. Simon, "Partnership," 42.
83. BTA, April 17, 1991, reported as "President Zhelev's Activities in Budapest Reported," *FBIS*, April 18, 1991, 3.
84. *Demokratsiya*, June 24, 1991, *FBIS*, July 1, 1991 [emphasis added].
85. Cottey, "Visegrád," 83.
86. ČTK (Czech News Agency), June 24, 1993, as "Suchocka, Klaus, to Sign Treaties," *FBIS*, June 25, 1993, 17.
87. See chapter 3.
88. *Republika*, October 2, 1993, *FBIS*, October 8, 1993, 21.
89. BTA, April 17, 1995.
90. "Czechs [sic] Plan Ties with Lithuania: Second Nation to Recognize Sovereignty," *Los Angeles Times*, February 16, 1991.
91. Kwaśniewski, 68.
92. Wolchik and Zięba, 133 and 136.
93. Wolczuk, 100.
94. Fawn and Drobysh; and chapter 8's Ukraine section.
95. *Polish Presidency Report, 2012–13*, 7, https://www.visegradgroup.eu/documents /annual-reports/report-pl-v4-pres-07-131209.
96. Okolicsanyi, 19; Bakos.
97. Życie Warszawy, October 8, 1991, as "Antall Interviewed on Central European Issues," *FBIS*, October 15, 1991, 18.
98. Quoted in Francis Harris, "East European [sic] States to Hold Talks on Free Trade," *Daily Telegraph*, April 9, 1991.
99. *Lidové Noviny*, May 24, 1996.
100. MTI, April 9, 1995.
101. Antohi, 68.
102. Krause, 250.
103. Bojkov, 516.
104. See, e.g., Nowak and Pöschl, "Assessment of Progress," 27 and 30.
105. Cited in Joe Schneider, "Slovakia: CEFTA Not 'Losing Its Breath' Says Czech PM," RFE/RL, September 9, 1996, http://www.rferl.org/content/article/1081537.html.
106. Emerging research on that emulation includes "V4 Support to Promote WB6 Common Regional Market: One Market for Post-COVID Recovery," November 1 2021–June 1, 2022, https://www.case-research.eu/index/?id=2ad268c32de4548f 7265e5c9ee87f6cb.
107. European Council in Edinburgh, December 11–12, 1992, *Conclusions of the Presidency*, Part D, External Relations, Sections 7 & 8, 94, https://www.consilium .europa.eu/media/20492/1992_december_-_edinburgh__eng_.pdf.

3

VISEGRAD
DESPITE ITSELF

MULTIPLE PATHS AND
MULTIPLE DEATHS, 1993–1998

Following Visegrad's swift and substantial successes in 1991 and 1992, it appeared to collapse into irrelevance. When, or rather, how often, and then why, remain unclear. Between 1993 and 1998 the Visegrad group suffered several apparent deaths before its ultimate resurrection.

This chapter determines if, how, and when Visegrad seemingly expired. It does so by identifying four destructive processes that individually hamstrung Visegrad and together as a minimum paralyzed it. These are: the consequences of Czechoslovakia's demise; the policies of independent Slovakia's new premier; similarly, the policies of the new Czech premier; and Hungarian nationalism. The chapter thereafter contends counterintuitively that Visegrad continued, through three means: with low-key activities; through the continuation of its original spirit among supporters; and in its offspring: the Central European Free Trade Agreement (CEFTA). The chapter also illustrates that Visegrad achieved international name-brand recognition when its functionality was lowest.

HOW DID VISEGRAD (SEEM TO) DIE?

Visegrad initially functioned effectively after the end of Czechoslovakia, the region's peaceable yet seismic event that was predicted to derail or end the cooperation. At first the official division of Czechoslovakia into Slovakia and the Czech Republic on January 1, 1993, did not affect the Group, which titularly morphed from being the Visegrad Three and the Visegrad Triangle to the Visegrad Four and the Visegrad Quadrangle. Four-way Visegrad cooperation continued throughout 1993 and into 1994. Outsiders also viewed the Four as a distinct entity in this period and beyond it, reflecting inaccurate momentum of name recognition unrepresentative of the Group's activity.

Just as Visegrad cooperation reached a height, its strength was sapped by four developments:

1. the perceived and actual geopolitical consequences of the breakup of Czechoslovakia;
2. changes in domestic political power in Slovakia;
3. changes in domestic political power in the Czech Republic; and
4. intensified nationalism in Hungary, itself partly but not only resulting from the first and second developments.

1. The Perceived and the Actual Geopolitical Consequences of the Breakup of Czechoslovakia

The damaging effects on Visegrad of Czechoslovakia's termination came from both the country's essential geographical location and the loss of key political personalities. Those who drove regional cooperation were either replaced or sidelined. Foreign minister Jiří Dienstbier was also leader of a small center-left party, which was unsuccessful in the June 1992 elections, and he resigned. Feeling increasingly powerless and sensing that other politicians willed the country's division, Václav Havel resigned as president in July. He was only reelected president of the new Czech Republic once Václav Klaus—his ideological heckler and, as will be elaborated, also a Visegrad detractor—had already assumed the Czech premiership. Briefly stated, the new Czech Constitution trimmed the president's powers. Havel, from his international stature, could still act, but the intention of the new government and the new country was to shift powers away from the presidency.

Czechoslovakia's expiration was seen by some as disastrous for Central European relations. Former Czechoslovak dissident Jan Urban perceived the post-1992 situation thus: "The dissolution of the CSFR will inevitably strengthen the position of Germany in Central Europe, leave Poland with unstable and most probably pro-German neighbours south of its borders, and open, once again, the border issue between Slovakia and Hungary." He additionally worried that existing tensions between Slovakia and Hungry over a dam, detailed below, would intensify and then inflame already-existing Hungarian nationalism, which "could turn the whole region into another potentially explosive area of Europe."[1]

Written in the year of Czechoslovakia's division, Urban's admonitions now seem outlandish. He was hardly alone. Czechoslovakia's passing posed severe challenges to Visegrad cooperation; commentaries at the time pronounced disaster. Petr Pithart—the erudite, measured, former dissident, legal scholar, and Czech premier within the Czechoslovak Federation—viewed the regional consequences of the Czechoslovak expiration similarly to Urban.[2] Czechoslovakia's breakup "undermined the fragile stability of Central Europe because the Czech and Slovak republics, alone or together, are not what Czechoslovakia was. Owing to our elongated shape, we were the East-West clamp of this rather unstable space." Visegrad, from such a view, would suffer. Czech-Slovak relations would be worse, with the governments of each republic "carrying out acts of ill will against each other."[3] The risks from the Czechoslovak annulment were deemed as dire, too, by outsiders and harmful even to Western Europe. Veteran RAND think tank analyst Thomas Szayna warned that Czechoslovakia's termination had "the potential to affect the western part of Europe in a most direct way of any changes in the region so far in the post-communist era."[4]

Such comments provide historical records of despair, even if later replaced by the positive metaphor of the country's "velvet divorce." Still, the country's termination presented new regional challenges. The very starting point was that Czechoslovakia served as the ideological parent and the geographic lynchpin of regional cooperation. From having been a relatively physically cohesive geographic area before 1993 (apart from the many strong claims of historical and cultural commonalities), the Czech Republic no longer bordered Hungary. That the Czech Republic was more removed, even insulated, from the unstable former Soviet Union—now having an independent Slovakia as well as Ukraine between it and Russia—was expressly part of the new Czech foreign policy worldview, as underlined in the country's foreign minister's inaugural speech.[5] The Czech defense minister, while unlike his foreign-ministerial counter, spoke of his fellow Visegrad ministers holding similar or identical views but nevertheless similarly said that Czechoslovakia's dissolution moved the Czech Republic "a few hundred kilometres further to the West."[6] Jeffrey Simon wrote in 1994, "New borders have caused the Czech Republic to turn westward, weakening the Visegrad Group and creating the potential for isolating Slovakia with reverberations extending to Ukraine."[7]

Czechoslovakia's end also meant the region's fragmentation into small states. Formerly totaling 15.5 million, Czechoslovaks, the second-largest Visegrad population, was reduced to 10 million Czechs, comparable to Hungary's 10 million, and the remainder generated its smallest population, Slovakia, with 5.5 million. For a formation that sometimes fears Polish dominance (but far less in practice than observers who simply asserted that Poland's size alone translated into ambitions of Group domination—when Warsaw was apparently not ignoring it altogether), the production of two smaller countries added to that perception. A Hungarian commentator wrote in 1992, "A small Czech Republic will obviously feel more *threatened* by Poland than a bigger Czechoslovakia,"[8] adding to the perceptions of luminaries like Pithart, who similarly expressed fears based on reduced size, for him of German influence that would consequently be (perniciously) greater against the smaller Czech Republic.[9]

The Czechoslovak breakup changed perceptions of Slovakia's geopolitical prospects, the president of the EastWest Institute warning in *Foreign Affairs* that Slovakia might "drift out of its west European trajectory into the maelstrom of the Balkans."[10] By 1994 Brzezinski, who encouraged usage of "Central Europe," no longer included Slovakia in that group and ceased mention when advocating the region's inclusion into Western institutions.[11] Slovakia's new premier did not physically or even metamorphically make it Balkan, but he certainly isolated it.

To be sure some analysts credit not so much personalities as "complex structural reasons," which could include geopolitics, in causing Visegrad's demise.[12] Certainly, the physical interaction of Central Europe was changed when Czechoslovakia ended, but the doomsday scenarios from that alone did not emerge. Rather, individual leaders and their specific policies undermined Visegrad. Its paralysis resulted foremost from domestic political developments in Czechoslovakia and, then, in its two successor states. The political field remained open to the winners of the June 1992 elections, ones contested not by Czechoslovak-wide political parties but those that ran only in the Czech or Slovak parts.

Two men, with incompatible political programs, were victorious: Václav Klaus in the Czech Republic and Vladimír Mečiar in Slovakia. They soon agreed on the practicalities of the Czechoslovak divorce, even if Mečiar contended that he did not want outright independence. Both men were principals in Czechoslovakia's dismemberment, and in trying to incapacitate Visegrad thereafter. Klaus endeavored proactively, Mečiar indirectly. Both succeeded. Visegrad suffered. Those acts follow, but first comes Hungarian foreign policy, which initially raised complications for Visegrad despite being the country that hosted its launch, then settled into a more cooperative outlook.[13]

2. The New Slovakia's Politics and Its Ambiguities over Central Europe

Independent Slovakia's new government started its foreign policy wanting to continue to be part of Visegrad. Even though, as we shall see, Mečiar turned Slovakia eastward, he did not do so immediately. And others in his circles remained in favor of both Visegrad and of a Euro-Atlantic foreign policy direction. In short: the Slovak leadership was not monolithic. Milan Kňažko—although a Slovak nationalist who had served some time as Havel's chief adviser on Slovak affairs and then as Slovakia's minister for foreign relations, and thereafter as Slovakia's foreign minister—stated that among the new country's foreign policy priorities included participation in the Visegrad Four.[14] (Mečiar had Kňažko dismissed from the foreign-ministerial post in March 1993, accusing him of misrepresenting Slovakia abroad.)[15] Martin Bútora and Zora Bútorová, noted researchers and the former later appointed as a senior Slovak diplomat, wrote at the end of 1993 that "a key area of concern" for independent Slovakia was "falling out of this [Visegrad] group and moving to a risky terrain of undefined character."[16] Even Mečiar said in October 1993 that he wanted to intensify cooperation with Visegrad, which he viewed as having acquired a political and moral lead that should not be lost. He said also that he would tell "Europe" of these cooperative intentions.[17] But at other times, hostility toward Visegrad under Mečiar's rule came to be expressed as follows: "Visegrád was often depicted in Bratislava as either a Czech plot to re-establish control over Slovakia or a Hungarian plan to annex Slovak territory."[18]

In addition to Mečiar's own gyrations regarding Visegrad, the Slovak government collectively provided jumbled signals. Slovakia's president, Michal Kováč, was consistently Western oriented and conciliatory toward his country's new neighbors. But he did not constitute the government, and he and Mečiar remained confrontational—to the extent that the Slovak Intelligence Services, headed by Mečiar ally Ivan Lexa, was accused of arranging the kidnapping of Kováč's son in 1995.[19] As a possibly related note on Slovak cooperation with Visegrad in this period, Lexa did not attend in 1995 what had become meetings of the Visegrad Four security services directors, convened under the auspices of NATO.[20]

The Mečiar government undertook policies that strained regional relations in four ways:

A. Slovak anti-Hungarian policies;
B. Mečiar's anti-democratic politics;
C. the Gabčikovo-Nagymaros dam; and
D. foreign policy reorientation eastward.

A. Slovak Anti-Hungarian Policies

Relations between Bratislava, still within the Czechoslovak Federation, and Budapest before 1993 were already strained. This friction intensified following Slovak independence without the counterweight of federal Prague against Slovak nationalism toward Hungarians. A contemporary American assessment warned, "No longer constrained by Prague, the mercurial Slovak prime minister [Mečiar] was free to pursue his populist-nationalist brand of politics."[21] Klaus was not himself particularly supportive of relations with Hungary, even referring to that country as not Central European but Balkan.[22] Unsurprisingly,

Klaus was "annoyed" that Hungary's Antall expected him to partner in pressurizing Slovakia to change its minorities policies.[23]

Mečiar's nationalism antagonized the 600,000 Hungarians in Slovakia, prompting the Hungarian government to attempt to derail Slovakia's entry into the Council of Europe (CoE) in 1993 (the two successor states of Czechoslovakia having to apply for new membership). Hungarian foreign minister Jeszenszky told the council that he hoped that certain countries, clearly meaning Slovakia, would not allow "red-brown, extremist forces" to prevent observance of their recommendations.[24] So bad were relations that, in July 1992, Hungarian academic Laszlo Antal wrote that it was "extraordinarily important to secure at least Czech neutrality in the case of an eventual conflict between Hungary and a nationalist Slovakia."[25] That entanglement was precisely what Prague's foreign policy officials sought to avoid,[26] and the Klaus government saw the Czech-Slovak annulment as "good riddance from the Slovak ballast."[27]

That said, CEFTA also facilitated some Slovak-Hungarian talks, especially after a change of Hungarian government in 1994. Even though the Treaty on Good Neighborliness and Friendly Cooperation was signed between the two countries in March 1995, tensions continued. The CEFTA meeting in September 1995 afforded some but insufficient continuation of previous informal bilateral discussions on Hungarian language rights.[28] In August 1996 Mečiar labeled a meeting of Hungarians in Budapest from neighboring states part of a "permanent effort" dating from 1920 "to renew a greater Hungary under various pretexts." His meeting with Horn was also cancelled, apparently postponed by mutual agreement.[29]

By August 1997 the Hungarian minorities' issue in Slovakia, despite Budapest's efforts to improve regional feelings, became so contentious and Mečiar so intent on confrontation that he told his Hungarian counterpart that the minority could be transferred to Hungary. Mečiar denied making the comments, while Horn said that they stirred sad and tragic memories, while Slovak-Hungarian leader Béla Bugár called that idea "ethnic cleansing."[30] Any such statements, and the sentiments that they incited, were venomous for regional cooperation.

B. Mečiar's Anti-Democratic Politics

The anti-democratic politics in this period drove an ideational wedge between Slovakia and the other three and also distanced Bratislava from NATO and the EU. The significance of Slovakia's exclusion is further contrasted by assessments of the value of the others' entry into NATO. Thus, as contrast to Bratislava, "in Budapest, the invitation to join NATO has been widely considered a prize for Hungary's democratic consolidation, successful economic transformation, and political stability."[31] Officials of the EU and NATO added to criticisms of individual Western governments of Mečiar's backsliding of democratic political developments, whose warning manifested into Slovakia's exclusion from those institutions' 1997 decisions to advance accession negotiations. The nationalist and anticonsultative practices of the Mečiar government seeped into and exacerbated other policy issues, including over the Gabčikovo-Nagymaros dam.

C. The Gabčikovo-Nagymaros Dam

At the time of the 1989 revolutions, Hungarian-(Czecho)Slovak relations were already also strained by the Gabčikovo-Nagymaros dam. Moscow in the 1950s proposed this massive hydroelectric project on the Danube to provide electricity for the ideologically driven industrialization of the Soviet bloc. The fraternal communist regimes in Prague and Budapest finally agreed in 1977 but ignored ecological or indeed political implications. These included the construction of enormous concrete aqueducts to lift and reroute the mighty Danube River, which would physically divide individual Hungarian-populated villages in southern Slovakia.

In the late 1980s a reformist communist regime in Hungary, sensitive to growing grassroots environmental concerns, began questioning its logic, aided by Gorbachev's easing of Soviet regional pressures. After the 1989 regime change and sensitive to Slovak concerns within federal Czechoslovakia, Prague continued to seek the dam's large-scale completion, while the Hungarian government decided unilaterally in 1992 to cease completion of its section. Slovaks had also come to see the project as "a potent symbol of the Slovak nation," and some understood that Budapest expected federal Czechoslovakia to stop the project.[32] Independent Slovakia would not face that risk and could and did continue with the project. Soon-to-be officials of the separate Czech Republic subsequently recounted their relief at jettisoning responsibility for the dam; the "sharp attacks" by Hungary against both federal Czechoslovakia and Slovakia for continuing the project would cease for the former.[33] The day the division of Czechoslovak assets was announced saw a top Czech daily lead with a cartoon of a Slovak and Hungarian, each wearing a dam-related T-shirt, squaring off for a match, the former saying, "This is it!"[34]

In October 1992 Czechoslovakia's final federal prime minister, Jan Stráský, pronounced his government "unable to make any decision on issues in which the two republics' interests clash." By contrast, so intent was the emergent Slovak state on the dam that its foreign minister (still within the existing Czechoslovak Federation), declared, "You can make any decision you want. Slovakia will dam the Danube anyway."[35] That was said just as the European Commission used a meeting with Visegrad to secure agreement from Budapest and

Bratislava to establish a multilateral fact-finding commission to evaluate the dam's future, itself indicating the dispute's increasing importance. The commission commended the outcome, which reflected "the spirit and willingness of cooperation which prevails between the Vysegrad [sic] countries themselves as well as between these countries and the Community."[36] This was a momentary reprieve; tensions only increased. No wonder that after Czechoslovakia's partition, Czech officials expressed relief that what they called a "Stalinist" industrial project ceased to be their concern, becoming exclusively Bratislava's.[37] As with Hungarian minority rights in an independent Slovakia, so too Klaus outright rejected efforts to have him mediate between Bratislava and Budapest over the dam.[38] On March 4, 1993, the Czech Foreign Ministry divested Prague of the matter in notes to Bratislava and the Hungarian embassy pronouncing Slovakia to be the only legal successor to the agreement establishing the dam.

Independent Slovakia still sought the project's full completion, while the referral to the International Court of Justice found both governments at fault for reneging on parts of the original agreement, although more with Slovakia. (The dispute was also viewed as one of the most important cases to come before that court.[39]) Ultimately dealt with not only peacefully but judicially, the issue nevertheless added additional strains to already fraught regional relations.

D. Mečiar's Foreign Policy Reorientation toward Russia

Mečiar reoriented Slovak foreign policy toward Russia. The degree to which it was doing so remains debatable, but it was more than enough to disrupt Visegrad itself and to undermine Slovakia's relations with NATO and the EU and, apart from the Group's domestic issues, further distancing itself from the rest of the Group's accession ambitions.

Some saw Mečiar's relations with Moscow as "close comradery,"[40] or an "absurd decision" that pitted his country against the West in an attempted new "cold war."[41] Other Central European states were concerned about lessening their dependence on Russian energy. (The Czech Republic had already initiated substantial infrastructure and contractual measures, which would serve it well for the later energy crises between Russia and Ukraine that led in 1999 to the first interruption of Russian gas supplies to the EU.) By contrast, Slovakia entertained joint ventures with Russia's energy conglomerate Gazprom; Slovakia's political opposition claimed the country "had succumbed to huge political and possibly financial pressure."[42] Slovakia was left without a national airline after the Czechoslovak breakup, and it was Russia's Aeroflot in 1996 that planned to provide aircraft. When Mečiar's hosted Russian prime minister Yevgeny Primakov in February 1996, regional media commented that Slovakia had become pro-Moscow and dependent on Russia.[43] Then, in April

1997, Russian prime minister Viktor Chernomyrdin called on Slovakia for three days, and signed sixteen agreements, the contents of which Mečiar attempted, poorly, to keep secret. The extensive economic and military engagement with Russia prompted prominent opposition politician Ján Langoš to say that Mečiar had "pulled Slovakia into an unbelievable dependence on the Russian economy and has made Slovakia dependent on Russia militarily as well."[44]

These militaries were still equipped with Soviet systems acquired during their decades in the Warsaw Pact. Prague decided, however, to cease purchasing Russian weapons. Budapest and Bratislava continued buying Russian MiG-29 fighter aircraft, the former as part of a debt swap with Russia in 1993. Hungary, however, ceased using the MiG-29s by 2010 and in 2019 began auctioning remainders; funds generated went, again, to offset Russian debts. At that point Hungarian retention of Soviet aircraft did not affect its NATO membership ambition, but Slovakia's continued retention was according to contemporary analyses due, extraordinarily, to fears of Hungary's "feverish military build-up."[45]

Slovakia's military involvement with Moscow extended to plans to purchase Russian air defense missile systems. That was additionally remarkable considering Slovakia's inclusion—with the other three—in the US Air Space Cooperation Initiative in 1994 (and expanded to Albania, Romania, and Slovenia in September 1995). By late 1995 Slovak military reforms, already "half-hearted," were failing enough to be "slipping off NATO's radar."[46] With added reason: already in 1993 independent Slovakia contravened understandings made at Kraków in October 1991, albeit by Czechoslovakia, that Visegrad would consult on foreign policy. Bratislava's Russian overture earned it disfavor as Visegrad's "weak link,"[47] although Russia's ambassador to Bratislava Sergei Yastrzhembskii complimented Slovakia for understanding Russia's fears of NATO expansion and "respecting" Russian concerns, unlike the others,[48] while undoing its own accession prospects.[49]

Slovak economic reforms were also seen as having slowed under Mečiar, even as his officials claimed otherwise. Additionally, unlike other Visegrad countries, which had reoriented trade from Russia to the EU, and were often owed money from the Soviet era, Slovakia developed a Sk17.8 billion trade deficit with Russia.[50]

Some Slovak foreign policy officials nevertheless asserted Slovak intentions of Euro-Atlantic integration, continuity that was vital for Slovakia's reinclusion in the Group in 1998–99. Rather than Mečiar's Slovakia being unambiguously anti-Western, its practices were differentiated. Indeed, Mečiar himself submitted Slovakia's membership application to both the EU and NATO. In December 1995 Slovakia accepted the North Atlantic Council's invitation for enhanced membership talks (offered to multiple countries), and

Slovak officials participated three times in the course of 1996, giving sufficient impression to outsiders that the Slovak government still sought Alliance membership.[51] Indeed, Kováč addressed NATO in 1996, not only speaking of Slovakia's Euro-Atlantic commitments but also stating expressly that Visegrad continued, and as a foursome.[52] Mečiar mistakenly "believed that Slovakia's strategic position as the only Visegrad country that borders the other three would, as a matter of course, ensure an invitation to begin NATO accession negotiations."[53]

Mečiar was apparently distressed when Slovakia was excluded in 1997 from NATO accession, an outcome blamed on the "incorrigibility" of Slovak leadership.[54] American diplomat William Hill later observed, Mečiar's "erratic and antidemocratic behavior" reduced Slovakia from having been "a shoo-in" for early NATO membership to a noncandidate.[55]

Regional tensions increased after Havel called Mečiar "paranoid" over Slovakia's exclusion from NATO. Undiplomatic, perhaps, but a statement that was grounded enough. Regional media thought Mečiar's reactions proved Havel's point: instead of disregarding the slight, the Slovak premier recalled his ambassador from Prague and reiterated demands for gold from the former federal Czechoslovak reserves.[56] Not only had Mečiar been claiming that both Hungary and the Czech Republic were actively defaming Slovakia to undercut its accession but also that the United States and Russia (however bizarrely unlikely) had conspired to exclude his country from NATO.[57] Mečiar demanded an apology; Havel declined but later conceded that his comment may have been "impertinent." Slovakia's ambassador to Prague was nevertheless recalled in protest. Jacques Rupnik summarized that Slovakia "could hardly reconcile the Visegrad process with its difficult relations with Prague and Budapest."[58]

If the policies of Mečiar's Slovakia were not enough challenge for Visegrad, they were often indirect—not targeting Visegrad itself but inflicting wounds. His Czech counterpart, Václav Klaus, cared enough about Visegrad to seek proactively to undo the cooperation. How and why he did follow now.

3. Klaus's Anti-Visegrad Policies

Another potent threat to Visegrad came from the seemingly intellectual reasonings of the Czech Republic's Václav Klaus. He intended to undermine Visegrad for four interwoven reasons, emanating from his ideological visions that made, or assumed, the Czech Republic to be the unequalled political-economic transformer of the entire post-communist world. Indeed, his mantra was that the Czech Republic had "transformed" so much that it was already a "normal" country comparable to those of Western democracies and economies.[59] His bravado was such that he declared that Prague would not apply for EU membership but wait for (and accept) an invitation to join (he was reminded that it was still Prague that sought to join the EU, and not vice versa). In this context, Klaus viewed Visegrad as an impediment to Czech success.

His first obstruction of Visegrad was dismissiveness, irrespective of its achievements and support in its early life. Rather than recognizing the cooperation's benefits, he explained sarcastically that "Visegrad is a hill and a castle in Prague, Visehrad in Czech pronunciation." Of course "Vysehrad," the standard English spelling, is a magnificent, elevated site on the eastern side of Prague's Vltava River, and the resting place of Czech literati. But the site and symbol of the cooperation were elsewhere, and Klaus's choice did not substitute for the intended one, except perhaps to articulate his Czech nationalism—that only a Czech "Vysehrad" mattered. A benefit of selecting Visegrád came from it being a Hungarian place-name ironically of Slavic origin, and interchangeable in the languages of Hungary's three Slavic partner-peoples. Klaus added that "a typical standard person in the Czech Republic doesn't know what the term means."[60] Often foreign policy tools and agreements are unfamiliar to publics, especially newer and smaller ones, so his slight seemed especially mistargeted. But it was one of many, including that Visegrad was "a poor man's club" from which his ever-more-successful Czech Republic had to distance itself.[61]

The second of Klaus's obstructions came from his ideological views regarding the preeminence of free trade. In this respect alone his rhetoric might have aided Visegrad cooperation, because of its early launch of regional trade liberalization. But while he later reduced Visegrad to only the Central European Free Trade Agreement, even the creation of that free trade area fell far short of his ideological expectations.[62] In some regards, Klaus was right about CEFTA's initial limitations. Signed in December 1992, CEFTA was supposed to liberalize further in 1995, and at that time the head of the Czech government's Weights and Measures Office said that trade barriers among CEFTA members were increasing due to insufficient standardization. Trade among Agreement members became *less* liberal than with nonmembers.[63] That said, the signing of new provisions on August 18, 1995, liberalized trade on almost all industrial goods,[64] and four years ahead of schedule. For Klaus, however, not even the EU (of which he has remained, for decades, a bombastic critic, saying that he would vote "no" in an accession referendum and later urging Prague to leave the union) and its unprecedented integrated market were sufficient. The only "free trade" he wanted was not even regional, that is, pan-European in terms of the EU, but worldwide. Indeed, his Euroskepticism became a highly potent force in Czech politics.[65] With such an unyielding perspective, CEFTA could never be adequate. For everyone else, CEFTA was triumphant. Indeed, outside observers, with comparative analysis, concluded that CEFTA was "generating a serious sense of momentum" and that its expansion could elevate it to a global-order free trade area.[66]

Thankfully, Klaus's misgivings toward CEFTA remained rhetorical. Although Klaus's government proactively disrupted the Visegrad cooperation, he even made use of and defended CEFTA; his criticisms then became that its members were not enacting trade liberalization fast enough.

Additionally, Klaus used CEFTA for bilateral discussions with his prickly Slovak counterpart, Mečiar, such as in Brno on September 11, 1995, and the first time that they met in person as premiers.[67] They suggested meeting more often, although unsuccessfully. CEFTA provided their only meeting platform. Klaus came to emphasize CEFTA's vitality and overall importance to the region. At its September 1996 Summit in Jasná, Slovakia, when others thought CEFTA was flagging, Klaus reassured that it was "not losing its breath." He also encouragingly rationalized that "it's easier to make large strides at the beginning. Once you get to the more sensitive stages, it becomes more difficult." Any seeming slowdown, Klaus accepted, was "simply a logical development."[68]

While he supported CEFTA, a third strand of Klaus's anti-Visegrad policies came from his Czech economic nationalism.[69] Manifestations of his nationalism included belief that his country would enter the EU of its own accord; he was so confident of his Czech transformation that already in 1993 he and his economy ministers spoke of the country not as "post-communist" or "transitional" but as entirely post-transitional. Regional analysis observed Czech political elite having been "contaminated by the virus of nationalism," manifesting Czech expressions of "intellectual superiority and "unrivalled perfection" of its reforms.[70]

This stance meant that the Klaus government did not submit an EU membership application until a year after Poland and Hungary, having rebuffed a joint Visegrad application. Klaus pronounced that Prague would have relations with *all* of its neighbors, including those formerly in the CMEA, but that it was also natural for the Czech Republic to engage with Germany and Austria. Marrying his economic nationalism with his jettisoning of Visegrad further showed Klaus's thinking to be that the Czech Republic was comparable to those advanced economies.

In July 1992, after the June election results that made Czechoslovakia's end likely, Klaus already said that because of the priority of domestic economy, the Czech Republic would be less interested in Visegrad (and the Hexagonale, which included the three Visegrad states and Austria, Italy, and Yugoslavia).[71] Not only was foreign policy secondary to internal reforms but the more internally organized the state became, he concluded, the fewer foreign policy issues it would have.[72]

Within two years of his Czech presidency Klaus decided (counterfactually) that Visegrad no longer existed. During the November 25, 1994, meeting of CEFTA prime ministers in Poznán, Klaus announced that "now the Czech Republic, in its dictionary, literally translates 'Visegrád' as 'CEFTA.'"[73]

And that view was coterminous with a growing Czech political view that Euro-Atlantic accession had to be not a group but an individual process for each state. Klaus's Czech defense minister Vilém Holáň attended a Visegrad Four (V4) ministerial meeting on June 1–2, 1995, the first time that the minister himself participated, but articulated that despite his attendance Prague did not support that cooperation, and its approach to joining NATO remained different from the other three, namely, to use and expand on the provisions provided through PfP. And while diplomats of NATO countries said in 1995 that cooperation among the Central European countries demonstrated that "that they would be capable of "cooperation within NATO," Holáň deadened even the prospect of common thinking among Visegrad states, saying that "our country wants to communicate . . . but that doesn't mean that we share the same beliefs."[74] Klaus's foreign minister Josef Zieleniec asserted, for example, on September 21, 1995, that—in contradistinction to earlier declarations—entry into the EU and NATO could not be a collective act.[75] These anti-Visegrad positions became pervasive and ideological; observers recorded that "in the Klaus administration, even the word Visegrád gradually became so suspicious that one couldn't even utter it as a metaphor for Central European cooperation."[76]

Visiting the Czech Republic, the Hungarian president and prime minister reversed their country's previously exceptionalist stance and its solo attitude toward accession. The Hungarian leaders declared that the two countries should "become partners rather than rivals on the road leading to European integration."[77] Klaus's Czech Republic abrogated the May 1992 Visegrad Summit agreement that pledged the countries to apply to the EC/EU together.

By 1994 the Czech Republic had adopted the same unilateral approach to NATO membership,[78] rather than using Visegrad to demonstrate regional stability. That came against the four-way Visegrad meeting with US president Bill Clinton in Prague at the start of that year. External analysts suggested that Klaus also opposed "further institutionalization" of Visegrad cooperation (as specifically limited as that already was) because that would hamper Czech chances of NATO accession, and a Czech general in 1994 told the US military that Visegrad was "of the past."[79]

A fourth and misleading aspect of Klaus's policy outlook was to deem Visegrad "an artificial creation of the West." To be sure, as this book argues, Visegrad was created partly because of the *absence* of Western institutional assistance and from the need to project positive images toward the EC/EU and NATO. Even if the West had an indirect influence on Visegrad—in the sense, as described elsewhere, of the absent hegemon that influences regionalism— Central European leaders created Visegrad. However, Klaus's argument was different as well as corrosive. In what proved also an early indicator of his anti-EU rhetoric, Klaus contended that Visegrad was created by Brussels, even suggesting (rather counterintuitively and with no evidence) that the Group was formed by the EU and NATO to *prevent* their entry.[80] Whereas Visegrad's originators were cautious not to make its cooperation too successful, also for fear of relieving NATO and the EC of responsibilities to them, Klaus's objections to Visegrad were different, suggesting that Visegrad originated from extraregional powers. Self-assured of the Czech transition relative to neighbors, Klaus combined his suspicions of Visegrad's origins with Czech nationalism: Visegrad was beneath the Czech Republic. Thomas Szayna observed contemporaneously, "The other Visegrád members and, for their own reasons, the EU and NATO greeted the Czech 'defection' from regional cooperation with resentment."[81] These "defections" included sending either inappropriately low-ranking Czech officials to Visegrad meetings—or none at all. Instead, the Klaus government stressed individual relations with countries over regional/multilateral ones; his foreign minister even proclaimed that the intensity of bilateral relations with Poland called for the "abandonment of the concept of Visegrad."[82]

Though the cooperation would be rescued from Klaus's enmity, his efforts to undermine it remain in official records. The Polish presidency report for 2012–13, refreshingly undiplomatically, named both Klaus and Mečiar as having made "clear attempts to reject the Central European identity." The Polish presidency report further felt the need to state that Klaus "was sceptical about the very idea of V4 cooperation" and that "in his opinion, the Czech Republic was part of Western Europe rather than Central Europe." The result, the Polish presidency concluded, was that Klaus's "attitude hindered cooperation in the hitherto format and called into question the Group's future existence."[83] Under Klaus, it seemed that some Central Europeans were more equal than others.

Havel earlier had disparaged Klaus regarding Visegrad and noted not only policy errors but also Klaus's personal arrogance. Havel reasoned that Klaus "railed against Visegrad" because he considered it "as some kind of left-wing intellectual expression of false solidarity," which could even cost the Czechs their "position as the crème de la crème."[84] Some even attributed to Klaus an "orientalist" view of neighboring states.[85]

The geopolitics of Czechoslovakia's breakup and the domestic ideologies and antiregionalist policies of Klaus and Mečiar might each have killed Visegrad. And in addition to them, early post-communist Hungarian policies also added complications to Visegrad relations.

4. Hungarian Nationalism and Wavering Regional Attitudes

Hungary's role in and attitude toward Visegrad in the mid-1990s shifted in two ways, one that removed hindrances to Visegrad cooperation and the other that encouraged and required the Group. That dual process salvaged Hungary from being a detractor to a proponent of the cooperation.

Despite Hungary hosting the founding meeting that became Visegrad, from 1990 the Hungarian government engaged in nationalist rhetoric and promotion of and even claims to its minorities living in adjacent countries. His first pronouncement on national television was that he was premier of 15 million Hungarians and that "the Hungarian nation stands united regardless of the citizenship that some of them may have obtained in the thunderstorm of history."[86] Even if, as some suggested, the comment arose from inexperience, it was nevertheless "inflammatory."[87] Three years later sentiments were that Antall had "shown virtually no signs of remorse over the remark," which still "incensed the region's leaders,"[88] even if his party back in 1990 had denied aims of reclaiming lost territories. In 1993 the Czech Republic's Klaus affirmed that he thought the Hungarian government was advocating for new administrative units in neighboring states that would then be able to assert self-determination,[89] in other words, to secede, join Hungary, and change the region's international borders.

For the prospects of Visegrad, Hungarian nationalistic and even irredentist statements matters especially toward Slovakia. These concerns abated somewhat when, upon assuming office in July 1994, Gyula Horn said that he would pay attention to coethnics abroad but that he was prime minister of 10.5 million Hungarians.[90]

Hungary, much like but separate from the Czech Republic, had also adopted a unilateralist view on Euro-Atlantic accession. Benefiting from the most, relatively speaking, liberal and free-trading economy in the socialist bloc, Hungary after 1989 continued with economic reforms. Its government was confident of early EU and NATO accession. Hungary by 1995 was so helpful to NATO in providing facilities to the Alliance for its Bosnian operations that US ambassador to Budapest Donald Blinken quipped that it was not Hungary that was joining NATO but, rather, NATO joining Hungary.[91] That both NATO and the EU made clear in 1997 that accession negotiations would not single out any one post-communist country while excluding others was added impetus for Hungary to coordinate with the Czech Republic and Poland.

The combined new attitude toward reducing nationalism and increasing cooperation, including toward Euro-Atlantic structure, changed the regional political atmosphere. Jiří Payne, chair of the Czech Parliament's Foreign Affairs Committee explained in 1995, "We had problems with the Hungarian government's preoccupation with the past. . . . Now the Polish and Hungarian governments have the same European priorities as we have."[92]

As elsewhere in the Visegrad region, foreign policy shifts often resulted from domestic considerations. The irony is the Hungarian government that came to power in 1994 and enacted these positive changes was then led by the same Horn, who in 1990 seemed to take little interest in the precursor meeting at Bratislava, which he left early and without issuing a statement. In 1994, however, Horn was credited with "seeking détente" with neighboring countries over the minority issue.[93]

Budapest gave priority to a treaty with Ukraine, where a Hungarian minority also resided (and Budapest would use Visegrad to criticize Ukrainian policies toward their coethnics after the Maidan Revolution of 2013–14). Budapest took time but did conclude treaties with Slovakia or Romania. Horn's government, in place from 1994 to 1998, described Hungary as "readier than ever for regional as well as international cooperation," which included ceasing his predecessors' "militance over minorities" pledges, something that improved Hungary's international reputation.[94] Some change, however, likely came from Western, especially EU, pressure on Budapest.[95] These Hungarian policy revisions came at an essential time: Visegrad was withering, and continued Hungarian hostility toward Slovakia may well have sunk the cooperation.

Many people and developments in the region between 1993 and 1998 worked hard to stymy and suffocate Visegrad. It was not entirely dead, however. Instead, a three-part puzzle emerges. First, did Visegrad really die? Second, if so, when exactly? And third, how do we know?

CHRONICLING A DEATH FORETOLD: WHEN, HOW, AND WHY DID VISEGRAD DIE?

Despite the strains that the breakup of Czechoslovakia and the new Czech and Slovak leaderships placed on regional relations in the early- to mid-1990s, many observers and actors inside and outside Visegrad continued to treat the Four as an entity throughout this period. This is inaccurate. The summation of analysts Michal Kořan or Vít Dostál are apposite: the Group was in "a vegetative state,"[96] a linguistic choice allowing for reawakening. That is often seen as the period from the end of Czechoslovakia to Visegrad's formal relaunch five years later. And Visegrad is now repeatedly referred to as having died, and then multiple times. Even Visegrad's website speaks of it as having "perished."[97] Did it? And if so, how and when? Phrasings from leading regional analysts speak of Visegrad's "many years of non-existence of Visegrad."[98] This section establishes and accounts for the multiple misconceptions and generalizations.

Confusion arises because Visegrad proponents afford one version. Analysis of events tells another, suggesting a slow death, which is contended here to have occurred by 1996, despite anachronistic references to Visegrad *outside the region*, and to be totally palpable by 1997. A third account results from (mis) perceptions, inaccuracies of reporting, and, ironically, the strength of Visegrad's name recognition—that outsiders attributed to Visegrad a continuity that it no longer possessed. Each of these is considered.

1. Visegrad Now Says Visegrad Never Really Died

In recording the meeting of the Czech, Hungarian, and Polish presidents in Budapest in 1998 in what became Visegrad's relaunch, the Group's website, as previously noted, maintains that the cooperation had "perished."[99] However, official accounts and celebrations signify uninterrupted continuity from 1991. Despite what was presented as a formal relaunch of cooperation in 1999, the anniversaries that Visegrad celebrates prominently date from 1991, jettisoning notions of interruption.

Practitioners and analysts also consider Visegrad to have continued. Inside the region, post-communist Hungarian foreign minister and Visegrad co-creator Géza Jeszenszky later wrote of the 1990s that "cooperation never stopped, even when it weakened, due to the attitude of certain leaders,"[100] of which we have now read. Is his view that of the favorably jaded relative? Regional analysts concur: "Security cooperation was never stopped completely and even during the worst crises in the relations between Visegrád countries at least some of its elements remained intact."[101]

2. Visegrad Lived to 1994

Visegrad functioned well in 1993.[102] The suggestion that Visegrad died immediately after and/or because of the breakup of Czechoslovakia is historically counterfactual. Despite doubts, in 1994 the Group had "defied all expectations of its durability."[103] Cooperation continued robustly into 1994, but it is in this year that its decline really began, once policies of both the Klaus and Mečiar governments corroded Visegrad.

Evidence began within days of the start of 1994, with a four-way meeting of the defense ministers that was convened in Warsaw on January 7. The matter was no less than formulating "a joint process" for NATO accession, and days in advance of President Clinton's visit to the region, at which he would announce the US government's revised and favorable view of NATO enlargement. This was the rotunda policy in the pantheon of Visegrad policy aims. The official version, still available when this book went to press, and using what already became a familiar abbreviation for the Visegrad Four, stated: "V4 Ministers of Defence meeting in Warsaw . . . jointly discussed the co-ordination of a joint process before NATO summit. The strategic goal and result of their meeting was full membership in NATO and resolve to obtain from NATO the promise of Alliance membership.[104] They welcomed the US offer for NATO to extend

Partnership for Peace as a "step in the right direction" but also signaled its insufficiency because it did not offer outright membership. (And as the program was also extended to almost all post-communist states, including to those of the former Soviet Union, it was hardly a security guarantee.)[105]

The meeting, however, was somewhat different than the official record suggests. As part of its antiregional ethos, the Klaus government refused to send its full-rank defense minister but only the deputy. Veteran contemporary observer and later an adviser to President Havel, Jiří Pehe wrote, "The Czech Republic's handling of the summit drew criticism from the other three countries' leaders, [Polish President Lech] Walesa in particular."[106] Further Czech contemporary observations noted "other Czech officials discounted the usefulness of such a meeting."[107]

Visegrad nevertheless wanted, and so continued to present, a common front. This official record a few days later reads:

11–12 January 1994
A meeting of Heads of States and Governments, Ministers of Foreign Affairs of the V4 countries and the American President, Bill Clinton, took place in Prague.[108]

In a possible egotistical turn, Klaus sought an individual, rather than a Visegrad group meeting, with Clinton during the Prague visit. And Havel managed his own time with Clinton during an evening in Prague's Reduta Jazz Club. There Havel presented Clinton with a Czech-made tenor saxophone, and the US president reciprocated by playing "My Funny Valentine."[109] But even the whole Czech political establishment was accused of "hijacking" an intended collective meeting with the American president.[110] Former Czechoslovak foreign minister Dienstbier said during Clinton's visit: "There is a tendency in the Czech Republic among politicians to think that the Czechs can make it alone." But, he continued, "the Czech Republic will be interesting [to the West] only if it will take its responsibility for stability in Central Europe."[111] And that meant meaningful, constructive engagement in regional relations, and the key, indeed historic, moment was held jointly among the four Central European leaders with Clinton. Clinton also referred to the gathered statesmen as "the Visegrad leaders," and the official US presidential records repeatedly refer to those events as being of and regarding "Visegrad," including also "Visegrad's security."[112]

Despite efforts at bilateralism during Clinton's Prague visit, others also took that meeting to be further evidence of the Visegrad Group as a coherent entity. France's ambassador to Prague wrote of Clinton's visit to the Czech capital as a meeting of him with the "Visegrad Four," as it indeed has been officially called.[113]

Similarly, Visegrad foreign ministries record that meeting as "Visegrad with Clinton"—and their acceptance at that point of PfP.[114]

Despite these highest-level recognitions of Visegrad's existence, a contemporary American analysis suggested otherwise: "In the Visegrad group, PFP legitimizes the Czech Republic's goal to achieve NATO membership first, rewards competition over cooperation, and undermines any further prospects for the group's development."[115] For earlier observers of Visegrad, the Prague Clinton-V4 meeting was the Group's last significant activity.[116] While a later section shows that Visegrad continued to be used after 1994, and also often including Slovakia, already in some parts of the US political system in that same year Visegrad was being recast as only the Three. Thus, Hungarian-born, Holocaust-surviving congressman Tom Lantos reiterated Brzezinski's stand that "the three Visegrad nations: Czechia, Hungary and Poland" should be considered for both EU and NATO membership.[117]

Another challenge to Visegrad began to crystalize in 1993 and 1994, and from, arguably, an unlikely source: Czech president Václav Havel. In October 1993 Havel returned from a state visit to Poland to say that unity within Visegrad was no longer necessary and that its objectives were achieved, particularly ending Soviet control over the region. The need for declaratory statements of unity were over, although, he said, when the countries still had common interests they could coordinate their foreign policies.[118] Clearly a parent of Visegrad, as chapter 2 determined, Havel also in 1993 reinitiated his experimentations with regional cooperation, which in 1990 were also broader than what became Visegrad. In that year he convened the president of Hungary (and not of Poland) with those of Germany and Austria. That formation then expanded in 1994, when Havel hosted in the Czech town of Litomyšl the same presidents with the addition of their counterparts from, this time, Poland, Slovakia, and Slovenia.

He called the meeting an informal one (as with Bratislava in 1990), one held away from formal diplomatic practices. Attending were the presidents of Austria, Germany, Hungary, Poland, Slovenia, and Slovakia (and therefore not Slovak premier Mečiar). Havel's alternative initiative, intended to revamp flagging regional cooperation, never had any firm outcomes to rival Visegrad's. Nevertheless, it continued meeting and coordinated also with the Central European Initiative. Although these meetings never became a competitor to Visegrad, Havel's foreign policy adviser and leading Czech diplomat Pavel Seifter even said that that cooperation made Visegrad "dead."[119] These "Central European" meetings once again gave evidence of a divide between countries in this broader region. The most "striking aspect" of the participation of some presidents was not that they were there but that others—such as Albania, Bulgaria, Croatia, and Romania—were not.[120]

Practical engagement with Visegrad as an entity nevertheless continued in this period, if more low key. The United States advanced a proposal to oversee the coordination and standardization of the control of the four countries' airspace. Such a proposed measure was also reported as a "very significant step regarding NATO entry." The presumption of Slovakia's inclusion in a four-way Visegrad format continued in 1995.[121]

The year 1994 appears to be the last one of coherent, sustained, and multiple forms of four-way Visegrad activity. And in that year Poland was seen to have come to pursue a "maximalist position towards Visegrád cooperation and the Poles to see themselves as the moving spirit behind the Visegrád Four."[122]

3. Visegrad Lives to 1995 and to 1996

To some extent, however, Visegrad continued into 1995. In February the Four signed an agreement on cooperation on customs issues. The most notable activity was again a meeting of the four defense ministers in Budapest on May 30, 1995.[123] But even with that meeting, and it being hosted by the Hungarians, it is in 1995 that prominent figures other than Klaus noted the Group's lack of utility. As Hungarian prime minister Gyula Horn said in Prague in 1995, "I agree with Mr. Klaus that it is not good to make a fetish" out of Visegrad or to "give it greater significance than it has."[124] Such regional views likely influenced external ones, so that in June 1995 a NATO official said of Visegrad, "There is not much of an effort to improve multilateral links."[125] Each Visegrad country pursued goals in Western multilateral platforms, which left questions as to how to achieve similar ones among themselves in Visegrad.

Unsurprisingly, international commentaries began to say that Visegrad was paralyzed. The *Financial Times* wrote that the Group was "lapsing into irrelevance as each country competes with its neighbours to join the European Union and Nato. Diplomats say co-operation among Hungary, Poland, the Czech Republic and Slovakia is at such a low ebb that the group could be wound up almost without anyone noticing."[126] An unnamed Central European diplomat added, "These days no one really thinks of being part of a foursome at all."[127] The only other event officially recorded for Visegrad in the second half of 1995 was an international seminar on foreign exchange regimes.

The case for Visegrad's outright demise in 1995, however, remains uncertain. Unwell, yes; deceased, not yet. Polish premier Waldemar Pawlak declared in January 1995 that Poland sought to "intensify regional cooperation" through Visegrad and CEFTA.[128] Hungarian ambassador to Poland Gábor Hárs wrote of a dinner meeting at his Czech counterpart in March 1995—billed expressly as a Visegrad meeting. Other Visegrad ambassadorial meetings continued that year, and Hárs also recounts that when in November 1995 he met with former dissident Bronisław Geremek, chairman of the foreign affairs committee of the Polish Parliament, they "talked primarily of Visegrad cooperation." He recollected the Visegrad cooperation further by noting "Prague's reservations regarding Visegrad had recently vanished. . . . Klaus seemed to have recognized that regional cooperation would not cast a shadow on bilateral relations with Euro-Atlantic organizations, but that on the contrary, a 'common voice' might improve the chances of each country."[129]

Other outsiders referred to Visegrad as "the four," including Slovakia, into 1995. For analysts, perhaps, this tendency may have been due to residue from the Clintonian references to Visegrad in 1994. Michael Mandelbaum's 1995 *Foreign Affairs* article, for example, wrote of the wider dangers posed by NATO enlargement to that group.[130] Equally, for Russia in 1995 Slovakia was viewed as part of Visegrad when considering threats to Russia from NATO's intensifying discussions on enlargement to Central Europe. (At other times, however, and for Russian-specific purposes, Russian politicians rather expressly considered Slovakia to be their anti-NATO ally in the region.)

That aside, both media and practitioners throughout 1995 repeatedly referred to Visegrad as the Four. Early in 1995 Slovene media deemed Slovenia's participation in Visegrad as part of the country's European integration strategy.[131] Germany's *Handelsblatt*, while not mentioning V4 activities, nevertheless continued to use Visegrad for the countries when it wrote in August that they had doubled exports to the EU since 1989.[132] In September 1995, the country manager for Hungary for the European Bank for Reconstruction and Development referred to the Four as Visegrad.[133] At the same time the *Economist* assessed the four as Visegrad in terms of readiness for NATO membership (and pronounced the Czech Republic to be the undisputed frontrunner).[134]

A dichotomy emerges for activities, and importantly, perceptions of Visegrad activities in 1995. The number of formal meetings were few; Visegrad supporter Ambassador Hárs speaks of dinner gatherings, and in only one of Visegrad capitals, rather than of any systematized meetings of the four governments, across sectors and across the region, let alone with external partners. Visegrad had entered international vocabulary—its resonance outlasted its functional rigor mortis. The Open Media Research Institute, OMRI (whose sources are among those used here), was an outstanding observer of the post-communist region. Its publications, including its annual reviews, used "Visegrad" as standard. OMRI reported of Visegrad in 1996 both its (unfair) view that Visegrad "remains more lip-service than practical business" but also that it had "become a bit firmed and deeper recently."[135] Outsiders still looked in on Visegrad and thought that they saw it.

As late as 1996, when Visegrad cooperation was clearly unraveling, many outside actors referred to Visegrad by name and, by the four countries, as its members. The US Congress, debating NATO enlargement, referred to them accordingly (and so continued into later 1997).[136]

Romanian president Ion Iliescu was described as expressing dismay about the positive position of the Group, and Romania's perceived contradistinction to them: "Upon returning to Bucharest, he expressed 'bewilderment' over statements advocating what he called a 'discriminatory approach' in favour of those Visegrad group countries, and he reiterated that the EU should offer 'equal treatment' and 'equal chances' to all candidates for full membership."[137]

Visegrad, then, was both perceived to be continuing in 1996 and was in fact but to a modest degree, thought more of as three rather than four. Despite the difficulties that the Czech and Hungarian governments had had with their Slovakia counterpart, each still pledged the desire to maintain some cooperation in the region and the desirability of having Slovakia admitted into Western institutions. But it was Poland's presidential successor to Wałęsa, Aleksander Kwaśniewski, who underscored the new divide between Poland, Hungary, and the Czech Republic, on the one hand, and Slovakia, on the other. In March 1996, more than a year before Agenda 2000, he stated in Budapest that only those three would qualify for EU accession, a comment international media called a "clanger."[138] Because of earlier statements of Polish support for Visegrad, Kwasniewski's statement hurt Slovakia to the point of protesting his statements and which he later qualified. But the implication was clear: Visegrad was down to Three.

And, then, not an active Three. The official Visegrad website lists for 1996 only three Visegrad meetings. One was a working meeting of V4 supreme audit authorities (see table 3.1). Rather than a statement of intensive quadrilateral high-level cooperation, that meeting was then recorded as having focused on "possibilities of bilateral co-operation."[139] (That cooperation did progress, and into annual meetings, and adopting for itself a later form of Visegrad outreach, the "plus" format, with the supreme auditors of Austria and Slovenia.) The second meeting—demonstrating the one sector in which cooperation continued—was of defense ministers, addressing "European security and NATO enlargement together," their experience of Partnership for Peace, and reform of their armed forces. Here it should be noted that the military cooperation was said to have continued uninterruptedly, and with little fanfare a working group of the four defence ministries was established, and by 2019 it met forty-two times.[140] The third—and longest of the three 1996 meetings—was of the national Red Cross organizations from V4 countries, a societal rather than a governmental set of actors.[141] Curiously, however, the *Economist*, which then and later has been astutely attentive to Visegrad, used that name and as the Four, in October 1996. It also contrasted Romania and Bulgaria negatively to the V4, and with the geocultural moniker of knowingly calling those two "more—to be

TABLE 3.1. The lingering life or multiple deaths of Visegrad

Month/year	1993[a]	1994	1995
Summation of the year	Despite calamitous warnings, especially from Czechs, of both regional instability and Visegrad collapse because of Czechoslovakia's demise, cooperation continues. — Havel, especially, undermines Visegrad but unsuccessfully.	Year of significant changes. Starts with Visegrad summit in Prague, with US president Clinton meeting with it by name. By end of year slowdown in cooperation and new Czech and Slovak premiers' antiregionalism start to affect Visegrad. — Havel, however, in the same month says that Visegrad was redundant.	Slowdown in meetings, though some continue. — Klaus and Mečiar hostilities tangible, but Poles endorse continued cooperation. — Many Western/international media and policymakers refer to Visegrad by name and include Slovakia.[b] Others, however, note Visegrad's weakness,[c] or "irrelevance."[d]
Summary life/death	Alive.	Very alive early year part of year, paralysis beginning in later.	Dying, with utterances that it is alive serving to show morbidity.
No month given	European Commission library: no Visegrad meetings between 1993 and 1998.[e]		
Jan.		7: V4 defense ministers meet in Warsaw — By name as Visegrad meeting with Clinton for PfP. — Clinton refers repeatedly to Visegrad.[k]	Polish premier wants to "intensify" Visegrad cooperation.[l]
Feb.			
Mar.	22: Klaus tells German press that Visegrad is "artificial," with no natural roots, and that Prague will cooperate with Visegrad countries as it does with other neighbors.[m]		

1996	1997	1998
Slowdowns and stoppages of cooperation, but international actors and observers still refer to Visegrad, possibly a mistaken holdover from the positive momentum Visegrad had created.	No recorded official cooperation, but supporters claim unofficial activities. Irony that EU and NATO accession confirmed but when Visegrad effectively defunct.	Change of governments in both Prague and Bratislava. Resumption of cooperation.
Deceased.	Deceased except for "spirit."	
At several points in 1996 both Russian and American officials refer to Visegrad, and as the Four,[f] as do neighbors such as Romania.[g]	Retrospective references that all four Visegrad defense ministries cooperating on human resources management.[h] — "Revival" (as Three) because of NATO accession.[i] — NATO official chides the Three's joint statement about early entry.[j]	
		Polish foreign minister Geremek says in major parliamentary address that Visegrad regained meaning.[n]

(*Continued*)

TABLE 3.1. (*Continued*)

Month/year	1993[a]	1994	1995
Apr.	The Four issued a statement asking for EU accession.		Hungarian and Polish PMs agree on need to maintain Visegrad cooperation.[o] — Lithuanian foreign minister says closer ties with Visegrad countries a main task.[p]
May			Hungarian ambassador to Poland says Klaus is moderating his (anti-Visegrad) stand and Visegrad relations are good.
June	21–22: Copenhagen European Council includes V4 countries (but not by that name) and Bulgaria and Romania. Central European leaders and analysts call this a blow to Visegrad.[s]	4: US secretary of state Warren Christopher repeatedly refers to Visegrad in address to the OECD.[t]	Czech defense minister says that Hungary, Poland, and Slovakia are "closer to the *former* idea of the Visegrad Four" than the Czechs, a cooperation which he says his country does not support.[u]
July			
Aug.			Independent; *Handelsblatt* refers to Visegrad by name for the 4.[z] — *FT* quotes diplomats saying Visegrad is finished.[aa]

1996	1997	1998
1–2: Meeting of V4 supreme audit authorities		
Visegrad Three in *Wall Street Journal*.q		Rudolf Chmel says Visegrad is dead but not buried; Adam Michnik says Visegrad is condemned to succeed,r each as evidence of a continuing Visegrad spirit.
	Czech, Hungary, and Poland as Visegrad, and not using name to avoid isolation of Slovakia.v — Regional commentary: no "political voodoo" could help Visegrad, and "Central Europe lives only in intellectuals' nostalgic dreams and in occasional speeches by presidents."w	
	8: NATO announced accession talks with the Three / Havel, Horn, and Kwasniewski give joint press conference at NATO: "Visegrad" not used, but they declare: "We are determined to intensify the political and military cooperation of our three countries."x — For some, this amounted to evidence that NATO accession was "the catalyst for further steps [of cooperation]."y Little immediately followed.	
November: "Andrzej Towpik, Undersecretary of State for foreign affairs, told me [Hárs] that Visegrad "does not exist, but it works."bb	22: Czech, Hungarian, and Polish prime ministers convene following NATO's accession statement. The meeting is not recorded on Visegrad website. Attendee Hungarian ambassador Hárs refers to the meeting as "long overdue" and as a Visegrad meeting that, on that occasion, occurred without Slovak representation.cc	

(Continued)

TABLE 3.1. (*Continued*)

Month/year	1993[a]	1994	1995
Sept.			*Economist*: Visegrad by name and as Four.[dd]
Oct.	Havel says that Visegrad could work with less conspicuous activities, ones that engaged regional social life, possibly suggesting a downgrading of its utility.[ee]		
Nov.			Hungarian Ambassador to Poland detects all fine in cooperation.[hh] — Hungarian ambassador to Poland Hárs recorded meeting with Geremek, and they "talked primarily of Visegrad cooperation."[ii]
Dec.			

a. No PM summits between 1993 and 1994 except with US president Clinton.
b. Commentary on US policy and Hungarian official on Kossuth Rádió, January 13, 1995, as "Briefing on U.S, Visegrad Cooperation Proposal," *FBIS* January 13, 1995, 5.
c. NATO official: "There is not much of an effort to improve multilateral link," in Timea Spitkova, "Visegrad's Usefulness in Doubt," *Prague Post*, June 13, 1995.
d. Tony Barber, "Eastern Europe: An Eastern Foursome Goes West," *Independent*, August 4, 1995. The first line read: "A race to join the EU and Nato has split the Visegrad states."
e. https://www.consilium.europa.eu/en/documents-publications/library/library-blog/posts/the-visegrad-group-v4/.
f. E.g., "Slovakia: Russian Ambassador on Joining NATO," as *Mladá fronta DNES*, February 6, 1996, *FBIS*, February 12, 1996. And "The Debate on NATO Enlargement, Hearings before the Committee on Foreign Relations. US Senate. One Hundred Fifth Congress. First Session," October 7, 9, 22, 28, and 30 and November 1997, 494.
g. Cited in Open Media Research Institute, 166.
h. E.g., "42nd Working Session of V4K Military Human Resources Management Working Group, 25–29 March 2019, Balatonakarattya, Hungary," *Visegrad Bulletin* 10 (1/2019), https://www.visegradgroup.eu/article-title-190201.
i. Examples of the three meeting as Visegrad include Khol, *Policies of the Visegrad*, 5; Burant, "Visegrad in all but Name."
j. RFE/RL Newsline, September 23, 1998.
k. E.g., in the Polish MFA timeline for NATO membership, accessed March 5, 2019, https://www.msz.gov.pl/en/foreign_policy/security_policy/nato/polands_road_to_nato/.
l. Cited in *La Libre Belgique*, January 13, 1995, as "Pawlak, Belgian Counterpart Discuss Relations," *FBIS*, January 17, 1995, 25.
m. As reported by Radiožurnál, March 22, 1993, *FBIS*, March 22, 1993.
n. Archived at http://orka2.sejm.gov.pl/Debata3.nsf/main/0078DB0D.
o. As reported in MTI, April 24, 1995.

1996	1997	1998
Mečiar pro CEFTA. — September 27–28: V4 defense ministers meet, an indication of the continuity of military cooperation.		
17: Slovak President Kovac to NATO. — *Economist*: "Visegrad Four."[ff]	October and November: US congressional hearing on NATO expansion and European defense repeatedly refer to Visegrad, and as the Visegrad Four.[gg]	
		Slovakia tells NATO: "It is in our highest interest to revive cooperation of the Visegrad Group as soon as possible."[jj]

p. Lithuanian Radio, April 4, 1995, in BBC Monitoring, April 6, 1995.

q. Gusztav Molnar, "NATO Membership for the Visegrad Three," *Wall Street Journal*, May 20, 1996.

r. As relayed in Libuše Koubská, "Looking for Visegrád," *New Presence*, June 1998, 8.

s. Had and Handl, 158.

t. Christopher.

u. As reported by ČTK, June 1, 1995, in SWB, June 1, 1995 [emphasis added].

v. As contended in Burant, "Visegrad in All but Name."

w. S. Majman, "A Gap Called Central Europe," *Warsaw Voice* 26/453, June 29, 1997.

x. Joint Press Conference by H. E. G. Horn, Hungary, H. E. V. Havel, Czech Republic, and H. E. A Kwasniewski, Poland," July 8, 1997, https://www.nato.int/docu/speech/1997/s970708h.htm.

y. Rhodes, 59.

z. Tony Barber, "An Eastern Foursome Goes West," *Independent*, August 4, 1995, https://www.independent.co .uk/news/world/an-eastern-foursome-goes-west-1594648.html.

aa. Barber, "Eastern Foursome."

bb. Hárs, 51.

cc. Hárs, 51.

dd. *Economist*, September 30, 1995.

ee. CTK, October 22, 1993, *FBIS*, October 22, 1993, 4.

ff. "Those South-eastern Laggards," *Economist*, October 19, 1996, 50.

gg. "The Debate on NATO Enlargement," 246, 320, 494, and 495.

hh. "It was pleasing that Prague's reservations regarding Visegrad had recently vanished. Prime Minister Václav Klaus seemed to have recognized that regional cooperation would not cast a shadow on bilateral relations with Euro-Atlantic organizations, but that on the contrary, a 'common voice' might improve the chances of each country," Hárs, 50–51.

ii. Hárs.

jj. Slovak Statement to NATO, December 8, 1998, https://www.nato.int/cps/en/natohq/opinions_26028.htm ?selectedLocale=en.

candid—Balkan."[142] One regional official who used the term was Slovak president Michal Kováč, and to NATO in October 1996.[143] That may well have been due, first, to his own efforts to retain Slovakia's Western foreign policy in the face of Mečiar's disruptions to it and, second, his longing for his country to be a member, even if the functionality was nonexistent.

4. Visegrad in 1997

In 1997 a solitary "Visegrad" meeting was recorded, and then that of the Red Cross societies of the four countries.[144] This was not a governmental activity of the V4. However, the V4 Military Human Resources Management Working Group was established in 1997 and has continued meeting since. That initiative, even if low-key, further indicates that some Visegrad activity certainly continued, especially among the militaries. It is one piece of evidence suggesting that Visegrad never completely died.

Nevertheless, 1997 was also the year in which NATO and the EU, separately, announced accession plans. The former offered that to only three of the four Visegrad countries, excluding Slovakia; the latter opened negotiations with those same three and also with two-non Visegrad countries, Estonia and Slovenia. Save for in 1997 what presumably must be holdover uses of the term, and then also including Slovakia,[145] 1997 really looked to be the year of Visegrad's total disappearance.

The reverberations of these accession negotiations were felt further in the former socialist world, and those in turn signaled also the end, or at least the dormancy of, Visegrad. A Ukrainian official said that the impact of the Three having been identified for NATO expansion "disrupted the very idea of regional cooperation."[146] From a practical viewpoint, then, "the other three Visegrád states had obvious disincentives to continuing defining themselves as a group with Slovakia" and by 1997 Visegrad as a group "had largely disappeared from the diplomatic map."[147] A Polish journalist concurred, damningly writing in the same year: "There is no use pretending. There is no Central European community. This won't be fixed by any political voodoo with the Visegrád Group. Central Europe lives only in intellectuals' nostalgic dreams and in occasional speeches by presidents."[148] One of those elevated to engage in such nostalgia was Bronisław Geremek, a leading former Polish dissident who had become foreign minister in 1997. He asserted then that Visegrad was still Four—if a "virtual Four"—and also that he and Polish premier Jerzy Buzek maintained the "empty chair" for Slovakia (even if Visegrad meetings themselves were hardly occurring).[149]

What comes of lingering dreams? Visegrad as a formal cooperation had stopped. However, what can be called the spirit of Visegrad still continued in 1997, albeit among the three states that received the go-ahead for EU and NATO accession. Czech diplomat Edita Hrdá commented of this time, "the cooperation [for accession] works very well. It is some kind of return to Visegrad, even if we don't think it makes sense to call it that anymore."[150] Slovak diplomat and Visegrad supporter Rudolf Chmel described the ethos in 1998: "Although Visegrad died, no one buried it."[151] It was still not entirely gone. The spirit of Visegrad allowed for the Group's formal revival in 1998 and 1999. In that vital way, Visegrad never expired, leaving enough potent legacy to be quickly and dynamically revived. CEFTA, too, played a role. How Visegrad still continued by other means in this period of supposed death deserves telling.

FALSE CHRONICLES OF A DEATH FORETOLD? VISEGRAD'S LIFE IN ANOTHER FORM

Just as Czechoslovakia disintegrated at the end of 1992, one of Visegrad's fast and remarkable achievements came to life: the Central European Free Trade Agreement. CEFTA continued to live—and indeed to prosper and expand in precisely the period of Visegrad's paralysis and death.

CEFTA was not merely the most active free trade arrangement among post-communist states, but it also served, sometimes intentionally and other times coincidentally, as a platform for diplomacy among the V4 when other channels were atrophied or blocked.

Under Mečiar, "Slovakia was a defiant member of both CEFTA and Visegrad."[152] But a member nevertheless. And noted also earlier in this chapter, both of these formations gained additional importance to Slovakia during the Mečiar-era isolation. Despite some aspects of Slovak foreign policy, opposition to Visegrad was not generally the case. Visegrad was not dead in some Slovak circles; instead, the more limited Slovakia's participation became, and along with that its related estrangement from Euro-Atlantic accession, a growing realization occurred within Slovak political circles of Visegrad's importance: as one outsider summarized, in Slovakia "marginalisation from the V4 [in the mid- to late-1990s] was seen as condemnation to the political periphery."[153]

Political marginalization notwithstanding, Slovakia's geographical location remained manifestly important. Uniquely among the V4, Slovakia bordered the three other members; Mečiar often asserted, mistakenly, that geography would ensure Slovakia's Euro-Atlantic accession. With the Visegrad Group having more than symbolic importance to Slovakia but less practicality in the mid-1990s, CEFTA could have meant even more to it. Thus Slovakia also continued participation in CEFTA, including chairing a summit in September 1996. The director of Slovakia's EU Integration Department at the Ministry of Economy stated that Mečiar wanted "to enhance cooperation" and "strengthen practical relations" among CEFTA members.[154]

So too did Klaus back CEFTA. At the Slovene-hosted Portorož Summit in September 1997, Klaus affirmed CEFTA as a model of a nonbureaucratic organization and took the further opportunity to extol CEFTA's virtue in comparison to the overbureaucratized and nonconsensual EU.[155]

Chapter 2 identified how, in its early years, Visegrad became a marker of success for other post-communist states. CEFTA provided the same. Broadly speaking, CEFTA could be unnoticed, being called "perhaps the least known and certainly the least publicized economic integration grouping in the world."[156] A 1998 Council of Europe Parliamentary Assembly report called CEFTA "a highly useful and efficient instrument for strengthening economic ties and economic development in central Europe, with the ultimate aim of stronger economic integration in the continent as a whole." The report noted that "since the establishment of CEFTA and largely thanks to it, trade among the participating countries has expanded and that their economic ties, which came under great strain at the beginning of the transition period, have now more than recovered."[157]

For neighboring countries, even more than Visegrad cooperation had become in the early 1990s, CEFTA provided economic gain and powerfully symbolized progress. The accession to CEFTA of Bulgaria, a country whose economic transition was lagging, was an opportunity to "stabilize its position."[158] Bulgaria continued to see the benefits of CEFTA; Prime Minister Ivan Kostov commented in 2001 of the "great importance" of economic benefits from relations with countries through CEFTA.[159]

In contrast to Bulgaria, and with the best-functioning nascent market economy outside the Visegrad countries, Slovenia too wanted CEFTA. Already self-identifying as a "typical central European economy,"[160] CEFTA membership showed that Slovenia had "more in common economically and politically with the Visegrad countries" than with former Yugoslav republics.[161] Indeed, Slovene media called CEFTA "an important instrument" for their country.[162]

Croatia similarly viewed engagement with CEFTA as a marker of success. Addressing the Croatian Parliament to mark ten years of Croatia's international recognition, Prime Minister Ivica Račan lauded its international achievements in 2002. Those included World Trade Organization (WTO) membership and NATO membership candidacy and "being on the way to becoming a full member" of CEFTA.[163] For Croatia CEFTA membership meant playing "a more constructive, rather than problematic, role in the wider region of South-East Europe,"[164] which also helped address Croatian ambitions that outsiders should "treat Croatia as an integral part of Central Europe separate from the turmoil of the Balkans."[165]

Even after Visegrad's relaunch in 1999, CEFTA served as a means for Visegrad outreach to other states and as a platform to ease regional tensions.

Romania's foreign minister commented in 2001 that the meeting of his prime minister with his Hungarian counterpart at the November 2001 CEFTA Summit would provide for "open and effective dialogue" to the point of providing "a new dimension" to their relations. The importance was underscored by him referring again to the Hungarian law asserting rights for its minorities, a measure that prevented their relations from being one of a cloudless sky.[166]

Just as Visegrad became the tightest expression of Central Europe, and thereby differentiated its member states from neighbors east and southward, CEFTA became a vehicle to move southeastern Europe toward the core of Europe—and away from the Balkans. In 2001 Slovenia's foreign minister Dmitrij Rupel encouraged the remainder of Yugoslavia to develop relations with CEFTA, calling it the "doorway to the European Union."[167]

The Czech Republic's Klaus's suggestion that CEFTA had become the embodiment of Visegrad held merit: Visegrad even continued through the mid-1990s in the form of CEFTA. But Visegrad would not remain merely as its trade-liberalization offspring. Why and how Visegrad renewed itself constitute the next chapter.

NOTES

1. Urban, 105.
2. Petr Pithart kindly offered two extended interviews in 1993 and 1994, and while much else could affirm the adjectives used here, neither conversation suggested anything shrill. The warnings therefore predicted for the region at Czechoslovakia's breakup seem particularly weighty.
3. Pithart, "Division/Dissolution," 228–29. Examples of early difficulties in Czech-Slovak relations are given below.
4. Szayna, "Breakup," 56.
5. On the new Czech foreign minister and the Czech Republic's transformed geography, see Fawn, "Reconstituting a National Identity."
6. *Pesti Hírlap*, March 24, 1993, *FBIS*, March 29, 1993.
7. Simon, "Czechoslovakia's," 482.
8. Laszlo Antal, op-ed, *Wall Street Journal Europe*, July 8, 1992 [emphasis added].
9. Pithart, "Division/Dissolution," 228–29.
10. Mroz, 49.
11. See, e.g., his "Normandy Evasion," *Washington Post*, May 3, 1994.
12. Dunay, "Subregional," 48.
13. "More" because as we shall see, Hungary improved on minorities' issues but also discarded the Visegrad cooperation regarding its Euro-Atlantic accession ambitions.
14. A US diplomatic confirmation is Hacker, *Slovakia on the Road*, 151. When France bestowed on Kňažko the Officier de la Légion d'Honneur in 2002, he gave a series of lectures that, although not on the Group, was nevertheless referred to as being on the development of the Visegrad countries. *Slovak Spectator*, April 17, 2002.
15. ČTK (Czech News Agency), March 19, 1993, *FBIS*, March 22, 1993.
16. Bútora and Bútorová, 732.

17. *Republika*, October 2, 1993, *FBIS*, October 8, 1993, 21.

18. Bugajski, "Visegrád's Past."

19. Lexa was acquitted of fourteen charges at home and in 2006 undertook to clear his name through the European Court of Human Rights. See "Lexa si chce očistiť meno v zahraničí" [Lexa Wants to Clear His Name Abroad], *Sme*, October 29, 2006, https://domov.sme.sk/c/2973224/lexa-si-chce-ocistit-meno-v-zahranici.html. Controversy still surrounds this case. Among retrospective reviews are the *Economist*, "Who Kidnapped the Son of Slovakia's President?," April 1, 2017.

20. See W. Williams and D. Deletant, 145.

21. Terry, "Poland's," 18.

22. Szayna, "Breakup," 62.

23. Pehe, "Choice," 16.

24. MTI, October 9, 1993, *FBIS*, October 13, 1993, 4.

25. Laszlo Antal, op-ed, *Wall Street Journal Europe*, July 8, 1992.

26. Frequently if politely stated in multiple interviews conducted in the early 1990s.

27. Nagy, 10.

28. Reuters, "Horn and Meciar Meet on Slovak Language Law," August 29, 1995.

29. Summarized in OMRI Daily Digest II, 160: 19, August 19, 1996.

30. RFE/RL (Radio Free Europe / Radio Liberty), September 8, 1997; Rupnik, "Joining," 40.

31. Barany, "Hungary," 74.

32. Fitzmaurice, 63.

33. Czech media tried also to present the bulk of the criticism as against Slovakia. Multiple interviews; *Lidové Noviny*, September 26, 1992, 3.

34. *Lidové Noviny*, September 24, 1992.

35. Both cited in Reuters, "Prague Is Spilt on Danube Dam Plan," *International Herald Tribune*, October 28, 1992.

36. European Commission Press Release (no title), October 28, 1992, https://europa.eu/rapid/press-release_IP-92-865_en.htm.

37. From interviews conducted in the early 1990s.

38. Bozóki, 94–95.

39. Okowa and Evans, 688.

40. Barany, *Future*, 51.

41. Tudoroiu, Horváth, and Hrušovský, 3. The article also offers succinct but powerful examples of Western opprobrium regarding Slovak politics.

42. Cited in RFE/RL, "Slovakia: New Gas Director Linked to Russian Deal," April 9, 1997, https://www.rferl.org/a/1084233.html.

43. *Mladá fronta DNES*, March 2, 1996.

44. Quoted in Jolyon Naegele, "Slovakia: Ties To Moscow Strengthen; Relations with Brussels Strained," RFE/RL, May 9, 1997, https://www.rferl.org/a/1084799.html.

45. Cited in Simon, *Czechoslovakia's*, 486.

46. "On Being a Bigger NATO," *Economist*, September 30, 1995.

47. Duleba, "Russia," 19.

48. "Slovakia: Russian Ambassador on Joining NATO," as *Mladá fronta DNES*, February 6, 1996, *FBIS*, February 12, 1996.

49. Fisher, with Szilagyi and Pehe, 380 and 378.

50. See, e.g., CSTK Ecoservice, July 27, 1995, in Reuter Textline, July 27, 1995. Slovak imports from Russia were Sk21.4 billion and exports only Sk4.1 billion in 1994.
51. See, e.g., Simon, *Slovakia*, 1.
52. "Address By H.E. Michal Kovac President of the Slovak Republic," October 17, 1996, https://www.nato.int/cps/en/natolive/opinions_25139.htm.
53. Burant, "After," 34.
54. Christopher Walker, "Poland's Eastern Challenge," RFE/RL, 2:46, March 9, 1998.
55. Hill, 135.
56. Zbyněk Petráček, "Havel jako diagnostik" [Havel as a Diagnosis], *Respekt*, April 14, 1997.
57. For contemporary analysis, see Jiří Pehe, "Tension between the Czech Republic and Slovakia," Reuters, *Prague Business Journal*, April 16, 1997, http://www.pehe .cz/clanky/1997/1997-Tensionbetweenczandsl.html.
58. Rupnik, "Joining," 40.
59. Radiožurnál, March 22, 1993, *FBIS*, March 22, 1993.
60. Cited in Fergus Pyle, "Trenchant and Formidable Advocate for a Czech Approach to the World," *Irish Times*, February 24, 1996.
61. Cited in Marek and Baun, 18.
62. See Hanley, *New*, esp. 192.
63. *Hospodářské noviny*, August 25, 1995. CEFTA could be criticized, including for not addressing competition among members in their still-important trade with post-Soviet states. Kupich, 101.
64. As reported in PAP, August 24, 1995.
65. A recent study of Klaus's determination of Czech Euroskepticism is Havlík and Mocek.
66. Kearns, 21.
67. Radiožurnál, August 29, 1995, reported as "Premier to Meet Slovak Counterpart in Brno on 11th September," BBC Monitoring, August 30, 1995.
68. Cited in Joe Schneider, "Slovakia: CEFTA Not 'Losing Its Breath' Says Czech PM," RFE/RL, September 9, 1996, http://www.rferl.org/content/article/1081537.html.
69. Pithy syntheses of Klaus's economic ideology and nationalism, and his rise and decline, are given in Dangerfield, "Ideology," Saxonberg, and Williams, "National Myths."
70. Leška, 78.
71. Comparative analysis of the Hexagonale, which became the Central European Initiative, and Visegrad are given in Fawn, "Regional Relations."
72. *Respekt*, July 8, 1992.
73. Cited in Vladimir Todres, "Czechs Reject Political Ties within Free-Trade Agreement," *Prague Post*, December 6, 1994.
74. Both cited in Timea Spitkova, "Visegrad's Usefulness in Doubt," *Prague Post*, June 13, 1995.
75. ČTK, September 21, 1995.
76. Libuše Koubská, "Looking for Visegrád," *New Presence*, June 1998, 8.
77. MTI, September 21, 1995, as "Hungary: Czech Minister Meets Hungarian President and Premier," in Reuter Textline, BBC Monitoring Service, September 23, 1995.
78. Wettig, 477.

79. De Santis, 66–67, 80.
80. For regional analysis of this Klausian view, see Samson, "Visegrad," 11.
81. Szayna, "Czech," 124.
82. *Lidové Noviny*, May 24, 1996.
83. *Report of the Polish Presidency of the Visegrad Group July 2012–July 2013*, 9, https://www.visegradgroup.eu/documents/annual-reports/report-pl-v4-pres-07-131209.
84. Havel, *Castle*, 156.
85. Antohi, 68.
86. Contemporary English-language accounts include Blaine Harden, "'Hungarian-ness' Back in Fashion," *Washington Post*, April 11, 1990.
87. Epstein, 158.
88. Stephen Engelberg with Judith Ingram, "Now Hungary Adds Its Voice to the Ethnic Tumult," *New York Times*, January 25, 1993, 3.
89. *Republika*, October 20, 1991, as "Klaus on Hungary's Border Change Intentions," *FBIS*, October 22, 1993, 5.
90. That this mattered, positively, is noted by international media coverage. The *Independent*, for example, called him "Conciliatory Horn," July 15, 1994.
91. Blinken.
92. Interview conducted by Rhodes, 61.
93. David B. Ottaway, "Hungary May Seek Detente with Neighbors," *Washington Post*, May 29, 1994.
94. Brown, *Grooves*, 201.
95. E.g., Vachudova, *Europe*, 147–51.
96. Kořan, "Visegrad Group," 201; Dostál, 181, the latter assigning the descriptor to 1992–98.
97. "Selected Events in 1998 and Earlier," accessed September 14, 2022, https://www.visegradgroup.eu/calendar/1998-and-before.
98. E.g., Luboš Palata, "Visegrád je už zavedená značka," Lidovky.cz, February 16, 2011, https://www.lidovky.cz/domov/visegrad-je-uz-zavedena-znacka.A110216_000027_ln_noviny_sko.
99. "Selected Events in 1998 and Earlier," accessed September 14, 2022, https://www.visegradgroup.eu/calendar/1998-and-before.
100. Jeszenszky, "Visegrád: Past and Future."
101. "Introduction" [no author], in Madej (ed.), *Cooperation on Security*, 5. It is the specifics of what remained intact that is essential to determining the extent to which, and how, Visegrad may have continued in this period.
102. See the earlier passages.
103. Whitehall Papers, 1994, 14.
104. http://www.visegradgroup.eu/calendar/1998-and-before.
105. See the earlier discussion.
106. Pehe, "Choice," 16.
107. Poláčková, 120.
108. "Selected Events in 1998 and Earlier," http://www.visegradgroup.eu/calendar/1998-and-before.
109. Recounted in Zantovsky, *Havel*, 442.
110. Adam LeBor, "Poles Accuse Czechs of Hijacking Prestige Visit," *Times*, January 12, 1994.

111. Cited in Carl M. Cannon, "Clinton Savors Prague, but Old Woes Won't Die," *Baltimore Sun*, January 12, 1994. Klaus issued a statement denying that he sought a solo meeting with Clinton.

112. "The President's News Conference with Visegrad Leaders in Prague, January 12, 1994," *Administration of William J. Clinton, 1994 / Jan. 12*, 41, accessed June 13, 2015, https://www.govinfo.gov/content/pkg/WCPD-1994-01-17/pdf/WCPD-1994-01-17-Pg41.pdf.

113. Benoit d'Aboville, "Prague Conference 21 February 2013: Twenty Years of Independent Czech and Slovak Diplomacy," Czech MFA website, June 13, 2015, https://mzv.gov.cz/file/956611/Konference_program_profily.pdf.

114. See, e.g., the Polish official chronology of NATO accession: "12 January 1994— The presidents of the Visegrad Group . . . at a Meeting with President Bill Clinton in Prague, Accepted the Partnership for Peace Programme," in "Poland's Road to NATO," accessed June 13, 2015, https://www.msz.gov.pl/en/foreign_policy/security_policy/nato/polands_road_to_nato/;jsessionid=56966AC2D8111A266D5213678B523569.cmsap2p.

115. Simon, "Partnership," 42.

116. See, e.g., Rhodes, 51.

117. "Hon. Tom Lantos of California in the House of Representatives," Congressional Record 140: 51 (May 3, 1994).

118. ČTK, October 22, 1993, *FBIS*, October 22, 1993, 4.

119. Rhodes. The CEI's limitations relative to Visegrad are shown by Austria's (almost-unrecorded) departure from it in 2018, and two supporters wrote in 2021 that "not a great deal" was come of it. Brix and Busek.

120. Jan B. de Weydenthal, "Central European Leaders Meet on European Integration," RFE/RL, June 9, 1996, https://www.rferl.org/a/1080705.html.

121. Budapest Kossuth Radio Network, January 13, 1995, as "Briefing on U.S. Visegrad Cooperation Proposal," *FBIS*, January 13, 1995, 5.

122. Kolankiewicz, 484.

123. Reported in *Népszabadság*, in Reuter News Service, May 31, 1995, although no content of the meeting is included.

124. *Telegraf*, February 27, 1995, cited in (and presumably translated by) Pehe, "Choice Between," 16.

125. The official is cited as unnamed, in Timea Spitkova, "Visegrad's Usefulness in Doubt," *Prague Post*, June 13, 1995.

126. Tony Barber, "An Eastern Foursome Goes West," *Independent*, August 14, 1995, https://www.independent.co.uk/news/world/an-eastern-foursome-goes-west-1594648.html.

127. Barber, "An Eastern Foursome."

128. Cited in *La Libre Belgique*, January 13, 1995, as "Pawlak, Belgian Counterpart Discuss Relations," *FBIS*, January 17, 1995, 25.

129. Hárs, n.p.

130. Mandelbaum, 9.

131. Ljubljana Radio Slovenia Network, February 6, 1995, as "Thaler, Hungary's Kovacs Sign Pact, Assess Talks," *FBIS*, February 8, 1995, 47.

132. *Handelsblatt* August 24, 1995, in European Commission Press Releases, August 24, 1995.

133. "Hungary, European Bank Official Gives Warning over Hungary's Credit Rating," Hungarian Radio, September 22, 1995, Reuter Textline in BBC Monitoring Service, September 27, 1995.
134. "On Being a Bigger NATO," *Economist*, September 30, 1995.
135. Open Media Research Institute, 375.
136. "The Debate on NATO Enlargement, Hearings before the Committee on Foreign Relations. US Senate. One Hundred Fifth Congress. First Session," October 7, 9, 22, 28, and 30 and November 1997, 494.
137. Open Media Research Institute, 166.
138. "The Visegrád Three . . . ," *Economist*, March 9, 1996
139. See "1–2 April 1996" at https://www.visegradgroup.eu/calendar/1998-and-before.
140. "42nd Working Session of V4K Military Human Resources Management Working Group, 25–29 March 2019, Balatonakarattya, Hungary," *Visegrad Bulletin* 10 (1/2019), https://www.visegradgroup.eu/article-title-190201. These meetings, including the apparent inauguration, are not recorded on the official Visegrad website of meetings.
141. "Selected Events in 1998 and Earlier: . . . 1997," http://www.visegradgroup.eu/calendar/1998-and-before/selected-events-in-1998.
142. "Romania and Bulgaria: Those South-Eastern Laggards," *Economist*, October 19 1996, 50.
143. "Address By H.E. Michal Kovac President of the Slovak Republic," October 17, 1996, NATO, updated November 5, 2008, https://www.nato.int/cps/en/natolive/opinions_25139.htm?selectedLocale=en.
144. Drawn from http://www.visegradgroup.eu/calendar/1998-and-before, accessed January 26, 2016; the page has shown this content for years.
145. Again, as per "The Debate on NATO Enlargement," 494.
146. Cited in Pavliuk, 352.
147. Cottey, "Visegrád Group and Beyond," 70 and 87.
148. S. Majman, "A Gap Called Central Europe," *Warsaw Voice* 26/453, June 29, 1997.
149. *Praca*, March 24, 1998.
150. Cited in Druker, 53.
151. Cited in Koubská, 8.
152. Ágh, 277.
153. Blackwell, 135.
154. Cited in Richard Lewis, "Bilateral Talks at CEFTA Summit," *Slovak Spectator*, September 11, 1996.
155. BBC, EE/3025 C2, 16/9/97, cited in Dangerfield, *CEFTA*, 84.
156. Nowak and Pöschl, 27.
157. Report of the Committee on Economic Affairs and Development, Rapporteur: Mr. András Bársony, Hungary, Socialist Group, July 9, 1998, http://www.assembly.coe.int/nw/xml/XRef/X2H-Xref-ViewHTML.asp?FileID=8604&lang=en.
158. Krause, 250.
159. BTA, May 17, 2001, as "Bulgarian-Hungarian Relations Viewed on Eve of Prime Minister Orban Visit," *FBIS*, May 17, 2001.
160. Miheljak, 120.
161. Wyzan, 102.
162. STA News Agency, July 22, 1995, cited in Reuter Textline, July 27, 1995.

163. HINA, January 15, 2002, as "Croatia: More on Prime Minister Racan's Address to Parliament," *FBIS*, January 15, 2002.
164. Stubbs and Zrinščak, 126.
165. Bebler.
166. *Magyar Hírlap*, November 9, 2001, as "Romanian Foreign Minister Views 'Optimistic' Bilateral Relations With Hungary," *FBIS*, November 9, 2001.
167. Tanjug, September 17, 2001, as "More on FRY, Slovene Foreign Ministers [*sic*] Discussing Relations," *FBIS*, September 17, 2001.

4

VISEGRAD'S RELAUNCH

FROM EXPIRATION TO RESURRECTION

Whether merely vegetative or thoroughly dead in the middle of the 1990s, Visegrad cooperation was revitalized quickly in 1998 and 1999. Better still, it became even more purposeful, multidimensional, and ambitious than before.

Five factors explain the prompt and robust resurrection. The first concerned the Group's physical incoherence without Slovakia, making what can be called immutable geographic influences and ones then open to subjective yet decisive perceptions of geopolitics. Second, despite the torrents of largely mistaken and certainly imprecise and collectively inconsistent pronouncements of Visegrad's death, aspects of cooperation never entirely ceased. This often-missed facet of both low-level and unofficial continuity deserves to be called the spirit of Visegrad. Lingering, positive vestiges of Visegrad's early cooperation existed, and were summoned and mobilized when auspicious circumstances returned, and by people in less prominent positions but remaining part of and committed to that past cooperation. More important, those legacies of early cooperation served new political leaders. Essential also to Visegrad's resurrection were the third and fourth factors: the political departure from state leadership of Václav Klaus in Prague and of Vladimír Mečiar in Bratislava. The implications of their leave-taking and replacement by others merit attention, expanding the preceding chapter's inklings that removal of their anti-Visegrad policies could only benefit cooperation. The fifth factor, one that needs only brief comment here, came from Budapest, which generally sought for its minorities' issue "compromise-seeking negotiations," including with pan-European international organizations.[1]

After discussing these considerations, the chapter determines how the revived Visegrad was to function and what it sought to achieve. The chapter then argues that Visegrad's rejuvenation created the means to overcome one of the foundational elements of Visegrad's earliest life, namely, that in its youth it was dependent on and vulnerable to political personalities and that it lacked regularized processes. True, personalities could and would continue to matter. After 1999, however, Visegrad established multiple frameworks of functionality that permitted it to endure divergent political agendas that individuals and governments at times would generate in the Group.

Before the chapter progresses to these discussions, mention is needed regarding the irony of Visegrad's resurrection in relation to Euro-Atlantic accession—exactly the aims that were unknown when the Group was formed in February 1991 but were not only enunciated but being pursued as Visegrad sought to rejuvenate itself in 1998–99. The irony is that Visegrad need not have renewed itself, making a further point that underscores regional commitment to it.

Visegrad cooperation resumed at precisely the time that its original and foundational rational disintegrated. The Visegrad of 1991 concerned bringing its countries back to Europe—intangibly by expressing through Visegrad the region's European values and tangibly by showing through Visegrad how committed and indeed suitable its countries were for Euro-Atlantic accession.[2]

In 1997, which chapter 3 determined to be Visegrad's low point, two developments occurred: first, the Amsterdam European Council in June pronounced that five counties were deemed eligible to begin the complex process of accession. Slovakia was excluded from both processes, puncturing Visegrad. The EU, previously having encouraged post-communist regional cooperation, jettisoned that idea by starting negotiations with not only part of Visegrad but also with Slovenia and Estonia, countries outside Visegrad.[3] Second, at its Madrid Summit in July, also in 1997, NATO decided that three, and not four, of the Visegrad countries would accede to the Alliance, in 1999. With this fundamental background, it is all the more remarkable that Visegrad could be and was revived. It would have been conceivable that ad hoc groupings could be made around common interests among accession countries, such as on the common agricultural policy or on EU constitutional issues. Nevertheless, Visegrad reasserted and then maintained itself. A V4 presidential summit in December 1999 produced the Tatras Declaration that reaffirmed the Visegrad cooperation, including with Slovakia, and its resolve to gain EU membership.

The second matter of timing came from Europe's other end: the Soviet Union, its military forces, and the Warsaw Treaty Organization (WTO) and the CMEA, and whatever threats and from them imperatives to regional cooperation had disappeared. That is not to say that Moscow presented no security concerns. The Central Europeans, for example, were distressed by Russia's extreme violence against separatist Chechens, including during Moscow's extensive and indiscriminate application of violence there between 1994 and 1996; these countries were arguably disproportionately supportive of Chechens in exile and of raising their plight in pan-European international organizations.[4] Visegrad continued seeking the hard security guarantee that was NATO membership. Nevertheless, the Visegrad states no longer had Russian military forces on their territory, nor overarching and controlling regional superstructures, and were further geographically insulated from Russia. Their big security concerns therefore also, by 1997, did not warrant joint lobbying or security collaboration. Yet, favorable geopolitical considerations at both ends of Europe did not dissuade these Central Europeans from resurrecting Visegrad. The Visegrad's four factors for resurrection feature next.

VISEGRAD'S FOUR FACTORS FOR RESURRECTION

1. The Foundational Facts of Visegrad's Geography

An inarguable fact of geography was that small Slovakia remained the physical lynchpin of the region, uniquely bordering the other three and providing regional corporeal coherence. Its absence from Visegrad and from the EU and NATO created a foundational problem. Unprecedented in NATO's history, the Alliance had admitted a country inaccessible by neither air, sea, nor land of an adjacent member country. Hungary would by physically isolated from the rest of the Alliance. Because the Czech Republic, Hungary, and Poland were acceding to NATO, it afforded foundational geographical impetus to renewed Visegrad cooperation.

As chapter 3 detailed, the breakup of Czechoslovakia and then the undemocratic and eastern turn of Mečiar's Slovakia already caused consternation because of the implications for the rest of Visegrad of its central geographic location. Even if Warsaw did not share such obvious geographic need for partnership with Slovakia, in contrast to Prague or Budapest, Polish defense minister Janusz Onyszkiewicz nevertheless exemplified geographic influence in April 1999, when Slovakia remained outside NATO while the other three joined: "To us Slovakia's entry into NATO is not only a question of sentiment [and] history, but also of geography and of our national interest."[5] Both the region and the EU wanted to avoid issues arising from Slovakia's possible exclusion from EU accession in 2004. That included also resolving disparities between the Czech Republic and Slovakia; the European parliamentary representative responsible for the latter, for example, advocated that the two countries accede together to avoid having to revise their bilateral border regime.[6]

Additionally, in terms of both preparations for EU accession and for any eventual membership, Slovak detachment was not simply a neutral matter but harmful. CEFTA had immediately upped regional trade, and its aim of creating

EU-compatible trade standards obviated the risk of new trade barriers. The Czech Republic and Slovakia also remained each other's main trade partners. The legacy of an integrated, if still socially planned, economy made them cojoined partners, now risking separation by a solitary accession to the EU. Not that the EU was thinking such overtly, but integrated transport and energy infrastructure would become increasingly important. Noncontiguous new member states would be highly disruptive to eventual and fundamental planning.

2. Visegrad's Enduring Spirit

A means to reintegrate Slovakia into Visegrad, and into the Euro-Atlantic accession process, came separately from recognizing hard geographic facts: this was the less tangible but important spirit of Visegrad cooperation from the past. That also returns to arguments about Visegrad cooperation's continuity in its low points between 1995 and 1997—even and especially in ways unrecorded in Visegrad's official and scholarly histories.

Just as the idea of Visegrad was conceived in and carried forward from communist-era dissident cooperation, so too did the cooperation after 1991 remain with those who had conducted it. Many former dissidents were catapulted to diplomacy, especially in Poland and Czechoslovakia and thereafter in the Czech Republic, if less so but still with some people in Slovakia and in Hungary.

Even when formal cooperation was abandoned, Gábor Hárs, Hungary's ambassador to Poland, spoke of "Visegrad" diplomatic dinners in Warsaw.[7] Czechoslovak diplomat Rudolf Chmel wrote similarly, while acknowledging that Visegrad was formally dead in the mid-1990s, the Group not only existed as a "psychological" unit but also continued to engage with Euro-Atlantic institutions.[8] Slovakia's Martin Bútora stated that Visegrad was reborn in Washington, DC, when the other Visegrad countries advanced their strategies together to convince American policymakers to admit them to NATO.[9] Regional analysis too suggests that while Visegrad cooperation stopped in other areas between 1993 and 1998, on NATO accession it continued.[10] The heights of Visegrad's extraordinary achievements were but a couple of years before; practitioners easily recalled them, and could conjure them anew.

An indicator of that spirit was that at some (three-way) Visegrad meetings, an empty chair was symbolically kept at meeting tables to represent Slovakia.[11] The official Visegrad chronology of events omits reference to any informal meetings. To those who convened them, these were still meetings of Visegrad—and also convoked with Slovakia in mind. But spirit or symbolism was one thing, formal cooperation another. While geography remained fixed and spirits

may have flown, the factor of leadership was the variable. Visegrad could not
be reborn without two leadership changes.

3. The Czech Dimension of Visegrad's Resurrection

That Václav Klaus, the Czech Republic's prime minister since 1992, had to leave
office in order for Visegrad to resume was painfully known among Visegrad
supporters at that time and recalled frequently later. His political departure
reopened some of the path back to a functioning Visegrad.

Despite international accolades for his Czech economic transformation,
and some impressive indicators—including pioneering voucher privatization
and having the lowest rate of unemployment in the post-communist space and
among Europe's lowest—by 1997 voters had become dismayed with an arrogance that masked emerging political and economic troubles.[12]

A combination of corruption and political leniency uniquely created a situation in which private bank accounts could be emptied by corrupt management, a process called *tunelování*, or tunnelling, that left many Czechs fleeced
of savings.[13] Meanwhile, successive revelations of political-party financing scan-
dals heightened popular malaise, especially raising questions over the probity
of Klaus's governing ODS party.[14] Havel, the former dissident and still Czech
president and whose moral standing outshone other public personalities,
increasingly applied his standing to question the Klaus government's behavior. A phrase attributed to Klaus for encouraging unfettered capitalism was
that there was no such thing as dirty money.[15] The questioning intensified,
and although Klaus survived a nonconfidence vote earlier in 1997, he had by
November to resign. Havel called the Czech political-economic situation "truly
a mournful one" in which the population believed that "the people in power
are again people who cannot be trusted and who are more concerned about
helping themselves than about the greater good."[16] He would never be far from
politics, however, already securing the speakership of the Czech Parliament in
1998, in a surprising and controversial deal with his left-wing political rivals,
and then in 2003 as Czech president. Klaus moderated his vehemence against
Visegrad later in his premiership, and as president from 2003 became positive,
even upbeat, toward Visegrad.

But before that, so influential was Klaus's personality and his quasi-
ideology to Czech politics in the 1990s that this young polity needed an
interim mechanism to manage the sudden disappearance of the only government that the country had had. A caretaker government was installed, one
auspicious also for Visegrad. The new government included another former
dissident, historian Jaroslav Šedivý, as foreign minister and who had previously
served as one of post-communist Czechoslovakia and the Czech Republic's

senior ambassadors.[17] He too brought dissident-era connections to public office, such as with Poland's Bronisław Geremek, who had likewise served as foreign minister and was then chairman of Poland's Parliamentary Foreign Affairs Committee. In contrast to the Polish comment of but a year earlier, that Visegrad was dead, in 1998 Geremek said of Klaus's departure: "The idea of Visegrad cooperation is considered now by the [Czech] political spectrum and by public opinion as a good project for the future."[18] He also internationally expressed Polish commitment to regional cooperation and said that Visegrad "had overcome past animosities in favor of a close partnership."[19] "The deflation of Klaus's seeming economic miracle also meant that the Klausian bombast lost credibility over the propagated belief that the Czech political-economic transformation had excelled beyond its neighbors and must not be impeded by them in Euro-Atlantic accession. The caretaker government was replaced by a Social Democratic government in later 1998, albeit with Klaus having negotiated an "opposition agreement," which was effectively a coalition arrangement, rewarding Klaus as speaker of the Czech Parliament. Nevertheless, the Czech Republic was committed to EU accession and accepted a conciliatory, even constructive, approach to Visegrad. It remained for Slovakia to return to the Group.

4. The Slovak Dimension

Although Mečiar's Slovakia was heavily criticized by Western states and by the European Commission and NATO for its undemocratic (and other) practices, the country nevertheless ran contestable elections, ones that allowed for full and peaceable handovers of power. Contrary to some external misperceptions, Mečiar lacked total power. In 1994 he was removed as premier in an overwhelming parliamentary no-confidence vote of seventy-eight to two.[20] And in 1998 he won a plurality of votes but too few to form a parliamentary majority.

Even so, warnings from former Czech dissident and premier Petr Pithart were flabbergasting: another Mečiar victory "would not only have spelled the end for Central Europe" because he would have employed the willing enemy in Hungary, resulting in "the Balkans expand[ing] to Europe, rather than the European Union expanding to the Balkans, and the balkanisation of Europe," which would in this scenario start at the Morava River, in the Czech lands.[21]

Slovakia slid behind the Visegrad Three in democratic development but retained mechanisms for political changeover.[22] The salience of that fact, in an entirely different context two decades later, was given by Dalibor Rohac in an op-ed entitled "My country had its own Trump. Here's how we beat him."[23] That "beating" was through successful electoral campaigning, aided by repeated statements of Western officials to the Slovak public of how much they had lost under Mečiar. In November 1998, with an 85 percent turnout, voters ousted Mečiar and a coalition government, including of parties representing ethnic Hungarians, replaced him.

The new Slovak government under Premier Mikuláš Dzurinda also recognized, unsurprisingly, that Slovakia's exclusion from Euro-Atlantic integration disadvantaged itself. But it also stated that that had harmed the collective interests of all four Visegrad states.[24] Dzurinda underlined the value to his country of Bratislava's renewed Visegrad membership and further declared that the cooperation would signal to the EU and NATO that Slovakia was democratic and could cooperate with its neighbors. That was language familiar from Visegrad's efforts to achieve collectively in the early 1990s the faith and backing of Western governments. Consequently, Dzurinda said, his government could "prove that we have adopted several measures which entitle us to enter the EU and NATO."[25] One measure was the cancellation of Mečiar's orders for Russian S-300 anti-aircraft missiles.[26] Slovak minister of foreign affairs Eduard Kukan added his assurance to NATO's Euro-Atlantic Partnership Council that "Slovakia is and will be an active and coherent element of regional cooperation in Central Europe." Kukan continued: "It is in our *highest interest* to revive cooperation of the Visegrad Group as soon as possible."[27] At the Group's relaunch he expounded that "Visegrad is no longer just a symbol—it is a very serious challenge for Slovakia and its V4 neighbours." He added: "Meeting this challenge will confirm Slovakia's maturity as a nation."[28] Such Slovak commentary paralleled that of aspirant countries to Visegrad, like Romania and Bulgaria, in the beginning of the 1990s.[29]

Visegrad membership's importance to Slovakia is already discernible from earlier assessments of Mečiar's policies. Worth reiterating was that Slovakia slipped quickly from the front line of transition states to a more backward position. Expressed as conceptual geography, Slovakia "had become a region specific country," as if it had come to inhabit a particular place of its own, "a borderline case between that of the more advanced Central European and lagging South-East European countries."[30] Slovakia had moved outside the "Central Europe" that Visegrad had created and so successfully promulgated. Visegrad also helped to secure Slovakia membership in the Organization for Economic Cooperation and Development (OECD), which in turn helped to augment the standing of its political-economic reforms.[31] Slovak geopolitical limbo proved impermanent, and governmental change swiftly let Slovakia exit the borderland into which Mečiar had shunted it.

With government change in both Prague and Bratislava, how was the new, or renewed Visegrad launched, and how was it different from its formative years?

VISEGRAD'S RELAUNCH

The prime ministers[32] of Poland, Hungary, and the Czech Republic declared in Budapest on October 21, 1998, "their interest in revitalizing Visegrad cooperation."[33] The meeting, held within days of the new Slovak government's installation, formally invited Slovakia to rejoin the Group. That act too suggests that Visegrad had not completely died but had become three-way ad hoc cooperation, using both existing and some informal means for engagement. Such presumptions reinforce the ideas of the last chapter, that the legacy of Visegrad remained conscious and that it could still run without all members active.

The Czech Foreign Ministry subsequently called the outcome of that 1998 meeting "The adherence of Slovakia to the Visegrad group."[34] That adherence needed to be operationalized. To that end, a formal Visegrad Summit was convened in May 1999 and, symbolically, in the Slovak capital of Bratislava.[35] There "Visegrad 2" was launched. That term was quickly dropped, reverting simply to unqualified "Visegrad," and subsequent commemorations date the cooperation from 1991, and uninterruptedly.

The cooperation was also called V4, and although "Four" had been used after the split of Czechoslovakia formally on January 1, 1993, and gained currency among observers, the Czech Visegrad presidency report (such reports also being an innovation of the new cooperation format) claimed that the countries met in May 1999 for "the first time in the new V4 format."[36]

Perhaps such counterfactual hyperbole was appropriate to mark Visegrad's relaunch. Of course, it had met as four before. But retrospective sources seemed to miss what we have detailed—the cooperation's breakdown in the mid-1990s. Some could write of 1998–99 as merely "a boost" to Visegrad endeavors when it was resuscitated.[37] Still others identify incorrect inspirations for Visegrad's relaunch. The *Economist* wrote, "Hard times and the war in Kosovo have sparked a revival of the Visegrad group." Was it "hard times," which were not defined in the article, that had suffocated Visegrad? And the decision to revive Visegrad occurred months before NATO began bombing Serbia/Kosovo in April 1999. Even if possibly off-target in its analysis, the *Economist*'s headline nevertheless showed that outsiders still saw merit in the Group, extolling: "Come back, Visegrad."[38]

The 1999 Visegrad Summit was not mere theater, perhaps in contradistinction to the castle settings and historical mythmaking of 1991. True, fanfare would remain, with occasional uses of other castles and greater, more systematized efforts at self-promotion. But unprecedented systematization and substance accompanied the rebirth. Visegrad restarted with a substantial program of cooperation and within that the establishment of multiple mechanisms to ensure regularized activity that also provided resilience when Visegrad faced internal and external challenges. These novel measures included statements of coordinated foreign policy on major contemporary issues; a range of socio-economic initiatives; and plans to improve regional transportation and tele-communications, and to confront organized crime and illegal migration.[39]

Strikingly, and long-lasting, cultural dimensions of cooperation were intro-duced into the partnership for the first time. That was in distinct contrast to earlier activities and generated a paradox. Initial Visegrad cooperation came from the conglomeration of artistic and activist personalities who had been propelled into diplomacy after the 1989 revolutions and who had spoken of the importance of their own, clandestine, cross-border cultural contacts under communism as foundations for the postrevolution cooperation that became Visegrad.

But people like Havel adapted to the realities of hard diplomacy; intention-ally or not, cultural imperatives disappeared. So too did the early and uncon-ventional diplomatic practice of including nondiplomats from "civil society." As we recall, rhetorical efforts and excuses were made in April 1990 in the precursor meeting of Bratislava to justify the inclusion of former dissidents who did not (yet) hold public office. Now the mature Visegrad could expand its activities and perhaps have the confidence to diverge from strict diplomatic and intergovernmental endeavors to reach back into its member' own societ-ies and across frontiers to others. Post-1999 Visegrad was going to include the civil-society dimensions from which its precursor necessarily grew but which it had previously neglected.

Even in advance of the 1999 Summit, Slovak foreign minister Eduard Kukan, keen to reassert Slovakia's geocultural place in the region and in Europe, told his Czech counterpart that the Four should cooperate on culture.[40] The 1999 Visegrad Summit included discussions of building regional awareness and identity, including the development of Central European television program-ming.[41] The reinitiated cooperation's immediately tangible achievement was the establishment of the International Visegrad Fund (IVF), which deserves separate attention. Briefly stated, the IVF, an abbreviation immune to its English-language fertility counterpart, began receiving annual funds from each government to foster common cultural projects and to cultivate Visegrad identity within and beyond the group by sponsoring individuals and activities.

Having traced the demise and collapse of Visegrad cooperation in the last chapter, one finds it all the more striking to see the intensity and range of cooperation undertaken already in 1999 and 2000. The details of activities in table 4.1 are not to burden the reader but instead to illustrate the new, expan-sive, and enduring features of that relaunched cooperation. Six new features to Visegrad cooperation furnished form and function, as did the new institution

TABLE 4.1. Meetings of "Visegrad 2" officials, 1999–2000

Date	Rank of meeting / national representatives (activity/outcome/statement)	Category/type
1999		
Apr. 13	V4 coordinators in Bratislava on the content of Visegrad Cooperation (preparation of the Bratislava Summit).	New internal organization
May 8	Ministers for the environment ("Joint Statement on Cooperation in the Field of Environmental Protection and Nature Conservation").	Ministerial
May 14	Prime Ministers' Summit in Bratislava. Formal relaunch of Visegrad cooperation, with Slovakia participating. Approval of the "Contents of Visegrad Cooperation 1999."	Prime-ministerial
June 23–24	Consultations of consular departments.	Foreign-ministerial functional
Sept. 7	State secretaries.	Ministerial
Sept. 21–22	Heads of National Border Services.	Agencies
Sept. 22	State secretaries.	Ministerial
Sept. 24–26	Ministers of culture.	Ministerial
Oct. 4–5	Chairmen of foreign affairs and defense committees of the Parliaments.	Parliamentary
Oct. 7–8	Ministers of health service.	Ministerial
Oct. 8–9	Ministers of culture.	Ministerial
Oct. 8–9	Ministers for the environment.	Ministerial
Oct. 15–16	Prime ministers.	Prime-ministerial
Nov. 4	Ministers of defense.	Ministerial
Nov. 4–5	V4 EU negotiators (in Brussels).	Accession
Nov. 5–6	Ministers of justice (recorded as informal).	Ministerial
Dec. 3	Presidents.	Highest-level
Dec. 9	Consular department directors.	Ministerial
2000		
Jan. 10–12	Geological surveyors.	Societal
Feb. 3–4	Visegrad coordinators and foreign-ministerial legal teams.	Ministerial, regarding the IVF
Feb. 15–18	Culture.	Ministerial
Mar. 22	Academies of science.	Societal
Apr. 6	EU negotiators.	Accession
Apr. 12–13	State secretaries.	Ministerial

(Continued)

TABLE 4.1. (*Continued*)

Date	Rank of meeting / national representatives (activity/outcome/statement)	Category/type
2000		
Apr. 25	National coordinators.	Ministerial
Apr. 26–28	Parliamentary chairs of the Foreign Affairs, European Integration, and Defense Committees.	Parliamentary
Apr. 28	Prime ministers with German chancellor Gerhard Schröder.	Higher-profile, internationalized
May 4	Prime ministers with French prime minister Lionel Jospin.	Higher-profile, internationalized
May 11–12	Ministers of environment.	Ministerial
May 30	Deputy foreign ministers.	Ministerial
June 1–3	Ministers of culture.	Ministerial
June 9	Prime ministers.	Highest-level
Aug. 4	Conference of youth delegations.	Societal
Oct. 9–10	Ministers of culture.	Ministerial
Oct. 12–13	Informal meeting of prime ministers.	Highest-level
Oct. 9–20	Ministers of the environment; and Sweden.	Ministerial and extraregional
Oct. 20	Ministers of the interior; and Austria.	Ministerial and extraregional
Oct. 21	Directors of geological surveys.	Societal
Oct. 23–25	General directors of railways.	Societal
Oct. 26–27	Deputy prime ministers and ministers of justice.	Ministerial
Nov. 13	Ministers of foreign affairs; and Slovenia.	Ministerial and extraregional
Nov. 23–25	Ministers of justice.	Ministerial

Source: Modified from http://www.Visegrád.org/v4/calendar.htm.

of the IVF and its decision to retain its original membership but create the outreach mechanism of its "plus" cooperation format.

Six Features of the New Visegrad

The first feature was that from 1999 Visegrad graduated from its occasional meetings in the early and mid-1990s to a series of set, highest-level summits. Visegrad would come to have presidential, prime-ministerial, and cabinet-level meetings on a regular basis. Unfortunately, some prominent sources misunderstood Visegrad's resumption and routinization after 1999. A European

Commission source wrote that Visegrad thereafter occurred "wherever possible" and "on an ad hoc basis" due to, it said, differences among members." To that it added its ad hoc nature was "made easier given the non-institutional character of the organisation." Curiously, also, the only supposed high-level meetings were of Visegrad prime ministers for coordination at the European Council.[42] Instead, Visegrad would from its relaunch institute multiple high-level and other levels of regular consultations and meetings, as table 4.1 illustrates.

The second feature was both the regularization and the deepening of activities. To that end, among the documents that the leaders approved at the May 1999 meeting was the "Contents of Visegrad Cooperation 1999." That succinct supplement formulated what it literally termed its "Substantive Elements of the Co-operation" and that also detailed the "structure of the Visegrad intergovernmental co-operation."[43] The latter specified the frequency and content of regular meetings among prime ministers; other government officials; state secretaries of foreign affairs; ambassadors, including that the Visegrad Four ambassadors in hosting countries were to meet at least four times annually; and the new post of Visegrad national coordinator.

To be meaningful rather than performative, those senior meetings naturally required tangible content, which propelled a process underway of its own accord: routine meetings of the four national ministries in sectors ranging from defense to culture. In later meetings with officials of regional foreign ministries, where Visegrad was and remains principally housed, it was striking to note over time comments about Visegrad's expansions across ministries.[44]

The breadth of activities and the need to synchronize them, and in recognition of Visegrad's growing reputation and activism resulted in, the foreign ministries gaining the specific, and permanent, posts of Visegrad national coordinator. As the title suggests, this was held in each foreign ministry by a specific person. Occasionally, that person could have parallel duties (in some cases, e.g., also serving as the ministry's point person for the Central European Initiative, another regional formation with some overlapping membership and interests).[45] But that office holder was normally aided, and full time, by other ministerial colleagues. Visegrad's "Content" Document also specified that these national coordinators were to meet in person regularly. My own visits to all ministries and national coordinators in 2012 and 2013 suggested that they were in very regular contact with each other and by multiple means, such as email and phone, with some indicating that that was daily, or even "all the time." The internal existence of these posts also meant that staff could be drawn from elsewhere in their ministries to assist when that country became responsible for the additional and demanding new features of renewed Visegrad cooperation.

The third involved the establishment of an annual and rotating Visegrad presidency, and the fourth constituted the accompanying annual Visegrad presidency program. Where Visegrad had been ad hoc before, now it had designated permanent, and indeed predictable, leaderships and responsibilities. While much interaction seemed good natured (and certainly as the series of working visits to all four national coordinators and their staffs suggested such), to outside observers a healthy competition could be said to arise. Annual presidency programs were and are achieved on a thoroughly consultative basis, in keeping with how Visegrad itself works, that is, on the basis of agreement.[46] But each Visegrad presidency program is branded as and by the country holding its presidency and gives the year a name and a logo, and each seems, arguably, to excel in the ambitiousness of its statements. Successive presidency programs have also generally expanded in physical length and in the range of topics proposed.[47]

A fifth new feature became the annual presidency report, a means to showcase that year's work and also to catch unforeseen developments arising in the presidency and the response to it. Some reports are mutual, that is, in recognizing overtly the past work of other presidencies, and usually the same refer to collaborative work. Others wrote more unilaterally of their work and sometimes even in a self-congratulatory way.[48] Regardless, the fact of annual presidency programs and reports created a public presence for Visegrad, and a drive toward activism, arguably one that was ever increasing in innovation, quality, and quantity.

It is at this point that we can say that Visegrad never sought "institutionalization"—that was an agreed and clear (anti)objective from Visegrad's outset. For its twenty-fifth anniversary, V4 leaders spent time declaring proudly, "We have also managed to achieve a unique quality of effective and flexible cooperation in the V4 without the unnecessary increase of institutionalization."[49] True, there was not a traditional secretariat and staff. But institutionalization is very much present, if in a less rigid manner and with tremendous responsiveness,[50] with likely significant cost savings.

A sixth feature involved Visegrad embarking on and expanding engagement with other partners. True, in its early days Visegrad had what can and should be called diplomatic experimentation, such as joint meetings with Benelux, the decades-old regional cooperation among Belgium, Netherlands, and Luxembourg, and the European Commission. After 1999 Visegrad upped its external engagement; in its first two years of its revamped format, the Group convened with German chancellor Gerhardt Schröder and with French prime minister Lionel Jospin. As Visegrad grew also in self-promotion and even self-congratulation, it would mark its founding anniversaries (again taking 1991 as the uninterrupted initiation) and would invite major European leaders to join them. Through these and other measures Visegrad ensured that it became a significant presence in its own region—and beyond it.[51]

Where comments on Visegrad back in 1991 warned that the new cooperation was "vulnerable to false starts, mixed signals, and accidental breakdowns,"[52]
less than ten years later Visegrad was seeking to avoid such problems through
regularized interactions throughout the Four's governments and bureaucracies. As table 4.1 shows, meetings convened in the first year after Visegrad's
relaunch. Four-way meetings of ministers were conducted repeatedly as part of
the renewed Visegrad and gave attention to regional identity, including committees for the establishment of the International Visegrad Fund, defense, and
the environment.

The quadrilateral cooperation expanded within the foreign ministries and
concerned foreign policy, consular services, and V4 EU negotiators. Table 4.1
illustrates also how wider public administration and even societal organizations were convening multilateral sessions, such as directors of the national
railways, geological surveyors, the academies of sciences, and heads of the
National Border Services. Important and novel too were meetings of V4 Parliamentary speakers and of the chairs of the four Parliamentary committees for
foreign affairs, European integration, and defense. The V4 started also inviting
other countries—such as Austria, Slovenia, and Sweden—and major European
politicians to meetings that were extraregional in content and higher profile in
form, including Germany's chancellor and France's prime minister.

Those events attracted international attention, but many other additions or
expansions of V4 multilateral ventures were often quiet but becoming engrained
in government activity. Interviews conducted in the early 2000s made clear that
V4 work was becoming routine in and across ministries. The 2016–17 Polish
presidency report affirmed unnecessarily what had become habitual: "Visegrad
cooperation in Poland involved all levels of government administration as well
as Parliaments and civil society organizations."[53]

Now that the chapter has shown the renewed Visegrad cooperation's
expansion throughout political circles and public administrations, its other
innovation deserves attention: its engagement with civil society and wider populations. And that calls also for an elaboration of the aims and work of the IVF.

The International Visegrad Fund and Visegrad
as Cultural and Regional Identity

The centrality of positive societal familiarity and interactions of a working
Visegrad neighborhood might best be expressed by the lamentations of Slovak
dissident Miroslav Kusý, published in the years of the 1989 revolutions:

> So far, no spontaneous grassroots process of integration has happened since
> the war and each of us secretly hopes that it never will in the near future.

Our mutual national antagonisms are still sufficiently alive as to push us in the opposite direction.

Your average Slovak still finds the idea of closer union with Hungary unthinkable. Czechs and Poles are hardly going to form a community with the Germans, but then nor are the Czechs and Slovaks with the Poles. . . .

[Even contact through tourism,] the universally accepted means for different nations to get to know each other[,] had a negative effect on the nations of the region. The actual effect is the contrary: sharpened mutual hostility and the entrenchment of our division.[54]

And a wider corroborative view came from decades-long regional analyst J. F. Brown, who nodded to Hungarian-Polish respect but contended that otherwise among all others, "it was often usually hatred, suspicion, and contempt. Forty years of socialism and [the socialist slogan of] the brotherhood of men had only solidified these sentiments."[55]

The renewed Visegrad cooperation wanted to tackle the low-political but essential objective: to nurture genuine societal contacts in the region. A handful of dissidents gave an ideational birth to Visegrad before 1989 through their transnational societal initiatives under communism. Cross-societal initiatives, however, were neglected in Visegrad's first life, even and especially as Havel spoke in 1990 and 1991 to the need to include those not in office in some official activities. Occasionally, some Visegrad proponents maintained that the societal side of Visegrad was strong, but those were members of the communist-era dissident community,[56] and could well have been speaking to their own initiatives and anything provided by the cooperation itself.

Consequently, Visegrad followed its renewal with specific ingenuities for cross-border societal engagement and regional identity building. A year after the relaunch, in June 2000, the Visegrad prime ministers met in Štiřín, a chateau with fifteenth-century origins as a fortress, southeast of Prague. There they elaborated plans for what became the International Visegrad Fund to support educational, scientific, and cultural programs in the region. To that end, the fund's mandate explicitly referred to the fostering of a Central European cultural identity, including these initiatives:

- creating Central European arts projects involving transfrontier festivals, performances, and joint exhibitions by young artists; operating creative camps; and supporting journalism focused on Central European themes;
- creating a list of existing national events open to participation from other V4 member countries;

- cooperating in the field of education of diplomats and civil servants, with a perspective of creating a joint educational facility (i.e., a diplomatic academy);
- founding a Visegrad Prize to honor personages and all institutions who have made serious efforts to promote cooperation between the states of the Central-Eastern European region;
- addressing the problems of human rights and cooperation with NGOs;
- improving cultural heritage, including protection of historic buildings and sites;
- offering scholarships and awarding prizes for an essay competition dealing with Central Europe;
- creating a common Internet Visegrád webpage;
- taking steps toward launching a foundation of a common TV program related to Visegrad issues in national TV stations; and
- taking steps toward creating a joint fund for financing joint activities in the fields of education, culture, and sports.[57]

While some of these initiatives were not undertaken, such as television or common academies,[58] for the first time a civic dimension emerged in Visegrad cooperation through the fund's establishment. Ironically for some, such as early director of the IVF, Urban Rusnák, culture and cross-border cooperation "were the natural choice" in light of Slovakia being behind in Euro-Atlantic integration, even perhaps as if that was a secondary option.[59]

But cultural cooperation was necessary, even imperative, for Visegrad, although now built on irony. Despite the foundational contribution of "civil society" actors like dissidents Václav Havel and Lech Wałęsa, and the fact, as chapter 2 noted, that concessions were made in 1990 and 1991 to include non-communists who were outside formal power, prior to the IVF Visegrad had lacked mechanisms for societal outreach. Havel had made brief mention in October 1993, when he also said that Visegrad need not remain united, that the formation could assume a new identity and with less "conspicuous" activities, namely, ones that engaged regional social life.[60] That suggestion was not followed through in the years before the foundation of the IVF. The aim of societal outreach mattered also because Visegrad supporters have wanted the Group to gain public recognition and were concerned about harm to it by certain politicians.

In that light it is striking that the Slovak presidency in 2014–15 wrote of both the importance of preserving the historical record of the dissident foundations to Visegrad and its presidency being "focused on strengthening the civic dimension of Visegrad cooperation."[61] The program devoted several paragraphs to enhanced communications, support of regionally focused NGO activity, and public events to raise societal awareness. A requirement of assessing funding applications was that they maximized regional interaction.

Past attempts were made outside of Visegrad to make a Central European identity. One such was funding from the philanthropic foundation of Hungary-born George Soros for a common monthly insert in one newspaper in each of the four countries, including ones with dissident-era pedigree. A. J. Liehm, who chaired the editorial board, said its aims were "precisely" the same as Visegrad's, namely, "overcoming the historical legacy of conflict through mutual rapprochement, better knowledge and understanding of one another."[62] Short lived, however, the effort was notable also as a rare initiative to develop "east-east" cooperation.[63] Instead, sustained cultural activity among the V4 needed the IVF. In turn the IVF would grow, its budget increased by the four national governments almost annually (and never decreased), as well as gain funds for distribution from external partners, including ones that were financially capable and with their own major diplomatic representations in the regions in which Visegrad operated on their behalf. These included Japan, the Netherlands, South Korea, and the United States.

The IVF's added importance has been its contributions to building a distinctive Visegrad–Central European identity. In no way is that to say that Visegrad or the IVF were seeking to monopolize the valuable epithet or to act exclusively—both and especially the fund were vehicles for outreach and for creating mutual understanding and consensuses beyond the four members. Many non-Visegrad people in the region recognized the IVF as Visegrad's soft power. The IVF and general outreach by Visegrad have also created public awareness of the Group. Already in 2001, as shown in table 4.2, affirmative responses to the question, "Yes, I have come across the term 'Visegrad Group' and I know what it means" were 52 percent among Slovaks, 27 percent among Poles, 35 percent of Hungarians, and 32 percent of Czechs. Two years later that recognition had grown in each country by at least 3 percent and as much as 12 percent.

While comparison to familiarity with other diplomatic cooperation or international organizations is unavailable, these figures are impressive for, at that time, a fledgling initiative that had also been dormant and had not yet had significant societal outreach.

The IVF's dedicated role of supporting cultural, educational, and research activities on Visegrad provides an essential if indirect reply to a concern raised by Czechoslovak diplomat and Slovak political figure Rudolf Chmel. For the Group's fifteenth anniversary, he applauded the introduction of culture into Visegrad's activities but noted that "culture ministers meet, even twice a year, but their plans become action only very slowly and sporadically." He lamented

TABLE 4.2. Responses to "Yes, I have come across the term 'Visegrad Group' and I know what it means"

	Slovaks	Poles	Hungarians	Czechs
2001	52%	27%	35%	32%
2003	56%	39%	44%	35%

Source: Adapted from the Institute of Public Affairs, as used in Fałkowski, Bukalska, and Gromadzki, *Yes to Visegrad*, 3. Such surveys are important correctives to ad hoc, even comical ones undertaken to suggest that Visegrad was unknown. See Zenker and Wartuschová for discussion of the latter.

that such formal provisions were "insufficient" because "ministerial bureaucrats do not always recognize good ideas."[64]

The IVF has been significant for developing a nexus of added policy thinking and regional awareness-raising; that is, from its support of think tanks generally and for what became the Think Visegrad Network. This is hardly undue "product placement" or paid self-promotion. Many international organizations offer fellowships and fund programs on themselves, such as by NATO and the EU. Others have been arguably belated, such as the Organization for Security and Co-operation in Europe (OSCE), with a country membership that exceeds those mentioned, albeit with internal dissension among participating states that the entry tests of NATO and the EU ostensibly eliminated.[65]

Some self-referential behavior may well emerge; people receive funds to work on Visegrad, creating more initiatives, which may in turn legitimate more funding, and more awareness raising. These activities have not only increased cross-regional contact but generated new ideas. Platforms like these have also increased awareness of Visegrad outside the region, by bringing in fellows from adjacent and other countries on the condition of researching, writing, and presenting about Visegrad's work.[66]

But the last feature of the relaunched Visegrad was something different, yet familiar again from its earlier history: that it would not expand membership, despite occasional internal interest and recurring external desire. Innovative Visegrad, however, created a format to bridge and harness the seeming contradiction of retaining its exclusivity while remaining open and being able to pursue its interests when issue-specific coalitions made sense.

Keeping Visegrad Membership and Introduction of the V4+

Visegrad's cultural initiatives for the enhancement of a "Central European" identity are all the more striking considering that the diplomatic relaunch deliberately forewent the opportunity to review, let alone reconstruct, Visegrad's membership.

This observation leads to a return to questions about an expanded Visegrad membership. After all, "Central Europe" by any historical, linguistic, or cultural definition extends beyond the Visegrad Four. And never did Visegrad suggest otherwise regarding those cartographically evasive denominators. Diplomacy, however, was different.

The decision of the governments of Poland, Hungary, and the Czech Republic to take Slovakia back into their fold was an opportunity to expand membership beyond the original group—which they consciously rejected. In 1998–99 Visegrad was already, and despite the stalling of the mid-1990s, an effective, even elite brand name. Nonexpansion was not a default option; successive Polish governments particularly had assumed the role of advocating the integration of the Baltic republics into European institutions, and chapter 2 illustrated Czechoslovak concern and advocacy for them also, while the Hungarian government often did the same for its southern neighbors: Slovenia, Croatia, and Romania.[67] Each of these countries could have proposed outsiders for membership, especially at the time of the relaunch. However, Slovakia's reinclusion was unique; membership was not, and would not, be extended to any other country, even if efforts to enlarge occasionally occurred from both inside and outside the Group.

Indeed, Slovenia, the first non-Visegrad member of CEFTA and an EU accession candidate, wanted to partake in "Visegrad 2," as Slovene premier Janez Drnovšek told his Czech counterpart in March 1999. But Czech prime minister Miloš Zeman was rare in Czech and Visegrad circles for frequently proposing membership expansions, particularly regarding Slovenia.[68] In so doing he was also repeatedly ignored. And Slovenia, understandably for some of the mixed signals Visegrad gave out, also misjudged Visegrad's ultimate commitment to exclusivity. Where in the 1990s Slovenia was characterized as thinking that association with Visegrad would hold it back from EU accession,[69] Drnovšek's chief of staff also showed the symbolic importance of Visegrad for EU accession. He explained retrospectively that "there was an open fear that we [Slovenes] would not be accepted in the first wave. We were behind the Visegrad group of countries."[70] However, such overtures to join Visegrad were rejected. Polish president Alexander Kwaśniewski acknowledged in February 2000 that both Slovenia and Ukraine expressed interest in membership and that foreign-ministerial consultations were being held.[71] And the Polish Visegrad presidency report of 2012–13 listed Lithuania, Slovenia, Romania, Bulgaria, and Croatia as having been mentioned as potential new members.[72]

Slovak premier Dzurinda and Polish premier Buzek stated in May 2000 that Visegrad was not a closed entity (though, very much, it was) but that most productive was the Group's current four-way format.[73] Enlargement was ruled out. As then Hungarian ambassador to the EU, Olivér Várhelyi, affirmed in an interview in 2017, "Visegrad is fit for four."[74] Outreach and collaboration with others, however, were possible and likely and eventually would become a flexible and strong feature of V4 activity.

The interest of others like Slovenia expressed after V4 renewal was understandable. As in the early 1990s, and when a de facto race among post-communist states existed to demonstrate their political-economic prowess at becoming more like the West, now membership of the renewed Visegrad also held capital for neighboring states, and consequences of being on the outside of Visegrad were considerable. A Slovene opposition politician asserted that "Slovenia made the mistake of not proving capable of forging in due time an alliance with the Central European, that is, Visegrad Group. Had it done so . . . it would have been automatically in the first round of NATO expansion, and it would have also been in a better position as regards the European Union."[75]

A further practice that Visegrad adopted in the relaunched period echoed that of the early 1990s: avoiding when communicating with others, but not within itself, the term "organization" or "institution," even in the face of all that was described above. "Alliance" or "bloc" was never uttered. Some of its new provisions for cooperation were left open-ended in the prime ministerial agreement of May 1999, probably as a flexible complement to the other structures introduced. Nonspecified government members would meet "as and when needs arise." But questions of the "how" remained.

That briefly aside, the coherence of the group helped it regain international familiarity and advance, as intended, Slovakia's standing in Euro-Atlantic accession. Slovak membership of Visegrad meant that the country was being addressed and treated as an "equal" to Poland, Hungary, and the Czech Republic. This included, as table 4.1 shows, meetings of the four Visegrad heads of states with German chancellor Gerhard Schröder in April 2000 and with French Premier Lionel Jospin in May 2000.[76] Such meetings, too, were a boast for Visegrad's own status, within the region and internationally as well as within Visegrad societies. Wojciech Przybylski wrote of the Polish experience, V4 meetings with German chancellor Angela Merkel and Japanese prime minister Shinzo Abe "meant a great deal in diplomacy as well as in how Polish public opinion began to appreciate the Visegrad Group."[77]

So successful became the projection of and familiarity with Visegrad abroad that Hungary's daily *Népszabadság* wrote in 2000 that "in the West's language, Visegrád is a far more common term than the four Visegrád countries perceive it [to be]."[78] Its hyperbole may have reflected, at that point, Visegrad's self-confidence more than universal recognition. Nevertheless, the V4 governments continued to assert that they were a coherent regional unit. Visegrad's renewal also contrasted with what some have called the "abject failure" of the CEI.[79] The latter, comprising the V4 as individual members and fourteen other post-communist states, also met regularly and, unlike Visegrad, created in 1996 a formal Executive Secretariat with permanent staff.

Visegrad squared the circle of not expanding its membership by devising its "plus" format, written with arithmetical symbol "+," and through that format literally added institutions and countries to its activities, one with less shared identity but common interests.[80] That equation proved effective when Visegrad asserted its interests in the EU, the subject of a chapter 5, and when it wanted to highlight or intensify relations with major actors, both European and international. Thus the European Commission became a "+" partner, as would, for example, the governments of Japan, Israel, South Korea, and the United States.[81] Taking Japan as an example, its foreign ministry writes of the "dialogues at the leader, foreign minister, and senior working levels and promotes V4 plus Japan cooperation in a wide range of areas, such as science and technology, assistance to third countries, disaster risk reduction, and the environment."[82]

Visegrad was fully functional, engaging with other partners inside and outside of the EU, and raising its profile within its societies. That said, not all Visegrad's activities proceeded in a linear fashion. Rather, the format took on an unexpected but important role—that as a vehicle for protest. The features identified from Visegrad's remake since 1999 allowed it to survive and respond, whereas years earlier, it might well have died—again. This next section illustrates Visegrad's internal resilience when it was held politically hostage by member states.

VISEGRAD'S RESILIENCE

For all its reinvigoration from 1999 onward, Visegrad was not perfect cooperation. Nor was it easy cooperation. Its members had conflict history and embers that could be and were easily ignited.

Cooperation almost broke down in 2002, when the Czech and Slovak governments boycotted a prime-ministerial level meeting of Visegrad after Hungarian prime minister Viktor Orbán called for the post–World War II Beneš Decrees to be revoked. The decrees, sanctioned by the Allies, allowed for the expulsion, sometimes violently and even fatally, of both Germans and Hungarians. Despite any moral questions about the decrees, they have been untouchable political issues (though some humanist Czech dissidents had thought differently even before the 1989 revolutions, and the collective moral responsibility toward the expellees was a subject of underground discussion and written debate).

The Slovak and Czech governments opted to boycott the Hungarian-organized Visegrad Summit. This was enough of an event that some contemporary media carried headlines referring (long before the "migrant" crisis, which did propel the Group's name into headlines) to Visegrad by name. Analyses close to the region, and therefore by those already familiar with it, asked if the cancelled summit provided "another nail" in Visegrad's coffin.[83] That was both because of the contentious issue—the postwar expulsion from Czechoslovakia of some 3 million Germans—and, more relevant to Visegrad, hundreds of thousands of Hungarians. The issue plagued foreign relations between Czechoslovakia on the one hand and Germany and Austria on the other. In 2002 a nationalistic Viktor Orbán sought to seize on the opportunity of EU accession having not yet been finalized to try to force Prague and Bratislava to rescind these postwar decrees. To do so he hijacked the Visegrad Summit that he was due to host, refusing to allow it to proceed if the decrees were not annulled. Prague and Bratislava replied by refusing to attend the summit.[84] Poland was not a party to the historical dispute, though Germans were forcibly expelled also from the lands reconstituted as Poland. Instead, in not so much as a statement of solidarity but of practicality, the Polish Foreign Ministry declared its nonparticipation on the basis that the absence of two members, irrespective of the summit even happening, made any attendance senseless.

That was not the end. Showing the severity of the reciprocal protest by Prague and Bratislava, a Hungarian government spokesman then chastised them for misusing Visegrad: "This is a regrettable fact because both Prague and Bratislava were referring to an issue which has nothing to do with our bilateral relations and nothing to do with Visegrad co-operation." But it was Budapest that had chosen to swell a "bilateral" issue into a multilateral one. The Hungarian representative continued Budapest's subsequent rationale: "As is well known, the question concerning the Benes decrees was actually raised by a member of the European Parliament. So the Hungarian Prime Minister responded to that, he gave a very clear and very balanced response."[85]

However, István Szent-Iványi, chairman of the Hungarian Parliament's Foreign Affairs Committee, rebuked the Hungarian prime minister and made a plea for upholding the Group's modus operandi. He stated that Orbán "did not choose the right place and right time to discuss that issue. The Hungarian position is very clear on that. We wouldn't like to put it on the agenda of the bilateral issue and of the international issues and he violated that basic rule and that was the problem with his saying in my opinion, in the sense that it was not good and not tactful to speak about that."[86] As much as some voices in Hungary criticized Orbán's misuse of Visegrad, the impact was serious. Noted Czech émigré author-activist Pavel Tigrid, culture minister for four years, warned that Visegrad was a direct victim of Orbán's resurrection of the issue of the Beneš Decrees.[87] No matter Hungarian ripostes; other Visegrad members saw Budapest as having misappropriated their common diplomatic venture.

While Visegrad had become a vehicle for two-way diplomatic protest, and regional media claimed that "political cooperation halted,"[88] the Group hardly ceased to function. That was due to two of Visegrad's characteristics. The first came from Visegrad's sectoral expansion and from the regularization of meetings. A scheduled Visegrad meeting of culture ministers occurred immediately after the thwarted prime-ministerial summit—something not in place just five years before. To symbolize Visegrad's continuity amid internal strife, that same meeting convened in Hungary. Better still, amid the public contention, Czech government spokesman Libor Rouček valuably injected that "because the [Visegrad] meetings are taking place regularly, we can expect that it will be held this year." He did caution about the continued impact of Orbán, who would go on to win the Hungarian elections for which he postured by raising the decrees in the first place. But Rouček's certainty was a result of Visegrad's institutionalization; it is hard to imagine Visegrad continuing to function in any form a decade earlier, without those established practices.

The second feature related to Visegrad's "spirit," and in this case older proponents of Visegrad—Hungarian activists and early Visegrad proponents who were not politicians like Orbán—challenged Orbán's apparent intentions to scuttle cooperation. They prevailed: differences were reconciled, and Visegrad continued.

That episode indicates how versatile Visegrad's functionality had become, including to its own members. Without the multilevel cooperation that Visegrad created in 1999, it is unlikely that Visegrad could have survived some of the disjunctures, even outright attacks on it.

But 2002 occurred before achievement of what was the original aim and purpose of the Group's formation, all members gaining full NATO and EU membership. Those triumphs are evaluated with knowledge that by 1999 Visegrad was restarted. Nevertheless, Visegrad's part in achieving EU and NATO accession remains paradoxical, requiring scrutiny.

NOTES

1. Reich, esp. 162.
2. See chapter 5.
3. EU and NATO decisions on accession and their impact on Visegrad are assessed in chapter 5.
4. Among literature making such a case is Fawn, "Bashing."
5. ČTK (Czech News Agency), April 6, 1999.
6. TASR (News Agency of the Slovak Republic), December 7, 2001.
7. Hárs.
8. Chmel, *Moja maďarská otázka*, esp. 23.
9. Bútora, "Miracle," 43; Strážay, "Visegrad: Arrival, Survival," 20.
10. Lukášek, 2, and chapter 3 of this book.

11. Specific reference to a fourth chair is made by Bútora but in the context of when he was appointed Slovak ambassador to Washington and his co-ambassadors reserving a chair for him at a breakfast meeting. Bútora, 90. Academic reference is made in Dangerfield, "Visegrád Group"; the empty chair is one of the "should know" items regarding Visegrad that *Visegrad Insight* highlights.
12. Dangerfield, "Ideology"; W. Williams, "National Myths."
13. The etymological development is particularly covered in Altshuler; see also generally Appel.
14. Among scholarly work, see Haughton, "When"; and Myant.
15. Klaus denied having said such, even once. *Mladá fronta DNES*, October 8, 1993. That view, however, came especially from a ČTK report in 1991 that had him explain that in privatization there was no way to distinguish dirty from clean money.
16. "Czech Republic: President Vaclav Havel Makes State of the Nation Speech" [verbatim speech, December 9, 1997], December 10, 1997, https://www.rferl.org/a/1087560.html. See also Pontuso.
17. He kindly granted an extended interview, even though his memoirs were about to be published. Šedivý, Čzernínský, and later *Diplomacie*.
18. Druker, 54.
19. Geremek, 117.
20. Haughton, "Vladimír."
21. Pithart, "European," 19.
22. At times, Mečiar's influence, let alone control, over Slovakia's political system was exaggerated to the point of caricature, especially in comparative non-region-specific literature of Slovakia. In his seminal article, and perhaps overkeen on alliteration, Fareed Zakaria paired Sierra Leone and Slovakia. Zakaria, 22.
23. Dalibor Rohac, "My Country Had Its Own Trump. Here's How We Beat Him," *Washington Post*, February 23, 2017, https://www.washingtonpost.com/news/democracy-post/wp/2017/02/23/my-country-had-its-own-trump-heres-how-we-beat-him/.
24. See the comments of the chairman of the Slovak Parliamentary Committee on European Integration, Frantisek Sebej, TASR, March 13, 1999.
25. TASR, November 21, 1998.
26. No NATO aspirant or member country would contemplate the same until Turkey, and that caused uproar with several of its NATO allies. That said, the Dzurinda government was condemned by part of the Slovak press after the 9/11 terror attacks for the cancellation as senseless "militant" ideology, claiming that the system could have protected Slovak airspace. *Pravda*, September 26, 2001. In this case, however, the S-300s were also part of a debt cancellation agreement with Russia. Slovakia's deputy defense minister said that the arrangements did not mean Slovakia was "returning to the East." Cited in RFE/RL Newsline, October 13, 1997. Slovakia received one communist-era S-300 system from the Czechoslovak divorce, and that system was transferred to Ukraine in April 2022 to be used against Russian airborne attacks. The US defense department then gave Slovakia a Patriot air defense system.
27. "Statement by H.E. Mr. Eduard Kukan Minister of Foreign Affairs of the Slovak Republic," December 8, 1998 [emphasis added].
28. Quoted in Daniel Gurlowitz, "Great Expectations Surround V4 Summit," *Slovak Spectator*, May 17, 1999.
29. See chapter 2.

30. Szomolányi, 60.
31. See such commentary as Visegrad "managed to lobby successfully to help Slovakia in its ambitions to join the OECD." "Central European Cooperation Goes into a New Gear," Radio Prague International, August 8, 2000, https://english.radio.cz /central-european-cooperation-goes-a-new-gear-8044956.
32. The Visegrad website refers to them as the three presidents; the official report of Czech Foreign Policy states, correctly, that it was the three prime ministers in attendance.
33. *1999/2000 Czech Presidency. Annual Report on the Activities of the Visegrad Group Bratislava—Budapest—Prague—Warsaw, 2000,* https://www.visegradgroup.eu /documents/annual-reports/1999-2000-czech-110412.
34. Ministry of Foreign Affairs of the Czech Republic, 45. By contrast, Radio Free Europe reported that the meeting "welcomed the possibility of Slovakia's return to the group." RFE Newsline, October 22, 1998, http://www.rferl.org/content/article /1141768.html.
35. The official Czech foreign policy report, however, does not mention the location of the meeting, let alone give attention to the choice of the Slovak capital.
36. *1999/2000 Czech Presidency. Annual Report on the Activities of the Visegrad Group Bratislava—Budapest—Prague—Warsaw, 2000.*
37. International Business Publications, 71.
38. "Come Back, Visegrad," *Economist,* May 20, 1999. As other citations reflect, the *Economist* has oscillated in its own view of Visegrad's utility.
39. Point 4 of the "Contents of Visegrad Cooperation 1999," https://www.visegrad group.eu/cooperation/contents-of-visegrad-110412.
40. ČTK, April 19, 1999.
41. The statement was given at www.visegrad.org/contents.htm.
42. "The Visegrad Group (V4)," July 5, 2016, accessed May 27, 2022, https://www .consilium.europa.eu/en/documents-publications/library/library-blog/posts/the -visegrad-group-v4/.
43. "Contents of Visegrad Cooperation 1999," https://www.visegradgroup.eu /cooperation/contents-of-visegrad-110412. Further specification came with the "Annex to the Contents of Visegrad Cooperation (2002)." https://www.visegrad group.eu/cooperation/annex-to-the-content-of. In particular, this annex established rules for Visegrad's "+" format of meetings, elaborated later in this chapter.
44. From interviews conducted regularly on this particular dimension of the cooperation, since 2004.
45. Comparison of the Central European Initiative to Visegrad is, inter alia, in Fawn, "International Transformation," and in "Regional Relations."
46. For issues of management including in times of dissension, some detailed below, see Fawn, "Visegrad."
47. These conclusions come from a content analysis of the reports by the present author. An unpublished draft of the finding is available.
48. Similarly, drawn from content analysis of the reports.
49. "Joint Statement of the Prime Ministers of the Visegrad Group Countries on the 25th V4 Anniversary," February 15, 2016, https://www.visegradgroup.eu/calendar /2016/joint-statement-of-the.
50. As per Visegrad coordinator interviews in Fawn, "Visegrad."
51. See also chapter 7, which has necessary analysis also of Visegrad's overreach.

RELAUNCH: EXPIRATION TO RESURRECTION   127

52. Tökés, 14.
53. *Report on the Polish Presidency of the Visegrad Group 1 July 2016–30 June 2017*, 6, https://www.visegradgroup.eu/documents/annual-reports/polish-presidency-report-180809.
54. Kusý, 92; in an interview in September 1995 in Bratislava, Professor Kusý said to me, perhaps unnecessarily, that that was a comment made in another time.
55. Brown, *Surge*, 266.
56. E.g., the statement of Geremek in 1998: "As far as the societies are concerned, this idea of Czech, Hungarian and Polish cooperation was always pleasant and always very strong." Cited in Druker, 47.
57. Modified from "Contents of Visegrád Cooperation Approved by the Prime Ministers' Summit, Bratislava, 14th May, 1999," http://www.Visegrád.org/v4/contents .htm.
58. The Štiřín prime-ministerial meeting proposed a diplomatic academy and not, e.g., a military one; it is exactly these initiatives that make sense but that, amid much else achieved, did not take root. The lack of common military training, despite intrinsic logic, is assessed in chapter 8.
59. Rusnák, "Future," 104–5.
60. ČTK, October 22, 1993, *FBIS*, October 22, 1993, 4.
61. *Slovak Presidency Programme 2014–2015*, 7, https://www.visegradgroup.eu /documents/presidency-programs/2014-2015-slovak.
62. Cited in Rhodes, 53.
63. Ash, *Freedom*, 138.
64. Chmel was particularly well suited to comment, inter alia having served as a postcommunist Czechoslovak ambassador to Hungary, Slovak MP, Slovak minister of culture, and president of the Open Society Foundation. Rudolf Chmel, "A Visegrad without Culture?," n.d., https://www.visegradgroup.eu/the-visegrad-book/chmel -rudolf-visegrad.
65. The OSCE Network was established after the IVF and the Think Visegrad Network and now has members across dozens of countries and significant activism. I add the disclaimer of having brought my home institution into the Network and participated in several events, including ones that were funded.
66. Disclaimer of interest: I was awarded a Think Visegrad Visiting Fellowship in 2013.
67. See the coverage of the April 1998 meeting of Polish president Kwaśniewski and Hungarian president Arpad Göncz in *Warsaw Voice* 17/496, April 26, 1998.
68. ČTK, March 5, 1999.
69. Orosz, "Relations of Slovenia." This attribution to Slovene views should be qualified as from a secondary source by a non-Slovene. Unlike for many other neighboring countries, my inquiries regarding Slovenia are more limited. These included interviews with Slovene diplomats in Central Europe, which suggested neither competitive nor derisive views toward Visegrad.
70. Quoted in European Stability Initiative, "Janez Drnovsek—New Age and Independence in Slovenia," September 16, 2009, https://www.esiweb.org/index.php?lang= en&id=391. At times other Slovenes asserted that Slovenia was ahead of Visegrad in Euro-Atlantic accession.
71. As reported by ČTK, February 22, 2000, *FBIS*, February 22, 2000.
72. *Report of the Polish Presidency of the Visegrad Group July 2012–June 2013*, https:// www.visegradgroup.eu/documents/annual-reports/report-pl-v4-pres-07-131209, 9.

73. ČTK, May 31, 2000.

74. Interview, Brussels, July 2017.

75. Reported as "SDS' Jasna Views Foreign, Domestic Issues," *FBIS*, February 11, 1998. Some contemporary analysis of Slovene efforts at NATO integration omitted reference to seeking relations with Visegrad. E.g., Bebler.

76. See the comments particularly in *Hospodářské noviny*, May 5, 2000. Jospin's meeting is recorded in the French Archives, with Visegrad by name but with no content. "Voyage officiel de Lionel Jospin, Premier ministre, en Hongrie Rencontre avec les chefs du gouvernement du groupe de Visegrad," https://francearchives.fr/en/facomponent/d3b7a20e3d05fdf4036a98c436ac5d22c22f970c.

77. Wojciech Przybylski, "The Ebb and Flow of the V4: There's No Need to Believe in the Visegrad Group—but Do Try to Understand It, *Visegrad Insight*, January 21, 2015, https://visegradinsight.eu/the-ebb-and-flow-of-the-v421012015/.

78. *Népszabadság*, April 8, 2000, *FBIS*, April 11, 2000.

79. Steves, 350. Comparison of Visegrad and the CEI and to other regional formations is offered in chapters 5 and 9.

80. Practice for the "+" format were established in "Annex to the Contents of Visegrad Cooperation (2002)," https://www.visegradgroup.eu/cooperation/annex-to-the-content-of. Cabada and Walsch, 116–17.

81. Limitations of the "+" format, including limiting its application, are discussed, e.g., in the context of relations with China in chapter 8, on Visegrad's non-European international relations.

82. "Third 'Visegrad Group Plus Japan' Summit Meeting," Ministry of Foreign Affairs of Japan, April 25, 2019, accessed May 26, 2022, https://www.mofa.go.jp/erp/c_see/page4e_001012.html.

83. Jolyon Naegele, "Central Europe: Is Summit Cancellation Another Nail in Visegrad Four Coffin?" RFE/RL, February 25, 2002.

84. E.g., David Cronin, "Visegrad Summit Cancelled as Orbán Salts War Wounds," *European Voice*, February 27, 2002, https://www.politico.eu/article/visegrad-summit-cancelled-as-orban-salts-war-wounds/.

85. Quoted in Radio Prague International, "Visegrad Four Dispute over Benes Decrees," February 27, 2002.

86. Quoted in Radio Prague International, "Visegrad Four Dispute."

87. *Mladá fronta DNES*, March 19, 2002.

88. ČTK, June 22, 2002.

5

VISEGRAD AND THE EURO-ATLANTIC ACCESSION PROCESS

Visegrad's self-reference to achieving Euro-Atlantic integration is so fundamental to its being, and the resistance it faced from NATO and the EU so great yet forgotten, that this statement deserves reprise: neither the EU nor NATO sought to embrace post-communist states immediately after the 1989 revolutions. Some engagement, yes; membership, no.[1]

When not contradictory, the totality of debate is cluttered and confused regarding Visegrad's roles in making those organizations change their perceptions toward Central European states. Additionally, Euro-Atlantic accession is considered by Visegrad supporters to be its greatest achievement; determining Visegrad's role becomes a fundamental part of the Group's and even Europe's history. Indeed, Visegrad's apparent centrality to gaining Euro-Atlantic membership is also subject to post-facto glorification, potentially clouding historical analysis, and also challenges scholarship on accession written outside the region that neglects Visegrad.

To recap: determining the extent of Visegrad's contribution to securing its countries' entry into NATO and the EU is important because

1. that has become part of Visegrad's official historiography;
2. it informs us of an otherwise missed dimension of the transformation of post–Cold War Euro-Atlantic security, including how those institutions decided upon and implemented their enlargement; and through that
3. it provides a corrective to some core literature on EU and NATO enlargement made with little or no reference to Central European regional dynamics.

The chapter proceeds by identifying perspectives from Visegrad practitioners on the Group's role in achieving Euro-Atlantic accession. It then determines the resistance that Visegrad faced and how Visegrad served to alter Western perceptions and Western policies. It contends that Visegrad did so through, first, projecting a positive image to the West; second, by undertaking regional cooperation that tangibly aided the accession process, foremost for the EU the establishment and intensification of the terms of the Central European Free Trade Agreement (CEFTA). In addressing oversights in major scholarly literature on Euro-Atlantic enlargement, the chapter contends that significant Visegrad initiatives have been missed, an omission likely caused by changes in *both* Western and Visegrad practices during the accession period. Ultimately, the region's own account of its history—and consequently that also of NATO and the EU—benefit from historical redress.

HISTORIOGRAPHIC OFFICIALDOM: VISEGRAD SAYS VISEGRAD MADE EURO-ATLANTIC ACCESSION

A starting point must be that Visegrad leaders have affirmed Visegrad's importance in fulfilling both accessions. Exemplary foreign policy architects from each of the V4 countries evoke Visegrad's centrality to Euro-Atlantic accession.

First is Martin Bútora, Slovakia's ambassador to the United States between 1999 and 2003, previously an adviser to Václav Havel. For Bútora, Visegrad "quickly found favour with the West, because it was a positive, sensible, stabilising, and constructive concept. Positive symbols are essential in politics and public diplomacy, and Visegrad quickly became just that."[2]

Michael Žantovský served as Havel's foreign policy spokesman after the Velvet Revolution, and Czech ambassador, like Bútora, to the United States, as well as to the United Kingdom and to Israel. Žantovský called Visegrad "a powerful negotiating tool" for gaining NATO membership and stated that Visegrad's "close and coordinated work . . . compelled American and Western European politicians to open the doors of the Atlantic alliance to us."[3]

"Compelling" Western leaders to open NATO is already an extraordinary tribute to Visegrad's influence. Hungarian foreign minister Géza Jeszenszky provides a third acknowledgment. Also ambassador to the United States during NATO accession, he heightens Visegrad's role with reference to what it surmounted: "Overcoming western reluctance and Russian opposition to NATO enlargement required considerable coordinated effort," and the 1999 accession "would not have taken place, or not as early, without Visegrád."[4]

As if three were insufficient, Poland's communist-era Solidarity dissident hero and post-communist president Lech Wałęsa provides a fourth: "The tangible fruits of this [Visegrad] cooperation can be seen nowadays in the integration of our countries with European and Atlantic structures. Today we can see that the Visegrad Group was an important platform for cooperation in achieving the integration aspirations."[5]

These are big claims. Are they accurate? Or perhaps glorified retrospectives? Differentiated responses are required to address those questions: that Visegrad played different roles and at different times, toward NATO and the EU. Additionally, at points, Visegrad cooperation obstructed accession. The only clear conclusion is where we started: Visegrad supporters continue to accord it tremendous importance in achieving that fundamental goal of Euro-Atlantic accession.

To assess Visegrad's role the chapter returns to establishing NATO's and the EU's reluctance to open their doors. The individual post-communist states and Visegrad collectively were fighting against tremendous resistance. They had to transform mindsets; establishing their starting point in relation to the two institutions is essential to any understanding. After that, the chapter contends that Visegrad's role in achieving accession was threefold: (1) ideational reassurance and reiteration of the West's values to itself; (2) practical preparations, including the role of CEFTA; and (3) as a pressure group. The chapter contends that the precise contribution that Visegrad made in securing Euro-Atlantic accession remains difficult to define because both it and its would-be partners changed their intentions in the process. But Visegrad most certainly made contributions to accession.

THE DOORS THAT DID NOT INTEND TO OPEN

Neither NATO nor the then-EC intended initially even to contemplate let alone offer the prospects of membership to post-communist states. Each offered proposals that consistently disappointed Visegrad. To appreciate Visegrad's accession achievement requires grasping the resistance those countries faced toward both Brussels-based international institutions, each assessed in turn.

NATO's Extraordinariness yet Insufficiency

What was NATO's perception of the immediate post-communist (in)stability of what became the Visegrad countries?[6] Again, a few statements immediately indicate the Alliance's hesitations. NATO secretary general Germany's Manfred Wörner warned in May 1990, "There are old national and ethnic rivalries that we thought had been overcome; border and minority questions are again rearing their heads."[7] Why would NATO accept as members countries in that predicament? The answer was clear enough: the Atlantic Alliance did not intend to do so. In 1991 a non-NATO analyst, one later serving as a Czech deputy foreign minister, wrote in NATO's leading means of public outreach that there was "no intention at NATO's Brussels headquarters or elsewhere in the West to extend the North Atlantic Treaty to cover any new commitments in Europe."[8]

NATO enlargement to Central Europe was a monumental consideration and faced continued opposition. Cold War historian John Lewis Gaddis concluded of American views on NATO enlargement: "Historians—normally so contentious—are in uncharacteristic agreement: with remarkably few exceptions, they see NATO enlargement as ill-conceived, ill-timed, and above all ill-suited to the realities of the post–Cold War world. Indeed I can recall no other moment in my own experience as a practising historian at which there was less support, within the community of historians, for an announced policy position."[9]

When NATO enlargement finally became policy, forty-six US foreign policy and Russia-specialist practitioners signed a letter to President Clinton declaring NATO expansion to be "neither necessary nor desirable" and "ill-conceived."[10] NATO's expansion," George F. Kennan, father of Containment, warned, "would be the most fateful error of American policy in the post cold-war era."[11] Other American officials applied provocative historical analogies: "NATO enlargement will encircle the Russian heartland in a huge military pincer movement like what the Germans tried in World War II."[12] Hungarian-born scholar and later a Hungarian member of European Parliament, George Schöpflin, exemplified regional views of Western disapproval of NATO enlargement: "The West seemed to be mesmerised by what was happening in Russia and was ready to subordinate" the interests of post-communist states "by effectively blocking access to Western security arrangements to the Visegrád countries."[13] Similarly, a prominent Central European study in 1993 concluded that "NATO's unwillingness to admit new members is clearly felt."[14]

NATO's first outreach in 1990 extended to almost all post-communist and post-Soviet states and concerned merely establishing relations. NATO's landmark, post–Cold War London Summit in 1990 suggested all of Eastern Europe could "come to NATO, not just to visit, but to establish regular diplomatic liaison with NATO."[15] Political dialogue and diplomatic relations constituted the Alliance's seismic policy change. Those were instead of any security guarantee or membership, and they also placed on an equal footing the Soviet colonizer and the East European colonized. Visegrad leaders wanted more.

As Central European policy coalesced in early 1991, and the Visegrad Summit of February 1991 enunciated the region's claims to Euro-Atlantic membership, NATO embarked on distractions. First, NATO put great store (as did the Central Europeans, and the USSR) on the Conference on Security and Cooperation in Europe (CSCE). However, as much as dissident-led post-communist countries supported Helsinki (and to a great extent their governments continue to today), that, too, was not a security guarantee. NATO support for the CSCE was part of an emerging strategy in response to the end of the Cold War, as the North Atlantic Council announced in December 1990, for a "framework of interlocking institutions in which the interests of all European states can be accommodated." Wörner's welcome address to Havel reiterated this Alliance view when he became the first head of a Warsaw Pact country to address NATO.[16] Havel and his fellow Visegrad leaders had pronounced the month before that they wanted nothing short of full NATO membership.

NATO's suboptimal offerings continued. In December 1991 it presented the North Atlantic Cooperation Council (NACC), itself a formalization of the gesture made at the London Summit of the preceding year. The NACC, however, involved thirty-seven NATO and former Warsaw Pact states and once again focused on dialogue, not security guarantees. Make no mistake—the Visegrad states accepted it, and because of American involvement, the formation was seen as Visegrad's "security institution of choice."[17] But NATO membership it was not, and this was the only measure offered, to which desperate and polite Central Europeans responded by saying, "We were slightly disappointed with the results" and reaffirming that they instead needed "some guarantees from the West concerning our security."[18]

NATO also deflected the Central Europeans away from itself and toward the Western European Union (WEU). Founded in 1954, the WEU might have become a West European NATO, except for lacking a military formation. In 1999 the Treaty of Amsterdam ended the WEU by dissolving it into the EU. How astute, therefore, of the Central Europeans not to place hope on the WEU—of which they were never offered full membership but only "associate" partnership. Even those supportive of the WEU's potential and of its significance to Visegrad's states indirectly reaffirmed what the Central Europeans felt: "As long as NATO exists and U.S. troops remain present in Europe, the WEU's original defense role [would] remain redundant."[19]

When—finally, from the Central European perspective—in 1997 NATO announced accession talks with Warsaw, Prague, and Budapest, US secretary of state Madeleine Albright still had to reject, and vehemently, assertions that those countries would be "second class" Alliance members.[20] NATO did not begin or continue in the post-communist period looking to embrace new members. Like NATO, the EU originally dampened and deflected Central European membership desires.

The EU: Keeping Its Distance

Perhaps it was totally unrealistic, and certainly part of the revolutionary euphoria, that crowds chanted in 1989 "Zpět do Evropy!" (Back to Europe!). A contemporary visual metaphor was the reproduction of a cartoon by Josef Lada in *The Good Soldier Švejk*. Ever intent on subverting mindless bureaucracy by acting the seeming fool to avoid combat in 1914, the apparently disabled and bandaged Czech literary character Švejk, flailing his crutches, is reproduced in 1990 in his wheelchair, exclaiming not his original Habsburg enthusiasm to fight to Belgrade but instead, now "To Europe."[21]

After decades of dysfunctional communist planning, Central European economies were stagnant and uncompetitive. The three countries' per capita GDPs were far below those of Spain or Portugal, themselves below-average economies, when they entered the European Community.[22] But comparative economic indicators mattered not to street protestors—nor particularly to post-communist leaders such as Havel, Wałęsa, and Antall. In their views, their countries and peoples deserved membership for intangible but formidable reasons: historical justice and the peaceable reunification of Europe. How did the EU respond?

The European Community (EC), as the present-day EU was until 1993, certainly extended aid and engaged in some trade talks with, relatively speaking, freer-minded communist regimes of Hungary, Poland, and Yugoslavia before 1989. Although the Treaty of the European Union Preamble affirmed that any "European" state could apply for membership if it were a democracy, had rule of law, and respected human rights, "Europe" geographically, remained undefined.[23] Most fundamentally, the EC was unprepared for the totality of change that sped through Central Europe.[24]

After the revolutions the EC engaged expanded aid and trade, without contemplating membership. If anything, several West European countries, foremost France, undertook to resist closer relations; French president François Mitterrand proposed a two-tier Europe—a measure unconnected with the later idea of a first group of EU countries being in the common-currency Eurozone and a second outside it. Mitterrand's plan went further—as Havel saw and ultimately argued successfully against—of creating a core and then a second-class Europe, to which post-communist states would be relegated. Had Mitterrand succeeded, Central European membership in the EU would have been significantly delayed or perhaps never realized.[25] Havel challenged Mitterrand over this important battle for the shape of post–Cold War Europe, and the French president's plan "failed completely."[26]

In a slowly developed position on membership, the EU enunciated the Copenhagen Criteria, four years after the 1989 revolutions, which merely demanded that the Central Europeans achieve what the Visegrad countries had already: cycles of free elections and lawful handovers of power, market economic reforms, and establishment of the rule of law. These actions were undertaken by the countries' own initiative and their good (political) sense, most likely all understanding that such was expected but not yet mandated.

Leading analysts from all four Visegrad countries in the mid-1990s concluded that it was "completely unclear when and under what conditions the EU will be willing to, *if at all*, enter into negotiations about the Visegrád Group countries' accession."[27] Even with some agreement within the EC toward Central Europe, a US ambassador to Czechoslovakia summarized these countries' fears of being placed in an "ante-room" that would become "a permanent limbo." While Association was accepted and even comforting, it was "doggedly rejected as the solution."[28] Eventually institutional language emerged that affirmed the EU had "an unavoidable duty to respond positively" to the changes in the former East European socialist states.[29] What Visegrad managed to change in its relation to the EU must be seen in light of the latter's resistance.

In determining also Visegrad's role in accession, the Copenhagen Council meeting of June 21–22, 1993, features in another regard: it torpedoed the Visegrad vessel. Copenhagen invited six post-communist countries—the V4 countries were present though invited not as a group but individually, as well as Bulgaria and Romania, who, at that point, could be said to have retained the same level of accession talks as the V3/4.[30] For leading regional analysts Miloslav Had and Vladimír Handl, the Copenhagen communiqué's omission of Visegrad created the impression that the West thought "Visegrad did not exist as a coherent significant entity," adding "even greater pessimism about the prospects for mutual cooperation."[31]

Visegrad's accomplishments included from its early existence that Visegrad achieved name recognition and became a negotiating platform with the EC. That alone hardly equated to Visegrad securing its goals from the EC. Instead, as with NATO, Visegrad continued to face serious challenges with the EC, although Visegrad's relations with it proved more fruitful than with NATO. Recall the Association Agreements mentioned in chapter 2, which the EC signed with the Visegrad states in December 1991. While all three states were present at the signing ceremony, the Agreements were concluded bilaterally. The Agreements made limited reference to eventual membership, not specifying how or when. An achievement of note for Visegrad: although the EC had considered waiting for ratification of the Association Agreements to occur also with similar ones with Bulgaria and Romania, Visegrad succeeded, as even the United States International Trade Commission observed, in having its agreements concluded without having to wait for the other two post-communist states.[32]

The EU, though, withheld the key trade concessions that Visegrad governments sought—namely, on agriculture, steel, and textiles. Visegrad lobbying could not obtain those, but these were also protected sectors of some EU-member-state economies.

This recasting of enlargement history is to reiterate what may be forgotten or taken for granted decades later: the EU and NATO needed convincing to allow accession. Prying open those doors was a momentous challenge. Certainly, Visegrad had some role. The question remains: What role exactly? As the chapter introduction summarized, that is determined through the identification of three Visegrad contributions.

1. IDEATIONAL REASSURANCE AND REITERATION OF THE WEST'S VALUES TO ITSELF

The book's first pages recounted Czechoslovak president Václav Havel's efforts in his earliest presidential days to remake Central European relations and seek Euro-Atlantic membership. He continued those themes in his invited addresses to Western institutions such as the Council of Europe and NATO. Although the Bratislava Summit of April 1990 was disappointing, it heralded the willingness of these countries to deliberate, organize themselves, and lay groundwork for constructive engagement with others.

But additionally, the absence of sufficient, meaningful overtures by NATO and the EC/EU to the Central Europeans contributed to their own recognition of the need to make cooperative inroads among themselves and in turn to use that evidence to impress upon both Brussels-based organizations that they were worthy, deserving members.

Visegrad contributed to accession by recognizing and filling what its drivers hoped would be only an intervening gap before accession could be possible. In that way also Visegrad steered a careful and commendable course, on the one hand, not to alarm an already-panicked Moscow and, on the other, not to be successful enough to release the EC/EU and NATO from help and even responsibility to them. If Visegrad worked too well, the nervous Atlantic and European institutions could continue happily on their existence paths of limited engagement. Even those dismissive of regional cooperation recognize, first, that the West was anxious about negative prospects in the region and, second, that a positive image was being projected.

Visegrad's efforts were foremost in informing the West that Visegrad meant peace and that the Visegrad formation itself was an exercise in the replication of European/Euro-Atlantic values in the previously fractured and isolated Central European region. To that invaluable Visegrad contribution to changing the Western strategic mind, a few contemporary reminders reflect the expectations of upheaval, even violence, in Central Europe. Russian geopolitical analyst Vladimir Kolossov warned that in Central Europe the "risk of aggravation of national conflicts and territorial disputes, new secessions, the instability of democratic regimes" was "rather high."[33] His views coincided with early warnings by Zbigniew Brzezinski after the 1989 revolutions. In *Foreign Affairs*, he counseled that all of the newly freed countries had "borders that are potentially subject to revisionist aspirations on the part of their neighbors." To that he added the possible exacerbation from the "historical immaturity" of the region's nationalisms, inclined as they were to be "more volatile, more emotional and more intense than those in the West."[34]

Where Havel perhaps became too philosophical and too open ended in his opening remarks and in lieu of an actual agenda for the April 1990 meeting (and chapter 2 also noted that that meeting produced no agreed statements), February 1991 was a formal act with a formal declaration—one that remains a cornerstone document. We saw earlier some of the very positive Western responses to Visegrad, and later literature recognizes the Visegrad cooperation's contribution, both to creating greater understanding among the countries and also to projecting that peaceable image toward the West.

Visegrad's founding Declaration implored the West to rethink its perceptions of Central Europe. The Group also expressed frustrations with the West's lack of understanding of the values Visegrad countries believed they shared with it. The Group knew that it had much to achieve within its ranks but that also the West needed to revise its own perceptions. At the Group's next summit, in Kraków in October 1991, Havel declared that the countries' common goal was to join "existing European associations" and that Visegrad possessed "no interest in the creation of any other bureaucracies." Reflecting the regional concern caused by the August Coup in the Soviet Union two months earlier, the Visegrad three also agreed at Kraków to coordinate their policies toward it, including abiding by the principle that they consult with each other in advance of signing any new bilateral treaty with Moscow.[35]

At its Prague Summit in May 1992, the Visegrad Group declared, "We regard it as crucial that in this spirit the Visegrád Three widen its co-operation.[36] We value very highly the co-operation achieved up till now." The Prague Summit also saw the three governments agree formally to coordinate their bids for EU membership and reiterate the need to reshape Western attitudes toward them:

> We are honestly disappointed in those that don't appreciate its significance and who believe that by disregarding it they can more quickly, and separately, enter the family of the European Community. We are disappointed, too, in those who feel that the Visegrád Three is a triple obstacle to rapid integration into NATO. It is our opinion that these organisations will more readily receive us together. Whoever sees advantage in following a separate path will sober up in a few months' time.[37]

Visegrad proved essential, as discussed previously regarding its formation, in projecting to the West an image not only of a stable Central Europe but of a region that fundamentally shared the same values as NATO and the EU. This it did through three messages. First, that it was fundamentally European, and by that it meant also its ability to surmount petty squabbles and historical hatreds. Second, Visegrad's economic-political reforms separated those countries from the rest of the post-communist world. A third facet was also enacted: Visegrad was informing the West of its own values and responsibilities. If NATO and the EU believed in expanding zones of peace and prosperity, then they should extend themselves to those who pledged the same. A contemporary analysis captured both Western inertia, including internal confusion in the EU, and Visegrad's innovativeness in asserting these values: "While political discourse on integration in Western Europe does not rise above the level of tabloid headlines or the Byzantine manoeuvres of the European Union's Brussels bureaucracy, the Visegrad states are championing something more fundamental that harkens back to views widely espoused in Western Europe in the first postwar decade following the Second World War."[38] That these aims were achieved are evidenced by contemporary analyses such as Pál Dunay's: "Visegrad was important in its early stage to counter the image of a disintegrated East as well and thus carried the message that the countries of the region could cooperate with each other and thus may be mature for western integration in due course."[39] George W. Grayson chronicled the influence of American politicians and American communities of Central European heritage on encouraging NATO expansion, but he also wrote that Havel "continuously reminded the U.S. leader [President Clinton] of the 'values of civilization' that the Visegrad countries shared with the West."[40]

To what extent did Visegrad's "civilizational" projections shift Western political mindsets? Central Europeans unequivocally thought they did so. According with views that opened this chapter, Czechoslovakia's Dienstbier recalled that "the ambassadors of the Visegrad 'Troika' in Washington or elsewhere [such as] in Brussels . . . showed the world that Central Europe was not a territory of post-communist chaos as [was the case in] certain other regions, but an area where the pragmatic joint activity of the Visegrad group contributed to stability."[41] Comments of these sorts are few, however, among Western policymakers. But we have ample evidence of the perceptions of concern and even chaos that many Western analysts and policymakers expressed about this region following its 1989 revolutions. Visegrad cooperation, therefore, did matter. Veteran regional analyst J. F. Brown wrote in 1997 that the "Eastern European state will never be taken very seriously by the West or each other until they themselves make some real effort at regional or subregional cooperation."[42] The Visegrad states had done that before the others.[43]

Commentaries on the fates of other post-communist countries substantiate Visegrad's role in starting accession or even getting noticed. Far from achieving NATO membership, others struggled merely to be noticed. Stephen R. Burant, for example, wrote, "Such non-members [of Visegrad] as Romania, Bulgaria and [even] the Baltic states have found it much more difficult to get on the West's radar screen."[44]

Having established that Visegrad raised awareness and positive images of its members, we should next evaluate how Visegrad managed negotiations and how it changed EC thinking. Indeed, despite achievements in name recognition, Visegrad had to lobby hard for its aims. An EC observer wrote of EC-Visegrad meetings in both Luxembourg and London in October, 1992 that they had not achieved "any significant results, either on the membership question or with respect to market access-issues. In fact, the situation had deteriorated markedly: the member states were now on the defensive, the British government has been defeated in its attempt to move policy ahead, and the Commission was divided."[45]

Visegrad cooperation arose in part precisely because the EC and NATO gave no meaningful indicators of membership. And the EU especially was deemed to be "promoting regional co-operation throughout Europe."[46] In this way, the comment of the Czech Republic's Klaus, if otherwise ill founded, that Visegrad was an artificial entity that the West created carries some merit. Poland's ambassador to the United States explained in 1992 that with Visegrad in existence, European and American partners wanted Poland to continue to cooperate in that format because doing so would coordinate their positions and increase scope for expanding relations with the West.[47] But no Western government or institution funded Visegrad's cooperation, an activity by which others judged EU efforts to "encourage multilateralism," as it did with the CEI.[48] Visegrad did arise, in part, because of the combination of lack of alternatives (as chapter 1 argued in terms of the absent hegemon) and of the Central European leadership design to re-project its region back onto West European and American decision makers as a place of shared values.

Passing and contradictory comments remain about how the West prompted Visegrad cooperation—the cooperation being, for example, "spurred by Western encouragement."[49] Or the cooperation—much more likely—arose because of what the Central Europeans perceived the West to want from them, an innate desire to project a positive regional image, *and* because no other viable options were then on offer. And where the EU was seen outright to "encourage multilateralism" among post-communist countries, that was usually deemed to be when it supplied aid directly to the regional initiative, such as the Central European Initiative.[50] Such was never the case to or for Visegrad.

Of particular salience was the sense of competition for accession that Klaus injected toxically into Visegrad's corpus. He repeatedly asserted both that the Czech Republic was the accession frontrunner and that the others must not hinder its prospects. That both the EU and NATO eventually undertook individual country assessment suitably for accession negotiations, and then evaluated those preparations on a case-by-case basis, also requires qualification of any argument about the salience of Visegrad. *Both* Visegrad governments *and* the two Euro-Atlantic institutions changed their stances on group approaches to accession. Analysis, therefore, of Visegrad's and CEFTA's roles in accession must be nuanced.

Although NATO and the EU ultimately decided the format for the accession candidates, cooperation through CEFTA helped to fulfill preconditions for the accession process to occur. Central European states, for example, originally wanted to retain their own quality standards and control for food and food products, but it was recognized that standardization was a crucial prerequisite for EU membership.[51] In the very early 1990s Visegrad members lobbied together, and the EC met with the individual countries together. Less in the public domain, Visegrad foreign policymakers maintain also that Visegrad (excluding Slovakia) *did* assist the NATO accession process in the mid-1990s.[52]

For its part, NATO recognized what Visegrad sought—and initially toiled to avoid it. Examples of evidence, and surprise, at that resistance came from outside Central Europe and appeared even in the Alliance-related forums, who commented that it was "striking how slowly the West has responded to those calls."[53] Furthermore, others assessed that "NATO itself began to discuss seriously the Visegrad proposals no earlier than 1993, and it realized that it was not prepared to swallow such a huge enlargement."[54]

Much was involved in making NATO enlargement possible. It is unrealistic to expect that any single actor, be it Visegrad or otherwise, could do so. Nevertheless, three personalities have been identified as most influential: US president Clinton, Václav Havel, and Lech Wałęsa.[55]

Already in 1993 the view was that "if the Visegrad group has achieved anything in its persistent attempts to move closer to the Atlantic Alliance since 1991, it has been to highlight NATO's need to confront the challenge of its future."[56] As Havel's dissident-era friend and former spokesman Žantovský wrote subsequently, by 1993 the Visegrad idea created by Havel at, specifically, Bratislava in April 1990 "began to pay dividends," as evidenced by US decision makers having begun to accept the radical idea of NATO enlargement.[57] Havel was perhaps understated, saying merely that he was uncertain whether NATO and EU enlargement would have "proceeded as smoothly as it did had it not been preceded by the cooperation of the Visegrad Group."[58] That Visegrad had a role in accession is a certainty. But it, and its offshoot CEFTA, have also been acknowledged for having "played a crucial role in the stabilization of post-bipolar East-Central Europe."[59] Visegrad as a whole, and of course through the influence of persuasive leaders like Havel and Wałęsa, managed to make the Alliance reflect about itself and to change its thinking.

Visegrad was alive; Visegrad was known; Visegrad was effective enough to get Clinton to say that his administration's project of PfP was insufficient for the Visegrad states.

Chapter 3 demonstrated how Clinton called the Visegrad counties by that name, in January 1994. Once the NATO Enlargement bill reached Congress, only three months later, no reference to Visegrad remained. It was, instead, a bill "to authorize the President to establish a program to assist the transition to full NATO membership of Poland, Hungary, the Czech Republic, and Slovakia by January 1999." Using "the Visegrad countries" would not only have continued the familiarity accorded to the Group by the president but also saved thirty-six words, with that long formulation being employed nine times. The relative insignificance of the Group is underlined by the bill's reference, not uniformly but frequently, by adding to four countries' names "and other European countries emerging from communist domination."[60]

Visegrad also contributed to changing international references to their region, from the socialist era, and generally pejorative, "Eastern Europe" to Central Europe. Thus geographers noted, if not so much Visegrad cooperation itself, then that Visegrad had succeeded in transplanting the Central Europeans "from a status as the western edge of the east to being once again the eastern edge of the west."[61] And these changes came within months of Visegrad's creation, so "Central Europe" and "Visegrad" were being used together in reporting on the early stages of negotiations in 1992.[62]

The "don't-hold-me-back" attitude that some Visegrad states held toward the others, especially the Czech Republic and Hungary, dissipated. The accession negotiations showed that none was deemed ready. In the case of Poland, despite it being initially perceived as an accession frontrunner, its implementation of EU legal requirements slowed at the end of the 1990s, placing it last among applicants. Polish officials said that a race among Visegrad was unnecessary.[63]

From Common to Separate Paths to the EU

"Sober up in a few months' time."

So said Hungary's leaders at Visegrad's Summit in May 1992 in Prague, of those who sought Euro-Atlantic integration alone.[64] For Visegrad adherents, another retrospective view is that Visegrad had agreed on and maintained group solidarity in the three or four countries' pursuit of NATO and EU accession. As Slovakia's Bútora recalled in 2006: "We agreed on two principles, that of solidarity and that of performance. The first meant that one candidate would not try to score points at the expense of another, while the second respected the fact that NATO would be judging us individually."[65]

Therein was acknowledgment that functioning as a group was no longer necessary for NATO (and EU) accession but that each country agreed not to detract from each other's efforts. That was, however, precisely what happened. We saw plenty of Klaus's ultimately unsuccessful Czechs-are-better-than-the-rest policy, one that meant also that his Czech Republic was not to be dragged backward by others.

Although the EU was once seen as treating countries as groups (and Visegrad also gave it one), once it and NATO started the accession process on a bilateral basis, Visegrad countries lost their "privileged position."[66] Nevertheless, Visegrad countries still sought to coordinate some changes the EU expected of them. Foremost were border controls for their countries' future entry into the Schengen Area—an issue also that prompted close, and successful, Visegrad coordination *after* accession.[67] Slovak premier Dzurinda said in 2001 that "the best way to combat illegal migration is to build standard Schengen borders at the Visegrad Four external borders."[68] Slovakia was concerned that the Czech Republic could still enter the EU unilaterally or earlier than Slovakia and thereby require a border between them.[69] Slovak president Rudolf Schuster reiterated similar views, in that case to his Austrian counterpart, whose country resisted extending Schengen to incoming states. He said that Slovakia had the strategic goal of entering the EU with its Visegrad partners to avoid Schengen borders being built between them.[70]

Even though some Visegrad countries intermittently sought or expected unilateral entry into NATO and the EU, the Polish view after entry into the former and completion of negotiations for the latter was that the countries did enter together.[71]

Although Visegrad countries were fragmented in their approach toward Euro-Atlantic membership by around 1994, they had engaged in another measure that was simultaneously both symbolically and practically preparing them as a group for EU accession. That was CEFTA—which deserves analysis for its contributions to changing Visegrad's place in Europe.

2. VISEGRAD'S PRACTICAL CONTRIBUTIONS TO ACCESSION, INCLUDING CEFTA

"CEFTA and Visegrád have done a remarkable job in creating the preconditions for and facilitating" what became the first rounds of EU and NATO accession negotiations, according to seasoned regional analyses.[72] Visegrad's practical contributions to accession were also seen as one of making work easier for Brussels: the Group's existence, wrote a British observer in the early 1990s, "would greatly relieve the overburdened EC Troika [of foreign ministers] and the Commission."[73]

Apart from these positive impressions, Visegrad expressly intended to assist regional economic transformation, that is, as the foreign trade dimension of their domestic economic overhauls. CEFTA fulfilled two related objectives. First, it reinforced what Visegrad had done, by projecting westward a cooperative regional image. Second, unlike in Visegrad activities, CEFTA worked to create specialized standards and practices, being as it was specifically dealing with trade, that very tangibly and directly helped its member states meet EU requirements.

Although CEFTA necessarily reflected the terms of the General Agreement on Tariffs and Trade (later the World Trade Organization), its preamble articulated EU language, including the signatory countries' reiteration of "their commitment to pluralistic democracy based on the rule of law, human rights and fundamental freedoms."[74] CEFTA reinforced the expressions of values that Visegrad knew the West wanted to hear. It was another layer of cooperation that reassured Western interlocutors that this region could come to grips with its own affairs, and in a productive and transparent way.

The economic cooperation was significant—not least because it was absent initially from regional discussions, in which consultations on political and security matters started immediately in 1990. The early participants instead even saw the economic dimension as "irrelevant."[75] Nevertheless, the Declaration signed in Visegrád in February 1991 pledged that the countries would not only build domestic liberal-market economies but also "support free flow of labor force and capital" through economic cooperation and to establish "mutually beneficial trade in goods and services." Aware that they would be competing for foreign direct investment to refire their capital-starved, antiquated domestic industrial plant, the Declaration pledged "to create favorable conditions for direct cooperation of enterprises and foreign capital investments, aimed at improving economic effectiveness."[76]

CEFTA also worked practically toward those ends. Pause to consider not only how distorted these socialist, planned economies had become on a national level but also on a regional one. These countries were intent on and succeeded in dismantling the CMEA. An achievement, to be sure. But its termination nevertheless added complications to these bankrupt, inefficient former socialist economies. A regional analyst wrote to a NATO audience: "No matter how irrational, unnatural or enforced those [CMEA] ties were, their immediate collapse represents substantial deterioration of the economic situation."[77] For years these countries had guaranteed markets for goods that were unsaleable on the world market. Suddenly major employers in societies protected from (official) unemployment for decades were exposed to immediate market competitors.

CEFTA was therefore a painful but also salutary way to rebuild trading relations—painful because it pitted comparable national economic sectors

against each other, where otherwise protectionism would naturally have followed. And some did impose protectionism, especially in the case of the Czech
Republic, which turned the former grand free trade area of Czechoslovakia into
a fortification of customs officials against Slovakia, prompting commentary
from those once in that country that said the successors were going backward,
"developing in the opposite direction" from the "Europe" that it supposedly
wanted to join.[78]

That CEFTA positively impacted regional trade relations therefore must
not be taken for granted. After a slow start, where only a quarter of industrial
goods had tariffs lifted, it accelerated and achieved genuine trade liberalization.
By 1994 trade had jumped among CEFTA's members: Hungary's trade with
CEFTA countries increased by 30 percent, the Czech Republic's by 26 percent,
Poland's by 30 percent, and Slovakia's by 37 percent. For all of the countries
the trade increases were twice the amount that they had with nonmembers.[79]

The Group began already in 1993 to plan to remedy the lack of full liberalization on the major sticking point of industrial goods, intending full removal
of tariffs to be completed not in eight but five years.[80] The internal enthusiasm
and commitment were evidenced by that goal reaching achievement in only
four years. International analysts of the EU recognized that CEFTA served its
members' "common wish to prepare for EU membership"[81] and made the Central European states' economies more efficient and competitive in advance of
accession to the EU.

External analysts confirmed that under CEFTA, "trade development
increased regional efficiency and industry specialization on the basis of comparative advantage." Extraordinarily, this assessment found, "in some cases,
competition within CEFTA was even stronger than the EU market pressure."
So much so that competition of steel products, for which the EU granted no
trade preferences to the Visegrad states, resulted in Czech and Slovak production eliminating Hungarian. Overall, "CEFTA accelerated the occurrence of the
adjustment costs that the [Central European countries] would have to face once
in the EU."[82] Comparative analyses of regional free trade arrangements ranked
CEFTA as "highly functional" and having "high effectiveness," comparable to
major initiatives such as the European Free Trade Association, composed of
the highly advanced and free-trading economies of Norway and Switzerland.[83]

In short, CEFTA analyst Martin Dangerfield assessed that already by the
mid-1990s, that is, within three years of its launch, CEFTA was already achieving positive changes. Moreover, "Not only had it become clear that CEFTA
co-operation was not a drag on their EU membership prospects, but useful economic advantages were increasingly evident." Trade among the CEFTA memberships shot up. Between 1993 and 1996 alone, Slovakia exported the least, while
its trade within CEFTA still grew 126 percent; the Czech Republic achieved the

highest, at 175 percent. The members decided to accelerate the total elimination of trade barriers on industrial products by four years, enacting full liberalization in 1997 rather than 2001.[84] The impact was not only regional. While the EU said relatively little of CEFTA, its architects and supporters in Central Europe were unambiguous on its use in preparing the countries for EU accession. Hungarian foreign minister Jeszenszky said, for example, CEFTA had prepared "the ground for barrier-free commercial relations" for joining the EU."[85]

These tangible improvements likely forced Klaus to recognize CEFTA's utility and achievements. He told his Polish counterpart in August 1995 that the Czech Republic would favor relations with post-communist countries and wanted them to be as strong as possible.[86]

The anti-regional-cooperationist Klaus endorsed CEFTA's contribution to Central European accession to the EU, despite that it was he who vehemently thought political cooperation would stall exactly that process. For him, CEFTA was creating conditions for highly liberalized flows of good and capital and that would facilitate faster integration with the West, along with ultimately EU membership. Among observers, CEFTA emerged uniquely among many regional initiatives that could "qualify as even hypothetical alternatives to the EU," even if that was not the intention.[87]

CEFTA, like Visegrad, also helped to differentiate among post-communist countries as more and less successful. In seeking membership for his country, Croatian premier Ivica Račan asserted that "CEFTA is very important for Croatia, because it allows us to be part of the European society and less part of the Balkans."[88]

At one point only CEFTA, ironically, became a tool for the EU to label post-communist states in a backward way, arguably unfairly. This was over bovine spongiform encephalopathy (BSE), a neurodegenerative disease tragicomically called "mad cow disease," which in 2001 swept through parts of Europe. The UK, where the disease first appeared, ultimately culled over 4 million cattle, and some 175 people died from contracting the human variant. In February 2001 CEFTA states proactively met to coordinate measures to avoid contagion in their region and to meet every other month. That proved an astute measure. In May 2001 the EU proclaimed all CEFTA countries to be at risk; yet none of them at that point had cases, while neighboring Germany, for example, planned to kill 400,000 of its cattle. CEFTA agriculture ministers issued a protest and insisted that their countries be moved to the EU's category of countries with minimal risk.[89] A CEFTA meeting in September secured the attendance of the European commissioner for consumer protection, where the CEFTA ministers signed an anti-BSE declaration.[90]

CEFTA also served as a platform for the advocacy of post-communist state interests toward the EU when those countries did not have a voice inside the union. CEFTA thus had additional importance as a bridge between Visegrad and other post-communist countries. The evidence for that includes the views of CEFTA's non-Visegrad members. By joining CEFTA, Croatia, keen to leave the ultranationalism and warfare of the Franjo Tuđman years, believed it could "play a more constructive, rather than problematic, role in the wider region of South-East Europe."[91]

CEFTA also withstood internal pressures arising from the seeming success of some member states in their EU accession preparations. A Czech agriculture minister in 2001 went as far as to say CEFTA would split into two groups, one consisting of economic liberalizers including his country, and the other of Slovakia and Hungary. That did not happen, and CEFTA remained, even in this cynical view, a "preparation" for those countries' EU accession.[92]

Already between the relaunch in 1999 and EU accession Visegrad had succeeded in creating a distinctive identity. Visegrad literally uses the term "trademark" for itself and confidently states that it is known not just across Europe but internationally. The Slovak presidency in 2002–03 concluded that the "trademark of the 'V4' symbol, is a well-known structure in the enlarging Europe, as well as in the entire international community."[93]

The official Hungarian government website carried a report of commentary by Zsolt Németh, chairman of the Hungarian Parliament's Foreign Affairs Committee. Not only did Nemeth call the V4 the most successful alliance in the EU but also affirmed that EU enlargement was one of the Group's most successful policies.[94] But he was not referring to the 2004 accession. Rather, the comment was about Visegrad's influence *in* the EU on further EU enlargement. How well, and on what, the V4 acted within the EU, after its members' 2004 accession, is the subject of the next chapter.

3. VISEGRAD AS A PRESSURE GROUP FOR ACCESSION

This essential feature draws across Visegrad's early history and could include the first observation: that of changing Western perception. Visegrad was a pressure group in the early 1990s, and it remained such even as NATO and the EU advanced accession procedures on a country-by-county basis. Visegrad did not lobby for everything but did so before and after accession on key issues. Examples are given in chapter 6.

Both perceptions of Visegrad and its actual activities changed in the accession process. Those multiple variables have clouded analysis of Visegrad's historical record in contributing to that process—when there is one.

Central European governments, reasonably, understood earlier in their engagement with NATO and the EU—that is, before they were even accession-candidate countries—that once both of those institutions had become open to enlargement, they wanted multilateral engagement with the Central European states.

In that way, Visegrad was valuable twice over. First, as outlined, Visegrad sent essential signals to the West that its members were "European" and "normal," as well as distinct from the rest of the chaotic, even backward and violent, post-communist space. Second, Visegrad itself became a discussion tool, as was very evident in 1992 with the EC, and when it repeatedly referred to and formally engaged with these countries as Visegrad.

But the process then changed: both NATO and the EU decided that accession had to be on a country-by-country basis. For some observers, that revised approach contributed in the mid-1990s outright to Visegrad's decline.[95] For practitioners, however, scope remained for a common voice. Hungary's Gábor Hárs reflected that during that same time even Klaus no longer fixated on bilateralism with NATO and the EU and "that on the contrary, a 'common voice' might improve the chances of each country."[96] Clearly, the EU and NATO shift from a group approach toward Central Europe to a country-by-country accession process caused Visegrad leaders to think of both unilateral and collaborative approaches.

Regardless, the good name that Visegrad had already given its members remained beneficial. But it was not enough; the omission of Slovakia from both opening rounds of accession talks gave definitive evidence. What then happened is that the formal system for accession negotiations "meant the end of the privileged position" that the Visegrad states had earned.[97]

But even with a country-by-country basis for acceptance into NATO and the EU, Visegrad states worked together, as Visegrad, in the later stages of accession to both organizations. Even though NATO announced enlargement in 1997 and at exactly the time that Visegrad was seen to be dead (Visegrad itself records, as we saw in the last chapter, no activities in that year), cooperation occurred among the three acceding countries' officials. For preparations for EU accession, both the rhetorical statements and the actual activities of the Visegrad states showed coordination.

A methodological observation, if such grand terminology may even be applied, arises from the acts of these practicing architects of foreign policy. Visegrad absolutely played *some* role in changing Western perceptions and making the EU and NATO (more) amenable to enlargement. That much should be undeniable. The degree remains important. What is partly difficult, and possibly an important assertion for this account of Visegrad's life, is that some of the activities that Visegrad practitioners think were essential to achieving accession and were in their minds done *as* Visegrad are not recorded that way. Thus meetings in Washington among (at that point) the Three and the lobbying that they achieved in the US foreign policy system are absent from Visegrad's official accounts. Chapter 3 noted how the only recorded Visegrad "meeting" in 1997 was of the national Red Crosses. But Visegrad ambassadors were working through this period to achieve this paramount Visegrad success. Hence Slovakia's Bútora states that Visegrad was reborn in Washington.[98] Regional analyses insist that despite the conclusion of NATO accession occurring bilaterally with NATO, three countries worked together to achieve that essential goal. One report writes that following NATO's 1997 Madrid Summit, which green-lighted Alliance accession, cooperation among Czechs, Hungarians, and Poles "involved various levels, from the Ministers of Defence to their deputies and chiefs of staff, and covered also regular meetings of a number of working groups on military reforms, defence planning, NATO infrastructure programmes, C3I, arms procurement, [and] human resources management."[99] That these accounts do not formally bear the name "Visegrad" is due in part to the absence of formal reporting of these apparently important meetings, it surely adds to the sense of Visegrad's inactivity and even irrelevance to achieving NATO admission.

And when it came time to formally begin the accession process, the three governments undercut the image of Visegrad contributing. When on July 8, 1997, NATO at its Madrid Summit invited the Czech Republic, Hungary, and Poland to join, the three leaders held a press conference together and issued a joint statement. They did not use "Visegrad," although they proffered that "we are determined to intensify the political and military cooperation of our three countries."[100] And when it came to their countries' actual accession in 1999, which involved presidential signature of the ratification document, even basic coordination was absent. The plan had been for joint signature. Despite prior agreement, the Office of Hungary's President Arpad Göncz appeared not to have anticipated the date and certainly had him out of the country. So he signed the ratification—unilaterally and early. The Czech foreign minister pronounced, "We were surprised"; the incensed Polish Foreign Ministry summoned the Hungarian ambassador.[101]

Although an occasion was held on March 12, 1999, for the three foreign ministers to sign the Act of Accession in the presence of US secretary of state Albright, the disruption of planning and the absence of references to Visegrad would lead observers examining purely the NATO-Central European interactions to miss the Group's roles.

That brings us to the methodological matter of the potential divide between studies on EU and NATO accession, on the one hand, and regional focuses, on the other. Certainly some EU-focused literature recognized Visegrad and CEFTA. Sometimes this occurred when the analytical lens was of EU-regional relations *broadly*, that is, seeking to assess many or all regional formations. Where Visegrad and CEFTA are recognized, so too has been the CEI, with the latter, unlike Visegrad, directly receiving EU funds. But the CEI's contribution to accession (or indeed much else) is limited, even nonexistent.[102]

But wider and non–Central European recognition of Visegrad's role in fashioning the groundwork for accession is missing. The preceding pages should give some strong indications that Visegrad was important to Central European policymakers, and even irrespective of those potentially subjective views, Western interlocuters—as individual officeholders or institutions—engaged with Visegrad and lent credibility and significance to it. More important, their views were changed by Visegrad itself. Rare in nonregional enlargement literature are assessments such as those of Duleba and Dunay. Some major studies that have focused expressly on either of both accession processes have *entirely* neglected Visegrad.[103] That may be because Visegrad's significant success in changing Western minds came in the early, and pivotal, 1990s, before the accession process formally began in 1997.

How much and in what ways did Visegrad contribute to making NATO and the EU behave differently? This is not a narrow question. The more we find that Visegrad made a difference—and considering just how momentous, for our lifetimes and beyond, the expansion of those institutions are—the more Visegrad changed the post–Cold War order.

Visegrad played a significant role. Foremost, but neglected by EC/NATO-focused studies, is that Visegrad transformed Western thinking about this region and dispelled negative associations. That was, and remains, a momentous achievement. Visegrad's own coordination in its very early years facilitated the Europe Agreements. Czechoslovak foreign minister Dienstbier said that it was thanks to their "mutual coordination that all three countries signed association agreements in Brussels as early as December 1991, only a year after they had begun talking about doing so."[104] Hungary's Jeszenszky called the joint signing of the Agreements "a very visible endorsement of the Visegrad model."[105]

Visegrad also, if retrospectively, claims that it did much to fulfill the final condition and requirements for accession in 2004. V4 leaders pronounced in 2016, on the Group's fifteenth anniversary, that the Group "served for harmonizing positions and advancing common interests during the accession process to the Euro-Atlantic structures."[106]

But it is not the overt, deliberate role assigned to it after the fact. It was more one of image projection rather than consistently active lobbying, as a group. And, after all, accession itself set the rules. NATO admitted three of the four countries, and at a point, in 1997, when Visegrad was not functioning. The EU, similarly, opened accession negotiations with three of the four, and then also with Estonia and Slovenia.

Nevertheless, Visegrad still featured in the later stages of accession negotiations. The V4 prime ministers met, for example, in February 2002 to coordinate

responses to what they deemed unfairly insufficient provision of direct EU
agricultural subsidies to their farmers upon entry. On this deeply sensitive
and politicized matter, facing the union's entrenched and lucrative agricultural
interests, the European Commission intended only to provide new-member
farmers initially with one-quarter of existing subsidies and to delay full subsidies for a decade after accession.[107] At a V4 meeting (including British representation) Hungarian official Zsolt Németh reaffirmed V4 unity and declared
it "bad" if EU farmers had better conditions than those of the V4.[108] Slovakia's
deputy prime minister for European integration Mária Kadlečíková said in 2002
that Visegrad needed to cooperate in negotiating EU agricultural subsidies,
confident that sufficient funds would be secured.[109] Clearly, the EU would have
been hearing from the V4, and Visegrad served as a loud and effective mega-
phone. But as Czech deputy prime minister Pavel Telička said of Visegrad, "We
agree that the EU should come with proposals first" and that the V4 were waiting for precisely those.[110] For analysts not looking at Visegrad, and also whose
focus started and remained with the EU, such Visegrad influence would likely
be missed. Instead, EU actions could be seen as originating not as a response
to the V4 and its early activism but instead as if entirely from Brussels.

Common Visegrad positions in the last years of accession were also advocated by those who dissented from Orbán's hijacking in 2002 of the Group over
the Beneš Decrees. Hungary's Parliamentary Foreign Affairs Committee chairman argued for Visegrad's importance to all member states in their preparations for EU accession, having "very much cooperation and a common platform
of the Visegrad Four countries. We are fighting, combating, for better criteria
for accession to the European Union. We need a common platform in order to
achieve a common agreement with the European Union. Under that circumstance, it is very dangerous to undermine the cooperation and cohesion of the
Visegrad Four countries."[111]

Orbán's use of Visegrad earned him criticism in Hungary, including that
he had engaged in "blackmail" and "disregard for national sensitivities" and
had caused "gross diplomatic offenses." The criticisms intimated that Orbán
had commandeered the Group for his purposes and also sought "to grind the
V4 down."[112] If so, he failed. His foreign minister, János Martonyi, agreed at
a meeting with his Czech counterpart that Visegrad had produced valuable
results and that the cooperation should continue as planned.[113] Martonyi also,
however, gave a very different account to the Hungarian Parliament's Foreign
Affairs Committee. There, in an atypically "confrontational" tone, he absolved
Orbán of blame for the Visegrad crisis and called the Czech and Slovak cancellation of participation in the Visegrad Summit "careless and hasty." Nevertheless, Martonyi said that Visegrad cooperation would continue and that the
Orbán government would "do its best" to promote it.[114]

Michael Žantovský—cited previously, and in the report by the 2002 Chairman of the Czech Senate's Foreign Affairs Committee—warned of Orbán's use of the decrees and the effect on Visegrad: "Nothing is more dangerous than politicians who play with the country's national interests to gain election support."[115]

The first case is one that should have disarmed the obituary writers: that accession itself would both raise opportunities for and also require cooperation as the V4 settled into the EU. Before that case is addressed, however, explaining why the V4 seemed defunct upon accession requires attention to two other developments of that time that contributed to a mistaken perception of Visegrad's impending, and final, demise: the Treaty of Nice and the EU's "Constitution."

The EU Constitution

The Treaty of Nice resulted from the EU's recognition of the need for updated practices to accommodate what would be the enlargements of 2004 and 2007. The treaty was signed on February 26, 2001, and came into force on February 1, 2003. Poland sought voting rights commensurate with its population of 38 million, which placed it among large-sized EU states.[116] Already Poland had been perceived by other V4 partners as seeking greater roles. The coming of accession and the weighted voting influence that Poland would carry after Nice was perceived as disruptive for Visegrad. Three analysts wrote:

> The acknowledgement and reflection of the "heavier weight" of Poland by the number of votes assigned to it within the institutional parameters of EU decision-making registered and preserved the stronger potential of Poland to shape policy-making processes in comparison with the individual possibilities of the rest of the V4 Group as new EU members. It had significant impact on the perception regarding the prospects of V4 partnership within the fabric of the European Union. . . [and] soon turned out to present a source of potential jealousy and criticism of its ambitions on the part of the three smaller Visegrad countries.[117]

What Poland achieved in voting rights was remarkable, with qualified majority voting that gave it numbers nearly equivalent to Germany's. While some of Central Europe's media nevertheless noted that the V4 would have many common interests to pursue in the EU, it is perhaps understandable that Poland's approach to the Nice Treaty and its substantial voting rights appeared to separate it from Visegrad.[118] Despite that, Polish officials routinely rejected that they engaged in competition for accession among Visegrad countries and instead supported common accession strategies.[119] It also continued to support and even rely on Visegrad to achieve aims inside and outside of the EU. After Britain's departure from the union, Central European analyses continued to consider Visegrad as a group and noted its relative increase in qualified majority voting from 12.91 percent to 14.53 percent, an outcome "considered very critical."[120]

Nor did NATO accession mean a reformulation of Visegrad military-security cooperation. To be sure, tangible coordination was hardly automatic and at points even refused. Having fulfilled the declared goal of helping Slovakia achieve NATO membership, thereafter Hungary declined to join the Polish-Czech military brigade (the Czechs and Slovaks having maintained a joint peacekeeping unit since the breakup of Czechoslovakia), which itself was created to aid Slovakia's renewed preparations for Alliance membership. As chapter 6 shows, Visegrad was advocating its interests in the EU and, even less expectedly, also in NATO, and that with public acclaim.

Part of the assessment of where Visegrad could survive Euro-Atlantic accession is surely how well Visegrad and its representatives signaled its post-2004 vitality. Despite views otherwise, the Group and its supporters asserted a post-accession life.

Among these were, when in 2001, former Czech dissident and a creative post–Cold War foreign minister Jiří Dienstbier, who, featured earlier, sagely advised that "cooperation among Visegrád members can be a tool for swifter adjustment to the demands of EU entry" and that "a common approach toward Brussels on many concrete issues could be as useful as it was in 1991."[121] István Szent-Iványi, chairman of Hungary's Parliamentary Committee on Foreign Affairs, said in 2002, "We need very much cooperation and a common platform of the Visegrad Four countries. We are fighting, combating, for better criteria for accession to the European Union. We need a common platform in order to achieve a common agreement with the European Union."[122] Those views were solidified in January 2003, when the chairs of all four parliamentary foreign affairs committees decided that Visegrad would continue and that it would not enlarge but be open to cooperation with other states. Slovakia's Ján Figeľ also said that in the EU Visegrad's cooperation would move to a higher stage.[123] The Czech Foreign Ministry summarized that all four countries' desired to continue with joint activities in the tried-and-tested format of Visegrad within the EU. Meeting at Tále, Slovakia, on June 24–25, 2003, the V4 prime ministers declared that with European integration "new opportunities" for Visegrad were "assured."[124]

Through 2003 Visegrad leaders intensified their post-accession claims. Slovak president Rudolf Schuster warned that "the accession countries will need to develop tighter cooperation." Not only consequently, he explained, did Visegrad have a future but also because the V4 would wield combined comparable votes to Germany and France, the EU would be—and with a remarkable word from a sitting president—"afraid."[125] Slovakia's Figel', who coordinated his country's EU accession (and within months would become Slovakia's first European commissioner), asserted in October 2003 that "although without an institutional basis, this cooperation is bearing fruit. I'm glad that after twelve years, the Visegrad cooperation is not ending, nor is it being questioned. On the contrary, [with EU accession] it is entering a new stage."[126] Václav Klaus, Czech president since 2003, quietly revised his anti-Visegrad repertoire of the 1990s. With accession materializing, his public denigration of Visegrad ceased. At a V4 presidential summit in Budapest in 2003 Klaus pronounced that he never opposed even deep cooperation among the countries, only "empty protocol meetings."[127] He attended Visegrad summits and posed with his Group counterparts jovially partaking in interlocking group handshakes.[128] He vocalized the Group's new-found benefits in the EU, and regional media disseminated his endorsements.[129]

Visegrad preparatory meetings gave tangible reinforcement to the assertions of heads-of-state declarations to dispel views of Visegrad's post-accession death. These also widened political and societal involvement within the Visegrad states. As an example, in October 2003 the four countries' parliamentary committees for foreign affairs, integration, and defense convened in the Czech Republic to elaborate post-accession V4 cooperation. In advance of accession V4 cooperation began in such sectors as tourism, transport, energy, information technology, healthcare, and agriculture.[130] Also in October 2003, the Visegrad Four convened with Benelux—the decades-old grouping of Belgium, Netherlands, and Luxembourg—and perhaps as an unintended historical parallel to when that formation extended assistance to Visegrad in 1991, even if one official report seemed to have forgotten that this cooperation was not new but instead was resurrecting the same from Visegrad's earliest post-communist period.[131] The Czech Foreign Ministry recorded that that and other initiatives, such as with the Nordic Council, were intended to make Visegrad cooperation "more profound and effective."[132] The Czech Visegrad presidency sought the "active cooperation" of the Four's Permanent Missions to the EU.[133] Cooperation extended beyond the EU; Visegrad prime ministers also held separate summits with their Japanese and their Ukrainian counterparts in 2003.[134] In short, Visegrad cooperation expanded on a sectoral basis and engaged in high-level diplomacy beyond the physical confines of the EU.

At the heart of these preparations was the EU's Constitutional Treaty, a draft of which was presented at the Thessaloniki European Council in June 2003 and was to be finalized at the Intergovernmental Conference (ICG) of existing EU states with associate states, including Visegrad, that convened in Rome in

October 2003. Key in the ICG was Visegrad's desire to ensure that the union delivered on the principle that each member state, including the new ones, was able to appoint a commissioner. On this objective Visegrad was not alone: other "smaller" EU states felt similarly and together were colloquially even called the "like-minded states." Visegrad prepared and asserted itself; as part of its preparations was a prime-ministerial summit on October 1, 2003, in advance of the ICG, and once more in a charming castle, that of Dobříš, outside Prague. Visegrad also appealed on the cultural and popular fronts, hosting a joint event in Brussels on the V4's economic prowess, followed by a gala concert.

Visegrad was coordinating in advance of the EU's top meeting, its intergovernmental conference, and the key one preceding the 2004 enlargement.[135] In short, far from dying off, Visegrad generated new life when Slovakia joined the other three in NATO in 2004, and when they all joined the EU also in that year. The next chapter determines Visegrad's activism its next life stage—in the EU.

NOTES

1. The European Union assumed that name as of November 1, 1993, and post-communist states engaged with its predecessor. For convenience, "EU" will generally be used irrespective of the time period.
2. Bútora, "Miracle," 43.
3. Žantovský, "Visegrad," 85.
4. Jeszenszky, "Visegrád: Past and Future."
5. Wałęsa, 81.
6. Adapted from Simon's summation, in his *NATO Enlargement*, 9.
7. Wörner.
8. Pick, "Demise," 16.
9. Gaddis, 145.
10. Dated June 27, 1997, https://www.armscontrol.org/act/1997-06/arms-control -today/opposition-nato-expansion.
11. George F. Kennan, "A Fateful Error," *New York Times*, February 5, 1997, A23.
12. Dean, 112.
13. Schöpflin, *Nations*, 206.
14. *Czech National Interests*, 56.
15. "Declaration on a Transformed North Atlantic Alliance," paragraph 7, last updated July 12, 2010, https://www.nato.int/cps/en/natohq/official_texts_23693.htm?.
16. *Statement on behalf of the North Atlantic Council by the Secretary General, Mr. Manfred Wörner, on the occasion of the visit to NATO by Mr. Václav Havel, President of the Czech and Slovak Federal Republic 21 March 1991, NATO Review*, 38:1, February 1990, 29–30.
17. Simon, "Czechoslovakia's," 495–96.
18. Jaroslav Suchánek, of Czechoslovakia's Foreign Affairs Committee, cited in Gerosa, 273.
19. Gordon, "Does," 130.
20. "Let me repeat. . . . There are not going to be any second class citizens in an enlarged NATO." "Secretary of State Madeleine K. Albright and Polish Foreign Minister

Dariusz Rasati. Remarks at photo opportunity, Department of State[,] Washington, D.C., March 13, 1997," https://1997-2001.state.gov/statements/970313a.html.
21. *Literární noviny*, December 13, 1990.
22. Taking 100 as GDP per-capita average for the EEC in 1988, Spain was 75 and Portugal and Greece 54, while Czechoslovakia was 52, Hungary 44, and Poland 37. By gross domestic product per person at purchasing power parity, Czechia overtook Spain in 2019. Antonio Maqueda, "Czech Republic Overtakes Spain in GDP Per Capita," *El País*, February 8, 2021, https://english.elpais.com/economy_and _business/2021-02-08/czech-republic-overtakes-spain-in-gdp-per-capita.html.
23. Discussion of (non)European boundaries for the European Communities receive particular attention in Wallace. The "Consolidated Treaty of the European Union" and current membership criteria are given at https://eur-lex.europa.eu/resource .html?uri=cellar:2bf140bf-a3f8-4ab2-b506-fd71826e6da6.0023.02/DOC_1& format=PDF.
24. Barnes and Barnes, 399.
25. Leading literature on accession processes identify the French plans as, minimally, "delaying tactics." E.g., Schimmelfennig, 56.
26. Quoted in Tiersky, 189.
27. Compiled in Richter, "Visegrád," 31.
28. Luers, "Harmonizing U.S.," 91.
29. Cameron, online, unpaginated. He was writing in a personal capacity while credited in the European Commission.
30. See chapter 2.
31. Bombik and Samson, 158.
32. United States International Trade Commission, *Effects of Greater Economic Integration within the European Community*, 140.
33. Kolossov, "Geopolitical Scenarios," 66.
34. Brzezinski, 3 and 4.
35. Duleba, "Russia," 19.
36. This meant among the Three, not, as chapter 2 showed, a widening of cooperation to other countries.
37. Antall, "Ties That Bind."
38. Whitehall Papers, 161–67.
39. Dunay, "Subregional Co-operation," 54.
40. Grayson, 87.
41. Dienstbier, "Visegrad," 19.
42. Brown, "Introduction: A Year of Productive Discontent," 8.
43. The EC's decision to extend Association Agreements to Bulgaria and Romania changed that dynamic, to that extent that Mayhew writes that for the Visegrad states, it "marked the end of their special relationship the Community, a relationship that they assumed would lead to rapid accession." Mayhew, *Recreating Europe*, 24.
44. Burant, "Visegrad in All but Name," 6.
45. Torreblanca, 185.
46. Cameron. CEFTA is given as an example but not Visegrad, which in any case was minimally active at that time of publication.
47. *Rzeczpospolita*, July 3, 1992, *FBIS*, July 10, 1992, 28.
48. Smith, 280.
49. Szayna, "Czech Republic," 122.

50. Smith, 280.
51. As per the comments of Hungarian agriculture minister László Lakos, exiting a CEFTA meeting; Reuters, "CEFTA Minister Reach Partial Farm Accord," August 15, 1995.
52. Including this chapter's early quotations.
53. Rodman, "NATO's Role," online version.
54. Dutkiewicz and Jackson, *NATO Looks East*, 131.
55. Goldgeier writes, with qualification, "Walesa and Havel may well have made a huge impression on a president open to emotional appeals. Still, given that Clinton cared so much about the fate of Russian reform, Walesa's appeal to bring Poland and other Central European nations into the West could hardly have been sufficient." Goldgeier, "NATO," esp. 100. See also his *Not Whether*.
56. Latawski, 91.
57. Zantovsky, "In Search," 53; Žantovský, *Havel*, 440.
58. Havel, *To the Castle*, 157.
59. Duleba, "Slovak-Ukrainian-Russian," 112.
60. "To Authorize the President to Establish a Program to Assist the Transition to Full NATO Membership of Poland, Hungary, the Czech Republic, and Slovakia by January 1999, H. R. 4210 (April 14, 1994)," https://www.congress.gov/103/bills/hr4210/BILLS-103hr4210ih.pdf.
61. Dingsdale, 213.
62. Anthony Robinson and Robert Mauthner, "EC to Step Up Links to Central Europe," *Financial Times*, October 29, 1992. Visegrad was used early in the article, though with the qualifier of "the so-called."
63. Polish prime minister Leszek Miller, Polish Radio 1, December 6, 2001, *FBIS*, December 6, 2001.
64. "Ties That Bind," 279.
65. Bútora, "Spirit," 92.
66. M. B. Williams, "Exporting," 34.
67. See the next chapter.
68. Cited in *Sme*, November 29, 2001, *FBIS*, November 29, 2001.
69. See comments of Slovak premier Dzurinda in ČTK, November 23, 2001.
70. ČTK, October 24, 2001.
71. *Rzeczpospolita*, January 2, 2002, as "Polish President Kwasniewski Talks about Poland's Role in Region, Europe," *FBIS*, January 2, 2002.
72. Duleba, "Slovak-Ukrainian-Russian Security Triangle," 112.
73. Batt, 43.
74. Central European Free Trade Agreement, accessed December 5, 2023, https://wits.worldbank.org/GPTAD/PDF/archive/CEFTA.pdf.
75. Żukrowska, 227.
76. Citing the unofficial English-language version, https://www.visegradgroup.eu/documents/visegrad-declarations/visegrad-declaration-110412-2.
77. Fingerland, "Central and European," 211.
78. See, e.g., Leška, 78.
79. MTI, April 13, 1995, in BBC Monitoring, April 13, 1995.
80. Per comments of Czech trade minister Vladimír Dlouhý, *Hospodářské noviny*, November 25, 1993.
81. Barnes and Barnes, 399.
82. Giusti, 146.

83. Slapin and Gray, "Depth, Ambition," esp. 96.
84. Dangerfield, "CEFTA," 309.
85. Jeszenszky, "Origins and Enactment," 62.
86. ČTK, August 11, 1995.
87. Dangerfield, "Subregional," citing the abstract.
88. Cited in Hina, November 16, 2001, in *FBIS*, November 16, 2001.
89. Slovenian Press Agency (STA) (Ljubljana), May 4, 2001, as "Slovene Agriculture Minister. CEFTA Members Discuss BSE Issues," *FBIS*, May 4, 2001.
90. "CEFTA Agriculture Ministers Sign a Declaration on Anti-BSE Measures," STA, September 13, 2001.
91. Stubbs and Zrinščak, "Croatian Social Policy," 126.
92. *Hospodářské noviny*, November 14, 2001.
93. *Annual Report of the Slovak Presidency in the Visegrad Group (2002–2003)*, https://www.visegradgroup.eu/documents/annual-reports/2002-2003-slovak-110412.
94. "Head of Parliament's Foreign Affairs Committee Says Visegrád Group Is the Most Successful Alliance in the EU," *About Hungary*, December 14, 2017, accessed June 28, 2018, http://abouthungary.hu/news-in-brief/head-of-parliaments-foreign-affairs-committee-says-visegrad-group-is-the-most-successful-alliance-in-the-eu/.
95. See, e.g., Tony Barber, "An Eastern Foursome Goes West," *Independent*, August 4, 1995.
96. Hárs, 50.
97. M. B. Williams, 34.
98. Bútora, "Spirit," 90–93.
99. Khol, "Policies of the Visegrad Countries," 5.
100. "Joint Press Conference by H.E. G. Horn, Hungary, H.E. V. Havel, Czech Republic and H.E. A Kwasniewski, Poland," July 8, 1997, https://www.nato.int/docu/speech/1997/s970708h.htm.
101. Luboš Palata's account and commentary in *Mladá fronta DNES*, as "Visegrad Tragicomedy about NATO Entry," *FBIS*, February 19, 1999.
102. Alecu de Flers and Regelsberger, 337. Conclusions on CEI include Fawn, "Regional Relations."
103. While retaining respect for the overall scholarly contributions, examples of heavily cited works on accession that do not refer to Visegrad include Jacoby; and Schimmelfennig. Examples of others that do, albeit at certain times, were cited earlier.
104. Dienstbier, "Visegrad—The First Phase."
105. Jeszenszky, "Origins," 62.
106. "Declaration of the Prime Ministers of the Visegrad Countries Visegrad, Hungary, 10 October 2006," https://www.visegradgroup.eu/official-statements/documents/declaration-of-the.
107. PAP, February 1, 2002, as "Central European Premier to Meet on EU Farming Subsidies," *FBIS*, February 1, 2002.
108. ČTK, January 10, 2002.
109. TASR, January 14, 2002.
110. Quoted in ČTK, January 10, 2002.
111. Quoted in Radio Prague International, "Visegrad Four Dispute over Benes Decrees," February 27, 2002, https://english.radio.cz/visegrad-four-dispute-over-benes-decrees-8058543.

112. Tibor Kiss, "Bankruptcy Procedure," *Népszabadság*, February 23, 2002, as "Hungarian Daily Calls PM Orban 'Gravedigger' of Visegrad Four," *FBIS*, February 26, 2002.
113. *Népszabadság*, March 1, 2002, as "Hungarian, Czech Foreign Ministers Agree on Restoring Visegrad Four Cooperation," *FBIS*, March 1, 2002.
114. As reported in *Népszabadság*, February 28, 2002, as "Hungarian Foreign Affairs Committee in Dispute over Benes Decrees Issue," March 1, 2002.
115. Cited in ČTK, February 26, 2002.
116. Only Germany, France, the UK, Italy, and Spain had greater populations, placing Poland ahead of nineteen other states of the EU in 2004.
117. Grúber, Kovács, and Törő, 49.
118. For a view on common interests, which is discussed also throughout this chapter, see *Hospodářské noviny*, December 11, 2003.
119. As referenced elsewhere. Poland could still after accession use its own larger votes for its interests, but the ethos seemed toward continued cooperation with Visegrad within the EU. It was also Poland that maintained what Group solidarity there was in the mid-1990s, when both the Hungarian and Czech governments engaged in unilateralism.
120. Kajánek, 184. More generally on Brexit's impact, see Brusenbauch Meislova.
121. Dienstbier, "Why," 10.
122. Quoted in "Visegrad Four Dispute Benes Decrees," Radio Prague, International, February 22, 2002, https://www.radio.cz/en/section/cetoday/visegrad-four-dispute-over-benes-decrees. In this case, Szent-Iványi was primarily criticizing Prime Minister Viktor Orbán for his comments on the Beneš Decrees. Szent-Iványi continued: "Under that circumstance [of needing to secure their countries' interests in the EU], it is very dangerous to undermine the cooperation and cohesion of the Visegrad Four countries."
123. Cited in TASR, January 13, 2003.
124. "Joint Statement Summit Meeting of the Heads of Government of the Visegrad Group, Tale, Slovak Republic, 24–25 June 2003," http://www.visegradgroup.eu/2003/summit-of-prime.
125. "Hungary: Slovak President Says Visegrad Four Need to Tighten Cooperation," *Magyar Hírlap*, October 18, 2003, 6.
126. Quoted in "Visegrad Four Demand Changes in EU Draft Constitution," October 13, 2003, https://english.radio.cz/visegrad-four-demand-changes-eu-draft-constitution-8079127.
127. *Magyar Hírlap*, November 4, 2003, *FBIS*, November 4, 2003.
128. 2003 Visegrad presidential meeting, Budapest, photo, http://www.gettyimages.co.uk/detail/news-photo/presidents-of-visegrads-countries-v4-rudolf-schuster-of-news-photo/2692861.
129. Peter Morvay, "Klaus otočil: Visegrád má zmysel" [Klaus Has Turned: Visegrad Does Have a Purpose], *Sme*, November 3, 2003, 11.
130. As recorded in *Report on the Foreign Policy of the Czech Republic: between January 2003 and December 2003*, 45, https://mzv.gov.cz/file/414924/Report_2003.pdf.
131. *Report on the Foreign Policy of the Czech Republic [2003]*, 130.
132. *Report on the Foreign Policy of the Czech Republic [2003]*, 45.
133. *Report on Activities of the Czech Presidency of the Visegrád Group (2003–2004)*, no pagination, https://www.visegradgroup.eu/documents/annual-reports/2003-2004-czech-110412.

134. "V4+Japan Foreign Ministerial Meeting," November 13, 2013, http://www.visegrad group.eu/v4-japan-foreign. The V4-Japan meeting was held on the margins of an Asia-Europe Meeting. Another decade passed before a prime-ministerial summit convened.

135. Comment by Prime Minister Vladimír Špidla in *Lidové noviny*, October 20, 2003. See also the *Annual Report of the Slovak Presidency in the Visegrad Group (2002–2003)*, for accession coordination within V4 and of V4 representatives with others in the EU, https://www.visegradgroup.eu/documents/annual-reports/2002-2003 -slovak-110412, no pagination.

6

ALIVE AGAIN
INSIDE THE EU

VISEGRAD'S DEFIANCE AND
POST-ACCESSION RESURRECTION

Having been written off for dead in the middle of the 1990s, Visegrad received its next set of erroneous obituaries, which at least acknowledged its lifetime achievement: its members having attained NATO and EU membership by 2004. Now not from failure but, ironically, from success did inapt obituaries decide Visegrad's death. And this time, seemingly, truly and permanently.

Eulogies pronounced that EU accession created a "crisis" of morbidity for Visegrad. Some epitaphs nodded to Visegrad's utility to *other* countries but otherwise presented its demise as inescapable: "Overnight the 'Visegrad Group' mark was no longer needed for members of the group as well as for other countries in the region."[1] Some wrote optimistically that 2004 represented these countries' accession to the EU's core and consequently resulted in the loss of both regional identity and even of the dissolution of regional structures.[2] Leading Czech analyst and past presidential adviser to Havel Jiří Pehe contended in 2004 that Visegrad would hardly survive EU enlargement.[3] Then and years since post-accession has been labeled a "dormant" period.[4] Others asserted, if oddly counterfactually to the following evidence, that in 2004 Visegrad leaders even asked about the Group's continued value and contemplated whether it should be "dissolved."[5] A region-based historian proposed that Visegrad was dead, while pleading via an article subtitle for the messenger not to be killed.[6] Another researcher suggested in 2005 that Visegrad in the EU was then "neither of primary nor secondary concern" to fellow scholars.[7] The *Economist* wrote in the same year, that with EU accession achieved, Visegrad was "falling, if not quite apart, then at least into insignificance. As outsiders, the four countries had to work together to get into the two clubs. Now, as insiders, they have wider choices of allies and policies."[8]

Some regional scholar-practitioners offered more moderate assessments, expecting little of Visegrad after EU admission: "In spite of the often feeble cohesion and solidarity within the V4 Group during the years of accession to the Union, some form of Visegrad cooperation inside the institutional fabric of the EU remained a sensible and logical, but not self-propelling option." Even in that analysis, Visegrad was only compensating for "the weakened bonds of real collaboration."[9] For some, there were but "few possibilities for the future of the Visegrád group."[10] Others deemed Visegrad in its early years of membership as merely "good pupils of the EU (2005–2009)" and only thereafter "learning of the possibilities,"[11] or that those "good students" just continued to implement EU routines.[12] For some, all that Visegrad apparently achieved in the decade prior to the "migrant crisis" "was lobbying jointly for more money from the EU's Cohesion Fund,"[13] cash intended to level economic and social disparities. The contention and correction here are that Visegrad mobilized and achieved aims within the EU already in those early years.

As per the *Economist*, the choice of (alternative) allies presents an effective means to judge Visegrad's durability. The "+" format discussed in chapter 4 already evidenced both Visegrad's adaptability and its ability to attach other countries and institutions to its lobbying and activities. In 2004 it should have been even more apparent that Visegrad was ready and well placed to serve as the springboard for its interests in the EU. The Visegrad region knew this too, and exactly such language of choice emerged. Polish foreign minister Włodzimierz Cimoszewicz reiterated Visegrad's post-accession utility shortly before EU entry, stating also that the group would "have more contacts, great opportunities for talks," could shoulder work better collectively, and could win over the rest of EU governments.[14]

And Visegrad has remained the formation of preference for its member governments, proving "efficient" and "especially important," as region-based analysts noted, for these countries after accession.[15] And Polish leaders addressed the seeming perennial fear of Poland breaking from the Four, in the EU arena with new ally-making opportunities, by routinely reasserting the Group's importance. As but one example was when upon becoming Polish prime minister in 2006 Jarosław Kaczyński asserted that the V4 would serve "to promote its [Visegrad's] joint interests in the European Union."[16]

Inasmuch as Visegrad had become the positive and practical embodiment of the concept of Central Europe,[17] that too was seen merely as a "way station in a Europeanization process."[18] Many Central Europeans said that with accession, the all-powerful geocultural expression of "Central Europe" could dissipate; the region was simply—and euphorically—"European." On that basis, too, Visegrad was expected also no longer to have purpose after 2004.[19] The collapsing of "Central Europe" into "Europe" was itself a misnomer; others in the region also indicated that Visegrad was not necessarily even foremost for the EU and NATO but rather and still intended for solving regional problems.[20]

How did so many get so much wrong on Visegrad's post-accession prospects? We first establish why some doubt could arise over Visegrad's future,
let alone vitality, after 2004. Thereafter, Visegrad achievements in the EU are
identified. Probably Visegrad's single-most-prominent endeavor in the EU—
stopping mandatory allocations of "migrants" in 2015—was so distinctive and
significant that chapter 7 is mainly devoted to it. Before that, however, it is
important to establish Visegrad's character inside the EU.

MISLEADERS OF VISEGRAD'S POST-2004 DEMISE

The year preceding accession, 2003, saw three issues that portended Visegrad's
demise. All concerned Poland—the geographic, economic, and demographic
giant among the V4. And to that, one could add, arguably also the most
militaristic.[21]

Of these issues portending a disintegration of Visegrad, the first was the
Iraq War, in which Poland became a war-fighting country along with the United
States and the United Kingdom. The other three did not. This stance, however, should not have been seen to divide the V4, nor did it. After all, post-
communist countries issued statements in support of the Anglo-American
position, even if they shocked anti-war Western intellectuals who could not
fathom that communist-era dissidents like Havel or Solidarity's Adam Michnik
could support war.[22] Nevertheless, an image of a decidedly activist Poland
emerged, one that was militarily allied to the Anglo-American world.

The second issue was that Visegrad could not maintain a consolidated position in what was the last round of pre-accession negotiations at the EU Summit in Copenhagen in December 2002. This view could have been all the more
convincing because, as noted earlier, the EU accession process moved from an
approach of grouping countries to individual assessments. And because of that,
both Hungary and the Czech Republic adopted, ultimately unnecessarily, policies of seeking to leave the other Visegrad countries behind. At the same time,
Poland seemed to have broken with an earlier Visegrad agreement jointly to
pursue direct payment from Brussels for Visegrad's farmers, causing Prague's
chief EU negotiator to declare displeasure with Warsaw.[23] Poland then negotiated firmly and successfully to reduce restrictions on its agricultural sales and
represented some of the interests of other accession countries.[24] Generally,
however, regional analysts felt that "it proved impossible" for the countries "to
frame a common strategy of action" toward the EU.[25]

Visegrad's appearance of failing to coordinate to pursue is common interests in the pre-accession period naturally contributed to perceptions of its
demise. A contemporary analyst wrote: "Several attempts among the candidates, especially among the 'Visegrád four' . . . to coordinate their positions

failed. So each country had to fight for itself in the end."[26] Others contended that this was a "setback," one consequently blunting Visegrad's "ambitions" to formalize itself into an alliance in the union after accession.[27] This outcome was, for others, even dissension among the Group and was remembered by the Polish Visegrad presidency even a decade later. Its 2012–13 presidency report boasted: "We have not repeated mistakes made before our accession [to the EU] in 2004. Back then, the V4 negotiated individually and our countries received different treatment, which led to mutual animosities."[28] Visegrad failed to have coherence throughout the final accession negotiations, but the Group ultimately endured and was perhaps even emboldened to improve on its coherence and determination accession, as that Polish statement suggests.

The translation of Poland's demographics into voting rights in the EU forms the third issue. Totaling nearly four times that of each of the Czech and Hungarian populations, and eight times Slovakia's, Poland's population was huge in the region. But in the EU it was significant also—displacing twenty-one other EU states to have the sixth-largest population in the enlarged union of twenty-seven states. Poland would enter the "exclusive" club of larger EU states and for some appeared the most "assertive" of all candidate countries,[29] creating a "cleavage" between itself and the other Visegrad states,[30] where Poland was "isolated" in the region.[31] Poland ultimately remained with Visegrad in negotiating the EU's new Constitution (and thereafter); for instance, one regional media source reported: "Visegrad Four demand changes in EU draft constitution."[32] Others saw Visegrad similarly but noted that it was not as strategic as it had been regarding the achievement of accession.[33] Even with caveats, these regionally focused analysts viewed Visegrad as still producing clear priorities to achieve inside the EU. Visegrad doubters might have heeded these proposals.

Others acknowledged that accession meant new roles and assertiveness for Visegrad: "Before 2004, the V4 could be characterized as a policy-taker with little or no intention to exert influence"; thereafter it was even becoming a policymaker in the EU, particularly toward the union's neighboring states to the south and the east, about which more follows.[34] After accession, Visegrad would not drive EU policy—not even France and Germany together, or the latter alone, do that routinely. Nor did it ever claim that it would. But Visegrad found plenty to do, and, as this chapter similarly contends, it could and did also shape some of the EU's major policies and activities.

Those achievements have been overtaken, or ignored, by the many who discovered Visegrad only because of its unprecedented international prominence in 2015. That came from Visegrad's approach to the "migrant crisis," when hundreds of thousands of people from desperate lands surged into the EU. For the uninitiated, Visegrad became a world phenomenon, the band of countries that seemingly resisted EU policies over this most televisual humanitarian crisis.

That episode, rightly if also sadly for how Visegrad gained its greatest international attention, gets covered in chapter 7.

The answer to Visegrad's post-accession life is in the analysis. To be sure, and in fairness to Visegrad's many post-accession critics, the V4 raised standards rather high. As we shall see, Visegrad pronounced a substantial program for itself upon EU entry. Judged by *those* standards, Visegrad falls short. Ironically, however, Visegrad's fiercest critics ignored Visegrad's own benchmarks when judging its post-accession utility, even as those criteria might make for the most compelling critique.

Despite Visegrad's ambition, it never intended to address every EU issue. Apt affirmation of this issue selectivity is that Visegrad "is not some kind of Central European 'bloc' . . . that automatically seeks to take joint positions across the whole range of EU business."[35] Some criticisms are just too unreal, presuming that Visegrad should always be acting. Nor can the cumbersome, multilayered EU be so easily informed, let alone policies changed. And when Visegrad had had impact, the analysis risked being skewed because some of its influence has been considered disruptive while Visegrad, always, considers itself to be constructive.[36]

To recognize Visegrad's achievements, and as often in the study of diplomacy generally, the aims need to be contextualized in terms of what was available to the campaigner and what resistance was faced. Several V4-EU interactions among Visegrad's post-accession interactions both help to identify, informationally, what the V4 have addressed in the EU and then how well, and why, they have achieved those aims. Testament to Visegrad's EU activism arises from the range of cases that are available for consideration. Examples have been selected, first, to offer sense of the diversity of issues on which Visegrad advocated. They have, second, been chosen in reflection of the divergent nature of policymaking. Some policy issues are very specifically defined and short term, lending themselves to discernible outcomes, while others are more open ended and longer term, where influence is more diffuse and measurable in less-tangible terms. Those cases are ones that involve shaping and prodding along an agenda, rather than securing an immediate outcome. And for both types, in the context of the EU's multilateral bargaining among more than two dozen states, essential also is the capacity to build alliances. Thus, this next section identifies first Visegrad's ability to be able to assert its new role as a lobbying platform generally; second, how it dealt with specific issues, ones with determinable outcomes; and third, longer-term interests where commitment had to be sustained. These three categories are broken down as follows:

1. role assertion: proactively advertising that Visegrad would remain alive after accession;
2. creating a new platform in the EU, for Visegrad and for others.

Specific and definitively achievable aims:

3. preventing Visegrad countries' exclusion or delayed entry into the
   Schengen area;
4. protesting and achieving food equality.

Examples of longer-term aims:

5. climate and environment;
6. energy security;
7. transportation infrastructure;
8. advocacy of further EU enlargement, specifically:
   a. the Western Balkans (WB);
   b. the Eastern Partnership (EaP).

Ukraine, the EaP's largest country, and Visegrad had forged an important
relationship since each of their births in 1991. Because that relationship also
became one of dealing with energy security and, from late 2013, territorial
annexation and conflict, it merits detailed attention in chapter 8. That chapter
too gives focus to hard security, including Visegrad's EU Battlegroup. V4's activities in the EU already form a substantial list, let alone for an entity whose future
many dismissed. We start with why this perception proved counterfactual.

1. VISEGRAD'S ROLE ASSERTION AFTER 2004

Visegrad stressed that it was going to live after accession. That role assertion
came in two parts: actions before accession and then after. Before accession,
the V4 enacted a strategy not only to assert its continued existence but also to
pronounce even greater dynamism following EU entry. The V4 knew in advance
of accession that it needed both to signal to all that it would continue as a
group and that it already had post-accessions on which to advocate. Chapter 5
indicated both reasons why Visegrad might have appeared to be less active, or
even divided, in the pre-accessions years of 2002 and 2003. But it also gathered
both testimonials and indications of Visegrad's activities related to remaining
active after 2004.

Preparations for Post-2004 Life

The prime-ministerial Visegrad Summit of 2003 made clear not only that
the Group intended to continue its activities once in the EU but also that
accession brought novel possibilities: "EU membership of the four countries

creates a new and unprecedented prospect for the further development of their economies and societies. The Visegrad countries are therefore willing to co-operate intensively in the areas of common interests in order to make this prospect realised."[37] The Czech presidency of Visegrad that coincided with EU accession adopted as its banner concepts "Continuity" and "Future."[38] The Czech Foreign Ministry's annual report noted both that efforts in 2003 made clear that cooperation would continue and that new areas of cooperation were created. These areas included tourism, transport, energy, information technology, healthcare, and agriculture.[39] Visegrad's biggest role was simply, but importantly, as a forum for lobbying in the EU. We will return to that presently.

Less visibly (including to doubters), but of substantive importance, Visegrad cooperation gained added dynamics because it moved beyond its previous perch of foreign ministries to coordinated work across most other ministries and other parts of V4 governments. A senior Hungarian diplomat responsible for regional cooperation advised in the year of EU accession that every level and every sectoral department of the Hungarian Foreign Ministry was coordinating with their Visegrad counterparts and likewise among other ministries. He also commented that regional cooperation received less attention because of the focus on accession, but regional cooperation remained a "vitally important component" of Hungarian foreign policy.[40] Slovakia's Magda Vašáryová similarly reflected in 2006 back on experience that Visegrad cooperation had become "a daily reality in the work of all government and state institutions."[41] Table 6.1 illustrates examples of ministerial cooperation across V4 administrations as accession approached. These also included functionalist units such as border guards, societal units such as education ministries on special needs, and ministries at the forefront of EU accession such as agriculture, interior, justice, and regional development.

2. STAKING THE CLAIM, AND WITH LOBBYING AND PLATFORM-BUILDING

Once inside the EU, Visegrad's self-promotion intensified. On May 12, 2004, Visegrad prime ministers issued the Kroměříž Declaration, in the Moravian town bearing a name clustered with Czech-language diacritics, making it far less pronounceable than even the linguistically ambiguous Visegrád. Despite the historic success of Euro-Atlantic memberships, Visegrad declared "their determination to continue developing" cooperation and to engage as a region with those institutions and neighboring countries.[42] The declaration continued: "The integration of the Visegrád Group countries into the European and

TABLE 6.1. V4 Sectoral ministerial meetings in advance of EU accession (other meetings for defense/NATO excluded)

Date	Location	Ministry/sector
September 11, 2003	Prague	Meeting of ministers of the interior
September 22–24, 2003	Bakonybél, Hungary	Meeting of experts from ministries of justice
September 28–30, 2003	Hungary	Meeting of directors of border guards
October 2–3, 2003	Čejkovice, Czech Republic	Meeting of ministers of the environment
October 29–30	Mojmírovce, Slovakia	Meeting of ministers of justice
November 13–14, 2003	Olomouc, Czech Republic	Meeting of ministers of culture
December 4–5, 2003	Tatranská Lomnica, Slovakia	Meeting of experts from ministries of finance to discuss the national funds
December 4–5, 2003	Bratislava	Meeting of deputy ministers of the interior (public administration)
January 12–13, 2004	Budapest	Meeting of working group for internal and external borders (ministries of the interior, police)
January 2004	Budapest	Meeting of working group for energy (ministries of industry)
February 2004	Brno	Preparation of "Visegrád: Exchange of Experiences and Development in Special Needs in the V4" (ministries of education)
February 5–6, 2004	Čejkovice, Czech Republic	Meeting of ministers of transport
February 25, 2004	Prague	Working group of border services (ministries of the interior, police)
February 25–26, 2004	Prague	Meeting of working group for combating extremism (ministries of the interior of the V4 countries and Austria)
March 2, 2004	Brno	Meeting of ministers of agriculture
March 5, 2004	Mariánské Lázně, Czech Republic	Meeting of ministers for regional development
March 8–10, 2004	Prague	Meeting of expert group for educational systems in public administration (ministries of the interior)
March 18–19, 2004	Prague	Meeting of expert group for modernization of public administration (ministries of the interior)

(Continued)

TABLE 6.1. (*Continued*)

Date	Location	Ministry/sector
March 25, 2004	Měřín, Czech Republic	Meeting of political directors of defense ministries
March 31, 2004	Prague	Meeting of expert group for computerization of public administration (ministries of the interior)
April 14–16, 2004	Kraków	Meeting of ministers of culture
April 15–16, 2004	Prague	Meetings of experts of ministries of finance to discuss the national funds
April 22–23, 2004	Budapest	Meeting of ministers for regional development

Euro-Atlantic structures opens up new opportunities and poses new challenges for their further cooperation on the issues of common interest."[43]

The Kroměříž Declaration was accompanied by "Guidelines on the Future Areas of Visegrad Cooperation."[44] These contained thirty-three points of cooperation. Just one of those, the "Mechanisms of Cooperation," encompassed another eight, which outlined how and with whom Visegrad would work. That made clear that the Visegrad states would coordinate the positions of its permanent delegations to intergovernmental organizations such as the EU and NATO, which should not have seemed novel after Visegrad's previous announcements to that end. It also informed that Visegrad coordination would occur in other international forums, such as in the Organization for Security and Co-operation, with fifty-seven participating states, in Europe; the Council of Europe, with forty-seven members, and the Organization for Economic Cooperation and Development; and, beyond Europe, the United Nations, and in the World Trade Organization. Not only was Visegrad alive; it dynamically planned European and global activism.

As before accession, directly after it the Group heralded these as more than declaratory intentions. V4 took the promulgation of its continued, even invigorated, existence to other countries and publics. Thus Visegrad ambassadors in various countries also wrote joint op-ed pieces at the time, in such outlets as Canada's *National Post*, to underline Visegrad's continued cooperation (and probably thereby also to alter a wider audience to the group's very existence). The V4 also mounted joint travel presentations at tourism fairs in the United States, Japan, Brazil, and China.[45]

Striking with respect to some of the dismissive accounts of Visegrad's utility after EU accession is precisely that the Group would have both new needs and new opportunities arising from union membership. Accounts that suggested Visegrad would die in 2004 appear even more unwisely dismissive of the Group's will to live, and thrive.

Alongside intensive coordination on government matters, Visegrad asserted its common regional identity. The Kroměříž Declaration announced that "the cooperation of the Visegrad Group countries will continue to focus on regional activities and initiatives aimed at strengthening the identity of the Central European region."[46] That aim was already part of Visegrad's relaunch in 1999 and was made tangible through the establishment of the International Visegrad Fund. But far from EU membership washing away a Central European / Visegrad identity, this new environment, Visegrad pronounced, could provide *more* possibility for Central European region building and its promotion. Slovak analyst Ivo Samson maintained that advancing a common "'Visegrad identity' appeared to be more real only after 2004 when all four countries did not have to bother about being regarded as part of a relatively prosperous, regional, multi-state institution that developed its relations with the EU on the basis of something like a 'privileged partnership.'"[47]

Despite announcing a new era for Visegrad, the Kroměříž Declaration was criticized for having "not set priorities of strategic perspectives comparable to the original aims of cooperation."[48] But, at the risk of necessary tautology, Visegrad of 2004 could not be the Visegrad of 1991: it had achieved the exemplary aim of Euro-Atlantic accession, one that also helped to reorder the Euro-Atlantic world. The criterion for judging Visegrad after 2004 has to be different. That should be judged by the roles Visegrad assigned to itself, which brings us again to the Kroměříž Declaration.

Visegrad Aims and Achievements after EU Accession

The Kroměříž Declaration prepared Visegrad to plan for the following:

- Consultations and cooperation on current issues of common interest;
- active contribution to the development of the Common Foreign and Security Policy (CFSP), including the "Wider Europe—New Neighbourhood" policy and the EU strategy toward the Western Balkans;
- consultations, cooperation, and exchange of experience in the area of justice and home affairs, and Schengen cooperation, including protection and management of the EU external borders, visa policy;
- creating new possibilities and forms of economic cooperation within the European Economic Area;
- consultations on national preparations for joining the European Monetary Union;

- active participation in the development of the European Security and Defence Policy (ESDP), as a contribution to the strengthening of relations between the EU and NATO and deepening of substantive dialogue between both organizations.[49]

This should sound like a substantial set of objectives. The first means by which to achieve anything would be for Visegrad to act as a lobbying platform. And that it did—and still does.

It first had to establish its continued name. Regional diplomats reflected Visegrad's growing confidence and recognition, stating that the Group was becoming a brand name or a trademark, one known not just in Europe but overseas, not only in diplomacy but also in international business, particularly in east Asia.[50] The Group was both a diplomatic platform and increasingly appearing as a coherent investment area. One of Slovakia's principle foreign policy architects, Pavol Demeš, similarly called Visegrad "a tried and true foreign policy trademark," one that, perhaps modestly, he then predicted, could last another fifteen years. The value of a name need not prove immortal, but Visegrad's certainly extended beyond EU accession.

More important than brand recognition was that Visegrad countries shared interests in the EU, making cooperation effectively instinctive. Many Visegrad activists, such as Havel, believe that membership itself did not preclude cooperation when it served the group, and, in addition, based on such interests, regional groupings exist within the EU and that Central Europe constitutes one of them. The issues pertaining to membership that Visegrad was coordinating before accession (which were fewer because of the EU's country-by-country approach) continued after, such as access to structural and cohesion funds and voting rights and commission seats. As Czech prime minister Jiří Paroubek wrote on Visegrad's fifteenth anniversary, "Fears that the activities of Visegrad Group would flag after the member countries joined the EU have proven unfounded."[51] And rather than diminishing, as Hungarian diplomat and parliamentarian Gábor Hárs upheld, Visegrad cooperation grew stronger with EU membership.[52] One regional practitioner qualifiedly noted, "On repeated occasions it [the Visegrad group] has been able to present a more or less united position within the European Union."[53] Perhaps it is an overestimation, but some argue not only that the V4 had new roles within the EU but also that their accession "brought a new dynamism to the EU."[54]

Visegrad sees itself as important to the internal and external dynamics of the EU. As an example, the Polish presidency 2012–13 program pronounced, "The Visegrad Group has come to epitomise successful systemic transformation, while intra group cooperation has been acclaimed as an important, constructive element of the European integration process."[55]

Post-EU Accession Lobbying

The first purpose was lobbying in EU. After accession, Visegrad representatives consulted ahead of council sessions, a practice to which veteran Visegrad analyst Michal Kořan said positively "no one really paid attention."[56] That was until 2009, when one of these previously ignored consultations provoked criticism from President Nicolas Sarkozy, showing "open irritation" that the V4 could organize,[57] and he warned the V4 not to meet before European Council meetings (despite France and Germany routinely doing precisely that). The French admonition demonstrated to Visegrad officials the Group's "viability and utility," even if it meant that the Group also sought thereafter to avoid generating a negative image.[58] And Sarkozy found himself attending a Visegrad summit in Prague on June 16, 2008, in advance of France's assumption of the European Council's presidency.

Lobbying for Visegrad interests openly continued, and regional commentators observed it to be a functioning institution that devised "pre-negotiation" positions prior to EU summits.[59] In an unstated rebuff to early French criticism, Slovakia summarized its 2014–15 Visegrad presidency as having "continued with the well-proven format of regular meetings of Prime Ministers before the European Councils, in order to coordinate common positions." It further noted those "regular" meetings allowed for Visegrad's "effective coordination" before EU Councils consultations occurred. The Slovak V4 presidency then named areas in which it successfully advanced its interests, including on the Climate and Energy Package, Energy Union, Digital Single Market, Eastern Partnership, and migration. The presidency's self-congratulatory summation was that the V4 was an integral part of the EU and had treated sensitive issues constructively.[60]

The V4's continued strength in the EU came also from pledging Group support when one of its states has held the rotating European Council presidency.[61] The Czechs were the first Visegrad country to hold one, and it was called a Visegrad presidency.[62] When Poland's Donald Tusk became president of the European Council in 2014, it was deemed a shared Visegrad achievement: "All this is not just Poland's ascent, but also that of Central Europe. Donald Tusk has spared no effort throughout his term as Polish prime minister to work together with other countries of the region, especially in the Visegrad Group. In spite of the different political profiles of the region's governments, he always believed that Central Europe has an interest in aligning its positions." That statement leads to how the V4 worked together to secure and to block senior EU appointments. Tusk's own selection as European Council president in 2014 itself was one of the "clear signs of Visegrad maximizing its clout."[63]

The V4 successfully challenged the candidacy in 2019 of Manfred Weber and Frans Timmermans for presidents of the European Commission. The V4 website pronounced, "V4 states oppose Timmermans as EC president."[64] Visegrad, with Romania and Bulgaria, produced a forthright, even embarrassing, public letter to Timmermans. It stressed the need for national levels of knowledge and omissions at the EU level, and the need for accuracy and comprehensiveness. The letter pointedly called for "reliable and solid information" and stated that "only a well-informed decision is a good one" as a prerequisite to secure agreement.[65]

Regional media went further in recognizing Visegrad's prowess: "Visegrad leaders claim victory in race for EU top jobs,"[66] and "Weber's campaign suffered a major setback when the Visegrad Four member states all came out against" him, for reasons of insufficient support for their conception of Christian Europe.[67] A regional analyst wrote that Germany's Ursula Von der Leyen "became European Commission president as a result of a secretive backroom deal between German chancellor Merkel, French president Macron and the Visegrád countries, who all shared profound concerns about Weber's suitability for the job."[68]

Orbán's spokesperson boasted colorfully of Visegrad's successes: "In our unity, the Visegrád Four have again demonstrated our growing strength and influence over the direction of EU. After defeating Weber, the V4 prime ministers have toppled Timmermans as well." And the spokesperson further tweeted that Visegrad "put on the EU table a package that is winning acceptance among a growing number of member countries" to support, ultimately successfully, German minister of defense von der Leyen as the new EU Commission president.[69]

Visegrad has had a multifaceted and potent presence in the EU. Its utility and strength intensified by serving not only as a platform for its members but for other new entrants also.

Visegrad as a Platform for Alliance Making within the EU

A principle Visegrad strength is itself: an existing platform, one flexible regarding content. That this was missed or discounted widely around accession time might speak of some observers, rather than of Visegrad. Indeed others saw V4 continuing as "a strong historical alliance."[70] And on an ad hoc basis alone Visegrad was attractive to others and easily allowed like-minded states, especially fellow accession countries, to align themselves with the Group. A representative statement is that the V4 "has experience in coordinating the positions in the previous negotiations and proved to be an effective basis for consultations with other like-minded states from the region (e.g. Bulgaria, Romania, Croatia, Slovenia)."[71] Post-communist states have clustered around Visegrad, even creating the new term "Central-Eastern Europe," defining themselves as those being in a different position in the EU from that of older, Western members. Indeed one argument for Austria's decision to apply and accede to the EU in 1995 was precisely to get itself both away from and ahead of the post-communist Central European in their ambitions toward EU membership.[72] It came to be that "the Visegrad Group was and is (wholly justifiably in regard to its own self-projection in Central-Eastern Europe) perceived as a leader of this "second" or "other" Europe," often viewed as a "spokesperson for the entire region of post-communist EU member states."[73]

That Visegrad would lobby for its interests should have been apparent. From their first year of EU membership Visegrad took stands. The Group successfully opposed the EU's draft budget for 2007–13, asserting that it would be disadvantaged.[74] Czech foreign minister Cyril Svoboda did not give an exact figure of what he thought his country would lose but put it at "tens of billions" of Czech crowns. The Central European press reported that debate on the EU budget, put forward by Luxembourg holding the rotating European Council presidency and supported by wealthier EU member-states, demonstrated Visegrad cooperation. Svoboda reiterated that Visegrad would coordinate a common position and indeed that the Group was "fighting" for pre-accession rules that would grant its countries the right to demand up to 4 percent of their GDP in EU assistance funds.[75] A high-level Visegrad report communicated the fact that at least 40 percent of EU cohesion funds for 2014–20 were allocated to their region as a "unique public investment."[76]

V4 introduced practical means for coalition building through its now-familiar structure of the "+" format. Countries with common interests could "click on" to Visegrad and together be force multipliers. By contrast, the older Benelux or Nordic Council formats, the much older yet comparable subregional formations within the EU, forwent functioning similarly.[77] The + worked—except for one example, with Germany when it assumed the European presidency in 2020—to allow "Visegrad positions on particular policy issues to Europeanise and upload them to the EU level."[78] Not every issue and not every post-communist country in the EU comes to Visegrad for advocacy. Nor is this the case for Benelux of the Nordic countries.[79] But Visegrad, when needs or opportunity arises, provides means and leadership. At the same time, Visegrad remained opposed to expanding its actual membership. So committed were members of these countries' political elites to retaining Visegrad's original membership that even the speakers of the Polish and Slovak national parliaments, used a press conference to criticize the idea.[80]

Meetings, even planning, and a lobbying platform are achievements. But has Visegrad achieved these in the EU? We start with how Visegrad tackled efforts to delay its citizens access to the EU's borderless Schengen area.

3. GETTING FREEDOM OF MOVEMENT,
ALL OVER AGAIN? SCHENGEN

Freedom of movement—including going to work and live in other EU states—
became commonplace. But for Central Europeans who were, say, among the
multitudes that constituted university-aged protestors against communist rule
in 1989, were already in their mid-thirties when their countries entered the EU
in 2004. Their expectations were ultimately to become full Europeans, with
mobility rights like all others. Most European states imposed some restrictions
on the citizens of accession countries. That these citizens could not, even with
that delay, benefit from the EU's borderless Schengen area was a further signal
of second-class citizenship. Worse, some member states, particularly Austria,
and the commission itself, sought to delay the removal of border checks at
frontiers with post-communist countries.

The resistance that Visegrad faced was the EU's retraction of a central
promise of accession. The EU's commitment to postpone access was substantial, though also sometimes presented cryptically. One of the excuses for the
delay arose when the European Commission decided for "technical reasons" on
September 11, 2006, to postpone the end of passport checkpoints on accession-
country citizens for at least eighteen months.[81] In addition, German and Austrian representatives claimed that Schengen access would flood their border
areas with "criminals and prostitutes."[82] The delays were substantial for people
waiting for and expecting free movement. Entering Schengen was "one of the
most vivid and tangible benefits" of EU entry for members of the public, and
doing so became a leading ambition of Visegrad governments in the preceding years.[83] Achieving that would amount to "an extreme transformation" of
the region's past borders—a deeply desired aim, both practically and metaphorically.[84] So moved, and perhaps with an eye to diplomatic theater, were
the Visegrad leaders by the Schengen delay that at one of their coordinating
meetings they gathered at the grave of liberal-humanist founding president of
Czechoslovakia, Tomáš Masaryk.[85]

Not only was Schengen access, therefore, of high value to Visegrad, but
the Group had to stop not one but two efforts to delay their entry. In 2006
it appeared that their proposed entry of March 2007 would be postponed as
late as to 2009. Czech foreign minister Saša Vondra, for example, said at a
V4 press conference in 2006 that it was not only major European states but
also the commission that sought to delay extending Schengen to new members. He also called on his fellow Visegrad foreign ministers to continue to
proceed together to prevent postponement and to put the onus on their EU
interlocuters to fulfill commitments.[86] Overall, EU commitment to enforcing
a delay was considerable.

Visegrad's impact on stopping the EU position was also considerable, the Group making a case in which Visegrad had changed or, rather, succeeded in reversing, EU policy. Visegrad invested in this aim. Already in 1999, well before accession, the V4 had coordinated in its preparations for Schengen, with the Czech Foreign Ministry calling that among its "most crucial tasks."[87] With exclusions on access to Schengen in place at accession, the V4, especially their interior ministries, continued coordination. The Czech Visegrad presidency report, which coincided with Visegrad's EU accession in 2004, recorded some of the anticipatory preparations to secure Schengen: "We also succeeded in promoting cooperation" on Schengen, establishing it as a "top" priority of the Czech presidency.[88] The ministries of the interior established expert groups. With delays looming to the end of the interim exclusion, the timing of the opening of Schengen became the forefront of Visegrad's activities in 2006.[89] In 2007 Visegrad made timely and full implementation of the Schengen *acquis*, or legal requirements, "an absolute top priority"; the V4 interior ministries' quiet, collaborative work may shroud those achievements.[90]

Czech president Klaus, that past Visegrad antagonist, declared at the Visegrad Summit of September 15–16, 2006, that "all four presidents stressed that Schengen is a clear priority and that discrimination should be removed." The V4 prime-ministerial declaration of their "fullest disapproval" of delays resonated across European media, often with reference to the EU's "discrimination" toward these states.[91]

Apart from Visegrad's collaboration to achieve technical proficiencies to meet Schengen requirements, the Group also mobilized a range of support, including early coordination of the V4 Parliaments, to increase pressure on the European Commission to adhere to its original terms. But its statement did far more, pointing out to the commission and other EU starts that the V4 countries had not only fulfilled EU requirements but also warned Brussels that it was risking its own credibility by backtracking.[92] One might feel an element of the original "Visegrad Declaration" reassert itself, saying, "We Central Europeans are doing our part, what you, Europe, expect of us, but in turn you have obligations to us." The V4 prime ministers asserted that "if this target date that was set and reaffirmed at the level of heads of state and government at the European Council in June 2006 was to be delayed for technical reasons it could result in a serious crisis of confidence from the populations in the new EU Member States. If the process of Schengen accession should be delayed, it will have an impact on the trustworthiness of European institutions."[93]

Two observers captured V4's spirit, stating that it "fought to gain the earliest possible entry into Schengen."[94] Visegrad reversed EU intentions to delay scheduled access to Schengen. Considering both the practical and the symbolic importance of gaining Schengen on time, and the resistance mounted against it, Visegrad secured a significant achievement. And when that occurred the V4 premiers (with their Slovene counterpart) resumed the language of European values, calling Schengen of "large symbolic value" and "a significant step to fulfilling the core ideas of the EU."[95]

Visegrad's activism kept Schengen entry as scheduled, at least toward the European Commission. However, Austria, bordering three Visegrad states, attempted anew in 2007 to delay the region's inclusion into the Schengen area. This may have been a relatively easy battle; the incoming Portuguese EU presidency disagreed with Austria. Nevertheless, Visegrad was astute to include Portuguese prime minister José Sócrates at its meeting. The V4 prime ministers again rejected any delay, using such phrases as "We have to stress to our Austrian colleagues that we don't agree" with their resistance to Schengen access. European newspapers carried Hungarian prime minister Ferenc Gyurcsány's pithy phrase to a Visegrad summit in June 2007: "There aren't two kinds of Schengen."[96] Gyurcsány captured Visegrad's potent diplomacy by saying that the V4 rejected plans to delay Schengen "politely, but decisively."[97]

That statement was targeted also at Austria, a leading proponent of delaying Schengen and who also intended to maintain its own border controls with Visegrad states, irrespective of EU decisions. Thus even after Visegrad entry into Schengen on December 21, 2007, Austria announced that it would continue to patrol those borders. At a Visegrad presidential meeting focused on Schengen, Hungarian president László Sólyom stated, "We [V4] do not agree with Austria's plan to guard its borders, there must not be differences between old and new members of the EU. We agreed that we will ask our governments to protest the plans of the Austrian government."[98] That they did, and, at last and nearly two decades from when barbed wire was ceremoniously cut on the Austro-Hungarian border, Visegrad could make its Western borders disappear.

With the migrant crisis (elaborated elsewhere) tossing the EU into chaos, the Visegrad countries were both unified in pressing for border closures and also for ensuring that Schengen—and freedom of movement for their citizens—remained. On December 3, 2015, prime ministers established the "Friends of Schengen" initiative, which, the Czech Republic's Bohuslav Sobotka explained, was created "to stress our common interest in protecting the external Schengen border and stress our common aim to maintain the Schengen area."[99] Visegrad took further measures to secure the EU's external borders while, as a Hungarian statement explained, resisting the EU's "opportunistic" and unacceptable measures that would limit freedom of movement.[100]

Visegrad changed EU policy on Schengen. That achievement alone might vindicate the Group's post-accession utility. Visegrad did not cease then; its ambitions extended to the further enlargement of the EU itself. Ironically,

Visegrad has advocated, and at time of writing unsuccessfully, with its previous Schengen foe Austria and with Slovenia also, for Romania, Bulgaria, and Croatia to be granted access to Schengen. Visegrad activism has arisen along with other seemingly discriminatory practices in addition to Schengen's delay, such as regarding the inequalities between products sold in different parts of the EU.

4. FOOD EQUALITY

Visegrad landed an ideal task when discoveries were made that major food producers were using different and substandard ingredients in the same branded products marketed in newer EU member states than in older ones.

The responses also reconfirm Visegrad's ad hoc but ready and beneficial lobbying capacity. When Slovak food-standards officials determined the practice in 2017 (as did separately Czech and Hungarian), Bratislava approached its Visegrad partners and the Group mobilized quickly to convene an "extraordinary" meeting on March 2.[101] Although equality of food products might seem inarguable, EU laws did not prevent such differences if ingredients were shown.

Visegrad's responsiveness received enthralled media coverage, including of it "readying attacks" on the commission.[102] In this case it also found allies, from other countries and the Czech Věra Jourová, who conveniently was commissioner for justice, consumers, and gender equality. Various Central European figures augmented attention with snappy metaphors for the problem, such as of a "food apartheid" and that their region had become the "garbage can" of the union.[103] The arguments that Visegrad advanced worked, again, on the basis of deploying the EU's stated values against it, for example, Slovak president Andrej Kiska pronouncing that "it is precisely the EC's role to ensure that every EU citizen is treated as equal."[104]

This was an easier but still demanding case for V4 action, because it had to deal with the EU's structural problem of being unable to enforce industry standardization. Western reports carried food manufacturers' defenses, even if counterfactual in view of Visegrad complaints, such as that they "tailor their brands to suit local tastes."[105] Visegrad stood firm, to the point of being commended for "victory" by getting the commission a year later to ban quality-level differences among products based on their intended sale location in the union.[106]

Although food inequality could remain an issue for lack of EU enforcement measures, it was nevertheless an issue for which Visegrad proved a ready and effective lobbying platform. It would so also for its interests concerning environmental and climate change policies.

5. ENVIRONMENT AND CLIMATE CHANGE

As with Schengen, on environmental and climate change matters Visegrad's influence came from resistance. This potent policy position derived from historical legacies. Despite overhauls of their economies and substantial foreign investment in production technology since 1989, the Visegrad and other post-communist states still retain highly energy-inefficient economies. Moreover, they contend that they should not be disadvantaged by West European economies that have benefited from longer technological innovation and can therefore engage in pollution reduction with less impact on their output and competitiveness.

Visegrad, to be sure, has declared itself in favor of *global* emissions reductions and said addressing climate change is crucial.[107] The Group has, though, succeeded in blocking EU attempts to introduce targets for carbon emission reduction. Analysts concerned with general EU practice (i.e., those who did not observe Visegrad routinely) have noted the Group's importance. The Visegrad Group "has become an active faction in the political landscape [in the EU] on the environment, and has exerted influence on the direction of European policy, for example in relation to emission reduction targets, aspects of the Emissions Trading Scheme, mitigation efforts in sectors outside the main industrial emissions, investment aid infrastructure including transport links, and various other measures." Visegrad is, additionally, seen as leading the position of other post-communist member states, with the result that it can be "more difficult to reach a common EU position in certain areas and has led to some special arrangements or concessions to a number of countries."[108]

The V4 challenged the EU's outlook on climate change. A Polish deputy minister at a V4+ meeting dedicated to responding to commission proposals stated, "Europe has a minor share in global greenhouse gases emissions. That is why the decisions concerning climate and energy policies of the European Union should consider the global process; otherwise, we will repeat the failure of Copenhagen, where unilateral measures taken by Europe did not meet with any response from others." The Group was openly critical of the commission, noting, "Discussion of new targets of the European Union should be based on transparent and reliable economic analyses broken down into Members States and sectors. The Commission did not specify what the new targets would be for individual countries, which makes it impossible for the V4+2 Group to adopt a position."[109]

Visegrad has been noted to be "widely perceived as an influential political alliance" so that any division among its members, in this case of climate change and energy, would be welcomed by others.[110] Indeed, some environmental groups and other EU member states have openly wished for Visegrad's demise, and others condemn its posture.[111] And diplomats of more environmentally friendly EU governments posted in Central Europe have frequently sought advice on how to encourage Visegrad to be more green.[112] Visegrad's stance, therefore, had been against significant support within the EU system and from many outside for carbon emission reductions. Visegrad's resistance also faces intensifying positions: "With Germany, the EU's biggest economy, joining a growing number of EU nations backing zero emissions by mid-century, momentum has built for leaders to agree the target at the summit."[113]

Visegrad has been vocal on some other of the EU's most challenging issues. The Polish presidency program of 2020–21 presaged the costs to its region of the European Commission's Green Deal, ones heightened by the 2020 pandemic: "It is necessary to secure ambitious financial resources for the realization of the climate policy objectives" in negotiations for the key Multiannual Financial Framework for 2021–27.[114] This is a consequential and an ongoing issue, and for which Visegrad has been both a blocker, and an initiator. V4 coordination on resisting the imposition of climate-change quotas led also to Visegrad's activism on energy security.

6. ENERGY SECURITY

As with industry, Visegrad countries retain legacies that differentiate them from many West Europeans. A brief summation is the "land of nuclear and coal."[115] The natural endowment in this relatively resource-poor region is lignite, or brown, coal. Even in communist times, in which regard for either the environment or for human health were negligible, lignite miners were given extra pay, nicknamed death or coffin money. The Soviet system pressed nuclear energy and bequeathed its dubious technology across these countries. Despite growing environmental campaigns, both within Visegrad societies and from neighbors, particularly Austria and Germany, which are officially non-nuclear-energy states, post-communist states have retained and even expanded the share of energy from nuclear sources. Additionally, as mentioned, communist-era factories were energy inefficient and also dependent on subsidies of Soviet fuel for their operation. A further metaphor on energy and the environment is that the post-communist countries retain coal but resist renewables, especially wind power. The proverbial question that then gets asked is if that renewal resource of wind ceases blowing north or east from nonnuclear Austria.

Finally, both geography and the legacies of integration of the Soviet bloc mean that the Visegrad states were linked to Soviet/Russian energy supply networks, both for their own consumption and for onward delivery to Western Europe. These decades-old infrastructure legacies play on today.

Russia's stoppage of gas through Ukraine in 2009 catapulted energy security onto media headlines and into Visegrad planning. Visegrad had previously

spoken of energy security. But the 2009 crisis had deeply affected its members. As a leading analyst stated, this was a crisis and "a critical juncture that
caused a change in the energy security policies of V4 countries—a change from
long-term proclamations to middle and short-term actions."[116] On Visegrad's
twentieth anniversary, two year later, V4 prime ministers declared their intention "to place strong emphasis on the need to foster European energy security
by extending and deepening the internal energy market and by enhanced V4
regional cooperation within the EU framework, to diversify the routes, sources
and suppliers of energy carriers and to develop the energy infrastructure, especially by the implementation of the North-South gas interconnections and
modernisation of the oil and electricity networks."[117]

Secure energy supplies are of course fundamental to Visegrad and to the EU
as a whole. Visegrad countries have relied on Russian supplies, but the different
types of energy requirements among them nevertheless posed the challenge to
"find a common strategy that would fulfil the expectations of all members."[118]
Hungary and Poland took different stands during the Russian-Georgian war
of 2008, primarily because of energy calculations.[119] In short, for Visegrad to
advocate a common energy strategy is hardly a given and would result from
serious internal discussions. To that end, the creation in 2009 of a permanent
Visegrad High Level Group on Energy Security was a proactive measure. The
Hungarian presidency organized in February 2010 a follow-up V4+ regional
prime-ministerial summit on energy security. It established tasks and priorities that became, according to Visegrad coordinators, essential to the Group's
ambitious and successful initiatives.[120]

Visegrad has since claimed that within the EU it has influenced institutional
and procedural changes on energy security. According to the Slovak presidency
summary, "The joint letter of the V4 Ministers of Economy helped to make
infrastructural projects in the region one of the top EU priories. This resulted
in establishing a High Level Working Group on North-South Interconnections,
coordinated by the European Commission (EC)."[121] Agenda setting on energy
seems evident in other cases. The Czech Visegrad presidency also pledged to
raise in the EU the region's support for the stalled Nabucco southern gas corri-
dor, a major initiative to bring gas across Turkey and the Balkans into Austria.
Practical common initiatives specifically for Visegrad have been advanced; the
Hungarian presidency in 2009–10 pledged to pursue "possibilities of creating
common underground gas storage facilities for the V4 countries."[122]

Some analysts suggest that V4's cooperation on energy security within the
EU amounted to no more than joint proclamations. Visegrad takes a very different view. As it stated in its 2012 Roadmap, "The Visegrad Group proved to
have a sufficient potential and ability for the promotion of common initiatives
and priorities of Visegrad countries at the EU level."[123]

Activism on energy was not just an issue area for Visegrad but also a means to assert identity in the EU. Czech trade minister Martin Kocourek called the 2011 energy declaration "a strong signal for our region to be perceived as one that is capable of claiming its rights."[124]

And also in an early stage of Visegrad activism, the Slovak prime minister stated, "I'm proud of the V4" for prioritizing gas connections, on which "our countries have shown active engagement from the outset."[125]

7. TRANSPORTATION INFRASTRUCTURE

One round of interviews with all four Visegrad national coordinators occurred after publication of an attractive, foldout, multicolored, detailed map of the V4 region.[126] Presentation of and reference to the map focused less on the bright lines indicating existing transportation routes but on those absent: ones running through the V4 countries from north to south. A Visegrad analyst verbalized the predicament: since 1989 only one new motorway was built anywhere among the V4 countries (between Poland and the Czech Republic), "and many of the rail connections seem to be poorer than in 1991."[127] A meeting in a V4-based Austrian embassy occurred in an office with an Austro-Hungarian imperial map mounted on a wall. The transport lines, especially rail, from 120 years ago were particularly visible, as if shouting how better integrated these lands had been.[128]

The V4 knows that regional infrastructure must improve. This is both economic and cultural, the latter in order to achieve the cohesive region to which Visegrad is committed. The national governments lack sufficient funds, and major interstate transportation is long term and costly. Enter the EU, and its Trans-European Transport Network (TEN-T) program for transportation improvement within the Union.[129] The program was open for bids, so on the surface, political organizing for access might be unnecessary. For the V4, it was. The Group therefore has repeatedly sought and succeeded, as a Slovak Visegrad presidency summarized, "to make infrastructural projects in the region one of the top EU priories." That had included the creation in the European Commission of the High-Level Working Group on North-South Interconnections.[130]

Visegrad countries still require redress to Soviet-era development, which built transportation lines not for organic regional needs but on a west-east axis to serve military production and deployments. Against an enormous structural legacy, Visegrad has worked within the EU to raise these issues and to begin funding redirections toward regional needs. Visegrad analyses are confident that without such efforts, little would change. In the early 1990s with regard to railway modernization, the V4 "basically followed Brussels' requirements and legislative measures."[131] Later, however, Visegrad served to adapt EU transport-infrastructural procedures to the region as "an optimal forum to agree upon joint lobbying positions before new railway regulations are approved by specified EU bodies or organizations."[132]

Outsiders like the *Financial Times* commend the Group's efforts: "Visegrad influence has also secured huge EU subsidies to upgrade eastern Europe's roads, railways and cities; [and] to pay for infrastructure to connect their energy networks."[133] Laudable, but insufficient, and V4 pressure continues. In 2018 V4 ministers criticized EU progress on regional infrastructure and cast that censure also in terms of urgent needs and benefits for the EU collectively, including even for the "proper functioning" on the whole European single market."[134]

In addition to working on long-term and costly initiatives such as infrastructure, it also has engaged actively in policies of EU accession and engagement with its key neighbors.

8. ENLARGEMENT ADVOCACY: THE EASTERN PARTNERSHIP AND THE WESTERN BALKANS

In their life-affirming statement of post-accession proactivity in 2004, the Visegrad prime ministers "reiterate their commitment to the enlargement process of the European Union. They are ready to assist countries aspiring for EU membership by sharing and transmitting their knowledge and experience . . . [and] are also ready to use their unique regional and historical experience and to contribute to shaping and implementing the European Union's policies towards the countries of Eastern and Southeastern Europe."[135] Visegrad has embraced those two geographic areas for its role in promoting EU enlargement. By "eastern" Visegrad meant post-Soviet states between the EU's new frontiers of 2004 and the Russian Federation. By the second, "Southeastern Europe"—a term that did not exist but was created by the EU—it meant Western Balkans, what became the EaP countries. The EU had a European Neighbourhood Policy (ENP)—a very broad program aimed at those countries and also the Mediterranean, including North Africa.[136]

Already in 2005, the V4 "continued to widen cooperation in the V4+ format on the European Neighbourhood Policy" and offered assistance to adjacent post-communist states.[137] Visegrad cooperation has consequently been called by its sponsors an "engine of a more dynamic EU policy towards Eastern and South-Eastern Europe,"[138] one able to export democracy and freedom throughout this region. As Poland's Lech Wałęsa commented after accession: "Cooperation between the Visegrad Group and other countries, especially those of Eastern Europe, has become an important assignment. . . . We can play an essential role as a bridge" between the post-communist states not currently in the EU and NATO and those institutions.[139]

Of particular relevance was the perception of keen analysts that Visegrad served as a role model: "V4 is becoming an ever greater inspiration for other regional initiatives in its neighborhood, specifically in the regions of Eastern Europe and the Western Balkans."[140] We turn to each, starting with the EU's Eastern Partnership.

The Eastern Partnership

The EaP—which has become so important and so contentious that it ultimately inflamed Moscow—was launched, perhaps symbolically, in Prague on May 7, 2009. The program is one of the EU's most important and ambitious, even a flagship program of the EU's external relations. It sought to retool the political, economic, and to an extent legal and administrative practices of the six post-Soviet states bordering the union to the east and adjacent to its Black Sea area: Armenia, Azerbaijan, Belarus, Georgia, Moldova, and Ukraine.

Russian accounts become useful indicators of Visegrad's influence within the EU; even if such analysis is double-edged, it is nonetheless telling of the Group's influence. A report from the influential Russian International Affairs Council wrote that "the Visegrad Four have taken a significant part of responsibility for the eastward enlargement of the European Union" and that the EU has gone as far as to "delegate" the EaP to Visegrad.[141] That is a statement that goes too far. But reflective of other perceptions of Visegrad's contribution to EaP include assertions that the Group "played an important role in initiating the EU Eastern Partnership" and sought "to support EU ambitions and the democratic transformation of the countries on the eastern EU border."[142]

These are ambitious endeavors. Indeed, Visegrad to an extent claims the birth of the EaP. Indeed, Czechs go as far as to consider that their initiative was developed within the Czech presidency of the V4 in 2007 in order to shape the EU's ENP more directly to its new eastern neighbors. The idea was then borrowed or adapted by Poland and Sweden, who, as one of the region's most astute analysts captured it, "were quicker in making the 'Eastern Partnership' accepted at the EU level."[143] Some point to the V4 governments' never having jointly "expressed the wish to take the lead on the EaP,"[144] despite convening V4 EaP forums. Others recognize that the "whole concept [of the EaP] draws on the experience of the Visegrad group,"[145] and even that the "V4 countries were instrumental" for the EaP's establishment, despite its official EU tag as Polish-Swedish.[146]

Issues of the EaP's parentage aside, Visegrad has influenced its functioning and thereby become a major player in the EU. Slovakia's leading diplomat Magda Vašáryová wrote that Visegrad's "engagement with Ukraine, Moldova and other neighboring states has increased the scope of the Visegrad Group's activities far beyond the border of simple regional cooperation."[147]

A Hungarian national coordinator said as early as 2004 that Visegrad had the "knowledge and experience" of democratization for such countries as Ukraine, Belarus and Moldova, and that experience "is highly appreciated in Brussels."[148]

Russian views are similar but with different end results: that the Eastern Partnership "triggered" the Ukraine crisis of 2013 onward. Additionally, Russian analyses attribute to Visegrad the EU's intensified engagement with EaP countries, especially Ukraine,[149] fashioning perhaps an unexpected vote of confidence in Visegrad.

The EaP has remained important to the EU, but Visegrad was intent on ensuring that it remained a central and sustained priority. Czech foreign minister Tomáš Petříček stated in 2020: "The Eastern Partnership is of strategic importance to the EU and therefore one of the priority topics in the context of the EU's external relations."[150] From the time of entering the EU, the V4 had sought to elevate and advance EU activism toward what would become the EaP countries. The V4 presidency approaching the launch of the EaP, held by Poland, directed the EU toward the ENP, the EaP being devised later. The Polish Visegrad presidency program deserves attention to reflect the Group's ambitions within the EU: "Recognizing the value of the experience acquired by Group countries in the process of building democracy and transforming their economic systems, the Polish Presidency will seek closer coordination of assistance undertakings, particularly those of a technical character, addressed to states in the V4 neighbourhood, i.e. Belarus, Moldova, Ukraine and the Caucasus, as well as promote pre-accession preparations in the countries of the Western Balkans."[151]

Visegrad states arguably have established themselves so well regarding the EaP that others expect their continued leadership. Zdeněk Kříž and Jana Urbanovska wrote: "Germany expects the V4 to intensively engage with the EaP countries . . . and to share their experiences from the political and economic transformation they underwent. The V4 countries, having regularly stressed the importance of deeper and wider cooperation within the EaP, have proved able to meet German expectations concerning their role in the EaP project." The German support of V4 activism on the EaP was also a major signal of Berlin's confidence in the V4 generally: "In a period marked by numerous disputes between the V4 states and Germany (with the migration crisis at the top of the list), the convergence of Germany's preferences with those of the V4 countries within the EaP initiative is an encouraging sign of a continuing intensive and deep cooperation among Germany and the V4 countries.[152]

In 2020, V4 took a lead within the EU to craft a program of COVID-19 assistance to the EaP countries (themselves having been among the worst affected in the EU).[153] Visegrad launched its own V4EastSolidarity program, pledging

€250,000 at one of its summits, which convened virtually.[154] As another step of Visegrad's coordination, applications would be reviewed by the V4 embassies in each EaP country.

Even in unusual circumstances, Visegrad remained committed to making a distinctive contribution to the EU's eastern neighbors. Among those states, the V4 gave particular attention to the geographically and demographically largest: Ukraine. This relationship merits particular attention, given in chapter 8, which discusses Visegrad and security issues.

The Western Balkans, or the WB6

At its European Council meeting in Thessaloniki in June 2003, the council endorsed the Thessaloniki Agenda for the Western Balkans, which established the way for European integration of the Western Balkan (WB) states. The EU also convened an EU–Western Balkans Summit, the statement from which pronounced that the EU believed the future of the Western Balkans was inside the union.[155] Visegrad, not yet in the EU at the time of Thessaloniki, does not claim ownership over such accession policy. However, the EU has since suffered enlargement fatigue, and the Western Balkans is a complex region where EU influence and European attractiveness are uneven. EU commitment to enlargement has weakened. Visegrad's, by contrast, has remained resolute. This is of additional importance in that some consider that Western Balkan countries have lacked their own "advocacy strategy aimed at promoting and speeding up their EU accession."[156] The V4 helps not only to provide that but also to advocate for Western Balkan accession. Indeed, the V4 uses language that it might have wanted to hear from others as they worked toward their own EU accession: that promises were made to them and that they would be kept. In this case, the V4 stridently lobbies for the WB countries and assures them of Visegrad's tangible support in meeting accession criteria and keeping EU doors open—no matter what. Hence V4 foreign ministers wrote an open letter in 2015 that ran in major media throughout the Western Balkans. The many issues within the EU, Visegrad insisted, would not be allowed to affect WB accession. And where Visegrad upended EU practices intended to confront the 2015 "migrant crisis" (detailed in chapter 7), to the WB the V4 promised not to allow that to be used to disrupt the WB's EU membership.[157]

What has been Visegrad's position? The V4 foreign minister said this as Croatia joined the EU in 2013: "Since their accession to the European Union, the V4 countries have been providing strong political support to the EU enlargement process by keeping this issue high on the EU's agenda and by transferring their unique experience in the field of European and Euro-Atlantic integration." The V4 ministers added that the back-to-back Hungarian and Polish presidencies

of the Council of the European Union in 2011, the "year of Central Europe,"
"succeeded in giving new impetus to the accession negotiations."[158] Hungary's
long-serving foreign minister János Martonyi reflected that Croatia might not
have acceded to the EU without Visegrad's advocacy.[159]

Visegrad further served as an exemplar: the Group's name "has permanently
entered the dictionary," defined as a "stable region" and then as "an example
of integration to other regions, such as the culturally and geographically close
Balkans."[160] The V4 began meetings with what similarly became another alpha-
numerical group, the WB6, as early as 2009. Visegrad has been the only group
inside the EU to do so.[161]

Visegrad's example of integration and advocacy for the Western Balkans
began long ago and in a manner almost forgotten. That historical reminder
returns us to CEFTA. As chapter 3 determined, CEFTA helped Visegrad and
other post-communist states prepare for EU accession. But instead of ceasing
upon some members' EU entry in 2004, this Visegrad product gained an additional role. It afforded ready means to build trade liberalization in the postwar
Western Balkans. The original members of CEFTA and those who joined the
EU in 2004 ironically had to leave CEFTA—EU accession meant the abrogation of preexisting trade agreements. But post-communist countries that had
CEFTA membership and did not accede to the EU in 2004—Bulgaria, Romania
and Croatia—continued in this format. Additionally keen to join were other
former Yugoslav republics, particularly Macedonia, which was under EU assistance substantial enough to ready itself for accession. CEFTA provided a viable
structure for preparation for EU entry.

Brussels could have chosen any name and format to encourage cooperation in the fractured Western Balkans (indeed, other forms *were* being tried—
such as the South-East European Cooperation Process). But the EU supported
a reinvigoration of CEFTA for this region. At the signing of the revised trade
agreement, the special coordinator of the Stability Pact for South Eastern
Europe, Erhard Busek, said in December 2006, "CEFTA is considered by many
as an excellent preparation for the highly demanding EU single market."[162]

Internal issues in the EU may halt or delay the accession of the Western
Balkans into the EU. France in 2018 derailed the preparations for Albania's
and North Macedonia's accession. The EU then decided to postpone those
countries' accession talks. With accession slowing generally for the Western
Balkans, Visegrad entered the fray. The V4 had already convened, as it did
with the EaP, its own meetings with Western Balkan states. At a V4 summit
with Western Balkan countries in Prague, the Visegrad leaders urged that
accession talks continue.[163] Orbán could not resist adding, in reference to the
migrant crisis of 2015, "If the EU hadn't slept on accepting North Macedonia
and Serbia as members, there would be fewer illegal migrants in Europe."[164]

Part of Visegrad's stand on the migrant crisis was that the WB needed to be brought into the EU and that Visegrad was physically protecting those borders, through deployments of its Visegrad border patrols and by its continued lobbying for WB accession, irrespective of and especially due to new hesitancies in the union toward that goal.[165]

Visegrad continued to convene an annual meeting of its foreign ministers with those of the Western Balkans. Visegrad includes others, notably the European commissioner for neighbourhood and enlargement. Visegrad uses the symbolic and powerful language for the accession of the Western Balkans to the EU that it used for itself in the 1990s: the imperative of achieving European reunification. Visegrad foreign ministers in their declaration resulting from the 2019 V4-WB meeting reiterated "their unequivocal support" for accession and "their firm belief that reunification of Europe cannot be complete without [Western Balkan states] joining the European Union.[166]

At their 2020 meeting, the V4 repeated "their long-term and unequivocal support for the efforts of the Western Balkan partners to join the EU." The Group affirmed that that aim applied to all states in that region,[167] positioning itself against some EU member states who were advocating selective accession. Visegrad was standing up on a contentious issue, one with intensifying national interests within the EU.

V4's support for WB accession raises, indirectly, a final question of how Visegrad has dealt with Kosovo/a.[168] Kosova's declaration of independence on February 17, 2008, was also a potential challenge to Visegrad's unity. Much like other EU states that fear secessionism and that did not recognize Kosova's independence (Cyprus, Greece, Romania, and Spain), so too Slovakia refused. But it was alone among the Four in not recognizing the unilateral declaration of independence, and this was a "very sensitive issue for Slovakia.[169] An observer further comments that "the Kosovo 'episode' seems to be one of the obstacles on the road to the creation of a common, regionally based approach towards political and security problems in Europe. The Czech Republic, Hungary and Poland obviously seem to see the recognition of Kosovo as a contribution to peace and stability in the western Balkans, whereas Slovakia still regards the declaration of the independence of Kosovo as an illegal act from the point of view of international law."[170]

The more that Kosova presented a challenge to Visegrad, the more it evidenced the Group's capacity for solutions. The Hungarian presidency for 2009–10 pledged to "further seek to find flexible solutions to open wider European perspective for the people of Kosovo. The Hungarian V4 Presidency attaches great importance to the continuation of the engagement of the international community in Kosovo. The role played by the EU and NATO and the strengthening of EU-NATO co-operation in Kosovo are particularly essential in that context."[171] According importance to bigger institutions for dealing with Kosovo/a was appropriate and not a measure of Visegrad's incapacity; where it had direct ability to act, it did so. Both the general integration of the Western Balkans and the IVF's activity therein have been important to Visegrad. Continued financial support for the Western Balkans was found, despite collective difference over Kosova's recognition, by making reference to "Kosovo" simply a technical matter, and using such phrasing as "countries and territories."[172] Finally, none of the Visegrad national coordinators, IVF staff, or foreign diplomats posted to Visegrad capitals interviewed for previous studies indicated that Kosovo/a, while not being recognized by all V4 states, presented any issue for the Group's work with it or indeed other WB states, including Serbia.[173]

The accession of the Balkan region will be an overall EU decision, but Visegrad has helped keep attention on its accession, and the Group gave technical assistance for accession and political support. Visegrad's exact influence is elusive, but again it has had some.

CONCLUDING ON VISEGRAD IN THE EU

EU officials and those of other member states are unlikely to diminish their own influence, or to overly credit Visegrad's, even if this chapter should have identified already sufficient external recognition of the V4's sway. In terms of other groupings within the EU, the majority of three dozen non-Visegrad diplomats based in Visegrad countries in 2013 felt that Visegrad was far more prominent and more effective in raising issues in the EU than Benelux or the Nordic Council.[174]

Some of Visegrad's work in the EU has been, as an IVF executive director Petr Vágner wrote, "ordinary work." And its relative absence from the public eye should not diminish it; moreover, those activities in the EU had the further effect of helping to maintain and augment the Group's internal cohesion.[175]

Nor will Visegrad members *always* act together in the EU. Individual Visegrad states, other EU member states, and EU officials and organs will see certain matters differently. The EU challenged Hungary and Poland on domestic political issues that did not apply to the Czech Republic or Slovakia. And in terms of financial negotiations in the EU in later 2020, the Group issued in September 2020 this general statement, one applicable at any time and on any issue: that its members "believe that initiatives and challenges in the financial field . . . require cooperation of the V4 Finance Ministers to ensure that solutions to be adopted at the EU level correspond to the interests of the countries of the region."[176] When it came to actual negotiations in December 2020 on the EU budget and on the rule of law, Budapest and Warsaw were not only on their own (and facing much EU criticism), but Prague and Bratislava purposefully kept away.

Many in Central Europe, and some outside it, recognize that Visegrad has changed at least some aspects of how the EU works and of policies.[177] A suitable summation could be "the visibility of the V4 in the EU has greatly increased, as have the ambitions of Central European leaders to shape the EU agenda."[178] Visegrad's ambition has grown from being largely a consumer of EU regulations to a producer. Poland's prime minister Beata Szydło signaled the inversion of the Visegrad-EU relationship in 2017: "We want the European Union to develop like the Visegrad Group."[179] By contrast, early on in her presidency of Slovakia, and concerned for Visegrad's reputation, Zuzana Čaputová said in Hungary that the V4 "has to be about promoting democratic values, the values of freedom and the rule of law, and the values of European integration, as was stated in the original agreement on whose basis the V4 was created."[180] The V4 countries are not united and should not be expected to unite on every issue in the EU. Ironically, that recurrent expectation speaks to how influential the Group has become.

And if all this still insufficiently illustrated a vibrant post-accession Visegrad life, its impact intensified in 2015 with the "migrant crisis." So important was that episode and its legacy that they merit separate analysis, in the next chapter.

NOTES

1. Bajda, "Visegrad," 32. The piece uses these points as a foil to show, as this chapter intends also, that Visegrad had post-accession utility. The contribution is indicative of views that Visegrad was already in trouble before accession and that accession, apparently, killed it.
2. Waisová, 66.
3. Jiří Pehe, "Skončí visegrádská spolupráce?" [The End of Visegrád Cooperation?], *Hospodářské noviny*, February 3, 2004, 9. An early key work assessing Visegrad in the EU gives credit to those noting challenges, but that work's premise, as here, is that those views proved incorrect. Dangerfield, "*Visegrad Group in the Expanded European Union*, 651–52.
4. Balogh, 191.
5. See Gerasymchuk, 43, which is also helpful on Visegrad's overlooked relations with Ukraine. See Fawn and Drobysh.
6. Jiří Vykoukal, "The End of Visegrád Cooperation, or 'Don't Kill the Messenger,'" Visegrad.info, March 27, 2004, accessed http://www.visegrad.info/index.php?ID=nazor&IDt=12.
7. Suwara, 46.
8. "Central Europe: From Visegrad to Mitteleuropa. Shifting Alliances among New Members of the European Union," *Economist*, April 16, 2005.
9. Grúber, Kovács, and Törő, 37.
10. E.g., Suwara, 45.
11. Gubová, esp. 120.
12. Copeland, 468, and secondary literature cited.
13. Szelényi, 342.

14. Polish Radio 1, February 25, 2004, as "Polish Minister Says Central Europeans Should Speak as Group in EU," *FBIS-EEU*, February 26, 2004.
15. E.g., Dubowski, 11. Later sections show that Visegrad did not expect, and should not be expected, to deal with *every* issue.
16. ČTK, "We rely on Visegrad Four cooperation—PM Kaczynski," August 4, 2006.
17. For one of many nonregional examples, see "Central Europe Used to Mean the Visegrad Group," *Economist*, April 16, 2005.
18. Neumann.
19. Both the ideas of "Central Europe" having served its (important) purpose and that Central Europe had simply become "Europe" were made in many sessions and interviews at the time.
20. E.g., Jan Urban: "We have a long list of regional issues and problems, which it is necessary to solve together. And I see the future of the Visegrad Group of course not so much focused on the European Union and NATO, but on some regional issues. I think the prospects for our group are quite bright and this structure can be very useful for all us." "What Is the Future for Regional Cooperation in Central Europe?," Radio Prague International, September 10, 2002, https://english.radio.cz/what-future-regional-cooperation-central-europe-8065731.
21. Chapter 8 identifies Poland's disproportionate contributions to leading Visegrad military initiatives.
22. Some views are in Fawn, "Alliance." Westerners disappointed, or worse, by these Central European views on war would have benefited from a (re)read of Havel's critique of Cold War Western peace and disarmament movements: Havel, "Anatomy."
23. *Lidové Noviny*, December 5, 2002.
24. See, e.g., Breffni O'Rourke, "2002 In Review: EU Creates 'New Europe' with Accession of 10 Countries," RFE/RL, December 17, 2002, https://www.rferl.org/a/1101702.html.
25. Gołembski, 60.
26. E.g., Heather Grabbe, "The Copenhagen Deal for Enlargement," Euractiv, January 18, 2003, https://www.euractiv.com/section/enlargement/opinion/the-copenhagen-deal-for-enlargement/836915/.
27. Marušiak, "Instead," 10.
28. *Report of the Polish Presidency of the Visegrad Group, July 2012–June 2013*, 27, https://www.visegradgroup.eu/documents/annual-reports/report-pl-v4-pres-07-131209.
29. "Profile of the Visegrad Countries in the Future of Europe Debate," Euractiv, September 18, 2003, https://www.euractiv.com/section/future-eu/opinion/profile-of-the-visegrad-countries-in-the-future-of-europe-debate/837616/.
30. Král, *Profil zemí Visegrádské skupiny*.
31. Bugajski and Teleki, 99.
32. The example is from Czech Radio, October 13, 2003, https://english.radio.cz/visegrad-four-demand-changes-eu-draft-constitution-8079127; see also "The Visegrad Four Are Determined to Amend Constitution Draft," Euractiv, October 3, 2003, https://www.euractiv.com/section/future-eu/news/the-visegrad-four-are-determined-to-amend-constitution-draft/.
33. Törő, Butler, and Grúber.
34. Végh, 443.
35. Dangerfield, "V4," 74.

36. See chapter 7, on the "migrant crisis," during which Visegrad presented itself as the enlightened part of the EU/Europe, the one working to save the EU both from migrants threats and from its own policies.
37. [Statement of the] *Summit of Prime Ministers in Tále (Slovakia), 24–25 June 2003*, https://www.visegradgroup.eu/2003/summit-of-prime.
38. *Report on Activities of the Czech Presidency of the Visegrád Group (2003–2004)*, https://www.visegradgroup.eu/documents/annual-reports/2003-2004-czech-110412.
39. *Report on the Foreign Policy of the Czech Republic: Between January 2003 and December 2003*, 43, https://mzv.gov.cz/file/414924/Report_2003.pdf.
40. Interview, László Püspök, Hungarian Foreign Ministry, November 8, 2004; and Püspök, "Experiencing the Change," mimeo, Visegrad Summer School, July 7, 2004.
41. Vašáryová, 78.
42. The formal name is "Declaration of Prime Ministers of the Czech Republic, the Republic of Hungary, the Republic of Poland and the Slovak Republic on Cooperation of the Visegrad Group Countries after Their Accession to the European Union, 12 May 2004," but officially it is also called the Visegrad Declaration 2004, and the Kroměříž Declaration and with the latter used hereafter. See http://www.visegradgroup.eu/2004/declaration-of-prime.
43. Kroměříž Declaration, second paragraph.
44. See http://www.visegradgroup.eu/cooperation/guidelines-on-the-future-110412.
45. As per the 2003/04 Czech Visegrad presidency report, under "Tourism," online only at https://www.visegradgroup.eu/documents/presidency-programs/2003-2004-czech-110412.
46. Kroměříž Declaration.
47. Samson, "Assessment," 10.
48. Grúber, Kovács, and Törő, 38.
49. "Guidelines on the Future Areas of Visegrad Cooperation," http://www.visegradgroup.eu/cooperation/guidelines-on-the-future-110412.
50. As the previous chapter noted, the Slovak presidency report for 2002–03, the last preceding EU accession wrote of the "trademark of the 'V4' symbol" as "a well-known structure in the enlarging Europe, as well as in the entire international community." *Annual Report of the Slovak Presidency in the Visegrad Group (2002–2003)* [no pagination, online], https://www.visegradgroup.eu/documents/annual-reports/2002-2003-slovak-110412.
51. Paroubek, 15.
52. Hárs, 50–53.
53. Čarnogurský, 35.
54. Simonyi, 96.
55. *Polish Presidency 2012–13* [no pagination].
56. Quoted in Daniela Lazarová and Michal Kořan, "Visegrad Is at a Crossroads," February 16, 2016, last accessed January 15, 2020, http://www.iir.cz/en/article/visegrad-is-at-a-crossroads.
57. Törő, Butler, and Grúber, 374.
58. Kořan, "Visegrad Cooperation," 123. See also "Sarkozy Warns Visegrad Countries Not to Make a Habit of Pre-summit Meetings," EUobserver, November 4, 2009.
59. See, e.g., Luboš Palata, "Visegrád je už zavedená značka," February 16, 2011, lidovky.cz, https://www.lidovky.cz/domov/visegrad-je-uz-zavedena-znacka.A110216_000027_ln_noviny_sko.

60. *Slovak Presidency Report, 2014–15*, 5, https://www.visegradgroup.eu/documents /presidency-programs/20142015-slovak.

61. See Slovak president Ivan Gašparovič's comments in "Gasparovic: Hungarian and Polish EU Presidencies a Chance for V4," SITA Online, January 1, 2011.

62. By 2022 the view could be different, with a leading regional analyst warning that the Czech presidency would downplay V4 interests. But that was also due to domestic Czech matters and the preeminence of the Russian war on Ukraine. Vít Dostál, "Expect Czech EU Presidency to Downgrade V4 Priorities," EUobserver, June 27, 2022, https://euobserver.com/opinion/155268.

63. Nič, 171.

64. "V4 States Oppose Timmermans as EC President—Czech PM," July 1, 2019, http:// www.visegradgroup.eu/news/v4-states-oppose.

65. "Joint letter from the the [*sic*] Visegrad Group /V4/, Republic of Bulgaria and Romania Environment and Climate Ministers to Mr. Frans Timmermans, Executive Vice-President of the European Commission on Impact Assessment (IA) for the European Union's 2030 Climate Ambition and the Action Plan," July 13, 2020, https://www.euractiv.com/wp-content/uploads/sites/2/2020/08/V4BGRO -letter-IA-2030_20200712.pdf. Media reported on the V4 initiative as pressuring "Timmermans to clearly spell out the 'real social, environmental and economic costs' of higher targets." Kalina Oroschakoff, "4 Things to Know about the EU's Battle to Cut Emissions," Politico, September 10, 2020, https://www.politico.eu /article/4-things-to-know-about-the-eus-battle-to-cut-emissions/.

66. Agata Palickova, "Visegrad Leaders Claim Victory in Race for EU Top Jobs," Euractiv, July 4, 2019, https://www.euractiv.com/section/eu-elections-2019/news/visegrad -leaders-claim-victory-in-race-for-eu-top-jobs/. See also *Visegrad Insight* editor Wojciech Przybylski, "Winning by Losing in the EU," July 3, 2019, https:// visegradinsight.eu/winning-by-losing-in-the-eu/.

67. Alexandra Brzozowski and Samuel Stolton, "Weber Forced to Stand Aside as EU Leaders Bypass Spitzenkandidaten," Euractiv, July 2, 2019, https://www.euractiv .com/section/eu-elections-2019/news/weber-forced-to-stand-aside-as-eu -leaders-bypass-spitzenkandidaten/.

68. Christian Schweiger, "Revisiting the Lisbon Treaty Ten Years after Its Ratification," CPD Policy Blog, December 12, 2019, accessed May 26, 2022, https://policyblog .uni-graz.at/2019/12/revisiting-the-lisbon-treaty-ten-years-after-its-ratification/.

69. @zoltanspox, July 2, 2019, https://twitter.com/zoltanspox/status/114605130184 0756738?ref_src=twsrc%5Etfw%7Ctwcamp%5Etweetembed%7Ctwterm%5E 1146051303128412162%7Ctwgr%5Eshare_3&ref_url=https%3A%2F%2Fvisegrad insight.eu%2Fwinning-by-losing-in-the-eu%2F.

70. Sejla Almadi, *Can the V4's Priorities Shape "Europe's Priorities"?: The Multiannual Financial Framework 2021–2027*, https://www.europeum.org/en/articles/detail /2382/can-the-v4-s-priorities-shape-europe-s-priorities.

71. Andrzej Sadecki, "Preparations for the EU Multiannual Financial Framework 2021–2027—Chances and Challenges for Central Europe," Europeum Policy Paper, February 5, 2018, https://europeum.org/en/articles/detail/1860/preparations-for -the-eu-multiannual-financial-framework-2021-2027-chances-and-challenges -for-central-europe.

72. Busek and Brix.

73. Cabada and Waisová, 13; M. Braun, *Politics*, 106.
74. Andrew Rettman, "Visegrad Four Mull over EU Budget Strategy," EUobserver, May 10, 2005, https://euobserver.com/economic/19031.
75. *Právo*, April 28, 2005.
76. High Level Reflection Group, 6. In making that point, the report was critical of how the Visegrad governments had not further developed regional energy and transport infrastructure.
77. Notwithstanding that these groups choose to meet with Visegrad.
78. Pavel Havlíček, "Czech V4 Presidency 2019/20: A Reasonable Way Forward," Lublin: Institute of Central Europe, 2020, https://ies.lublin.pl/en/komentarze -commentaries/czech-v4-presidency-201920-a-reasonable-way-forward-pavel -havlicek-237-140-2020.
79. Useful comparisons are Braun, *Politics of Regional Cooperation*; and Kirch.
80. PAP, March 30, 2005, as "Polish, Slovak Speakers against Expansion of Visegrad Group," *FBIS*, March 30, 2005.
81. For Visegrad reactions, see Kristina Alda, "Country Shut Out of Border Treaty," *Prague Post*, September 20, 2006.
82. "Czechs and Slovaks 'Reunited' by Schengen Passport-Free Zone," Euractiv, December 21, 2007, https://www.euractiv.com/section/social-europe-jobs/news /czechs-and-slovaks-reunited-by-schengen-passport-free-zone/.
83. Writing of the Czech experience, see Beneš and Braun, "European Dimension of the Czech Foreign Policy," 71.
84. Havlíček, Jeřábek, and Dokoupil, "Schengen Phenomenon," 50.
85. The visit seems theatrical, but I am unaware of intention or of reactions to it regarding lobbying against Schengen delays. Mention of the visit is in Znoj, 110.
86. SITA, "V4 chce do Schengenu v pôvodnom termíne" (V4 Wants Schengen Entry by the Original Date), hnonline.sk, September 5, 2006, https://hnonline.sk/autor /sita-7729.
87. *Report on the Foreign Policy of the Czech Republic: 1998–1999*, 274, https://mzv .gov.cz/jnp/en/foreign_relations/reports_and_documents/report1998_1999.html.
88. *Report on Activities of the Czech Presidency of the Visegrád Group (2003–2004)*, no page, https://www.visegradgroup.eu/documents/annual-reports/2003-2004-czech -110412.
89. See, e.g., Marušiak, "Slovak Presidency," 100.
90. Kořan, "Visegrad Cooperation," 125.
91. E.g., Agence France-Press, "Central European Presidents Denounce EU 'Discrim- ination' over Schengen Extension," September 15, 2006.
92. See "Closing Declaration of the Presidents of Parliaments of Visegrád Group Countries on the Threats Associated with the Possible Postponement of the Enlargement of the Schengen Area by New Member States of the European Union, Košice, Slovakia November 13th 2006," http://www.visegradgroup.eu/official -statements/documents/declaration-of-the-110412. This statement remains on the official Visegrad website.
93. "Declaration of the Prime Ministers of the Visegrad Countries: Visegrad, Hungary, 10 October 2006," http://www.visegradgroup.eu/official-statements/documents /declaration-of-the.
94. Marek and Baun, 117.

95. "Joint Statement, V4 + Slovenia Prime Ministers' Meeting. Ostrava, December 9–10, 2007," https://www.visegradgroup.eu/2007/joint-statement-v4.
96. Quote in, e.g., "V4 Group against Austrian Plan to Delay Schengen Zone Extension," *Austria Today*, June 22, 2007; and *Der Standard*, June 19, 2007.
97. Quoted in Michaela Stanková, "Gyurcsány: 'There Aren't Two Schengens,'" *Slovak Spectator*, June 27, 2007, https://spectator.sme.sk/c/20005406/gyurcsany-there-arent-two-schengens.html.
98. Cited in Jan Richter "Presidents of the Visegrad Group Countries Meet on Lake Balaton," Radio Praha, September 25, 2007, http://www.radio.cz/en/section/talking/presidents-of-the-visegrad-group-countries-meet-on-lake-balaton.
99. Cited in Reuters, "Central Europeans Set up Group to Keep Schengen Zone Alive," December 3, 2015, http://www.vlada.cz/en/media-centrum/aktualne/joint-statement-of-the-visegrad-group-countries-137816/.
100. Cabinet Office of the Prime Minister [of Hungary], "Visegrád Group to Reject the idea of "Mini-Schengen," December 3, 2015, http://www.miniszterelnok.hu/visegrad-group-to-reject-the-idea-of-mini-schengen/.
101. Regional coverage includes "Extraordinary V4 Summit over 'Garbage Can's Food Quality in Central and Eastern Europe," February 28, 2017, https://visegradpost.com/en/2017/02/28/extraordinary-v4-summit-over-garbage-can-food-quality-in-central-and-eastern-europe/.
102. Georgi Gotev, "Visegrád Readies Attack against 'Double Standards' for Food," Euractiv, March 2, 2017, https://www.euractiv.com/section/agriculture-food/news/visegrad-readies-attack-against-double-standards-for-food/. Visegrad's initial statement is at https://www.visegradgroup.eu/calendar/v4-statement-on-dual.
103. Euractiv, "Eastern Europeans Bite Back over 'Food Apartheid,'" July 3, 2017, https://www.euractiv.com/section/agriculture-food/news/eastern-europeans-bite-back-over-food-apartheid/.
104. "Kiska at the V4 Summit: We Have a Very Strong Perception of Extremism," October 14, 2017, https://www.prezident.sk/en/article/prezident-na-samite-v4-extremizmus-vnimane-velmi-silne/.
105. E.g., BBC, "New EU Tests to Tackle 'Rip-Off' Food Complaints," April 12, 2018, https://www.bbc.co.uk/news/world-europe-43741545.
106. See, e.g., "Victory for the V4: The European Union Bans Double Quality of Brand Products," *Visegrad Post*, April 16, 2018, https://visegradpost.com/en/2018/04/16/victory-for-the-v4-the-european-union-bans-double-quality-of-brand-products/.
107. "Joint Statement of the 14th Meeting of the Environment Ministers of the Visegrad Group Countries 24–25 May 2007, Prague, Czech Republic," https://www.visegradgroup.eu/jointstatement.
108. Baldock, 185.
109. Quoted in the Polish government statement "The Visegrad Group about the Climate," December 12, 2014, http://klimada.mos.gov.pl/en/2014/02/12/the-visegrad-group-about-the-climate/.
110. Philipp Thaler, "Cracks in the Visegrád Group Are Good News for EU Climate Ambition," ECG, March 4, 2017, https://www.e3g.org/publications/cracks-in-the-visegrad-group-are-good-news-for-eu-climate-ambition/.
111. Among many indicators, see Linda Zeilina, "Why Visegrad 4 Need to Get Real about Climate Change," EUobserver, July 2, 2019, https://euobserver.com/opinion

/145293. Discussions to which I was invited to present to other EU member states on Visegrad have made the latter point clear.

112. From multiple discussions especially in late 2019 and early 2020.

113. "Visegrad Group to Agree Common Stance on EU's 2050 Climate Goals: Hungary," Reuters, June 20, 2019, https://www.reuters.com/article/us-eu-climate-visegrad-idUSKCN1TL0UF/.

114. *Polish Presidency Programme 2020–21*, 5, https://www.visegradgroup.eu/documents/presidency-programs/2020-2021-polish.

115. Adéla Denková, Edit Zgut, Krzysztof Kokoszczy, and Pavol Szalai, "V4 Energy Security: The Land of Nuclear and Coal," Euractiv.com, March 16, 2017, https://www.euractiv.com/section/electricity/news/v4-energy-security-the-land-of-nuclear-and-coal/.

116. Mišík, "Crisis" 57.

117. "The Bratislava Declaration of the Prime Ministers of the Czech Republic, the Republic of Hungary, the Republic of Poland and the Slovak Republic on the Occasion of the 20th Anniversary of the Visegrad Group (15 February 2011, Bratislava)."

118. Strážay, "Visegrad—Arrival, Survival, Renewal", 29.

119. Samson, "Assessment," esp. 39.

120. Interviews at the Hungarian Ministry of Foreign Affairs in interviews, February 5, 2012; and communications from the Hungarian Visegrad coordinator staff, March 7, 2012.

121. *Annual Implementation Report*, 2011, bolded emphasis removed from the original.

122. *2009/10 Hungarian presidency*, https://www.visegradgroup.eu/documents/annual-reports/2009-2010-hungarian-110412.

123. "Road Map towards the Regional Gas Market among Visegrad 4 Countries," https://www.premier.gov.pl/files/files/v4_road_map_eng.pdf.

124. "V4 Countries Seek EU Support for North-South Energy Link Project," SITA Online, January 26, 2011.

125. TASR, February 4, 2011.

126. *The Visegrad Group Countries*.

127. Gniazdowski (no title), in Przybylski et. al, 125.

128. Generally, Austrian diplomats, of whom several have been interviewed across the region over several years, tend to avoid any reference to the empire. Even when a positive reference—including from communist-era dissidents who spoke positively of the late Habsburg Empire as one of high culture and a relative ethos of tolerance—is made, engagement with that past has otherwise been muted.

129. See "TEN-T," https://ec.europa.eu/inea/en/ten-t.

130. "Annual Implementation Report," 2011 [bolded emphasis removed from the original].

131. Tóth, 160.

132. Tóth, 158.

133. Henry Foy and Andrew Byrne, "Splits over EU Test Relations between Visegrad Four," *FT*, October 6, 2016, https://www.ft.com/content/f5d017f8-84b2-11e6-8897-2359a58ac7a5.

134. "Joint Declaration of Ministers Responsible for Transport, Development and EU Funds concerning the Future of Transport Financing in the 2021–2027 Financial Perspective," October 6, 2018, https://www.visegradgroup.eu/calendar/2018/joint-declaration-of-181213.

135. "Declaration of Prime Ministers of the Czech Republic, the Republic of Hungary, the Republic of Poland and the Slovak Republic on Cooperation of the Visegrad Group Countries after Their Accession to the European Union, 12 May 2004 (The Kroměříž Declaration)."

136. See "European Neighbourhood Policy," https://eeas.europa.eu/diplomatic-network/european-neighbourhood-policy-enp_en.

137. *Report on the Foreign Policy of the Czech Republic: Between January 2005*, 65, accessed 2005, https://www.mzv.cz/jnp/en/foreign_relations/reports_and_documents/report2005.html.

138. Simonyi, 97.

139. Wałęsa, 82.

140. Strážay, "Visegrad Four," 12.

141. L. N. Shishelina, "Introduction," in *Russia and the Visegrad Group*, 4. The Russian International Affairs Council, which published the study, was established by President Vladimir Putin and has been chaired by Foreign Minister Sergei Lavrov.

142. Lucia Yar and Radovan Geist, "V4 No Longer a Role Model for Eastern Partnership Countries," Euractiv.com, October 27 and 30, 2017, https://www.euractiv.com/section/europe-s-east/news/v4-no-longer-a-role-model-for-eastern-partnership-countries/. As the title indicates, this article suggests that domestic political developments in some V4 countries meant that they might pay less attention to the EaP and also, through their populist and seemingly anti-EU streaks, diminish their capacity for influence in the region as role models.

143. Tulmets, "Countries," 214.

144. Merheim-Eyre, 99.

145. Cianciara, 3.

146. Braun, *Politics*, 105.

147. Vašáryová, 78.

148. Interview, Budapest, November 4, 2004.

149. See, e.g., the opening page of "Introduction" in Shishelina, (ed.), 4: "The Eastern Partnership that triggered the Ukrainian crisis. . . . The Visegrad Four have taken a significant part of responsibility for the eastern enlargement of the European Union."

150. Cited in "V4 Foreign Ministers Discussed the Future of the Eastern Partnership," April 9, 2020, http://www.visegradgroup.eu/v4-foreign-ministers-200409.

151. "III. Priorities of the Polish Presidency," in *Programme of the Polish Presidency of the Visegrad Group (July 2008–June 2009)*, https://www.visegradgroup.eu/documents/presidency-programs/2008-2009-polish-110412.

152. Kříž and Urbanovska, citing the abstract.

153. The V4 presidents also made a joint appeal to their populations calling for vaccination and acknowledging that "our region is facing a dire pandemic situation." This statement presumes not just a public recognition of Visegrad but that such a statement should have salutary impact on popular actions regarding personal health. "Joint Appeal of the Presidents of the Visegrad Group Countries Regarding the COVID-19 Situation; Nov. 30, 2021," https://www.visegradgroup.eu/download.php?docID=473.

154. "V4 Foreign Ministers Discussed the Future of the Eastern Partnership," April 9, 2020, http://www.visegradgroup.eu/v4-foreign-ministers-200409.

155. "EU-Western Balkans Summit. Thessaloniki, 21 June 2003, Declaration," June 21, 2003, https://ec.europa.eu/commission/presscorner/detail/en/PRES_03_163.
156. European Movement in Serbia, 1.
157. "V4 Ministers in Joint Article: We Offer You Our Helping Hand on the EU Path," November 11, 2015, https://www.visegradgroup.eu/calendar/2015/v4-ministers-in-joint.
158. "Joint Declaration of the Foreign Ministers of the Visegrad Countries and Croatia on the Occasion of the Croatian Accession to the EU," June 26, 2013, http://www.visegradgroup.eu/calendar/2013/joint-declaration-of-the.
159. "Nasza własna Europa" [Our Own Europe (interview with Martonyi)], *Rzeczpospolita*, October 27, 2012.
160. Bukalska and Bocian, 19.
161. Juzová et al., 2.
162. "Speech by Erhardt Busek at the Signing of the Agreement to Amend and Enlarge the CEFTA," December 19, 2006, http://www.stabilitypact.org/pages/speeches/detail.asp?y=2006&p=470.
163. "V4 Statement on the Western Balkans," accessed December 11, 2023, http://www.visegradgroup.eu/documents/official-statements/v4-statement-on-the-190912.
164. Cited in Georgi Gotev, "Visegrad Countries Back Opening of Accession Talks with North Macedonia, Albania," Euractiv, September 13, 2019, https://www.euractiv.com/section/enlargement/news/visegrad-countries-back-opening-of-accession-talks-with-north-macedonia-albania/.
165. The V4 foreign ministers' letter of November 2015, "V4 Ministers in Joint Article," is strong evidence of these Visegrad views.
166. "V4 Statement on the Western Balkans," September 12, 2019, http://www.visegradgroup.eu/documents/official-statements/v4-statement-on-the-190912.
167. "Joint Statement of the Ministers of Foreign Affairs of the V4 countries on the Western Balkans," February 27, 2020, http://www.visegradgroup.eu/documents/official-statements/joint-statement-of-the-200323.
168. The use of "Kosova" does not disregard the fact that the country lacks universal recognition. Kosovo/a is a representative but clumsy formulation.
169. Interview, Slovak MFA, February 9, 2012.
170. Samson, "Assessment of Visegrad Cooperation," 28.
171. *2009/2010 Hungarian Presidency Report*, https://www.visegradgroup.eu/documents/annual-reports/2009-2010-hungarian-110412.
172. Interview, International Visegrad Fund, February 2012.
173. The relevant interviews including that subject were conducted in 2012 and 2013. Visegrad documents mentioning "Kosovo" give the standard caveat that its designation "Kosovo" is used "without prejudice to positions on status and is in line with UNSCR 1244/1999 and the ICJ Opinion on the Kosovo declaration of independence." E.g., September 12, 2019.
174. Visegrad Fellowship Report and Fawn, "External Perceptions."
175. Vágner, "Can the Visegrad Group Serve," 10. This is cited separately, but Petr Vágner was a most welcoming host to the IVF and deeply insightful.
176. "Joint Declaration of V4 Finance Ministers on the Cooperation in the Financial Area," September 4, 2020, https://www.visegradgroup.eu/calendar/events-in-2020/joint-declaration-of-v4.

177. This was also a summary finding of the perceptions in 2013 of three dozen foreign diplomats based in Visegrad capitals. Fawn, "External Perceptions."
178. Groszkowski, citing the abstract.
179. Quoted in *Report on the Polish Presidency of the Visegrad Group1 July 2016–30 June 2017*, 6, https://www.visegradgroup.eu/documents/annual-reports/polish -presidency-report.
180. "President of the Slovak Republic Zuzana Čaputová on a Foreign Visit to Hungary: Cooperation in the V4 Region Mustn't Be Just about Safeguarding Regional Interests," July 11, 2019, https://www.prezident.sk/en/article/testang/.

7

FROM LIBERAL TO
ILLIBERAL VISEGRAD

THE "MIGRANT CRISIS" AND
TOXIC INTERNATIONAL FAME

From bike rides to book publications, Visegrad has sought to boost its profile. Nothing in the Group's considerable history, however, catapulted its name internationally more than its reactions to the "migrant crisis" that began in 2015.

Throughout the summer of that year, hundreds of thousands of people landed on the Italian and Greek coasts, while still others came overland from Turkey. Many, but not all, were escaping war-ravaged Syria, where a brutal civil war had begun in 2011 and increased in summer 2015, as Russia began military operations in that country. Some refugees arriving in southern Europe continued northeastward, through Bulgaria. Others traveled through former states of Yugoslavia. The first EU border attained by the many marching across Serbia was Hungary's. Numbers quickly increased. In August 2015 some 107,500 migrants per month were reaching the EU; the EU at that point estimated total figures for 2015 would climb to the already-significant number of 750,000.

Just four months later, the figure, including for affiliated EU countries like Switzerland, had nearly doubled to 1,300,000.[1] That enormous tally was twice the previous figure of 1992, caused particularly by the expanding violence in what became the Yugoslav wars of secession, even if there were far lower numbers than feared from the disintegration of the Soviet Union. Before final estimates were made, the influx had become Europe's worst refugee crisis since World War II.

Although the crisis affected many parts of the EU, especially Mediterranean littoral states, Hungary gained particular televisual focus, images appearing worldwide of beleaguered masses crammed into Budapest's Keleti train station. Politicized debate began about whether the crowds were primarily of single, working-aged males, or of families; the former served to underscore the argument that these were not conflict-fleeing refugees but rather economic opportunists and thus "migrants." In the event, the latter epithet stuck overwhelmingly.[2] And the EU faced the quandary of where to place the multitudes who were then firmly inside the union's boundaries.

Written in early 2015, before this demographic crisis arose, a book-length study of EU resistance to unwelcome arrivals, entitled *Fortress Europe*, observed, "Europe has shown no sign of abandoning the fortress model of border enforcement. . . . On the contrary, both the European Union and many of its member states have stepped up their attempts to reduce and prevent immigration."[3]

Now "Europe," and primarily the EU, had a challenge that was unforeseen and colossal. French president François Hollande and German chancellor Angela Merkel began plans for resettlement of the migrants across the EU. But Visegrad convened its own "extraordinary summit" and was already opposing any requirement of accepting the arrivals. Hollande attended a second part of the V4 summit. At that, Orbán stood his ground on refusing numbers and asserted that Hungary had already received more people than Italy or Greece, the coastal countries in which so many migrants had originally landed. French and German officials produced a common position in September 2015, and Hollande explained that this plan would involve EU member states accepting a "permanent and mandatory mechanism" to settle migrants in their states.[4]

In unveiling this response to a humanitarian crisis, one meant to be of and for the whole EU, Hollande also responded to Visegrad's "extraordinary summit on migration" of September 4. At that the V4 leaders issued a detailed and determined response of their own.[5] They expressed sadness at the loss of life, and indeed some of those fleeing died. Two days before the V4 convened, global media palpitated with images of the dead body of two-year-old Syrian Alan Kurdi, face down on a Turkish beach.

Amid this increasingly emotive crisis, Visegrad also enunciated its understanding of EU values; those included "preserving the voluntary nature of EU solidarity measures—so that each Member State may build on its experience, best practices and available resources." Those, perhaps, more gentle words, were followed with defiance: "Any proposal leading to introduction of mandatory and permanent quota for solidarity measures would be unacceptable." But to the V4, "mandatory quotas" for settling migrants in their countries were what Hollande and Merkel were demanding. The V4 concluded its statement by making clear that its contents provided the basis for the V4's position in advance of and for the extraordinary meeting that the EU itself was convening eleven days later.[6] The V4 was seeking to reset the EU agenda.

In taking their view the V4 member states continued to be in direct confrontation with the Franco-German stand, which Hollande particularly reiterated as ethical obligations of EU states: "What has been done now is not enough anymore, and there are countries that do not meet their moral obligations." He intended still more: he meant Visegrad. And media that had not previously used "Visegrad," or perhaps not even heard of it, began using that name even as a familiar adjective in explaining Hollande's statement, such as that the French president was making "a direct jab at Visegrad-type views."[7]

Visegrad continued to oppose Franco-German or wider EU proposals. The V4 convened a summit around its twenty-fifth anniversary, on February 15, 2016. Considering Visegrad's penchant for using anniversaries (a practice elaborated in chapter 9), a celebratory meeting was likely, perhaps with another high-level European leader. The first part of this "extraordinary" (but still anniversary) summit was commemorative; a second part included Macedonia's president and Bulgaria's prime minister, in what Visegrad announced in advance was to devise "opportunities to assist those states currently bearing the brunt of migratory pressures as they seek to protect their borders." The Visegrad statement also criticized the insufficiency of an EU measure to contain migrants in Turkey and pronounced Visegrad intended not only to aid Greece (and a recipient of the Visegrad border force) but also "Macedonia, Bulgaria and other countries along the Balkan route to protect their borders."[8] The V4 called on the EU to seek a "reduction of the mixed migratory pressure on Europe"—terminology implying that not all of the population flows were deserving. Visegrad also wanted systems to determine "genuine asylum seekers" and coordination of EU external policies, work on site in "hot spots" outside the EU that were causing population displacements, and protection of the Union's external borders.[9] The EU convened an "informal" summit of twenty-seven heads of state in, perhaps fittingly, Bratislava on September 16, 2016. This was the first meeting since Britain's Brexit referendum three months before but also one at which Visegrad pressures were addressed. Indeed, the V4 had just met in the very same venue: the Slovak capital's castle. The EU's resulting "Bratislava Declaration" pledged vapidly to "broaden EU consensus on long term migration policy and apply the principles of responsibility and solidarity."[10] Jacques Rupnik likened the EU's term of "flexible solidarity" to adjectival additions that strip nouns of substance, like "fried snowballs" or, with aching reference to the region's recent communist past, "socialist democracy."[11]

No matter what linguistic terms were used, Visegrad arrived at its apogee of influence and international name-recognition. This it achieved, as its proponents stridently contended, by becoming the best advocates of Europe's core values. But for Visegrad's detractors, whose numbers rocketed, the Group's stance destroyed its own founding values and made in one go the cooperation's brand name toxic.

This chapter identifies and assesses the reception of Visegrad in international media during and following that crisis. Because of the volume of V4 coverage around just the European Council Summit of June 2018 regarding migrant quotas, the chapter gives that meeting particular attention. The significance of that focus should itself not be understated: countless major news agencies worldwide reported on Visegrad by name, even if, by explanation, the membership of the group was routinely added.

This chapter categorizes a selection of online English-language media in and beyond Europe to determine how Visegrad's handling of the crisis was perceived internationally. A later section covers what did *not* receive attention by foreign media, from familiarity with Visegrad government statements and regional press, and what that also says of Visegrad. A final section contends that the "migrant crisis," while elevating and even empowering Visegrad, has only in certain media been (re)associated with "Eastern Europe." After all, as we saw earlier, the introduction of the term "Central Europe" was integral to the post-communist project of reasserting the region's Western geocultural identity. To have the reapplication of Eastern Europe to the region by outside interlocutors would have been tantamount to a political reversal of some of Visegrad's greatest achievements of the preceding quarter-century. While Visegrad gained intense negative publicity, its stance at least did not remake its region back into Eastern Europe. Nevertheless, this episode is full of irony because past Visegrad supporters saw its 2015 initiatives as undermining all that the Group had stood for in the years since its creation. Before the migrant crisis, advocates wanted Visegrad to adopt more good causes to enhance its soft power.[12] The Visegrad leaderships, however, at that time, believed and argued that it was they who were morally correct and were teaching Europe about itself and also saving it. As the chapter concludes on that particular point, it finds that only saddened regional analysts began renaming Visegrad's region Eastern Europe.

An additional irony for Visegrad from its assertiveness over the migrant crisis was that it began to be credited unduly for unity. Differentiation over the quality of foreign media reporting can be made by those who recognize that the strident and coherent position that Visegrad adopted over quotas for relocating migrants was unusual for it. By contrast, reporting on the rejection in September 2017 of Slovakia and Hungary's application to the European Court of Justice to stop the mandatory relocation demonstrated degrees to which foreign reporting appreciated the capacities for Visegrad unity and activism.

THE "MIGRANT CRISIS" AND VISEGRAD IN THE EU

If anyone might still think, after the last chapter, that the V4 had not recognized, and furthermore, not successfully pursued its self-defined interest in the EU, Visegrad's resistance to the mandatory allocation of migrants surely persuades.

How did Visegrad react? Attempting a brief objective narrative (categorizations of interpretations follow), one can say that Visegrad jumped to international attention by advancing a common position on the return of these peoples to their countries of origin, rather than accepting them into EU states. In pure statistical terms, Visegrad achieved what it wanted: accepting few or no "migrants."[13] Apart from numerous statements and assertiveness in the EU, Visegrad also increased its prominence and activism by producing a joint-border patrol. Guards from each of the four countries were sent to Greece and patrolled together, each wearing purposely commissioned four-country emblems. These patrols and symbols formed part of the pictorial display in the official commemoration of the V4's twenty-fifth anniversary.[14]

The "migrant" crisis was unquestionably Visegrad's greatest leap into the international imagination but also its most unfavorable.[15] But even saying that is tricky. While, as will be outlined, Visegrad received negative press, its drivers seized on the negative criticism to make Visegrad sound virtuous: the Group asserted that it was nobly, and uniquely, speaking the truth in and to the EU and serving all of the EU's interests.[16] Indeed, Visegrad's stand also won it commendations. Nevertheless, the "migrant" stand generated commentary that stood starkly in opposition to Visegrad's own founding principles of inclusiveness and tolerance. The next sections analyze the frequency and quality of references to Visegrad in English-language media. Visegrad's actions are discerned and categorized into five forms: resistance, "dissent" and reversal of policies, the extraction of concessions, leadership (and even an "axis" thereof), and unity.

Resistance to Germany Particularly, and the EU Generally

At the June 2018 EU Summit the V4 blocked passage of a compulsory migrant quota for each member state. Additionally, individual Visegrad states took few or no migrants. As one source summarized: "The numbers speak for themselves. The Czech Republic should have relocated 2,691 refugees from Greece and Italy. It relocated 12. Hungary should have accepted 1,294 people but allowed none in. Poland was to take in 7,082 refugees and hasn't accepted any. Slovakia was supposed to relocate 902 asylum seekers. But it relocated 16 people—all single mothers with children."[17] For contrast to these accepted numbers of displaced peoples in Visegrad countries, Germany accepted 800,000— the highest in absolute terms. Sweden received 162,877 asylum applications in 2015, in a country of under 10 million, by far the highest per capita in Europe.[18]

How Visegrad Was Perceived

For its successful resistance to the EU's mandatory migrant allocation, Visegrad was recognized as a strong actor in being described as standing up to Germany and the remainder of the EU. Common, if neutral, coverage included

such as that of the BBC, which observed that Visegrad "rejected" the EU proposal.[19] Britain's *Observer*, the Sunday counterpart of the *Guardian*, wrote that
Visegrad's stance of opposing EU measures against Poland and Hungary for
resisting migrant quotas had "sharpened into all-out confrontation."[20] Some
of the language was even more firm and graphic. For Reuters, Visegrad was
"pushing back" and telling Brussels "to back off."[21] Other language from the
British tabloid press included "Brussels bosses . . . Combat Visegrad Defiance."[22]
Belgian premier Charles Michel (and from December 2019, president of the
European Council) declared of Visegrad that "By stubbornly, repeatedly, sys-
tematically refusing to show a minimum of solidarity, these countries automatically open the political debate about the Schengen area," from which he
proposed their expulsion.[23]

   Considering such commentaries already, the following from Bne IntelliNews is hardly surprising: "Visegrad Four claim EU migration summit as their
own success."[24]

More than Resistance: "Battles," "Dissent," and the Reversal of Policies

Resistance was not all that Visegrad had achieved; it had turned the tables
on the rest of the EU. No longer was the V4 merely lobbying in the EU, but
rather the EU now had to deal with the V4. *Politico* wrote of "Brussels' battle
to tame Visegrad rebels."[25] The UK's *Observer*, with implied reference to Brexit,
contended that "Europe faces a threat to its cohesion. But this time it's on the
eastern front, not the western."[26]

   In a striking, and perhaps unintended, contrast to the historical origins of
Visegrad among communist-era dissidents, the *New York Times* quoted a former Italian diplomat who asserted that Germany's Merkel would need to "tame
the Visegrad dissidents."[27] That comment then gives context to the Associated
Press's assessment (and representatively so) of the V4 as an "anti-migrant force"
in the EU, already a well-established view. The AP then asserted that the Group
had proved sufficiently potent to "hurt" Germany's Merkel (a comment itself
curious perhaps for focusing on Merkel rather than on the EU collectively).[28]

   Such comments aside, other media expressed understanding for the V4's
objections to intended EU policy on migrant quotas. The *Economist* wrote,
"The V4 felt (literally) marginalized by Angela Merkel's decision to keep her
country's borders open to refugees at the peak of the crisis in 2015. Without
consultation, it seemed to them, the chancellor had turned them into transit
corridors for undesirable migrants drawn by the promise of a cushy life in Germany. Their irritation turned to anger when she later urged every EU state to
admit a quota of refugees."[29]

Arguably less-reasoned coverage—such as in Britain's popular, anti-EU tabloid the *Express*—proclaimed that Visegrad had achieved a "Brussels slap down," and that the V4 had "slapped down the bloc," here "bloc" surely being a negative description of the EU.[30]

It is also in the context of the label of "dissent" that reference was made to the V4 being in such contention with Brussels as to be in a "cold war." That phraseology was adopted by none other than Czechoslovak dissident-era foreign policy thinker, and Visegrad parent, Alexandr Vondra.[31] In addition to reversing policies, and closely related to that, the V4 was seen also as extracting concessions from the EU.

Extraction of Concessions

The Group did not simply stand up to and "battle" with Brussels. It might have done so, unsuccessfully. Instead, its achievements were often reported as extracting concessions from Brussels.

Thus, under V4 pressures the EU agreed that "controlled centres" for migrants would be established in member countries only on a voluntary basis. This was written as "a concession made to the Visegrad countries . . . which have signaled their staunch opposition to the arrival of migrants on their territory."[32]

Britain's Euroskeptic *Express* reported of Hungarian prime minister Orbán's Facebook claims for the V4 on June 29, 2018, that he "declared victory for the so-called Visegrad Group."[33] But reportage went even further than stating that the V4 had been "victorious" over the EU. Some asserted that the V4 was becoming a leader of resistance in the union.

(Axis of) Leadership

The V4 was reported in a new light: as giving leadership in the EU, one to which other member states were joining. As chapter 6 showed, this was an activity that Visegrad had undertaken since EU accession. To be sure, those familiar with Visegrad know of its V4+ format, which allows any like-minded state to join the V4 in lobbying on a case-by-case basis. However, reporting was not merely referring to leadership in achieving modest goals but in a wholesale approach toward the EU, and on a critical, divisive, and sensitive matter. Thus the UK's *Independent* wrote: "The formation of an anti-immigration Axis between the core EU states would build on the work of the Visegrad group. The V4 countries . . . have been resistant to migration, and led opposition to EU quotas to take pressure off southern European countries."[34]

The *Observer* similarly reported, "The populist nationalist approach, long championed by the Visegrád bloc, is gaining wider traction, with the interior

ministers of Austria, Italy and Germany announcing a new 'axis' of cooperation on security and immigration," where again the term "axis" featured.[35] The
BBC quoted a Hungarian-government-sponsored institute head who stated
that "the V4 view of Europe is catching on."[36] What is also striking is that the
Visegrad stance was being recognized as, if unstated, providing opportunity
for dissension within the national governments of EU states. Thus Germany's
interior minister was at odds with Merkel over migrant quotas and relocation,
and such reporting suggests that Visegrad provided a forum for that expression. Non-European English-language media, however, did not appear to give
the "leadership" dimension significant attention.

The British summations accorded with how the Group expressed both confidence and demonstrated leadership by aligning with Austria in advance of the
European Council Summit. A joint V4 statement pronounced, "We are con-
vinced that we can achieve positive results at European level by our joint efforts
made through the effective cooperation of the Visegrad Group and Austria."[37]
In seeing that other countries joined with Visegrad, foreign media actually
overplayed Visegrad's own unity. That deserves attention in its own right and is
considered through analysis of coverage of Slovakia and Hungary's failed application to the European Court of Justice to block migrant quotas.

UNITY AND DISUNITY

Perhaps unsurprising, considering plaudits already noted, media generally took
the Group's unity for granted. That came from a misguided focus on very specific events and issues, namely binding migrant relocation. Thus Brussels-based
Euractiv could write, "Visegrad nations united against mandatory relocation
quotas."[38] Still other media, however, noted previous and even current discord. A British tabloid could accurately note (perhaps informed by a leading
Central European analysis and policymaker quoted in the same article) that
"unity within Visegrad has run hot and cold ever since the group was founded
in 1991."[39] Those approaches suggest a higher degree of familiarity with and
insight into Visegrad's history and how it works (and does not). A key view
would be Visegrad is selective on what issues it undertakes. The V4 has a tautological issue-selection process, which means that many divisive issues are a
priori excluded from discussion, let alone action.[40]

Despite the international attention Visegrad gained from its antimigrant
policies, and the claims by especially Hungarian premier Viktor Orbán and his
foreign minister about Visegrad's power, some reportage even noted that the
Group's influence would weaken after 2018.[41] Indeed, the "migrant crisis" and
its sensational media coverage distracted from differences among V4 countries
and the many issues on which they disagree.

Particularly telling of such reporting oversight came from coverage of Slovakia and Hungary's application to the European Court of Justice to challenge the legality of September 2015 European Council decisions that set compulsory migrant quotas for member states (the two countries challenged the second decision, which relocated a larger number of migrants). Slovakia and Hungary's case was dismissed outright on September 6, 2017. That only two of the four countries brought the case demonstrates divergence among the Group; yet all reportage above suggested Visegrad's unity. Many news outlets made no reference to Visegrad, even when belatedly the Czech Republic and Poland (and non-Visegrad Romania) supported the application. Astute reporting, instead, noted differences among the countries, particularly (though not necessarily immediately germane) that Slovakia was unique among the Group for being in the Eurozone.

And shortly after the court rejection, media noted specifically that the migrant crisis was a recent issue for unity but that many other issues were driving the Four apart. These included Poland and Hungary's divergence from the Czech Republic and Slovakia on backing France's proposals to restrict regulations on employees working outside their native states. Some commentary suggested that Visegrad was dividable, noting that French president "Macron has openly cultivated the leaders of Slovakia and the Czech Republic, who are generally regarded as pragmatic" and indicating that he met with both in August, while avoiding "Visegrad's more difficult half."[42] Notable commentators also encouraged divergence of national policies among the V4. The *Financial Times'* (*FT's*) Tony Barber used the fiftieth anniversary of the Warsaw Pact's crushing of the Prague Spring to reiterate that "in western European capitals this foursome [of the V4] is suspected of caring far too little for the EU's values" and to warn Prague and Bratislava that such is a "dangerous trend" that goes against their historical values and their current national interests.[43] For all that was said about Visegrad, aspects of its activities were also missed in international media.

VISEGRAD INITIATIVES AND WHAT WAS NOT COVERED IN ENGLISH-LANGUAGE MEDIA

Relevant to any study of media should also be what remains unreported. Three issues arose: the V4 and Libya, Visegrad as a "brand," and the return of "Eastern Europe," which will be discussed in a longer section on the downsides of foreign media coverage.

Visegrad's Migrant Crisis Response Mechanism

Effectively ignored was that Visegrad introduced a Migrant Crisis Response Mechanism, open to any EU state, to increase border cooperation at the union's external frontiers to limit (illegal) entry into the EU. Already it was seen by regional analysts as having little prospect of use and impact on the migration crisis.[44] Arguably, the mechanism and associated activity became internal to V4 and therefore less noticeable. The Migration Analytical Centre was created at the Office for Foreigners in Poland, with an initial task of reviewing *EU* data on migrants. Input into studies that followed came from across the V4 but not more widely.[45]

The Missed Plaudit: Libya

On December 14, 2017, the V4 and Italy agreed on a project to prevent "illegal migration" by creating facilities in Libya. The initiative was pronounced on all V4 government websites, but English-language foreign attention was very limited.[46] Initial Visegrad support, before the December summit, had received some attention, but that was often after the fact, and in the context of further developments, such as on the establishment of overseas migrant centers.[47]

Once this initiative was formalized, in 2018, European Commission president Jean-Claude Juncker made an overture to the V4, by commending its initiative. But he also said, as the present media scan affirms, that few west Europeans were conscious of the contribution of the Visegrad countries in assisting refugees from Libya. He said that the €35 million that the V4 had made available to Italy was "an effort others didn't do."[48] Not only had it not been done by others; the act went unreported as well. A search for "Visegrad Libya" generated multiple Central European news and official statements but extremely few English-language (or indeed other language) news sources. As an indicator, the terms together produced no relevant news stories on the Associated Press, in the American *Wall Street Journal*, or the *New York Times*; similarly, none in the UK's *Independent* and one in the *Guardian* but without direct connection. Where the V4's Libya plan received attention was in the *FT*. That article again noted Visegrad as "hostile" to the EU regarding quotas, gave attention to critiques of human rights activists that the funding might support a Libyan coast guard suspected of human rights abuses, and then focused on Italian prime minister Paolo Gentiloni, who chastised Visegrad: "The paradox is they [Visegrad] say it's time to commit to support a policy that delivered results [on Libya], but at the same time they say no to share the redistribution. We need a compromise, but the compromise is not doing nothing. We have to do both things."[49] By contrast, the Hungarian prime-ministerial web page announced the Libya border funding, and in applauding terms: "The V4 are making a significant contribution to the defence of Europe's maritime borders,"[50] and national contributions, such as Prague's, were not only reported but rightly as a Visegrad initiative.[51] Much later, in February 2023, when the first of several search-and-rescue ships was given by the European Commission to Libya to deal with migrants, the official press statement recognized that that initiative had been "significantly financed by the Visegrád Group countries."[52]

Also Missing: The Fact of Name Recognition and Visegrad as a "Brand"

What also was *not* so much commented on in English-language media was the fact of Visegrad's recently gained recognition. As some analysis already suggests, Visegrad has become a "brand," but negatively.

Nevertheless, within the region and particularly in an official capacity attention was given to how Visegrad had become such. Thus Hungary's foreign minister pronounced on February 2, 2018:

Visegrad cooperation definitely became a *brand* and the Visegrad Group is the most effective and the tightest alliance within the European Union. The cooperation within the group is tighter and more effective than ever—I can say that without exaggeration. It is cooperation based on common sense and rationality which is of the utmost importance now. Because during these challenging times for Europe debates in the EU have tended to easily swing to emotions, and emotional and stigmatizing debates will never bring you a solution.[53]

Visegrad already saw itself as a "brand," one able to endure challenges. A leading regional analyst, for example, could comment in 2011 that the "V4 brand" had weathered well the multiple challenges of 2010.[54] Of the four rotating Visegrad presidencies, it was the Hungarian one that referred most often (in its 2013–14 annual report) to Visegrad being a "brand."[55] That Visegrad has gained a reputation through its handling of the "migrant crisis" was the starting point of this chapter. Readers will know that the media attention was double-edged, and we are familiar with the antiliberal exclamations. However, what has not particularly happened is the reassociation of the region with "Eastern Europe."

THE NON-RETURN OF "EASTERN EUROPE"

As chapter 2 asserted, Visegrad started life formally in 1991 to reassert a positive, recognizably European image of the region to the West. To a high degree, that geocultural reformulation worked. Indeed, with Euro-Atlantic accession completed by 2004, many in the region asserted that "Central Europe" was finished because the region had consequently become one or all of the following: European, the EU, or Euro-Atlantic.

What did Visegrad's responses to the "migrant crisis" achieve for negative perceptions in reporting? Considering the range and frequency of positive reporting (if casting the V4 against the EU) in the chapter's first section, English-media reporting does not present as negative an image of Visegrad as might be expected.

The terminology here is that the V4 members have been uncooperative and toxic, but that these views are also used to show Visegrad's disunity. Thus, rather than being virtuous in their resistance, Visegrad was reported as obstructionist, to the point of the Group being called "eastern refuseniks."[56]

The V4 was labeled as toxic, but that view generally came from quotations emanating from Central Europe itself and from those dismayed by positions of their own governments. Despite the seeming unity of the Visegrad, the *FT* quoted an unnamed Czech official as evidence of dissension within the Group ("It is getting less and less comfortable to be seen as part of the bloc" and also that "V4 is a toxic brand"[57]).

Robert Anderson, with extensive regional reporting connection, wrote that "the united front of the V4 was always exaggerated anyway, both by Hungary and Poland (to bulk up their own significance), and by Western media, which as always prefer to hype a sexy story rather than tease out the little known region's complexities."[58]

Perhaps counterintuitive is that the negative coverage of Visegrad, particularly from its migrant stance, has not made for a renewal of "Eastern Europe." Some analysts from the region note, and lament, the return of Eastern Europe when the region falls out of disfavor.[59] Despite the negative coverage of Visegrad, the use of Eastern Europe since 2015 occurs in instances either when issues *other* than the "migrant crisis" are discussed, or in media more geographically removed from Central Europe (with the exception of Canada).

Even in a positive sense—here their economic performance—Visegrad countries are again called Eastern Europe. Thus Economics Nobel laureate and *New York Times* columnist Paul Krugman referred to "the so-called Visegrad economies of *eastern Europe*" when he commended their economic performance.[60] Ironically, when the *FT* wrote more recently of Visegrad countries (by name) "running out of steam," it also only called them "Central Europe."[61] The UK's *Independent* called the Group (in a headline) "Eastern Europe," but that was regarding a post-Brexit arrangement that could curtail its workers' rights in Britain.[62]

Although another study could cross-check individual news sources over time to determine any slippage *back* into a usage of Eastern Europe, the V4 positions on "migrant crisis" have not generally caused that, or only years after, when for example Visegrad opposed a compulsory solidarity mechanism for migrant relocation in 2020. Then the Visegrad heads were "Eastern European."[63]

The second categorization of Eastern Europe for Visegrad occurs from a (nonquantitative) analysis indicating that the more geographically removed the news headquarters is from Central Europe, the greater the tendency it has toward calling the Group Eastern European. Exceptions exist; for instance, an article in the relatively proximate Brussels-based Euractiv had repeated the use of "Visegrad" in its text and was entitled "Eastern Europe could pay to avoid taking in refugees."[64] This use, at close publishing proximity to "Central Europe," seems anomalous.

Even in negative reporting of the V4, British newspapers retain "Central Europe." Thus with references to "populists [who] are undermining the EU" and "descending into authoritarianism," the region is still "Central Europe."[65]

By contrast, at the western end of Europe, Spain's English-language EFE wrote of "Eastern Europe's Visegrad Four nations,"[66] and in the Middle East, Al Jazeera called the group "Eastern Europe."[67] Reuters, by contrast, used "central European states."[68] Likewise, *Politico*, titled another article referring to Visegrad in its text "Central Europeans to boycott migration summit they weren't invited to."[69] More unusually, the UK's *FT*, however, referred to "the Visegrad group of countries from Eastern and central Europe" (the uppercase of "Eastern" being in the original).[70] *Politico*, too, implies distinctions between "Central Europe" and "Eastern Europe"—the former are Visegrad, and other countries (like the Baltic states) join with it to, presumably, constitute the "Eastern."[71] In the British press, however, "Eastern Europe" occurred not in respect to the V4 but individual leaders. Representative of this pattern might have been when former Europe minister Denis MacShane wrote in the *Independent* of "eastern European illiberal clerical nationalists like Jaroslaw Kaczynski . . . and Viktor Orban."[72]

Extending from Europe to North America, Canada's more news-savvy newspaper (in this author's view) the *Globe and Mail* had but a single reference to Visegrad in a three-year period. Then, however, it referred to the "central European states."[73] The *Toronto Star* referred firmly to Visegrad as "Central European," even if in that case the paper was running AP stories with a Slavic-sounding byline.[74] Canada may be the geographic exception to the use of Central Europe.

In contrast, many US news outlets used "Eastern Europe" with reference to the region. A *New York Times* article specifically naming the V4 countries is entitled "In Eastern Europe, Populism Lives, Widening a Split in the E.U." Within it "Central Europe" appears—but in reference to Germany.[75] CNN similarly referred in print to Hungary and "several other eastern European states" still refusing to accept migrants.[76]

"Central Europe" was set to stay. A significant part of Visegrad's migrant-crisis-era undertaking was the redefinition of "Central Europe" as the enlightened part of Europe that was defending the continent's civilization (and especially Christian) values. For some this rebranding of "Central Europe" constituted a reversal of the political freedom achieved and signified by 1989. Rather than the regional metaphor re-becoming "Eastern Europe," it was instead that of a disappearing or even failed light.[77]

The rejection of resettlement of non-Europeans in and since 2015 contrasts with Visegrad's position toward Ukrainians. The Czech 2023–24 presidency specified not simply that it would assist those millions fleeing Russian aggression but also integrate them into Visegrad societies.[78]

FINAL OBSERVATION ON APPELLATIONS AND VISEGRAD'S IMAGE AFTER THE MIGRANT CRISIS

Visegrad's stand in the EU on migrant quotas produced various interpretations of its purpose and prowess. Gone were doubts of Visegrad's utility, let alone its existence. Perhaps oddly, with the V4 having had a twenty-seven-year history by the time of the June 2018 European Council meeting, and extraordinary international coverage since 2015, many reports still called Visegrad "the so-called." Readers here will not need, and will probably not agree with, such a doubtful appellation. It may be surprising still to appear in specialist news outlets, such as RFE/RL.[79] For all the media coverage, a further observation is of the infrequency with which Visegrad is simply called that. That means without "the so-called" and, perhaps to raise expectations higher, also without the qualification of stating membership (one case where the Group's composition remained unstated was in the *Observer*[80]). Even region-focused outlets still demonstrate a need to identify the Group's membership. That aside, the Group has received unprecedented international recognition since 2015. One measurement is if Visegrad need not be prefaced by "so-called"; another is if its members are not named, presuming name recognition.

Visegrad gained extensive media-recognition from the Group's name being used in countless headlines. Even if the Group was then explained, the "migrant" crisis surely gave the Group unprecedented international attention. Migrants, too, became a "region builder" for Visegrad, providing an often elusive ingredient for common supranational identity: new normative content to juxtapose Visegrad against the EU.[81] But it will also have done so at some cost to the liberal, inclusive, "European" values that those previously familiar with Visegrad had admired in it. Years on from the crisis, Czech foreign minister Tomáš Petříček conceded that counteracting Visegrad's "toxic label" still required work and that "it will take time to close the ditches that we have dug."[82]

Even with apologetic statements from part of one Visegrad government, the prime ministers continued their objections, including in a meeting on September 24, 2020, with European Commission president Ursula von der Leyen, against German-led plans attempting again to use relocation quotas.[83] The plan had just been announced, with Visegrad's alacrity in organizing the meeting also being noted.[84] In keeping also with Visegrad's preparation in advance of major EU meetings, it convened before an EU leaders' summit.

Visegrad's self-interpretation following the migrant crisis was that it was fundamentally European and a defender of those values, and for all of the EU. Both in ideational and practical terms, Visegrad governments continue their own work on the migrant issue. They note that effective policy cannot be developed without accurate information; to that end, and thereby also not relying on others' information and analysis, they have convened the directors of the V4 Migration Office and established the joint V4 Migration Analytical Center. The Group pronounces that it remains in "absolute" agreement on the need to deal with potential migrant issues in the countries of origin, and have expanded its own experimentations to those ends, including in Jordan.[85]

Similar thinking arose in late 2021, when migrants from outside Europe massed on the Belarusian-Polish border. Poland's defense minister joined a V4 foreign-ministerial meeting in Budapest to laud the V4's support and to pronounce the Group's renewed efforts to protect the EU's borders, while also questioning the meeting's external guest, its Egyptian counterpart, on that country's existing border controls.[86]

The unparalleled visibility and arguably, as well, the potent influence that Visegrad gained from the migrant crisis could also backfire. The intensity of its resistance, particularly toward Germany, suggested for some that instead of recognizing the group's seeming power Berlin might seek instead to work around Visegrad, undercutting its hard-earned past clout. It might mean that Germany could align with other countries instead of with Visegrad and develop policies unsupportive of Visegrad interests in, for example, energy and cohesion policy.[87]

While Visegrad cooperation at the state level gained labels of toxicity, the same name—hitherto associated with state-to-state relations—was adopted and grafted successfully onto other levels of cooperation and with alternative messages. Hungary, where Orbán and his supporters were known to intend to retain power for the next two or three decades,[88] saw the election of the Greens' Gergely Karácsony as mayor of Budapest in October 2019. All four Visegrad states had by then mayors of their capitals openly in opposition to the policies, even ideologies, of their national governments. The four mayors branded themselves as Visegrad and on December 16, 2019, pronounced their Pact of Free Cities. Clasping hands together, as Visegrad premiers had done before, the four leftist-liberal mayors said that they would seek EU funding directly to their cities. They also pledged to promote tolerance and liberal values, even as parallel liberal responsibilities were disregarded. In diverging from its original values of inclusiveness and of removing barriers, illiberal Visegrad at the state level helped to spawn alternative forms of itself.

NOTES

1. For the high figure see Pew Research Center, "Number of Refugees to Europe Surges to Record 1.3 Million in 2015," August 2, 2016, https://www.pewresearch .org/global/2016/08/02/number-of-refugees-to-europe-surges-to-record-1-3 -million-in-2015/.
2. That said, in certain key documents other terms were used, such as from the European Court of Justice, which used "displaced persons" and "asylum seekers." Even there it also used "migrants." Court of Justice of the European Union, Press Release No 91/17 Luxembourg, Judgment in Joined Cases C-643/15 and C-647/15 Slovakia and Hungary v. Council, "The Court Dismisses the Actions Brought by Slovakia and Hungary against the Provisional Mechanism for the Mandatory Relocation of Asylum Seekers," September 6, 2017, accessed September 13, 2018. https://curia .europa.eu/jcms/upload/docs/application/pdf/2017-09/cp170091en.pdf.
3. Carr, *Fortress Europe*, 271.
4. See, e.g., "France's Hollande says binding system needed to take in refugees," Reuters, September 3, 2015. In announcing the plan publicly, Hollande referred to Merkel's support and was accompanied by Irish Prime minister Enda Kenny.
5. "Joint Statement of the Heads of Government of the Visegrad Group Countries," September 4, 2015, https://www.visegradgroup.eu/calendar/2015/joint-statement -of-the-150904.
6. "Joint Statement of the Heads of Government."
7. "Visegrad States Meet on Refusal of Refugee Quotas," EUobserver, September 4, 2015, https://euobserver.com/migration/130115.
8. "Extraordinary Summit of V4 Prime Ministers on the Migration Crisis," February 15, 2016, https://www.visegradgroup.eu/extraordinary-summit-of.
9. "Joint Statement of the Heads of Government of the Visegrad Group Countries. Prague, September 4, 2015," https://www.visegradgroup.eu/calendar/2016/joint -statement-on.
10. "The Bratislava Declaration," September 16, 2016, https://www.consilium.europa .eu/media/21250/160916-bratislava-declaration-and-roadmapen16.pdf.
11. Rupnik, "Migrants," 130.
12. Katarzyna Pisarska, "How Visegradians Can Emulate Scandinavians," USC Center on Public Diplomacy, 2014, https://uscpublicdiplomacy.org/pdin_monitor_article /how-visegradians-can-emulate-scandinavians#_ftn13.
13. This is detailed in the next section.
14. In the foyer of the Czech Ministry of Foreign Affairs. Author's notes (and photographs).
15. Although this chapter gives some data for recent appearances of the word "migrant" in major English media, this present assertion is impressionistic, although also based on observation of and writing on Visegrad throughout its history. For the purposes of this chapter, this author prefers to use the term "migrants" in quotation marks.

16. Multiple examples exist and might be representative of a Hungarian Foreign Ministry press release: "V4 have proven on numerous occasions that their sometimes controversial policies serve the interests of the people who live here and all Europeans." "A Strong Visegrád Voice Is Also in the EU's Interests," July 9, 2018, accessed September 13, 2018, http://www.kormany.hu/en/ministry-of-foreign-affairs-and-trade/news/a-strong-visegrad-voice-is-also-in-the-eu-s-interests.

17. Euractiv, "Visegrad Nations United against Mandatory Relocation Quotas," July 23, 2018, accessed on September 13, 2018, https://www.euractiv.com/section/justice-home-affairs/news/visegrad-nations-united-against-mandatory-relocation-quotas/).

18. Even countries that were "welcoming" of asylum applications took measures to limit entry and residency after 2015; Sweden, for example, increased border controls and legislative restrictions, and the site sweden.se recognized negative media that presented "an image of intolerance and financial restraints, far from the otherwise often utopian image of Sweden." "Media and Public Opinion," current as of February 1, 2023, https://sweden.se/migration/#2015.

19. BBC, "Migrant Crisis: EU Summit Divided amid Migration Row," June 28, 2018, accessed September 13, 2018, https://www.bbc.co.uk/news/world-europe-4463 3606. See also "Italy Still Wants Mandatory Relocation of Migrants across the EU, but the Visegrad Group . . . Rejects It," accessed September 13, 2018, https://www.bbc.co.uk/news/world-europe-44656471.

20. "The Observer View on the EU's Eastern Bloc," *Observer*, January 7, 2018, accessed on September 13, 2018, https://www.theguardian.com/world/commentisfree/2018/jan/07/observer-view-european-union-eastern-bloc-hungary-poland.

21. "Eastern EU States Tell Brussels to Back Off," *Reuters*, January 26, 2018, accessed on September 13, 2018, https://uk.reuters.com/article/uk-europe-hungary-visegrad/eastern-eu-states-tell-brussels-to-back-off-idUKKBN1FF1TL.

22. "Brussels Bosses Accused of 'Divide and Conquer' Tactics to Combat Visegrad Defiance," *Express*, May 27, 2018, accessed on September 13, 2018, https://www.express.co.uk/news/world/965773/european-union-visegrad-group-hungary-poland-slovakia-czech-republic-eu-news.

23. "Belgian PM Suggests Visegrad Countries Should Be Expelled from Schengen," schengenvisainfo.com, December 18, 2018, https://www./news/belgian-pm-suggests-visegrad-countries-should-be-expelled-from-schengen/.

24. "Visegrad Four Claim EU Migration Summit as Their Own Success," Bne Intelli-News, July 2, 2018, accessed on September 13, 2018, http://www.intellinews.com/visegrad-four-claim-eu-migration-summit-as-their-own-success-144423/.

25. Matthew Karnitschnig, "Brussels' Battle to Tame Visegrad Rebels," *Politico*, May 24, 2018, accessed on September 13, 2018, https://www.politico.eu/article/visegrad-poland-hungary-czech-republic-slovakia-brussels-battle-to-tame-visegrad-rebels/.

26. "The Observer View on the EU's Eastern Bloc," *Observer*, January 7, 2018, accessed on September 13, 2018, https://www.theguardian.com/world/commentisfree/2018/jan/07/observer-view-european-union-eastern-bloc-hungary-poland.

27. Steven Erlanger, "Germany's Far Right Complicates Life for Merkel, and the E.U.," *New York Times*, September 25, 2017, accessed on September 13, 2018, https://www.nytimes.com/2017/09/25/world/europe/germany-merkel-europe.html.

28. Vanessa Gera, "Anti-Migrant Force Builds in Europe, Hurting Merkel's Quest," AP, February 15, 2016.

29. "Germany's Troubled Relations with the Visegrad States Show the Limits to Its Power," *Economist*, June 16, 2018, accessed on September 13, 2018, http://media .economist.com/news/europe/21744073-poland-czech-republic-slovakia-and -hungary-dont-much-care-what-angela-merkel-thinks-germanys.

30. "'Treat Members EQUALLY' EU Rebels Demand Brussels Backs Down over Poland Punishment," *Express*, January 26, 2018, accessed on September 13, 2018, https://www.express.co.uk/news/world/910567/Visegrad-European-Union -rebels-Brussels-back-down-Poland-punishment. The *Daily Express* is regarded as "hating" the EU, e.g., "So. . . Why does the Daily Express hate the EU?," *New States-man*, March 13, 2013, accessed September 13, 2018, https://www.newstatesman .com/media/2013/03/so-why-does-daily-express-hate-eu.

31. Alexandr Vondra, "Cold War between Visegrad and Brussels," Global Intelligence Services, June 27, 2018, https://www.gisreportsonline.com/cold-war-between -visegrad-and-brussels-gis-global-trends-video-reports,201,v.html.

32. "'Controlled Centres' for Migrants—Not 'Hotspots,' Say EU Leaders," Euractiv, July 2, 2018, accessed September 13, 2018, https://www.euractiv.com/section /future-eu/news/controlled-centres-for-migrants-not-hotspots-say-eu-leaders/.

33. "Orban Celebrates VICTORY over EU on Migrant Crisis: 'We Managed to FEND OFF Brussels'" [uppercase in the original], accessed September 13, 2018, https:// www.express.co.uk/news/world/981692/viktor-orban-eu-migrant-crisis-hungary -european-council-summit-immigration.

34. Jon Stone, "Austria's Chancellor Calls for Anti-migration 'Axis' with Germany and Italy," *Independent*, June 14, 2018.

35. "The Observer View on Migrants Dying Because Europe Is Pandering to Popu-lism," June 17, 2018, accessed September 13, 2018, https://www.theguardian.com /commentisfree/2018/jun/17/observer-view-europe-migration-policy-populism -rescue-ship-aquarius.

36. "Visegrad: The Clash of the Euro Visions," *BBC*, January 30, 2018, accessed Sep-tember 13, 2018, https://www.bbc.co.uk/news/world-europe-42868599.

37. "Visegrad Group and Austria Summit Declaration on 'Setting up a Mechanism for Assistance in Protecting the Borders of the Western Balkan Countries,'" Buda-pest, June 21, 2018, accessed September 13, 2018, http://www.visegradgroup.eu /documents/official-statements/joint-declaration-of-the-180626.

38. "Visegrad Nations United against Mandatory Relocation Quotas," July 23, 2018, accessed September 13, 2018, https://www.euractiv.com/section/justice-home -affairs/news/visegrad-nations-united-against-mandatory-relocation-quotas/.

39. "Brussels Bosses Accused of 'Divide and Conquer' Tactics to Combat Visegrad Defiance," *Express*, May 27, 2018, accessed September 13, 2018, https://www .express.co.uk/news/world/965773/european-union-visegrad-group-hungary -poland-slovakia-czech-republic-eu-news.

40. See other parts of the book and Fawn, "Visegrad: Fit for Purpose?" for exam-ples, based also on interviews with V4 officials on these points, including what is excluded from Visegrad's agendas.

41. Robert Anderson, "Visegrad: Europe's Axis Is Shifting West Not East," Bne Intelli-News, February 13, 2018, accessed on September 13, 2018, http://www.intellinews .com/index.php/visegrad-europe-s-axis-is-shifting-west-not-east-136694/.

42. "Visegrad 4 Cools on Europe, and Each Other," Politico, October 31, 2017, accessed September 13, 2018, https://www.politico.eu/article/visegrad-4-cools-on-europe -and-each-other/.

43. Tony Barber, "The Prague Spring Still Haunts Europe," FT, August 13, 2018, accessed September 13, 2018, https://www.ft.com/content/98ead96c-9a34-11e8 -ab77-f854c65a4465.

44. Bauerová, 105.

45. As explained in Wrona, Jankowska, and Grudziąż, 8.

46. E.g., Government of the Czech Republic, "Czech PM Babiš Agreed with Other V4 MPs on a Joint Project on Prevention of Illegal Migration," December 14, 2017, accessed September 13, 2018, https://www.vlada.cz/en/media-centrum/aktualne /czech-pm-babis-agreed-with-other-v4-mps-on-a-joint-project-on-prevention -of-illegal-migration-162216/.

47. E.g., BBC, "Migrant Crisis: Italy Backs Force to Police Libya Shore," July 28, 2017, accessed September 13, 2018, https://www.bbc.com/news/world-europe -40750994.

48. Georgi Gotev, "Juncker Upbeat on Slovak Presidency of Visegrad," Euractiv, April 13, 2018, https://www.euractiv.com/section/central-europe/news/juncker -upbeat-on-slovak-presidency-of-visegrad/.

49. "EU Widens Contentious Libya Migration Work. Central European States Back Plan Despite Allegations of Abuses," FT, December 13, 2017, https://www.ft.com /content/df52dd00-e021-11e7-a8a4-0a1e63a52f9c.

50. The Hungarian Prime Minister, "The V4 Are Making a Significant Contribution to the Defence of Europe's Maritime Borders," December 14, 2017, accessed August 3, 2018, http://www.kormany.hu/en/the-prime-minister/news/the-v4-are-making-a -significant-contribution-to-the-defence-of-europe-s-maritime-borders.

51. "Visegrád finančně podpoří ochranu hranic v Libyi, Česko dá 220 milionů," iDnes, December 14, 2017, accessed September 13, 2018, https://zpravy.idnes.cz /eu-summit-brusel-premier-andrej-babis-migrace-kvoty-cesko-pmb-/zahranicni .aspx?c=A171214_093753_zahranicni_ert.

52. "Commissioner Olivér Várhelyi Attends the Handover Ceremony of EU-Financed Search and Rescue Vessels to Libya," February 6, 2023, https://neighbourhood -enlargement.ec.europa.eu/news/commissioner-oliver-varhelyi-attends-handover -ceremony-eu-financed-search-and-rescue-vessels-libya-2023-02-06_en. In a per- sonal interview with Hungarian ambassador to the EU before his Commission appointment, Várhelyi had spoken very favorably of Visegrad.

53. Quoted in "Hungarian Foreign Minister on Visegrad Group: We Strengthen Each Other" [emphasis added], Czech Radio, February 2, 2018, http://www.radio.cz/en /section/curraffrs/hungarian-foreign-minister-on-visegrad-group-we-strengthen -each-other.

54. Strážay, "Second," 112.

55. Drawn from a draft paper by the author, available on request.

56. "The Observer View on the EU's Eastern Bloc," Observer, January 7, 2018, accessed on September 13, 2018, https://www.theguardian.com/world/commentisfree /2018/jan/07/observer-view-european-union-eastern-bloc-hungary-poland).

57. Quote in "Splits over EU Test Relations between Visegrad Four," FT, October 6, 2016, accessed on September 13, 2018, https://www.ft.com/content/f5d017f8 -84b2-11e6-8897-2359a58ac7a5.

58. Anderson, "Visegrad: Europe's Axis Is Shifting West Not East."
59. Růžička.
60. Paul Krugman, "Leprechauns of Eastern Europe," *New York Times*, December 4, 2017, accessed on September 13, 2018, https://krugman.blogs.nytimes.com/2017/12/04/leprechauns-of-eastern-europe/.
61. James Shotter, "The Big Read: Visegrad. Central Europe: Running Out of Steam," *FT*, August 27, 2018, accessed on September 13, 2018, https://www.ft.com/content/21c2d25e-a0ba-11e8-85da-eeb7a9ce36e4.
62. "Eastern European Countries 'Will Veto Any Brexit Deal That Diminishes Rights of Their Citizens Who Live and Work in UK,'" *Independent*, September 18, 2016, accessed on September 13, 2018, https://www.independent.co.uk/news/world/europe/brexit-eastern-european-countries-citizens-rights-robert-fico-slovakia-czech-republic-hungary-poland-a7314306.html .
63. DW, "Eastern European Leaders Get Tough on Migration Plans," September 24, 2020, https://www.dw.com/en/eu-migration-policy-eastern-european-leaders-get-tough-on-new-plans/a-55040039.
64. Euractiv, "Eastern Europe Could Pay to Avoid Taking in Refugees," June 28, 2018, accessed on September 13, 2018, https://www.euractiv.com/section/justice-home-affairs/news/eastern-europe-could-pay-to-avoid-taking-in-refugees/.
65. "East vs West: The New Battle for Europe," *Spectator*, January 27, 2018, accessed September 13, 2018, https://www.spectator.co.uk/2018/01/the-fight-for-europe-is-now-between-east-and-west/.
66. EFE, "Eastern Europe's Visegrad Four Nations Will Skip EC's Migration Mini-Summit," June 21, 2018, accessed September 13, 2018, https://www.efe.com/efe/english/world/eastern-europe-s-visegrad-four-nations-will-skip-ec-migration-mini-summit/50000262-3657447.
67. Al Jazeera, "Poland: Eastern Europe Remains Firm on Anti-Migrant Stance," June 26, 2018, accessed on September 13, 2018, https://www.aljazeera.com/news/2018/06/poland-eastern-europe-remains-firm-anti-migrant-stance-180626141653561.html.
68. "Visegrad Group Boycotts EU Mini-Summit on Migration," June 21, 2018, accessed September 13, 2018, http://www.euronews.com/2018/06/21/visegrad-group-boycotts-eu-mini-summit-on-migration.
69. "Central Europeans to Boycott Migration Summit They Weren't Invited To," *Politico*, June 21, 2018, accessed September 13, 2018, https://www.politico.eu/article/viktor-orban-hungary-poland-central-europeans-to-boycott-migration-summit-they-werent-invited-to/.
70. James Politi, "Italy Stand-Off Looms as Migrants Left Stranded at Sea," *FT*, June 24, 2018, accessed September 13, 2018, https://www.ft.com/content/df5d3962-7798-11e8-bc55-50daf11b720d.
71. "Visegrad 4 Cools on Europe, and Each Other: Central Europe's Unity Is Cracking," Politico, October 31, 2017, updated November 8, 2017, accessed on September 13, 2018, https://www.politico.eu/article/visegrad-4-cools-on-europe-and-each-other/).
72. Denis MacShane, "Angela Merkel Should Become the President of the European Commission," *Independent*, September 3, 2018, accessed on September 13, 2018, https://www.independent.co.uk/voices/angela-merkel-president-european-union-commission-brexit-a8520301.html.

73. Using Reuters: "Italy, Germany Clash as Migration Cuts to the Core of EU Unity," *Globe and Mail*, June 21, 2018, accessed September 13, 2018, https://www.the globeandmail.com/world/article-italy-germany-clash-as-migration-cuts-to-the -core-of-eu-unity/.

74. "Central European Leaders Reject EU Migration Rules," *Toronto Star*, March 28, 2017, accessed on September 13, 2018, https://www.thestar.com/news/world /2017/03/28/central-european-leaders-reject-eu-migration-rules.html.

75. See "In Eastern Europe, Populism Lives, Widening a Split in the E.U.," November 28, 2017, accessed on September 13, 2018, https://www.nytimes.com/2017/11 /28/world/europe/populism-eastern-europe.html.

76. CNN, "A Hungarian-Italian Bromance Could Become Europe's Trojan Horse," accessed on September 13, 2018, https://edition.cnn.com/2018/09/01/europe /orban-salvini-european-elections-analysis-intl/index.html. Space prevents consideration of the extent to which and, then, why Canadian and US terminology on the Visegrad region might have varied.

77. Kalmar, 111, referencing Applebaum, and Krastev and Holmes.

78. *Programme of the Czech Presidency of the Visegrad Group 2023/2024*, 16–17, https://www.visegradgroup.eu/documents/presidency-programs/v4-program -20232024.

79. "Talk of Unity, but Little Progress at EU Mini-Summit on Migration," RFE/RL, June 24, 2018, accessed on September 13, 2018, https://www.rferl.org/a/eu -germany-italy-immigration-crisis-summit/29316852.html .

80. "The Observer View on Migrants Dying because Europe Is Pandering to Populism," June 17, 2018, accessed September 13, 2018, https://www.theguardian.com /commentisfree/2018/jun/17/observer-view-europe-migration-policy-populism -rescue-ship-aquarius.

81. Kazharski, 771.

82. Interviewed in Aneta Zachová, "Czech FM: Visegrad Countries Will Continue to Promote EU Enlargement," January 21, 2020, Euractiv (EURACTIV.cz), https:// www.euractiv.com/section/enlargement/interview/czech-fm-visegrad-countries -will-continue-to-promote-eu-enlargement/.

83. "Visegrad Four Grouping Push Back on New EU Migration Plan," Reuters, September 24, 2020, https://www.reuters.com/article/us-europe-migrants-hungary -idUSKCN26F1T6.

84. E.g., in the headline "Visegrad Countries Immediately Push Back on New Migration Pact," by Eszter Zalan, EUobserver, September 25, 2020, https://euobserver .com/rule-of-law/149537.

85. "Meeting of Directors of Migration and Asylum Offices, 12–13 March 2019, Bratislava," https://www.visegradgroup.eu/article-title-190201.

86. "The Visegrad Group in Solidarity on the Protection of the EU Borders," October 11, 2021, https://www.gov.pl/web/national-defence/the-visegrad-group-in -solidarity-on-the-protection-of-the-eu-borders.

87. See Milan Nič and Vít Dostál, "Central Europe's Outlook on the EU and Foreign Policy," January 8, 2016, https://carnegieeurope.eu/strategiceurope/?fa=62423.

88. Lendvai, and Szelényi detail these plans.

8

VISEGRAD DEFENSE AND SECURITY COOPERATION

HARD AND GLOBAL?

Visegrad is ambitious. A voracious security consumer in its infancy, Visegrad matured to be a provider, both in NATO and in the EU, then a pioneering security bridge between the two organizations. Additionally, Visegrad's activism has sought to be pan-European, especially toward its eastern and southern flanks, and global. For all of its attributes and some impressive achievements, even with correctives offered to some of the misperceptions circulating about Visegrad, on security and worldwide matters the Group has become unnecessarily, and unsuccessfully, overambitious, even as its supporters continued to suggest possibilities.[1]

This chapter steps away from Visegrad's engagement inside the European Union, which remains the Group's primary focus and forum. Attention here shifts instead to Visegrad's internal efforts at military and defense cooperation, and its self-projection and diplomatic activities beyond the union. The chapter first establishes the ironies of Visegrad's military-security efforts that, even with substantial backing, never materialized—ironic because Visegrad nevertheless generated an unexpected military-security contribution to both the EU and NATO and then developed unique linkages. Thereafter, Ukraine's place in Visegrad's thinking along with related opportunities and challenges are assessed. The argument is that Visegrad initially was an important advocate for Ukrainian interests in the Euro-Atlantic community and also a role model for Ukrainian internal and external policy. However, as pressures increased on Ukraine from Russia even before the 2022 invasion, that role model relationship evaporated, and even commonalities among positions within Visegrad ceased. One of Visegrad's most visible and significant external policy arenas became counterproductive.

A final section identifies how Visegrad has sought to project itself beyond the Euro-Atlantic region and how those attempts show that lack of necessity to do so, and indeed significant constraints on them. For its many other achievements, as well as some global glimmers, Visegrad's worldwide ambitions have proven unnecessary and too grand.

VISEGRAD AND MILITARY COOPERATION

No one expected, let alone demanded, military cooperation among the Visegrad countries. In the early 1990s, as chapter 2 determined, Visegrad strove *not* to project any sense of being a multilateral military formation, even to the extent of eschewing multilateral defense cooperation and sticking to bilateral forms. Contemporary observers were dismissive of Visegrad's early military cooperation efforts as both "half-hearted" and "with no security commitments" made to each other.[2]

That absence makes sense. Visegrad sought to balance two challenges that face any political leadership. The first concerns the pooling of defense provision and production, that is, of personnel and expertise, and the facilities and economy of building weapons. Any state considers it a challenge, on the one hand, to retain sovereignty and self-reliance and, on the other hand, pool such capabilities regionally. Visegrad's foremost security ambitions were always toward and then within NATO, rather than exclusively among its member countries. Alliance membership meant redirection of training and of production and procurement to NATO standards—all further impediments to regional defense programs.

That Visegrad would embark on serious military cooperation and defense production is the anomaly rather than the expectation. However, retrospectively, some Visegrad statements ambitiously claim military cooperation, providing markers against which to judge its ultimate achievements (and disappointments). That these countries should cooperate made sense from the early post-communist period. A Czech defense minister summarized in 1993 the situation of the Four: "We inherited similar armies, command structures, and almost identical military technology and equipment from the Warsaw Pact, and we are struggling with almost identical problems. For this reason, we frequently have to exchange our experiences and coordinate our steps."[3] The Visegrad web page containing links to defense declarations begins: "Since the very beginning of the Visegrad Group, the efforts to develop and strengthen regional cooperation in the military and defence context has been in the heart of it." Objective bases for doing so were apparent, but the record in the early 1990s for such makes this comment appear as retrospective wishful thinking. The Visegrad website section later says that Visegrad defense cooperation took "a new direction in recent years."[4] Why and when?

By the early 2010s onward, Visegrad had repeatedly attempted to combine procurement and modernization of major weapons systems and to undertake joint military education and training. Unlike for trade liberalization—which became the formal, multilateral Central European Free Trade Agreement,[5] and for which some argument exists that the EU wanted such cooperation[6]— external interlocutors presented no expectation for collective military activities. Ironically, Visegrad downplays the military coordination that occurred among the three and often in the name of Visegrad after the Czech Republic, Hungary, and Poland knew in 1997 that accession would occur. Not only did the three military chiefs of staff meet in January 1998 and agree to establish a joint working group for common arms procurement; the Czech chief of staff even said that six related working groups had already been created.[7]

NATO accession in 1999 and membership thereafter, however, did not increase military cooperation among Visegrad states, even if some regional observers suggested that accession allowed the Group "to base further military cooperation on the structures of the Alliance."[8] Others also reasonably expected that "in the process of adjusting to the requirements of alliance membership, [they] will confront the issue of joint weapons acquisition."[9]

Instead, Visegrad admits that once its members all entered NATO by 2004, the "intensity of the V4 cooperation in the area of defence *decreased*."[10] That a Visegrad document acknowledges such speaks to the Group's realism. Why, after having secured admission to potentially history's most successful military, should the Four seek a military formation among just themselves within that far larger entity? And indeed in its early inclusion in Euro-Atlantic institutions, Visegrad in its own records affirms that its countries' "focus shifted to joint projects and activities in the framework of NATO and the EU."[11] The foremost aims were not to cooperate militarily, and certainly not exclusively, among themselves.

In addition, V4 statements reiterate that the Group's countries' Euro-Atlantic membership afforded historically "unprecedented security."[12] Finally, Central Europe's protracted historical experience of unsuccessful alliances made within the region or outside the region but against some of its members could be put to rest and instead replaced by genuine multilateralism and real collective security.

Visegrad military cooperation, both before and after EU-NATO accession, was all the more unlikely because of the mismatch of assets among its members. Poland's military capacity, personnel, spending, and arguably also volition toward using its military instruments have exceeded those of the other three Visegrad states combined. It also uniquely possesses a navy. In defense production Poland alone is considered to have a sufficient national base.[13] And in policy, Poland was an active and influential security player, being a war-fighting Anglo-American coalition partner in Iraq, administering territory thereafter. Influential regional practitioner-analyst Valášek, who did not address Visegrad specifically, counseled that even Poland might share similar strategic cultures with some (and not even all) of its immediate post-communist neighbors: "The trouble with big countries is that they do not always take smaller partners seriously."[14]

When the V4 has cooperated militarily, in its combined Battlegroup, which is elaborated below, Poland has been the primary contributor, been the lead country, and headquartered the formation in its southwestern city of Kraków. Making such differences even more notable among the Four, the other three Visegrad states joined in separate military cooperation from June 2010 as the Central European Defence Cooperation (CEDC)—including the similarly smaller states of Austria, Slovenia, and Croatia—with Poland having only observer status.[15] The CEDC involves training and capability development, to the extent that within two years the initiatives were worthy of comparison to established ones like the Nordic Defence Cooperation (and Nordic cooperation members have sometime referred to Visegrad as a lesson provider).[16] The CEDC also claimed that it was, with seven members, the largest Central European forum for security and defense matters,[17] thus a potential rival to Visegrad. Some argued that that was preferable to the "more institutionalized, less flexible frameworks" of V4 defense cooperation,[18] a seeming compliment that might have aggrandized Visegrad security cooperation at the time.[19] But rather than CEDC becoming a competitor to Visegrad, the V4 engaged with it in Visegrad's "+" format.[20]

In terms of additional Visegrad security name-recognition, when the leading security think tank RAND analyzed NATO's northern security capacities, including naturally Nordic cooperation,[21] its Euler diagram also included Visegrad, the only such named group to straddle the EU and NATO.[22]

Even so, the region's historically unprecedented security nevertheless had Visegrad determined to show that NATO-EU accession would not end its own cooperation and that it would create a new role from itself with the double accession. A kernel of military-security cooperation was created—but not used—in the 2004 Kroměříž Declaration. In addition to what chapter 5 determined about Visegrad's activism in the EU accession, in security matters the Group also pledged "active participation in the development of the ESDP [European Security and Defence Policy], as a contribution to the strengthening of relations across the EU and NATO and deepening of substantive dialogue between both organisations."[23]

Despite such declarations, it did not pursue this policy immediately (and security cooperation among member states decreased after EU accession). That was partly because, unlike with the EU, in which Visegrad fought and won several struggles, the Group found no cause to oppose NATO policies, let alone to introduce alternatives. Nevertheless, the seed of military cooperation was present among Visegrad, and it could germinate with a combination of regional initiative and Alliance encouragement. As part of NATO's new eastern flank, Visegrad was deeply sensitive to developments to its east. And a NATO drive to increase its own contributions, yet economically, through "smart defence," together moved Visegrad forward. Costs savings were important to Visegrad states, even before NATO nudged its members into "smart defence."[24] Russian aggression against Ukraine in 2014 awoke NATO to the need for new cooperation, and the inarguable imperative of geographic proximity refocused Visegrad and Baltic activism between the member countries and within NATO.

But while Visegrad stood up to potential and actual EU policies both before and after accession, demonstrating its influence, finding the same of Visegrad in NATO is harder. The premise of NATO membership is surely that states within NATO can work with each other, collectively. And NATO outreach throughout the 1990s, as in the North Atlantic Cooperation Council and Partnership for Peace and combined peacekeeping missions especially in the Balkans, increased information exchanges and expanded interoperability. Consequently, an expectation of, say, distinct Iberian military cooperation within NATO never arose.[25] And Central European experts pointedly remind of other military-cooperation efforts in Western Europe, as between France and Germany, who established a joint brigade but never employed it, or of initiatives that amounted to "howlers," delayed by years and overbudget when not collapsing entirely.[26] Visegrad ostensibly wanted to avoid failures and to be a constructive security partner. That road was inauspicious; Visegrad tried but flopped on outwardly basic cooperation, including pilot training and military education and defense procurement.

Pilot Training and Military Education

An instance of cooperation, despite the official history noted above, were the plans advanced already in 2004 for a Visegrad joint pilot training program. That could have made remarkable sense, least with the integration of Slovakia at that time also in NATO. Nevertheless, Visegrad countries opted for alternative aircraft acquisition. The Czech Republic and Hungary had decided on Swedish Jas-39 Gripen fighters; Poland had contemplated buying up to 60 Czech-made training jets but ultimately purchased American F-16s.[27] Slovakia still flew Soviet-era MiG-29s, and even regional analysts were saying that that country lacked an air force.[28] Far from keeping and modernizing its MiG-29s, Hungary sought to swap them back to Russia in exchange for Russian military helicopters and was buying the Swedish Gripens.[29] Even more fighter-aircraft diversity among Visegrad states arose when Poland agreed to buy in September 2022 South Korean FA-50s to replace those same MiG-29s.

Despite possession of different aircraft among Visegrad militaries, the Czechs noted at a 2005 V4 defense ministers meeting the lack of economic sense in training Visegrad pilots separately and were optimistic that the four would use a common training facility at Dęblin, Poland.[30] In March 2005 V4 defence ministers reiterated the idea, with the Czech minister offering to supply trainer jets, a worthy proposal in view of international recognition for its trainer aircraft. At times, the Czech government even made use of their L-159 training jets a condition.[31] Outsiders watched these developments; Chinese media wrote that "Visegrad Group countries agree to promote defense cooperation."[32] Still, this took time, and in 2010 Visegrad states had finally established joint pilot training. The Group announced its virtues: "We naturally want to achieve savings in logistics to make the training as much efficient as possible and at the same time to reduce its costs."[33] The initiative, however, has not gone further. Instead, attention then went to joint training for helicopter pilots, a measure in that instance to build on a Czech facility.[34] The Central European Policy Institute (CEPI) report listed the helicopter-pilot training not only as one that would build on existing facilities, and thus presumably would be easy to achieve, but also as a Tier 1 smart defense project in NATO.[35] So much logic, support, and rationale; so little outcome.

Another logical area for military cooperation included general defense education. This easiest part has not happened, as a regional assessment wrote in 2019: "Real cooperation between V4 military academies is non-existent."[36] Nevertheless, the V4's 2020 "Long Term Vision" for defense pledged as a priority the improvement of combined military education but while also promising to "devote more attention" to joint education and language training, and then with reference to e-learning.[37] The Slovak presidency program for 2022–23 presented amid Russia's invasion of Ukraine, contained proposals for joint training and information sharing but none pertaining to Visegrad military education.[38] The logic of such cooperation exists, as does a stated historical intention, if most stated by Czechs. Czech defense minister Jaroslav Tvrdík said in 2001, "Since the beginning [of V4 cooperation] there has been an effort to somehow coordinate the arming of the Visegrad Group countries."[39] And, ten years later, the 2011–12 Czech Visegrad presidency proposed multinational military capacity building, especially for air force capacities.[40] Doing so could be low cost and high value but remains underutilized, even and perhaps especially in the face of real military need. Defense equipment modernization and procurement share similar logic and similarly limited outcomes.

Defense Modernization and Procurement:
The Mi-24, the T-72, and Radar

Military and weapons cooperation among the four specifically—that is, with all of and only with the Four rather than in combination of some of V4 with other partners—has been limited. This section considers Visegrad military production first as an idea, then its practice in three areas.

In short, as an idea, Visegrad's approach remains declaratory—despite rhetoric otherwise. The Polish presidency program for 2020–21 promised "Pragmatic V4 consultations to *revitalise cooperation* between defence industries of the V4 countries." The "revitalise" might be a telling word—revitalization, however, of what? The same presidency program then references past "efforts to intensify military and technical collaboration envisaged in the memorandum of Polish, Czech, Slovak and Hungarian defence ministers of 26 January 2009."[41] That document appears neither available nor referenced in succeeding documents.

Specific efforts at collaborative defense production occurred in three areas. The first intended V4 cooperation was on military aircraft, with proposals that never flew. As noted, the Four pursued different acquisition plans, and even when both Prague and Budapest planned for the Swedish-designed Gripen, it neither coordinated with other members nor consulted within the Group.[42]

The V4 did, however, make declarations regarding the Mi-24 helicopter, codenamed Hind by NATO—a Soviet design unveiled in 1966 and still in service in Visegrad militaries. The four countries agreed in 2002 that they would all benefit from the helicopter's modernization and that collectively they had approximately one hundred, making the modernization cost effective. The idea was welcomed with the mix of noting the Group's past inability to agree even on a single similar project, and its multiple advantages, including for the troop mobility the helicopters could provide in future NATO operations,[43] while also being upgraded with onboard equipment to meet Alliance standards. Slovakia's defense minister enthusiastically noted that this first such cooperation was "economically interesting, effective and purposeful."[44] This first venture remained as "lofty ambitions."[45] Even as the Czech defence minister announced the joint plan, he stated that Hungarian participation remained uncertain.[46] An additional hindrance was that the Mi-24 remained under Soviet-cum-Russian license, which may explain immediate Hungarian reticence toward the project, despite Visegrad's initial efforts. And just as it launched the idea, the Czech Visegrad program for 2003–04 also caveated this cooperation: the Mi-24's joint modernization would have "a looser, more flexible form of cooperation based on the implementation of a prototype in the national conditions of the individual countries and on mutually beneficial cooperation under bilateral agreements in sub-areas of modernization."[47]

The Four Visegrad governments signed an agreement in February 2003 to upgrade jointly 105 helicopters, resulting finally in a "Visegrad Contract" (won by Britain's BAE Systems).[48] Logical division of labor was even created, with each country responsible for a core element of modernization and research and development costs divided equally.[49] Yet the agreement was abandoned, and V4 governments ultimately undertook separate contracts. The Czech Republic, which was to provide the core of the V4 helicopter modernization and had been the project's leading political advocate, ultimately signed a unilateral agreement with American Bell for two types of military helicopters in 2019.[50] The collapse had wider political-military significance, with the jointly modernized helicopter having been intended for use in combined forces, and internationally.[51]

Visegrad again experienced initial high expectations with the T-72 main battle tank, the second of the three areas of military production. Commonplace across Warsaw Pact militaries and produced in satellite states under Soviet license, the T-72 was neither defunct nor incompatible with NATO. Rather, Poland's prime minister pronounced as late as 2019 that this tank, even with his country in NATO, would make the Polish army "really be better equipped and better prepared for the defence of our territory."[52] And those tanks would be desperately wanted by Ukraine to repel the Russian invasion after February 2022. Whatever military virtues the revamped Soviet T-72 had, Visegrad countries again could not advance common plans or even individual commitments: the Czech Republic, for example, undertook less than one-tenth of the planned upgrades, and each government defaulted to separate national arrangements, despite the encouragement, and then lamentations, of regional analysts and practitioners.[53]

Despite those failures, Visegrad continued its experimentation, including in 2013 on a third asset: mobile 3D radar. In June 2014 Visegrad agreed to develop cross-regional defence production, a key part of which would be that radar system. A memorandum of understanding was even completed across regional defense industry producers. Despite these initial successes, ultimately all four Visegrad countries "were blaming each other for favoring national interests over the success of the project."[54] Industry experts contended that the four countries could neither consume enough of the radars themselves to justify investment, nor compete in a saturated international market to make the initiative economically viable.[55] Within weeks, however, Poland decided to withdraw, impairing the capacity of the three smaller countries to continue the project.[56] Some consideration was given to the other three countries continuing to collaborate, but a Czech decision, in September 2014, again ended collaborative prospects, when Prague decided on international tenders.[57] Slovakia became the last to leave the arrangement when, in March 2021, it signed a bilateral agreement with Israel to purchase its own 3D radar.

With none of these military initiatives resulting in common programs, alternatives were also occasionally mentioned. In pronouncing a "New

Opening" in V4 defense cooperation in 2014, V4 prime ministers mentioned none of the above attempts but continued with the ideal of "mutually beneficial industrial cooperation," now proposing universal tracked platforms or wheeled armored personnel carriers.[58] From plans to modernize together key military hardware and acquire others, Visegrad reduced defense cooperation to the most mundane: exchanging experience on military human resources management. This was pronounced with fanfare that explained that working sessions of senior officials and experts had been organized among the four defense ministries "to exchange experience on current human resources by respective countries."[59] Rather than being innovative, this was the continuation of consultations begun in 1997.[60]

Important as it may be, human resource management itself does not produce common training or armaments production or purchasing. Visegrad reasserted its ambition with its 2020 "Long Term Vision," which stated, "Joint procurement will stay high on the V4 agenda." Being on the agenda is itself not action, and Visegrad recognized multiple obstacles, ranging from technical to political, economic, legal, and organizational.[61] A working group was created for discussions on surface air defense. A four-day meeting produced "fruitful discussions" and agreement on "the detailed structure" and each country's tasks for an analytical study to be delivered at a following workshop.[62]

In 2021 a realistic note on joint procurement was announced, taking forward a proposal from 2019. On January 21, 2021, the four signed a letter of intent to buy small arms munitions through NATO's Support and Procurement Agency. The Czech defense minister summarized in 2019 Visegrad's limited history in this area, despite declarative desires: "We refrained from exaggerated ambitions and plans. We want to start with something real, and that is the joint purchase of ammunition."[63]

Thus, Visegrad recognizes that its potential in defense matters "has not been fully used."[64] Further consultations in 2022 resulted in the signing of four-way pledges to develop military cooperation, including procurement,[65] and the Czech presidency for 2023–24 pledged to continue to work toward that.[66] Vít Stříteský summarized that the Visegrad countries have several prerequisites for successful defense cooperation and production, but "a rich experience with failures of common defence projects,"[67] a view likely to hold in the aftermath of Russia's full-scale onslaught against Ukraine.

Despite the limitations in internal Visegrad defense cooperation and weapons production, the Group became a successful military actor in both the EU and NATO, then between them. Visegrad's intrinsic Euro-Atlantic nature explains why this important area succeeded where others, and seemingly easy ones, failed.

INCREASING VISEGRAD MILITARY COOPERATION
AND FORGING IDENTITY IN NATO AND THE EU

As chapter 6 contended, Visegrad changed EU policies. As stated earlier, it need not have engaged in large security matters either in NATO, nor tried to resist or change policies there, nor tried to interfere or innovate between NATO and the EU. Yet it has done so. The principal means of determining that is to identity what its partners have said and to identity comparisons for those contributions.

Despite limits to defense cooperation before 1999 and 2004, and then with little even by Visegrad's admission in the years that followed, what prompted change? Four processes converged to create momentum for military-security cooperation.

First, Visegrad had both a rhetorical and functional basis for security cooperation, even if such went unused. Visegrad had from its outset pledged to make its region more secure, and had established, as in every other sector, continuous working relations between defense ministries and military personnel. Indeed, in many cases a holdover of fraternal experience from the era of the Warsaw Pact also aided this process after 1989.[68]

Second, all the Visegrad states had shared experience, if unevenly, in NATO outreach programs, particularly in the North Atlantic Cooperation Council and Partnership for Peace,[69] and then in NATO-led operations in the Balkans and Afghanistan. PfP, despite Visegrad reservations that it was a policy for postponing NATO membership, already within its first months conducted its inaugural exercise with six former Warsaw Pact and six NATO militaries (and Ukraine), and in Poland.[70] Such cooperation therefore was not hypothetical, or even functionally only bilaterally between Visegrad counties themselves or with Western partners, but enjoyed on-the-ground, multilateral experience from which to draw. These two reasons already assist to explain the 2011 Visegrad decision to create its combined EU Battlegroup, albeit one that would, even when assembled, only be on standby in 2016.

Third, NATO officials and certain member states frequently mentioned burden sharing or that some Alliance members persistently underspent on defense. Central European states knew that they had been financial under-payers, even if they had consciously and perhaps in a compensatory way given key assets to NATO and other missions. Slovak premier Robert Fico in 2012 summarized regional sentiment: "We have never seen NATO as just a strong 'umbrella' under which we can hide. We are ready to share the burden."[71] It may also have been that the noncontributions of Visegrad states to NATO's military operation in Libya the year before prompted calls for greater involvement, such as Fico's. Outside observers wrote that the "Visegrad damaged themselves within the Alliance" and that the Group would risk diminished political relevance.[72] In 2011 the Visegrad states not only appeared as bystanders but even free riders, while pressures mounted for all NATO members to increase their contributions.

A fourth reason came from NATO. At the 2012 Chicago NATO Summit, Secretary General Anders Fogh Rasmussen proposed the concept of "smart defence." That idea came in response to the growing pressures on member-state budget austerity and the continuing lack of fulfilment of defense-spending expectations and to operational challenges within the Alliance and what the Alliance, even before the multiple crises that would hit Ukraine from 2014, deemed to be an increasingly uncertain security environment.[73]

This chronology already provides an important corrective against some later assertions that Visegrad became more engaged in military matters because of Russia's 2014 aggression against Ukraine. Accurate instead is that "the Ukraine/Crimea Crisis is an important context but not a primary cause" of Visegrad's military cooperation.[74]

From these impetuses, Visegrad quickly established a more visible role and identity in NATO. In 2013 Rasmussen acknowledged to the Polish military that its "multinational approach," including specifically through Visegrad, was "already helping us to fill some of our serious capability shortfalls," and in both the EU and NATO.[75]

In 2014 Rasmussen commended Visegrad's regional defense cooperation as a model for the Alliance. First noting problems among NATO allies concerning "gaps in our military capabilities," he reiterated his call for "smart defence" projects and "closer regional cooperation" in the Alliance, that is, that groups within NATO could and should do so. The NATO chief said of the Group's emerging new efforts, "The Visegrad countries continue to demonstrate that this is a pragmatic way to build greater security together."[76]

And while the Baltic states have had common military training and activities since 1994 (and with such conveniently tagged as, e.g., the Baltic peacekeeping battalion, BALTBAT, and with its own emblems), even cited as a role model for Visegrad,[77] Visegrad still has the most recognized military identity in the Alliance. When the Baltic states and Poland, sharing borders with Russia, felt threatened by Moscow's March 2014 annexation of Crimea and its support for insurgencies in eastern Ukraine, the V4 pledged forces for deployment there. That month, the V4 reconvened in Visegrád and issued its detailed "Long Term Vision of the Visegrad Countries on Deeping Their Defence Cooperation." It called for the EU and NATO to work better together and defined their own role, an expressly regional one, in urgently helping to do so: "It is crucial for all European allies and EU member states to spend their defence budgets more efficiently and strengthen their defence cooperation as much as possible. Regional cooperation has an added value and an important contribution to make. Recognising this, we set the objective to strengthen European and transatlantic capabilities by deepening our defence cooperation, modernizing our armed forces and better using our available resources."[78]

The V4 Joint Logistics Support Group Headquarters was established, and each of the four countries rotated forces in and out of the Baltic area. Other NATO allies, to be sure, made deployments. Nevertheless, NATO's Warsaw Summit Communiqué of 2016 offered commendations for the V4, welcoming "the decision of the Visegrad Group to provide rotational presence in the Baltic states in 2017 to conduct exercises in support of Allied activities."[79] In the communiqué's 139 paragraphs, Visegrad was the only grouping within NATO to receive mention.

The V4 continued to project group distinctiveness in NATO, one observed far afield. Visegrad prime ministers and defense ministers convened at a military base in Poland in 2019 to mark the twentieth anniversary of accession to NATO (and occasionally noting that Slovakia joined separately five years later, although that added the symmetry of a fifteenth anniversary of accession). This was not a celebration with or of other post-communist states that joined the Alliance.[80] That occasion was in turn noted by international media; China's news agency called the Group a "cultural and political alliance" to advance its "military, cultural, economic and energy cooperation."[81]

To be sure, skepticism remained regarding Visegrad's military capacity, even after its Battlegroup was formed. That seemed to miss the point, and effort, of creating and maintaining it. And it found immediate purpose in deployment under that name to the Baltic in 2017, though in stages where each nation sent forces separately. The recognition received substantiates Visegrad's claim in 2020 in its revised "Long Term Vision for Defence" that the Group continues to "enhance its footprint" in both NATO and the EU, while also "strengthen[ing] the cohesion of the Alliance and the Union."[82] The Group produced distinctive Visegrad badges for its combined unit, worn below the national emblem of each country.

Certainly, V4 chiefs of defense suggested that NATO and their EU Battle Group partake in the "high visibility exercise" of Trident Juncture 2015. They noted that no official relationship then existed between the EU and NATO (and they stressed also that they observed existing frameworks) and that their formation could partake in Alliance exercises that could create greater cooperation with the EU.[83]

V4 military leaders continue such claims and encourage, even admonish, the EU and NATO to work in step. Visegrad defence ministers in 2018, for example, "welcome[d] the significant results of deepening NATO-EU cooperation," which they had supported, urged "sustaining this momentum," and sought still more between the two organizations.[84] In 2022 Visegrad defense ministers said that EU defense initiatives "must be consistent and complementary to NATO activities" and that Visegrad wanted military capabilities to be able to "serve both organizations."[85]

The idea of shifting V4 defense cooperation forward gained enough momentum to be the subject of review and recommendations by a high-level civilian and military panel of quadrilateral experts in the 2012 program of "Defence Austerity: A New Paradigm for Defence and Security Cooperation in the Visegrad Region."[86]

In October 2013 V4 leaders pledged increased military cooperation to improve the ability of both the EU and NATO to respond to security challenges.[87] NATO recognized these efforts. The Alliance's Secretary General Rasmussen commended Hungarian prime minister Viktor Orbán in 2013: "You are also making the most of your cooperation with your neighbours in the Visegrad group. . . . Such cooperation benefits NATO, and it benefits Europe.[88] This sentiment was reiterated by, for example, NATO deputy secretary general ambassador Alexander Vershbow in 2016: "And I want to congratulate you, for example, on the role you play as part of the Visegrad 4 Group. NATO knows as well as any organisation that we are all stronger when we work together. In this regard, I am pleased by the news that the Visegrad-4 will contribute a military unit to NATO's forward presence in the Baltic States."[89] As EU military-security initiatives have developed, Visegrad leaders restated that "we reaffirm our support for strengthening EU Common Security and Defence Policy in full complementarity with NATO."[90]

A further measure of defense cooperation is what Visegrad sets itself, such as that "the V4 Training and Exercise Strategy was endorsed to increase interoperability among the V4 countries' armed forces and thus visibly contributing to NATO's robust exercise program."[91] Visegrad's military efforts for and in NATO have never been to the exclusion of the EU but instead fashioned expressly as a means to bond the two formations, including through its creation of the Visegrad Battlegroup.

In 2021 the V4 prime ministers called on the EU to increase its own military capacity, but also "wherever possible complementing NATO," and said that they "looked forward to working on a new, ambitious EU-NATO Declaration . . . to reinvigorate this strategic partnership and improve both organisations' ability to respond jointly to threats and challenges."[92] The Group's position and commitment to enhancing EU-NATO military cooperation are unambiguous.

The Visegrad Battlegroup and Bridging Security across NATO and the EU

Visegrad's achievement in military-security matters are foremost its Battlegroup and in building security connections between the EU and NATO. Evidence comes from a variety of practitioners and observers.

Some skepticism has been noted, but others are positive to the point of calling for more military integration to follow.[93] Leading regional practitioner-analysts also suggest that combined military formations would enhance trust between Slovaks and Hungarians,[94] even and as those tensions could and do reemerge.

Visegrad experts suggested that the Group could "become an exemplar" in the EU and NATO of regional security initiatives.[95] The European Commission began to recognize Visegrad's military bridging role. In a factually erroneous summary, the body nevertheless correctly observed of Visegrad governments that they "share a strong Transatlantic link, with all of them welcoming the presence of the NATO's forces in their territories." It further noted that under the then Czech Visegrad presidency, "the four countries continued to build the permanent V4 military structure."[96]

V4 work on security remains open and ongoing, as the 2021–22 Polish presidency program stated: "Security cooperation will be crucial for V4. This cooperation will concern the development of a coherent V4 position on key defence policy issues discussed in the NATO and EU."[97]

Despite the slowness of Visegrad's military cooperation and production, the Group also became a model for others. From 2014 Visegrad had committed to annual joint military exercises, and the establishment by 2016 of the Visegrad Battlegroup,[98] a force consisting of 3,900 troops. Longtime NATO analyst Michael O'Hanlon wrote, "Internal NATO dialogues intended to foster greater defence collaboration and efficiency among key subgroups of states . . . should be unapologetically continued"; Visegrad was named as the example.[99] Visegrad defense cooperation is an activity in itself. But the Group outrightly wants that that cooperation also serve to raise the V4's profile.[100] And Visegrad has achieved a profile, and tangibly much more, in NATO.

All V4's security preparations, however, were tested with Ukraine—when in 2013 and 2014 that country endured domestic political turmoil and violence, followed by the territorial amputation of Crimea by Russia and open conflict in its southeastern region of Donbas.

UKRAINE

The multiple crises in and concerning Ukraine from 2013 rocketed the country to the top of European security concerns—although not sufficiently, considering that even larger-scale Russian aggression in 2022 has been at least partly explained by the timidity of Western responses then. The loss of Crimea to the Russian Federation, after a hastily organized if not entirely farcical "referendum" and "hybrid warfare" remained unresolved a decade later. At best, high-level negotiating formats remained and international monitors under the fifty-seven-state Organization for Security and Co-operation in Europe (OSCE) could at least track illicit supplies weapons and outbreaks of violence. The biggest powers in the Euro-Atlantic arena could not change these dynamics. That is the scenario into which Visegrad both ventured and was called upon.

Ukraine expected much of Visegrad in its times of troubles. We already saw that the V4 had anointed itself with a special, even directing role of the EU's EaP and that Ukraine, by virtue of its geographic position and size and population, was the centerpiece.

Long before the Ukraine crisis of 2013+, Visegrad devoted attention within itself, and then to the EU and NATO, about drawing Ukraine closer to Euro-Atlantic institutions. The Czech presidency in 2003–04 specifically pledged to assist Ukraine's implementation of the NATO-Ukraine Action Plan and to strength Ukraine's relations with the transatlantic community.[101]

Visegrad's own relations with Ukraine are assessed later; attention here is on how Visegrad raised relations within the EU toward Ukraine. Part of that dynamic is that Ukrainian governments—irrespective of whether they were, simply put, Moscow- or Western-oriented—had strong interests in Visegrad, as a means for that country also to increase its profile positively in the West.

Ukraine, however, has become a case of both misplaced expectations imposed on Visegrad and ultimately an instance of Visegrad overreach. Before the 2009 gas crisis, in which Russia pressured Ukraine (and parts of Europe) by curtailing gas supplies, let alone Russian annexation of Crimea and war in Donbas since 2014, the Slovak V4 presidency in 2006–07 declared that it would "endeavour to coordinate the activities of V4 countries with regard to support for bringing Ukraine closer to the EU and NATO."[102] Ukraine's defense minister was included in some V4 defense minister meetings, and Ukraine has been the only non-V4 country mentioned in the Slovak presidency's plans for defense cooperation. A stated aim was "organising discussions on a joint approach towards supporting Ukraine's NATO accession process."[103] In April 2008, V4 defense and foreign ministers declared their support for Ukrainian membership in NATO and the EU. This was a deeply contentious matter, one that effectively split NATO in view of the muddled declaration the Alliance made at its Bucharest Summit in 2008. NATO, on the one hand, proclaimed that Ukraine and Georgia would become members but, on the other, made clear that the two countries had a long and difficult path to that end. This ambiguous statement may well have both alarmed and emboldened Moscow to attack Georgia later that year. After all, NATO's declaration told Moscow that the countries would enter the Alliance but gave both time and means to derail that process. The year 2008 marked a watershed in European security, one in which the V4 took a very clear position and one which likely added to security dilemmas for Europe.

In addition to what we saw of the Polish V4 presidency's commitment to raising EU's attention to the ENP, it also pledged "greater engagement of V4 in the negotiations on an enhanced cooperation agreement between the EU and Ukraine." Not satisfied to assert only that aim, the presidency program continued,

> Poland will seek greater V4 commitment to the intensification of talks on a new, enhanced EU-Ukraine agreement, so that it can be given a partnership association character, offering the perspective of EU membership for Ukraine and qualitatively new institutional cooperation of the EU with Ukraine. The Polish Presidency will also promote a strong V4 support for the conclusion of a Free Trade Agreement between the EU and Ukraine, which will be a crucial component of the new EU-Ukraine agreement.[104]

Ukrainian president Viktor Yanukovych was supportive of and supported by Moscow. Nevertheless, he held public discussions in Poland in 2013 with all four of his Visegrad presidential counterparts about accepting EU association status for Ukraine and had pledged to the V4 that he would sign the Association Agreement and Deep and Comprehensive Free Trade Agreement (DCFTA) with the EU.[105] It was his sudden refusal, almost certainly made under pressure and incentivization from Moscow, to sign those agreements, that prompted in November 2013 what became in Kyiv the Maidan, or the Revolution of Dignity, which unseated him.

Irrespective of 2014 and Russia's annexation of Ukraine's Crimea and the war in eastern Ukraine, Ukraine would have continued military and other cooperation with the V4. The Ukrainian Defense Ministry refers in its annual reports to military cooperation with Visegrad.[106] After 2014 the fate of Ukraine is a principally European security issue. The V4 was profoundly ambitious to draw this large country closer to both the EU and NATO. Visegrad achieved some of that objective and contributed perhaps simultaneously to greater insecurity in Europe by heightening the competition over Ukraine, and to heightening Euro-Atlantic recognition of the imperative of paying close attention to this pivotal post-Soviet state.

In 2014 Visegrad advocated to EU officials for Ukraine's suitability to sign an Association Agreement and also, in what was likely a clever throwback to claims made after 1989, a moral right.[107] Coming out of a summit with EaP countries, the V4 declared its support for Ukraine's territorial integrity and condemned Russian threats but stopped short of named military assistance, let alone preparations. Visegrad's emphasis remained on Ukrainian preparations for and accession to the DCFTA and Association Agreement.[108]

Poland appeared to break out of Visegrad by using its Weimar Triangle cooperation with France and Germany. Initially the three countries' foreign ministers, including Poland's foreign minister Radek Sikorski, negotiated with the Ukrainian government in 2013–14.[109] After Yanukovych's departure to Russia and the increasing Russian-backed subterfuge in Ukraine, Poland also turned to the Weimar Triangle to clamor for European responses to these threats.[110] However, negotiations continued without Poland, so any argument of Polish abandonment of Visegrad became irrelevant.

After Yanukovych's hasty departure from Kyiv to Russia in February 2014, the V4 became more active in aiding the interim government that replaced him to hasten its Euro-Atlantic ties. Ukrainians' new president, Petro Poroshenko, referred to the Visegrad countries' experience of EU accession as "extremely important" for his country. A November 2014 meeting between Poroshenko and the V4 presidents agreed to "establish a new format of collaboration," including "continuous interaction on the ministerial level of foreign affairs and defence between the V4 countries and Ukraine."[111]

The Four devised a division of labor to assist Ukraine is specific areas of preparation for accession to the terms of the EU agreements. However, as Russian interference in Ukraine continued, Visegrad's utility and even its rhetorical common stance frayed. Hungary advocated for minority rights in Ukraine, made more intense by Kyiv's 2017 law echoing Russian demands for de facto federalization of the country, a position that was also but separately advocated by Russia and that provoked Kyiv's ire.

Russian-Ukraine interactions became even more hostile, when, on November 25, 2018, overtly marked Russian naval forces attacked small Ukrainian naval vessels at the Kerch Strait and took hostage two dozen Ukrainian sailors. The International Institute for Strategic Studies called the clash "a potentially serious escalation of a conflict."[112] In this newest crisis, Ukraine turned to Visegrad for additional support.[113] Three days later, on November 30, political directors of the four Visegrad foreign ministries convened with their Ukrainian counterpart, an immediacy that on the surface suggested both internal Visegrad unity and solidarity with Ukraine. And indeed Ukraine sought Visegrad's support, specifically asking it "to demand the immediate release" from Russia of its captured sailors.[114] Ukrainian media, too, expressed hope that Visegrad would advance a "consolidated political position" to help Ukraine through that crisis.[115]

Visegrad issued a statement, but its online records even omit mention of this meeting. Instead, Visegrad's website suggests the opposite of any coherent and meaningful Group denunciation: separate accounts and the absence of any collective denunciation of Russian actions. Listed instead were that the Czech Senate (only one part of the country's bicameral legislature) condemned the detention of the Ukrainian vessels. It then stated that "Poland's position on [the] Kerch Strait incident [is] in line with NATO" and that Russia breached international law.[116] A Visegrad member reiterated NATO's stand—but not Visegrad's, for none was to be had.

In early 2022, as Russian forces increasingly encamped on three sides of Ukraine, officially only for "exercises," NATO states neighboring or near Russia asked for or received deployments from other Alliance members. By contrast, Hungary's foreign minister brazenly maintained that his country needed no NATO forces and that the Hungarian military could deal with any eventuality. As the Russian onslaught against Ukraine continued, and Western countries intensified sanctions to include Russian energy, it was Hungary solely that declared that it would block EU sanctions. Not only was a Visegrad position on Ukraine impossible, but reaching consensus on actions regarding Ukraine was difficult also in the EU and NATO. As Russian forces assembled on Ukraine's borders in January 2022, Hungary's foreign minister blamed Ukraine: "I have told our EU and NATO colleagues frankly that if the Ukrainians do not back down from this policy, it will very much limit the Hungarian government's ability to provide any kind of support to Ukraine."[117] The foreign minister later explained why Hungary, unlike any other NATO country, would refuse Alliance troops in another creative phrasing, explaining counterintuitively that "we have already NATO's troops on the territory of the country," which he also said were the Hungarian armed forces and sufficient for defense.[118] That was a telling departure from the Hungarian Visegrad presidency report of 2017–18, which (in a new bullet-pointed format that used abbreviated language) promised "further deepening defence cooperation; joint military exercises" in their region.[119]

With the Russian invasion underway by only days, on February 28, 2022, the editorship of the region's prominent *Visegrad Insight* wrote that Hungary "was acting as an anti-Ukrainian agent inside the EU and NATO."[120] Visegrad, under a Hungarian presidency, did manage a joint communiqué, on March 8, 2022. In that the Group pledged assistance to Ukrainian refugees, complementing bilateral initiatives, thereby indirectly noting the enormous differences in national responses, with "a joint act of tangible solidarity," which principally meant applications to the IVF for use of an additional €1 million to aid Ukrainians already in a V4 country.[121]

After the Russian invasion and ever-increasing displacements and deaths of Ukrainians, Hungary opposed intensified EU sanctions on Russian energy. The initial justification was that Hungary needed between €15–18 billion to rework its energy infrastructure, and Budapest put onus on the EU to offer a plan. Hungary unilaterally dispatched representatives to Moscow to secure energy. Other leaders derided Hungarian tactics; Lithuania's foreign minister said that one member held the whole Union "hostage."[122] The prospect of a common Visegrad position on Ukraine became even more remote, when Orbán pronounced in July 2022 that the EU should not side with Ukraine. Rather, Orbán said, Ukraine could not win the war and Brussels should "position itself" between Ukraine and Russia; he also pronounced that it was Russia that had security concerns.[123]

Ukraine presented Europe with a security and humanitarian crisis that exceeded even the Yugoslav wars of the 1990s. Visegrad could not be expected to deal with even a portion of that. But it also showed, especially though Hungary's pronounced self-interest, that it could not even maintain rhetorical unity. Having been a champion of Ukraine's Euro-Atlantic ambitions, Visegrad's commonality not only disintegrated but generated, once more, protest and hostility. Warsaw, Prague, and Bratislava withdrew from a two-day V4 defense ministers' meeting in Budapest; Budapest in turn cancelled the meeting. Czech defense minister Jana Černochová tweeted in Czech that she would not personally go to Budapest but added fiercely that she will always back Visegrad; "I am very sorry that cheap Russian oil is now more important to Hungarian politicians than Ukrainian blood."[124] Regional analyses warned that Hungary's posture could be the final nail in Visegrad's coffin.[125] Despite close Polish-Hungarian cooperation against the EU effort to penalize their abrogation of separations of political and judicial power, Polish statements emerged declaring that cooperation with Hungary could not continue, including most damningly from Orbán's long-standing Polish ally Jarosław Kaczyński, and advocacy emerged for a V4 without Hungary to be replaced by a Polish-Czech-Slovak triangle.[126]

Ukraine was once a country of common and high-level purpose for Visegrad, but the Russian pressures and then full-scale invasion terminated this area of V4 cooperation. However, if and as peace may return and Ukraine undertakes to meet the terms of the accession status it was granted by the European Council on June 23, 2022, Visegrad may well regain preeminence in assisting in that fundamental process. The war itself, however, unsurprisingly challenged Visegrad's capacity. Necessarily, the war went to a much larger regional level, as evidenced in the coordination of all "eastern EU/NATO member-states in the Bucharest 9 format, and a muting of Visegrad's own capacities. The 2023–24 Czech presidency program's section on Ukraine made no reference to joint Visegrad military assistance, instead offering declaratory and other support.[127]

Ukraine was not the only front on which the V4 had unfilled ambitions, albeit these carried no lethal consequence. Foreign policy experimentation might be laudable—indeed, early Visegrad was exactly that—but mature Visegrad has lacked the means to achieve all of its ambitions in taking itself global.

VISEGRAD SEEKS THE GLOBAL

Even before Visegrad completed its foundational aim of EU accession and was preparing a new life in the union, it saw itself as bigger still. Thus, the last Visegrad presidency before accession, Slovak's in 2002–03, contended that "V4" was a "well-known" symbol not only in Europe but also "in the entire international community."[128] To these ends, Visegrad has discussed or experimented with common consular activities, joint military operations overseas, coordination of their policies in international organizations other than the EU and NATO, and expanding relations with countries and organizations beyond the Euro-Atlantic area.

Diplomacy and Consular Services

In terms of diplomacy, Visegrad countries operate internationally as part of the EU. The countries therefore have an extraordinary network of representations. Nevertheless (and not, it seems, as a competing counterpoint to those EU presences), the V4 governments have attempted group diplomacy. But the first try became the last, despite supportive rhetoric.

Regional analysts proposed the idea in 2006 and tested the idea with reference to Moldova and Ukraine. Among their findings was that V4 cooperation could be formalized quickly and the Group, then still new in the EU, could be "forerunners among EU Member States."[129]

Visegrad's Cape Town House opened in 2010, in a facility that was previously used as a Czech consulate until 2008 but closed to save costs. The new facility also served as the Common Presentation House for the V4, with each contributing to running costs.[130] Discussions apparently arose in 2011 of joint V4 representations in Odesa, Sevastopol, Santiago, and Rio de Janeiro.[131]

The 2012–13 Polish presidency program effused about prospects (without naming cities), wanting to expand the concept of "Visegrad Houses" modeled on Cape Town, and for consular services generally it planned for "intensifying and broadening this cooperation by tapping all possible options for V4 collaboration."[132] The 2013–14 Hungarian presidency program deemed the Cape Town initiative "a good example of a new type of cooperation" and forming the basis for further combined consular practices in other countries. It even said that the Group deemed the Visegrad House "as exemplary" and that it "attaches great importance to the endeavour," and planned to expand it, including to Vietnam.[133] Ultimately, that was limited to some "cultural activity," with the Hanoi Times TV noting that a "Visegrad corner" would bring Central Europe closer to the Vietnamese people,[134] and an essay competition with a cash prize was offered by the Polish Embassy in Hanoi.[135] The following Slovak presidency, however, did not mention Cape Town, only pledging further consular cooperation where existing Visegrad capacities allowed.[136] And by the next Polish presidency report (those also tending to be the longest and most detailed), combined consular initiatives received no mention. Common Visegrad consular provisions in some post-Soviet countries were also considered but not initiated.[137]

While those efforts dissipated, less evident were other forms of diplomatic coordination, often arising only as an administrative procedure. In overseeing the V4's own COVID assistance to EaP countries, applications for emergency funding were made to the designated V4 embassy in that country and then were assessed jointly by the four V4 embassies.[138] An unexplored possibility might be the establishment of a "Visegrad desk" in, as Brussels's embassies are called, EU representations abroad.

Practical diplomatic activity clearly can and does arise, and no harm and only good comes from such foreign policy experimentation, but the overall record suggests that expectations need to be calibrated.

Visegrad Military Activism beyond Europe

Visegrad's biggest military roles have been in the EU and NATO, and in the European theater. Its militaries, as said, have now a long record of individually having served in larger formations in operations overseas.

Within the EU and NATO, however, Visegrad has occasionally also advocated for further, collective, international roles. It enunciated for the NATO 2012 Summit that regarding operations in Afghanistan, "we remain committed to the principle of 'in together—out together.'"[139] Most important for operations has been the promise of the Visegrad Battlegroup, and at points its existence has suggested that V4 might have deployment far from Europe. A 2021 collaborative analysis of leading V4 practitioners and commentators noted their countries' contributions to stabilization efforts in Afghanistan and Iraq and added that "even more distant mission areas are regularly introduced in V4 discussions, such as a number of conflict-prone countries in the Sahel region." The report at once said that "the V4 is willing to bear the responsibility for allied action" but with the proviso that it was "to the extent of its capabilities."[140] These remain aspirational rather than actioned.

Visegrad's International Relations beyond the Euro-Atlantic

Visegrad has sought to raise its brand name internationally. The V4+ format has had engagement with as geographically disparate countries as the United States, including in defense even before it had done so in Europe, and Israel, South Korea, and Japan. Some of these relations show promise; others demonstrate limitations.

The latter is most shown in how Visegrad has not succeeded in a China format—with Beijing instead fashioning its own choice of 16+1, where Central, Southeast European, and Baltic states are grouped into one. (Greek accession in 2019 made it 17+1. It returned to 16+1 when Lithuania withdrew in 2021, saying the forum gave it no benefits, and encouraged others to follow.) The 2012–13 Polish Visegrad presidency pledged that "V4 contacts will continue to be developed with China, Taiwan."[141] The latter has not seemed to bother China, though advocacy for Taiwan, or hosting of the Dalai Lama, disrupts bilateral relations with Beijing. The lack of issue may be because Visegrad has failed to register as a significant partner with China, even if occasional Chinese research notes that the V4 accounts for over 70 percent of all Chinese trade with and Chinese investments in those 16 countries. China acknowledges that the V4 has an "important role" in the EU but simultaneously notes "poor V4 cooperation within the EU," attributed well before 2022 to Orbán (and with reference to his speech in China in which he detailed Hungary's isolation amid Germans and Slavs).[142]

Visegrad-based foreign policy analysts have advocated for a V4-China format—but within that, caveats were made to avoid disrupting Sino-EU relations and to recognize that that relationship remained paramount; also, it was emphasized, any such V4 endeavor with China must prevent the Group from being perceived as or becoming a Chinese trojan horse inside the Union.[143] China has referred to the V4 as "the most dynamic force" in the EU and believes that "the V4 is able to provide new impetus for the building of the European integration."[144]

It may be that the V4 continues to jockey for its own format in relations with China. Regional commentators noted that some 16/17+1 governments protest China's regional influence by sending ministers to the first-ever summit with Chinese leaders; the V4 governments all provided heads of state. Instead, China has indicated that it wants the V4 to lead the (then) 16+1 format,[145] an outcome unlikely to materialize.

Rather, some of V4's other, if selective, engagements in Asia may indicate elements of balancing China's growing European influence. The V4 and Japan began meeting in 2003, with the latter referring to itself as the V4's "+1". Meetings initially, such as two years later, produced a few words stating that discussion of UN reform and of future cooperation.[146] The cooperation has continued, and V4-Japan relations receive encouragement from regional analysts, in part because of the latter's significant investments in Poland and the Czech Republic but foremost from an identification of common, even strategic, interests and ones that suggest modest rebalancing against Chinese influence.[147] Having started modestly, within a decade, and coinciding with that anniversary, a prime-ministerial summit produced a lengthy declaration, reaffirming commitment to seeking UN reform and common values and security views, both in Asia and in Europe. Japan expressed within that statement its recognition of the V4's roles in the EU and especially regarding the Eastern Partnership. Expanded and regularized ambassadorial consultations were mentioned, as were continued foreign-ministerial and even prime-ministerial meetings.[148]

Visegrad has developed regularized relations with other overseas partners. Its annual forum with South Korea produced ten points of cooperation, including discussions on expanded cooperation in national defense and defense production.[149] Both parties speak of their relations as intensifying.

Coordination in International Organizations

Some of Visegrad's earliest coordination and initiatives occurred in international organizations. Hungarian diplomats, in laying claim to Visegrad, asserted its birth by them at the Conference on Security and Cooperation in Europe in 1990.[150] Early Visegrad statements were made in that and other forums, including on the wars in former Yugoslavia. It is not surprising perhaps that Visegrad might coordinate in other forums, as it had started in the 2000s to do especially regarding the EU.

The Polish presidency advocated for Visegrad coordination in the UN. The succeeding Hungarian presidency then aimed to create a V4 consultation mechanism regarding the UN and its specialized agencies. It recommended V4 coordination in the OSCE and the Council of Europe, including regarding nominations to senior posts in each.[151] The Slovak presidency that followed in 2014–15 was positive of these developments: "We will use the coordination and consultation mechanisms of the V4 in relevant international and specialized organizations of the UN."[152] The extent to which this has happened remains to be determined. Visegrad presidency programs rarely mention the CoE, OSCE, or UN, let alone plans for coordinated V4 positions. Poland was assuming the Chairmanship-in-Office of the OSCE in 2022. Its V4 presidency program made no mention. By contrast, it started with reference to the EU, pledging a "Strong V4 in a strong Europe" and "Consultation and coordination of V4 at EU political level; strengthening of V4 countries influence on the EU decision-making process."[153] There seems little need, and less action, for Visegrad to make claims regarding international organizations when its attentions and priorities, understandably, remain in and with the EU and NATO.

If successful, these Visegrad initiatives also risk either duplicating or clashing with EU positions, with, after all, that organization having a global strategy for international affairs and an established bureaucracy to pursue those aims.

In the past when Visegrad's consistent and core values have been to reembrace its pre-1989 struggle for human rights and democracy, it has been a powerful voice. At times that has been to the consternation of other EU states and over such countries as Myanmar/Burma, Cuba, and North Korea.[154] This may be a role that Visegrad returns to in later years, and the rhetorical and diplomatic support for beleaguered human rights defenders could be once again an appropriate and a workable international goal for the Group.

CONCLUSION

Visegrad has evolved from security consumer to producer. It has forged a place for itself in both the EU and NATO—and then, significantly, between them. But the Group also has limits; those have been foremost demonstrated in the Group's (non)responses to Russian aggression against Ukraine. This should be a distressing development for Visegrad, in view of the centrality given Ukraine in Visegrad's outreach, before and after the crises of 2013–14.

But Visegrad lacks formal mechanisms to determine common threats. In that absence, it is hard for the V4 to be the security actor that it sometimes, even often, proclaims itself to be. Of course, that absence conceals differences, until those differences become too apparent. Worse yet, when the achingly obvious threat emerged from Russia in 2014 and especially in and after 2022, dissension within the Group led to paralysis.

Visegrad need not, and should not, have made the claims of security and global diplomacy with the bravura that it has. Instead, and with little need or expectation, Visegrad has overextended itself; without so stating, it has retreated from many of its international intentions.

Policy experimentation and adaptation—including foregoing options— provide markers of foreign policy ability. This book's final chapter assesses what makes Visegrad cooperation work and the lessons that can be extracted for regionalism more generally.

NOTES

1. Kugiel.
2. Dick, Dunne, and Lough, 391.
3. *Pesti Hírlap*, March 24, 1993, *FBIS*, March 29, 1993.
4. See "Visegrad Group Defence Cooperation" [n.d.], accessed June 5, 2020, http:// www.visegradgroup.eu/about/cooperation/defence, printout retained.
5. While originating from Visegrad's Prague Summit in 1992, CEFTA was nevertheless seen as arising at least from indirect or even direct EU pressure.
6. See chapter 5, on EU and NATO accession.
7. See Burant, "Visegrad," 7.
8. Kowalczyk, 65.
9. Burant, "Visegrad," 7.
10. "Visegrad Group Defence Cooperation."
11. "Visegrad Group Defence Cooperation."
12. See, e.g., "Long Term Vision of the Visegrad Countries on Deepening their Defence Cooperation (Visegrad, 14 March 2014)," mimeo.
13. Střítecký, "Doing More for Less," 78. I will declare a seeming interest in that that researcher was one of my postgraduate students. His experience, publications, and reputation all speak separately to the cogency of using these findings.
14. Valasek, *Surviving Austerity*, 23.

15. The proliferation of other regional, even "Central European," cooperation, as noted elsewhere, is both commonplace and not a distraction from Visegrad.
16. "The Visegrad Group, this dynamic quartet, presents to us in the northern part of Europe another interesting example for regional cooperation. We are eager to learn from the Visegrad experience, and when possible, think of ways to put into practice the successes achieved in its cooperation." "Opening statement by Secretary of State [of Finland] Perti Torstila at Seminar on Visegrád Regional Cooperation in Hungarian Cultural Institute in Helsinki on 5 November 2013," accessed April 21, 2016, http://formin.finland.fi/public/default.aspx?contentid=292115.
17. See https://cedc.info/, as accessed September 18, 2022.
18. Németh and Csiki, 11.
19. And others note the disparities between declarative intentions and tangible results in both interstate security initiatives. Rieker and Terlikowski.
20. See "the Visegrad Group is dedicated to building partnerships with other countries in the V4+ format" including with CEDC, "Visegrad Group Defence Cooperation" [n.d.], https://www.visegradgroup.eu/about/cooperation/visegrad-group-defence; and "V4 + CEDC Defence Policy Directors Meeting, 10–11 April 2019, Brussels," https://www.visegradgroup.eu/article-title-190201.
21. The Nordic Battlegroup in the EU predated Visegrad's and, unlike the latter, contained a mix of NATO and non-NATO countries: Estonia, Norway, Sweden, Finland, and even Ireland. The "different security policy choices" among the eight Nordic-Baltic countries was "not regarded as a problem." Rebane and Pajula, 46–47.
22. Black et al., 31.
23. Kroměříž Declaration (which Visegrad lists as "Visegrad Declaration 2004"), https://www.visegradgroup.eu/documents/visegrad-declarations/visegrad-declaration-110412-1.
24. Valášek and Šuplata, 5. For the discussion, see Zetocha.
25. In a rare instance of specific Iberian military cooperation, the two defense ministers said that a joint statement on defense industries *would* be made and then that within the context of the EU, with no explanatory reference to NATO. See the Spanish government website, "Spain and Portugal to Work Together to Boost European Union and NATO Defence Policies," February 17, 2020, https://www.lamoncloa.gob.es/lang/en/gobierno/news/Paginas/2020/20200217eu-nato-defence.aspx.
26. Valášek and Šuplata, 3.
27. "Poland Interested in Buying Czech Fighter Aircraft," AFP (Agence France-Presse), June 23, 2004.
28. Racz, 68.
29. MTI, "Hungary for Deal on New Russian Helicopters, Says DefMin," June 26, 2007.
30. ČTK, March 4, 2005.
31. See the comments of Czech defense minister Karel Kuehnl in *Právo*, June 21, 2005.
32. Xinhuanet, March 4, 2005.
33. "Visegrad Countries' Air Forces Sign Memorandum on Pilot Training," ČTK, September 19, 2010.
34. Valášek, and Šuplata, *Towards a Deeper*, 13.
35. Valášek and Šuplata, *Towards a Deeper*, 13.
36. Jurak Krupa, "Visegrad Four Defense Cooperation: Years of Missed Opportunities," *Warsaw Institute Review*, June 24, 2019, https://warsawinstitute.review/issue-2019/issue-2-2019/visegrad-four-defense-cooperation-years-of-missed-opportunities/.

37. Long Term Vision (2020), 3, 4, https://www.visegradgroup.eu/documents/official-statements/the-long-term-vision-of.
38. Programme of the Slovak Presidency of the Visegrad Group (July 2022–June 2023), "Cooperation on Defence, Hybrid Threats and the Police," 4, https://www.visegradgroup.eu/documents/presidency-programs/programme-of-the-slovak.
39. ČTK, September 10, 2001.
40. Innovative Visegrad: Programme of the Czech Presidency of the Visegrad Group 2011–2012, https://www.visegradgroup.eu/documents/presidency-programs/innovative-visegrad.
41. Polish Presidency Programme, 2020–21, "Cooperation between Defence Industries" [emphasis added], 29, https://www.visegradgroup.eu/documents/presidency-programs/pl-v4-pres-programme.
42. Lazar, 297.
43. *Hospodářské noviny*, January 30, 2002.
44. ČTK, May 30, 2002.
45. Nicolini, Žídek, and Pšida, 312.
46. Media coverage of the V4 statement wrote, e.g., that "Státy Visegrádu se budou podílet rovným dílem na obnově vrtulníků" [the Visegrad countries will participate equally in the reconstruction of helicopters], *Hospodářské noviny*, May 30, 2002.
47. "Programme of the Czech Republic's V4 Presidency (July 2003–June 2004)," under "Defence Issues," http://www.visegradgroup.eu/documents/presidency-programs/2003-2004-czech-110412.
48. John Fricker, "BAE Systems Wins Lead Visegrad Contract," *Aviation Week*, May 1, 2004.
49. Lubomir Sedlak, "Visegrad Nations to Tie up on Hind," *Flight Global*, February 12, 2002, https://www.flightglobal.com/visegrad-nations-to-tie-up-on-hind/41471.article; ČTK, May 30, 2002.
50. ČTK, September 18, 2019.
51. Gniazdowski, "Possibilities"; Khol, *Perspektivy*.
52. "T-72 Tank Overhaul Deal a Historic Moment—Polish PM," PAP, July 22, 2019; tellingly also carried on the Visegrad website, https://www.visegradgroup.eu/news/72-tank-overhaul-deal.
53. Behr and Siwiecki, 9.
54. Jurak Krupa, "Visegrad Four Defense Cooperation: Years of Missed Opportunities," *Warsaw Institute Review*, June 24, 2019, https://warsawinstitute.review/issue-2019/issue-2-2019/visegrad-four-defense-cooperation-years-of-missed-opportunities/.
55. Nicholas Watson, "Czechs Abandon Visegrad Plan to Build Local Radar Defence System," Bne IntelliNews, September 30, 2004, "https://www.intellinews.com/czechs-abandon-visegrad-plan-to-build-local-radar-defence-system-500428710/?archive=bne.
56. Henry Foy, "Poland to Withdraw from Visegrad Defence Radar Project," *FT*, September 14, 2014.
57. Radio Prague International, "Czech Military to Spend up to CZK 1.7 Billion on New Air Defence Radar System," September 30, 2014, https://english.radio.cz/czech-military-spend-czk-17-billion-new-air-defence-radar-system-8282382.
58. "Budapest Declaration of the Visegrad Group Heads of Government on the New Opening in V4 Defence Cooperation: June 24, 2014," https://www.visegradgroup.eu/calendar/2014/budapest-declaration-of.

59. "42nd Working Session of V4K [*sic*] Military Human Resources Management Working Group, 25–29 March 2019, Balatonakarattya, Hungary," https://www.visegradgroup.eu/article-title-190201.

60. See chapter 3 also for how this four-way initiative provides a counterexample of Visegrad's "death" in or before 1997.

61. Long Term Vision, 4.

62. "V4 Surface Based Air Defence (SBAD) Modernization Working Group, 26–29 March 2019, Liptovský Mikuláš," https://www.visegradgroup.eu/article-title-190201.

63. Cited in "Visegrad Group Moves into Collective Procurement," Shephard News Team, February 2, 2021, https://www.shephardmedia.com/news/defence-notes/visegrad-group-moves-collective-procurement/.

64. "Visegrad Group Defence Cooperation," [n.d.], accessed April 13, 2022, https://www.visegradgroup.eu/about/cooperation/defence.

65. "Framework for an Enhanced Visegrad Group Defence Planning Cooperation," November 9, 2022, https://www.visegradgroup.eu/documents/official-statements/framework-for-an-221208.

66. *Programme of the Czech Presidency of the Visegrad Group 2023/2024*, 8, https://www.visegradgroup.eu/documents/presidency-programs/v4-program-20232024.

67. Střítecký, "Doing," 78.

68. Kořan, "Visegrad Cooperation," 124; Szitás, 2.

69. See chapter 5 for NACC and PfP.

70. Asmus, *Opening*, 69.

71. TSAR, "Fico dúfa, že NATO sa rozšíri o nových členov" [Fico Hopes NATO Expands to New Members], April 12, 2012.

72. Bell and Hendrickson, 159–60. Visegrad inaction on Libya did not, however, feature in discussions in Central Europe as a motivation for the contributions that Visegrad proposed thereafter.

73. Among contemporary analysis is Giegerich.

74. Dangerfield, "Defence," 1.

75. "A Strong Europe for a Strong NATO: Speech by NATO Secretary General Anders Fogh Rasmussen at the Academy of National Defence in Warsaw," June 6, updated June 10, 2013, https://www.nato.int/cps/en/natohq/opinions_101323.htm. He also mentioned Poland's participation in the Weimar Triangle.

76. "Standing up for Freedom and Security: Keynote Speech by NATO Secretary General Anders Fogh Rasmussen at GLOBSEC 2014," May 15, 2014, https://www.nato.int/cps/en/natohq/opinions_109859.htm?selectedLocale=en.

77. The CEPI Report refers to the Defence College in Tartu. See Valášek and Šuplata, *Towards a Deeper*, 13. The Baltic states had embarked on multiple sets of military cooperation from the early 1990s.

78. "Long Term Vision of the Visegrad Countries on Deepening Their Defence Cooperation (Visegrad, March 14, 2014)," 1, https://www.visegradgroup.eu/download.php?docID=253.

79. "Warsaw Summit Communiqué Issued by the Heads of State and Government participating in the meeting of the North Atlantic Council in Warsaw 8–9 July 2016," https://www.nato.int/cps/en/natohq/official_texts_133169.htm?selectedLocale=en.

80. The Hungarian prime-ministerial press release stated that the Hungarian leadership would celebrate the "20th Anniversary of the Visegrád Countries'

NATO Accession Together with Their Czech, Slovak and Polish Counterparts," accessed June 26, 2020, https://www.kormany.hu/en/the-prime-minister/news /v4-heads-of-government-to-celebrate-20th-anniversary-of-nato-accession-in -warsaw.

81. Xinhua, "PMs of Visegrad Group Countries Celebrate in Warsaw 20 Years of NATO Accession," March 11, 2019, http://www.xinhuanet.com/english/2019-03 /11/c_137884264.htm. As noted elsewhere, the Chinese Foreign Ministry contains no reference in English to the Visegrad Group.

82. "The Long Term Vision of the Visegrad Countries on Their Defence Cooperation (Prague, 24 June 2020)," mimeo, 2.

83. Letter from and signed by V4 chiefs of defence staff to General Knud Bartels, Chairman, NATO Military Committee, May 2014 [no day given], mimeo, included in the Hungarian presidency 2013–2014 of the Visegrad Group, https:// www.visegradgroup.eu/documents/annual-reports/2013-2014-annual-report.

84. "Joint Communiqué of the Visegrad Group Ministers of Defence," March 27, 2018, https://www.visegradgroup.eu/calendar/2018/joint-communique-of-the-180329.

85. Website of the Republic of Poland, "Strengthening the Visegrad Cooperation," March 1, 2018, accessed July 20, 2022, https://www.gov.pl/web/national-defence /strengthening-the-visegrad-cooperation.

86. Valášek and Šuplata "Towards a Deeper."

87. "Budapest Joint Statement of the Visegrad Group Heads of Government on Strengthening the V4 Security and Defence Cooperation (Budapest, October 14, 2013)," http://www.visegradgroup.eu/calendar/2013/budapest-joint-statement-140929.

88. "Opening Remarks by NATO Secretary General Anders Fogh Rasmussen at the Joint Press Point with Prime Minister Victor Orban in the Hungarian Parliament," July 1, 2013, https://www.nato.int/cps/en/natohq/opinions_101963.htm ?selectedLocale=en.

89. "Our Security Cannot Be Taken for Granted: Keynote speech by NATO Deputy Secretary General Ambassador Alexander Vershbow at the Jagello Conference, Prague," May 29, 2016, https://www.nato.int/cps/en/natohq/opinions_131609 .htm?selectedLocale=en.

90. "Joint Communiqué of the Visegrad Group Ministers of Defence (March 27, 2018), https://www.visegradgroup.eu/calendar/2018/joint-communique-of-the -180329."

91. "Joint Communiqué of the Visegrad Group Ministers of Defence [April 23, 2015]," https://www.visegradgroup.eu/calendar/2015/joint-communique-of-the.

92. "Statement of the Presidency of the Visegrád Group 13 December 2021," https:// www.visegradgroup.eu/download.php?docID=485.

93. Molnár and Szenes.

94. Valášek and Šuplata, *Towards Deeper*, 9. The High Level Reflection Group wrote that military cooperation could prevent potential tensions between Slovakia and Hungary: *Central Europe*, 7.

95. High Level Reflection Group, 7.

96. "The Visegrad Group (V4)," July 5, 2016, accessed May 27, 2022, https://www .consilium.europa.eu/en/documents/publications/library/library-blog/posts/the -visegrad-group-v4/.

97. *2020/2021 Polish Presidency: Back on Track* [original emphasis removed], 6, https:// www.visegradgroup.eu/documents/presidency-programs/2020-2021-polish.

98. "Long Term Vision of the Visegrad Countries on Deepening their Defence Cooperation (Visegrad, 14 March 2014)," mimeo.
99. O'Hanlon, *Beyond NATO*, 102.
100. "Long Term Vision of the Visegrad Countries on Deepening their Defence Cooperation (Visegrad, 14 March 2014)."
101. "Programme of the Czech Republic's V4 Presidency (July 2003–June 2004)," 5.
102. "I. The Foreign Policy and European Dimensions of Visegrad Cooperation," in *The Programme of Slovakia's V4 Presidency*, 2006/2007, https://www.visegradgroup.eu /documents/presidency-programs/2006-2007-slovak-110412.
103. "12. Defence," in *The Programme of Slovakia's V4 Presidency*, 2006/2007.
104. "III. Priorities of the Polish Presidency," in *Programme of the Polish Presidency of the Visegrad Group (July 2008–June 2009)*, https://www.visegradgroup.eu /documents/presidency-programs/2008-2009-polish-110412.
105. "Visegrad, Ukraine Presidents Start Debates in Wisla," PAP, July 3, 2013.
106. Ministry of Defence of Ukraine, 77.
107. The letter is dated formally but incorrectly March 13, 2013, https://www.visegrad group.eu/download.php?docID=241.
108. "Statement of the Ministers of Foreign Affairs of the V4 Countries on the Occasion of the V4+EaP Informal Ministerial Meeting," April 28–29, 2014, https:// www.visegradgroup.eu/calendar/2014/statement-of-the.
109. Also cited elsewhere, Sikorski wrote an extremely supportive preface to the Polish Visegrad presidency report under his tenure. The short-lived involvement in Weimar during the Ukrainian crisis did not detract from the overall value Warsaw ascribes to the V4.
110. "Joint Statement on Ukraine of the Weimar Triangle Foreign Ministers Frank-Walter Steinmeier (Germany), Laurent Fabius (France), and Radoslaw Sikorski (Poland) in Weimar," March 31, 2014, https://www.auswaertiges-amt.de/en/news room/news/140331-gemeinsame-erklaerung-zur-ukraine/261272.
111. Velvyslanectví Ukrajiny v České republice, "President: New Format of Interaction between Ukraine and the Visegrad Group Has Been Initiated in Bratislava," November 17, 2014, accessed April 7, 2021, https://czechia.mfa.gov.ua/cs/news /29726-u-bratislavi-zapochatkovano-novij-format-spivrobitnictva-ukrajini-z -vishegradsykoju-chetvirkojuglava-derzhavi.
112. "The Kerch Strait Incident," *Strategic Comments* 24:10 (2018): i–ii.
113. Ukrainian source materials draw from Fawn and Drobysh.
114. Ministry of Foreign Affairs of Ukraine, "Visegrad States to Further Support Ukraine in Countering the Russian Aggression," November 30, 2018, accessed April 6, 2021, https://mfa.gov.ua/en/news/69092-krajini-vishegradsykoji-grupi -i-nadali-pidtrimuvatimuty-ukrajinu-u-protidiji-rosijsykij-agresiji. For hopeful Ukrainian media coverage, see "Kyiv zaklykav Vyshehrads'ku chetvirku vymahaty vid RF zvil'nennya ukrayins'kykh moryakiv" [Latinized], *Ukrains'ka Pravda*, November 30, 2018,: https://www.pravda.com.ua/news/2018/11/30/7199892/.
115. "Ukrayins'ka pryzma: Zovnishnya polityka 2018— Znovu 'chetvirka z minusom" [Latinized], accessed April 6, 2021, Prism UA, http://prismua.org/ukrainian -prism-foreign-policy-2018/.
116. PAP, "Poland's Position on Kerch Strait Incident in Line with NATO," November 28, 2018, accessed April 7, 2021, http://www.visegradgroup.eu/news/poland -position-on-kerch.

117. Cited in Vlad Makszimov, "Hungary: Kyiv's Minority Rights Stance 'Limits' Any Support in Conflict," Euractiv, January 27, 2022.

118. Euronews, "Ukraine Crisis: Hungary Won't Accept More NATO Troops on Its Soil, Says Foreign Minister Szijjártó," February 10, 2022, https://www.euronews.com/2022/02/09/ukraine-crisis-hungary-won-t-accept-more-nato-troops-on-its-soil-says-foreign-minister-szi.

119. *Achievements of the 2017/18 Hungarian Presidency*, 2, https://www.visegradgroup.eu/documents/annual-reports/2017-2018-annual-report.

120. Editorial Team, "The Position of the V4 towards War in Ukraine," *Visegrad Insight*, February 28, 2022, https://visegradinsight.eu/the-position-of-the-v4-towards-war-in-ukraine/.

121. "Joint Communiqué on Providing Joint V4 Assistance to Refugees from Ukraine 8 March 2022," https://www.visegradgroup.eu/download.php?docID=489.

122. Quotations from Jennifer Rankin, "Hungary 'Holding EU Hostage' over Sanctions on Russian Oil," *Guardian*, May 16, 2022, https://www.theguardian.com/world/2022/may/16/hungary-sanctions-russian-oil-embargo-eu.

123. "Orban Calls for U.S.-Russia Talks on Ukraine War; Says Kyiv Can't Win," RFE/RL, July 23, 2022, https://www.rferl.org/a/orban-ukraine-war-us-russia-talks/31956804.html.

124. Jana Černochová, Twitter [now X] post, https://twitter.com/jana_cernochova/status/1507390311307554821, March 25, 2022.

125. Matej Kandrík, "The Defense Impact of the Ukraine War on the Visegrád Four," German Marshall Fund, July 28, 2022, https://www.gmfus.org/news/defense-impact-ukraine-war-visegrad-four.

126. Kaczyński told Poland's extensive radio network Radio Plus: "When Prime Minister Orbán says that he does not see exactly what happened in Bucha [sight of suspected mass killings of Ukrainian civilians under Russian occupation], he must be advised to go to an ophthalmologist" and that "We cannot continue to cooperate [with Orbán] . . . a change [in relations] would be a very good thing, but only if Viktor Orbán changes." Cited, e.g., in "Kaczyński Criticises Orbán's Approach to Ukraine: 'We Cannot Cooperate If It Continues," *Notes from Poland*, April 8, 2022, https://notesfrompoland.com/2022/04/08/kaczynski-criticises-orbans-approach-to-ukraine-we-cannot-cooperate-if-it-continues/; and Paweł Musiałek, "V4 No More? Time for a Polish-Czech-Slovak Triangle," *Notes from Poland*, July 19, 2022, https://notesfrompoland.com/2022/07/19/v4-no-more-time-for-a-polish-czech-slovak-triangle/.

127. *Programme of the Czech Presidency of the Visegrad Group 2023/2024*, 16–17.

128. *Annual Report of the Slovak Presidency in the Visegrad Group (2002–2003)*, https://www.visegradgroup.eu/documents/annual-reports/2002-2003-slovak-110412.

129. Kaźmierkiewicz et al., 67.

130. ČTK, March 26, 2010.

131. "V4 Joint Embassies Planned in Ukraine and South America," April 19, 2011, *Slovak Spectator*, https://spectator.sme.sk/c/20039575/v4-joint-embassies-planned-in-ukraine-and-south-america.html.

132. *Visegrad 4 Integration and Cohesion (Polish Presidency Program 2012–2013)*, 11, https://www.visegradgroup.eu/documents/presidency-programs/2012-2013-polish.

133. *2013–2014 Hungarian Presidency: Hungarian Presidency in the Visegrad Group (2013–2014)*, 14 and 13, https://www.visegradgroup.eu/documents/presidency -programs/20132014-hungarian.

134. "'Visegrad Corner' Brings Central Europe Close to Vietnamese People," https:// hanoitimes.vn/visegrad-corner-brings-central-europe-close-to-vietnamese -people-317940.html.

135. Duy Nguyen, "V4 Heritage: Chance to Explore Diverse Cultures," Hanoi Times, April 12, 2021, http://hanoitimes.vn/v4-heritage-chance-to-explore-diversified -cultures-316988.html.

136. *Slovak Presidency Programme, 2014–15*, 34, https://www.visegradgroup.eu /documents/presidency-programs/20142015-slovak.

137. Marušiak, "Instead of Introduction," 14–15.

138. See, e.g., "V4 East Solidarity Programme: Call for Proposals from Azerbaijan to Be Delivered until 10 June 2020," Czech Embassy in Baku, posted May 22, 2020, https://www.mzv.cz/baku/en/v4_east_solidarity_programme_call_for.mobi (printout retained).

139. "Declaration of the Visegrad Group—Responsibility for a Strong NATO," April 18, 2012, https://www.visegradgroup.eu/documents/official-statements/declaration -of-the.

140. *V4 towards a New NATO Strategic Concept*, 18, https://www.europeum.org/data /articles/the-v4-towards-a-new-nato-strategic-concept.pdf.

141. *2012/2013 Polish Presidency: Visegrad 4 Integration and Cohesion*, 10, https:// www.visegradgroup.eu/documents/presidency-programs/2012-2013-polish.

142. Zuokoi, 56, 58.

143. Dubravčíková et al.

144. "Wang Yi Meets with Deputy Foreign Ministers of V4 Countries," Ministry of Foreign Affairs of the Republic of China, March 23, 2018, https://www.fmprc.gov .cn/mfa_eng/gjhdq_665435/3265_665445/3225_664752/3227_664756/201803 /t20180327_579043.html.

145. "Wang Yi Meets with Deputy Foreign Ministers of V4 Countries."

146. "Foreign Ministers' Meeting of the Visegrad Four and Japan (V4+1)," June 22, 2005, https://www.mofa.go.jp/announce/event/2005/6/0622.html.

147. Particularly useful analyses are in Rudolf Fürst, "Japan and the Visegrad 4: The Unsensational Strategic Partners," May 19, 2020, https://www.iir.cz/en/japan-and -the-visegrad-4-the-unsensational-strategic-partners-2.

148. "Visegrad Group plus Japan Joint Statement Partnership Based on Common Values for the 21st Century," June 16, 2003, https://www.mofa.go.jp/files/000006466.pdf.

149. "Joint Statement on the Occasion of the Second Summit of Prime Ministers of the Visegrad Group and the President of the Republic of Korea" (November 4, 2021), esp. para. 8, https://www.visegradgroup.eu/calendar/2021/joint-statement -on-the-211105.

150. See chapter 2.

151. *Hungarian Presidency Programme, 2013–14*, 14.

152. *Slovak Presidency Programme, 2014–15*, 34, https://www.visegradgroup.eu /documents/presidency-programs/20142015-slovak.

153. First point of the "Presidency Objectives," *Polish Presidency of the Visegrad Group July 2020–June 2021 Presidency Programme*, 4, https://www.visegradgroup.eu /documents/presidency-programs/2020-2021-polish.

154. Within Europe, Fawn "Bashing"; for Visegrad internationally, Mikulova, who wrote in 2013–14, "As outspoken advocates of human rights and former satellite countries who have 'been there,' the Visegrad states have engaged in fierce verbal shoot-outs (often to the irritation of "old Europe") with dictatorships," 67. More generally, see Hornat.

9

LESSONS FOR REGIONALISM
FROM THE VISEGRAD GROUP

Visegrad has decades-long history; a range of policy initiatives, inside, between and also outside of the EU and NATO; and an ambitious program of identity creation and advancement not just in the Euro-Atlantic world but internationally. Visegrad offers insights on regionalism more generally, and it holds those also because of its uneven history. Far more can be extracted from a record of challenges and defeats than from uninterrupted, linear progression. At least thirteen lessons from Visegrad's experience can inform the study and practice of wider regionalism.

1. HAVE A BIG BIRTH AND KEEP CELEBRATING BIRTHDAYS, AND NOISILY, THEREAFTER

Visegrad had an inauspicious beginning: it started clumsily in Bratislava in April 1990 and sputtered before it became Visegrad. Disagreements persist among the countries as to when the cooperation was started and particularly by whom. The cooperation commenced earnestly only in February 1991, when a combination of the lack of overture from the European Communities and NATO and Soviet killings of unarmed protestors in the Baltic states the preceding month compelled the three to consolidate their foreign policy aims into tangible cooperation. Visegrad ignored initial failure and continued. The cooperation continued because of need and opportunity, and while the reordering issues of the post–Cold War period will not reappear in the same form, that period showed the perseverance of the states in seeking cooperation. The multiple national claims to creating Visegrad further demonstrate its value.[1]

Similarly, the big issues surrounding Visegrad's birth are unlikely to reappear: namely, reordering the politics of its region after forty years of domestic communist rule and the need to dismantle the Moscow-imposed, seemingly multilateral institutions of the Council for Mutual Economic Assistance and the Warsaw Treaty Organization.

International reordering times like those following the 1989 revolutions and the Soviet Union's demise are rare. And regional formations in Visegrad's geographical area proliferate irrespective of systemic changes: births are common but few register and gain support, let alone sustain it.

In view of the opportunities (and needs) in 1990 and 1991, the Visegrad originators did not act so well to advertise their initiative. Fortunately, media expressed interest, and, as chapter 2 showed, it was not Visegrad's parents who named their prodigy but journalists. That said, Visegrad has learned to proclaim itself, especially on anniversaries. And these announcements, we have seen, even have questionable provenance, including from the question of whether the Group dates from 1990 and where it has continuity. Visegrad raises its profile also by celebrating itself in and with major forums, such as in and with NATO officials, and with major heads of state.

Against expectation, as chapter 5 illustrated, Visegrad wanted to continue after its EU accession in May 2004. It astutely mobilized to make that decidedly clear, not only through its Kroměříž Declaration but also by public pronouncements such as op-eds produced abroad by Visegrad ambassadors and the convening of public events regionally and internationally.

Additionally, Visegrad has worked with major partners, including but not limited to NATO and the EU, to mark its anniversaries and to reinforce the facts of its continued activism. In addition to using its own anniversaries, Visegrad has built on others. The 1989 revolutions have been used, and on the thirtieth anniversary Visegrad prime ministers convened with German chancellor Angela Merkel, and also produced a joint statement.[2] Her engagement with Visegrad was seen by some of the German political spectrum as important to redeveloping Germany's relations with the region.[3] Latitude on dates can be permitted (presumably convening all five leaders proved challenging), for this anniversary meeting was held in February 2019, when changes in the region started with landmark but still only partially free election in Poland in June, 1989 and east Germany and Czechoslovakia had revolutions in November. Separately, the German chancellor and the German president issued a joint statement thanking, specifically by name, the Visegrad countries for making those revolutions.

Visegrad also uses major anniversaries to engage with both general publics and especially think-tank and scholarly communities (elaborated below), which then generate more familiarity with the formation. Birthdays are part of Visegrad's success in developing what it now refers to as "region-ness"— the establishment and promotion both internally and externally of a common regional identity.[4]

2. UNEVEN STATE SIZE NEED NOT TROUBLE
LET ALONE TRUMP INTRINSIC VALUE

Numerically, the four countries are an unequal, and an unlikely match. Poland is almost four times more populous as the Czech Republic and Hungary, and eight times more than Slovakia. Poland routinely sees itself as one of the six large EU states, and, when it first held the rotating European Council presidency, it came with ambitions commensurate with that status.[5]

The then Czechoslovakia easily rebuffed immediate Polish efforts in the post-communist period, not just to be a seeming regional leader but to propose a federation with it. In January 1990 Polish officials and the Polish-born former US national security adviser Zbigniew Brzezinski advocated a federation of that country with Czechoslovakia, arguably even following a tradition of suggesting the same after the two other reordering periods in the twentieth century, following each of the world wars. The Czechoslovaks successfully declined those nascent Polish overtures.

The possibilities of Polish dominance of Visegrad have appeared throughout the Group's life. At Visegrad's commencement a leading observer suggested that "Poland was reluctant to work in this [security] field with two small players such as Hungary and Czechoslovakia."[6] Some call Poland a "hegemonic power";[7] others assert that the "three smaller V4 states tend to be suspicious of Poland" and that it acts as "the bigger partner up-loading its policy priorities" onto them.[8] Polish "hegemony," however, has not materialized and, it is argued here, has not meaningfully been attempted. Instead, Polish analyses contend that Warsaw attached "great importance" to Visegrad for the Euro-Atlantic accession process, as well as after.[9] A high-level study by analysts from across the Visegrad countries recognized Warsaw's other foreign and security policy initiatives and concluded that "Poland seems to recognise strategic advantage" of its Visegrad cooperation with smaller partners and that it handled its status well by involving those countries, reducing cause for distrust of its size. Better still, the report asserted the opposite of Polish domination, submitting that the others could "abuse Poland's much larger size and willingness to lead as pretext for free-riding."[10]

Nor has Poland abandoned Visegrad, even though as Slovak analyst-practitioner Milan Nič notes, Warsaw always "had more opportunities to join other coalitions and alliances," including the Weimar Triangle.[11] That grouping also provides an example of when Polish stature could elevate it above Visegrad, by partnering the country since 1991 with the European heavyweights of Germany and France. Rather than enjoying the routinized practices of Visegrad, Weimar, however, has stalled when not functioning ad hoc. The French foreign ministry recorded that the three partners on their fifteenth anniversary "decided to breathe new life" into the format.[12] Even with the new gust, the last Heads of State meeting was in 2011, and the once-annual foreign-ministerial meetings lapsed between 2016 and 2020. True, a de facto Weimar format was tried in 2014 to deal with the emerging crisis in Ukraine, and a case where Polish activism sought major Western powers in lieu of Visegrad. Even so, as chapter 8 demonstrated, Visegrad collectively was dynamic toward Ukraine, and Kyiv saw the Group as an essential partner. Weimar's thirtieth anniversary was marked, at the provincial level of Thüringen, the German *Land* housing Weimar, with Polish representation only at the ambassadorial level, and with no French.[13] Visegrad commemorations, by contrast and as the first point suggested, are intensively choreographed and gather diverse and high-profile audience when in their capitals, marked also in major international organizations.

The expectation, seemingly contradicting this first assertion, that Warsaw would abandon Visegrad in pursuit of other alliances, has not come true either. To the contrary, Poland has reiterated in official foreign policy documents and in the speeches of major officials its commitment to Visegrad and to doing so on equal footing. Polish foreign minister Radek Sikorski, the same minister who negotiated with France and Germany in Ukraine in 2014, stated in 2013, "We can safely say that the Visegrad Group is Central Europe's most effective regional cooperation forum—and one which still carries untapped potential."[14] And big Poland has routinely carried Visegrad with it. When Poland's former prime minister Donald Tusk became president of the European Council in 2014, Polish commentary said that "this is not just Poland's ascent, but also that of Central Europe. Tusk has spared no effort throughout his term as Polish prime minister to work together with other countries of the region, especially in the Visegrad Group."[15]

If such is only rhetoric, then reference to national interests serve to reinforce Visegrad's importance in Polish foreign policy. A representative view is that Poland remains a "very active member" of the Group because it "aims at exploiting the group to pursue its national interests."[16] Each member does that—irrespective of size. If that ambition is true, then it affirms Visegrad's attractiveness and utility. But irrespective of any big power ambition, instead collegiality is expressed routinely by Polish officials, as, for example, in a foreign-ministerial statement to the *Sejm* in 2013: "A strong Poland in the EU also means a stronger Visegrad Group."[17] A Poland "acting big" wants Visegrad even more and sees mutually reinforcing interests and benefits.

Poland certainly exercises alternative foreign policy options, but so have other Visegrad members. And divisions over key foreign policy issues have occurred across the region, not simply by Poland. One seeming disunion was that Poland alone actively participated in the Anglo-American-led invasion of Iraq and also became (partly as recognition for its war-fighting contribution) an administrator of postwar Iraqi territory. Much forgotten, but the Czech premier refused to attend a Visegrad meeting because of Poland's participation in the invasion. That was a singular event with no sustained impact. Poland was also seen to have jettisoned its Visegrad partners when it launched the Eastern Partnership (EaP) with Sweden. Although Visegrad collectively maintained an interest in countries to its east (and south), and support for further accession was part of its 2004 Declaration, the EaP did not arise from the V4. If anything, Czechs often claim the genesis, and the EaP was launched in Prague. More important to Visegrad's role regarding the EaP is not its innovation but that the V4 has convened annual summits between itself and the corresponding post-Soviet states.

Poland has repeatedly returned, or better said remained, with Visegrad. Those presuming that size would end Poland's participation should have heeded and should continue to heed Warsaw's proactive comments about its adherence to the group, when of course, as for any multilateral formation, it serves each and all members' interests.

Size alone fails to explain dissenting political behavior in Visegrad. Rather, smaller states have both prompted policy reorientation, or even taken the cooperation hostage. Hungary—with but one quarter of Poland's population—moved the whole group in 2015 to oppose EU plans for mandatory reassignment of migrants to EU member states; Warsaw originally accepted the proposal. Visegrad states take different views on Russia, to the point even that some Czech leaders have been considered apologists for Moscow's annexation of Crimea.[18] In financial matters, Slovakia in 2009 entered the Eurozone and remains Visegrad's solitary member. Smaller Hungary provoked, again, challenges for Visegrad after Russia's full-scale invasion of Ukraine in 2022. Not only was, as chapter 8 noted, Hungary's position incompatible with those of other Visegrad governments, but within a month of the invasion a Visegrad defense-ministerial meeting in Hungary, the country holding the Visegrad presidency, was boycotted by Prague and Warsaw, resulting in Budapest cancelling the meeting.[19]

But resumption, resilience, and the long view remain integral to Visegrad and to the lessons that it offers. Divisions within the Group from Russia's Ukrainian invasion did not stop it from convening in November 2022, and that forum gave leaders the opportunity to chastise Hungary's Viktor Orbán.[20] Visegrad's continuity remains significant in the face of other regional choices.

3. DO-IT-YOURSELF INSTITUTIONALIZATION

Visegrad officially repeats that it is uninstitutionalized: "Visegrad cooperation is not institutionalized in any manner. It is based solely on the principle of periodical meetings of its representatives at various levels."[21] Its only institution—and frequent are the reminders—remains the International Visegrad Fund.[22] The fund principally advertises for, reviews, and then finances cultural, educational, and societal initiatives; scholarships (including for within the region and to bring non-Visegrad students and scholars to it); and publications.

Meant positively, these claims are misleading. The Secretariat of the Fund serves as an archive of official activities and a support to current ones. It already does far more to underpin diplomatic pursuits than a strictly cultural-educational fund.

Nor are diplomatic institutions matters of buildings and staff. Despite Visegrad's declarations, it conducts affairs through means readily recognizable in other international institutions.[23] With Visegrad's relaunch in 1999, of which the fund's establishment constituted one part, the Group enunciated a series of processes and practices to regularize cooperation. As chapter 4 detailed, these include timetabled meetings of presidents, prime ministers, and foreign ministers, and of almost all other ministries. Additionally, an annual rotating presidency was instituted in 1999 and continues decades later. Each presidency establishes a presidency program, detailed in dozens of pages, encompassing all major sectoral activities and with engagement of major actors, especially the EU and NATO, as well as globally. Annual reports showcase achievements and provide opportunities for accountability; many reports are also dozens of pages and just their compiling, let alone the work represented, are indictive of substantial staffing investments. Ceremony has also been built into some formalized arrangements, including prominent handover events between annual presidencies, in addition to the summits and anniversaries.

Visegrad national coordinators oversee these responsibilities, in positions established and maintained in each Visegrad Foreign Ministry. They could, instead, work in a Visegrad headquarters; separate interviews with them and their staff in all four ministries uniformly affirmed that they were in regular, even daily and effective contact, and none spoke to the need of any central, physical structure, while mentioning the costs saved. Coordinators do meet, having done so first after the positions were created to organize Visegrad's relaunch in 1999. The 2004 Kroměříž Declaration elaborated these roles, specifying "Intensified communication of V4 national co-ordinators" and recording "their key role in internal and inter-state co-ordination."[24]

Visegrad has therefore established its own form of internal institutionalization, and rhetoric to the contrary simply serves to underline both the Group's cost-effectiveness and occasional arguments about the Group's postulated informality. Indeed the latter could also serve as an astute tactical device to avoid engagement on certain issues.

4. WORRY NOT OF
SEEMING-COMPETITOR REGIONALISMS

Visegrad's region remains flooded with overlapping and competing interstate initiatives. As with mistaken analyses of dangers to Visegrad from Poland's size, the many claims that Visegrad would be overtaken by other state formations so too have proven exaggerated.

Already around Visegrad's birth in 1991, its member states enjoyed alternative formats.[25] One was the Pentagonale, championed as recognizable from the Italian name, by Rome's active foreign minister Gianni de Michelis in 1990, as a counterweight to the power of a soon-to-be united Germany.[26] Under the refashioned name of the Central European Initiative, the formation grew to have eighteen countries, including the four Visegrad states. But it has few concrete results, and countries have not sent appropriately ranking representatives, or representatives at all, to some meetings.[27]

Although the CEI, both in name—invoking that all-valuable term "Central Europe"—and membership could seem a rival to Visegrad, it has foundered. Its secretaries general have exclusively been Austrian or Italian, suggesting either proprietorship (likely in Italy's case), or a lack of interest or capacity among the membership.[28] Despite some publicity, the CEI has delivered few results comparable to Visegrad's. Austria, which has made overtures to Visegrad, in 2018 ended its CEI membership.

Throughout Visegrad's history new formations and reformulations of existing ones have emerged—and disappeared. Václav Havel, a diplomatic entrepreneur as well as playwright, sought to bridge the CEI and the Danish-German–initiated Council of the Baltic Sea States. That never happened, foregoing the opportunity of landlocked Czechoslovakia being the geographic connector between two European seas. In 1993, it was Havel suggesting that Visegrad had limits, and he began partaking in and then leading an alternative meeting of "Central European" leaders. As chapter 3 noted, Havel's key foreign policy adviser even said that this new format showed Visegrad to be dead, and Havel engaged in other forms of regional interactions, ones that are commemorated as part of his political legacy. Regardless, regional observers contend that with historical comparative insight, "the Visegrad Group has played a much more significant role" in European affairs than either the CBSS or the CEI.[29]

Other efforts have presented challenges to Visegrad. Czech, Slovak, and Austrian cooperation in the "Slavkov format" that began in 2015 had been mooted even as a slayer of or a successor to Visegrad.[30] Some even saw Germany's Merkel and France's Macron seeking in 2017 to use Slavkov to "weaken" or even "dismantle" Visegrad.[31] Merkel, instead, as noted elsewhere in this chapter, reinforced Visegrad's presence in 2019. Rather than challenging

Visegrad, the Slovak Foreign Ministry thought that Slavkov "could be helpful in stimulating new projects,"[32] and that Slovak presidency in 2019–20 "persistently underlines directing the S3 format in [a] flexible and pragmatic way," noting, "We deem it complementary and consistent with other already established regional platforms."[33]

Vienna has presented regional cooperation since 2001, including some bearing the imaginative title of "Regional Partnership," involving the four Visegrad states and Slovenia convening with Austria. The Czech Foreign Ministry's views of the formation's utility was politely forthright: while it participated, Prague's "regional priority remains the Visegrad co-operation in V4 or V4+ format." Austria, this inferred, could join with Visegrad initiatives—but not vice versa. If that was insufficient, the Czech Foreign Ministry deemed "the Regional Partnership more as a complement to Visegrad co-operation."[34]

With the larger membership of twelve states, the Three Seas Initiative (TSI) was also, separately, launched in 2015. The presidents of twelve EU states fronting or close to the Baltic, Adriatic, and Black Seas pledged to improve regional physical connectivity and increase transatlantic diplomatic ties. US president Donald Trump attended the TSI's 2017 Summit, and European Commission president Jean-Claude Juncker its 2018 successor. It is smart for new formations to lure giant-named international figures. Visegrad was a leader in doing so. The TSI's international fanfare has yet to produce deliverables.[35] Any increase in the TSI's significance might only benefit Visegrad rather than overtake it: the V4 countries are called "leaders" of it.[36]

Visegrad has been deemed defunct or superseded many times, and by many apparent alternatives, yet continues successfully and in the face of multiple competitors. One Visegrad lesson is not to worry unduly about competition (and those who raise it). A second is to embrace content and delivery. A way to do that is to have offspring—and in that way Visegrad has also differentiated itself from putative equivalents.

5. CREATE OFFSPRING

Visegrad serves well for wider lessons of smaller-state multilateralism because, as noted at the outset, it was at various points of collapse, including in the middle of the 1990s. Nevertheless, during precisely that time of paralysis, one of its earliest and enduring results continued that cooperation. It also attracted substantial interest and the accession to it of other countries. This was the Visegrad progeny of the Central European Free Trade Agreement (CEFTA). Launched in 1992, CEFTA increased interregional trade among its three-cum-four members, even if it was created with the expectation of Association Agreements with the EU and eventual accession negotiations at its heart.[37]

CEFTA was real cooperation in its own right through both creating trade liberalization among its members and by reinforcing to the EU that its aspirant members were committed to full-scale transformation from communist-era command economies that could withstand competitive pressures generally and be able to converge wholesale into the world's largest integrated market. As chapter 3 showed, CEFTA also became a substitute for Visegrad's diplomatic cooperation when it crumpled in the 1990s. Regional heads of state who antagonized their counterpart populations and undercut Visegrad nevertheless attended CEFTA summits and used them for bilateral and multilateral matters. While Klaus disrupted and denigrated Visegrad, he keenly supported CEFTA. His 1995 comment that in his dictionary Visegrad was defined only as CEFTA belied his engagement with Visegrad through this format. As chapter 6 indicated, CEFTA allowed for diplomatic interactions that otherwise might not have occurred, including of Hungarians with Slovaks, and of Klaus with his Slovak counterpart Mečiar.

CEFTA did more than sustain Visegrad during its immobilization. The European Commission adopted it as the framework for trade liberalization among accession and other countries in the Western Balkans. The entry of existing CEFTA members into the EU in 2004 and 2007 required their conclusion of other trade agreements. The EU borrowed that format, retitling it (perhaps unimaginatively) as CEFTA-2006, the latter for the year of its commencement.

Having offspring is also representative of Visegrad's success of engaging different policy initiatives in different forums and sectors of cooperation. In 2002 a public spectacle of a Visegrad breakdown occurred at the prime-ministerial level. Hungarian prime minister Orbán demanded that the Slovak and Czech governments annul the post–World War II decrees—sanctioned by the United States, Great Britain, and the Soviet Union—that supported the expulsion from Czechoslovakia of ethnic Germans and Hungarians. The Czech and Slovak prime ministers protested the comments and underscored their dismay by boycotting the upcoming heads-of-state Visegrad Summit—which happened to be also in Budapest. The Polish prime minister opted also not to attend, although whether he did so out of solidarity with Prague and Bratislava, or because a bilateral meeting was unattractive, remained unclear.[38]

The IVF remains, officially, Visegrad's only "institution." It also serves as offspring, and additionally shows how a regional state formation can and should do more: provide models and pursue emulation.

6. LOOK FOR, OFFER, AND ACCEPT EMULATION

Related also to offspring, and another marker of success in its own right, is emulation. Not only was Visegrad's CEFTA embraced and reapplied to other countries, but so has its funding body and primary mechanism for enhancing regional societal interlinkages. The IVF has been adopted among the post-conflict countries of former Yugoslavia. The V4 prime ministers declared that the Western Balkans Fund, established based on the IVF model, "underlined the determination of the Visegrad Group countries to continue supporting extensive regional cooperation, good neighbourly relations, and reconciliation in the Western Balkans also through the International Visegrad Fund's grants (Visegrad+ Grants), scholarship programmes or assistance to the Western Balkans Fund."[39]

Kosovo was included as a participant, despite the continued opposition of fellow member Serbia, which refuses to recognize the former's independence. Perhaps more significant, the V4 has been divided—with Slovakia uniquely among the Four not recognizing Kosovo's February 2008 declaration of independence. The V4 navigates the issue by avoiding reference to Kosovo's status, and, in a joint statement Visegrad welcomed the Stabilization and Association Agreement between the EU and the former Serbian province.[40] Despite the political disagreement over Kosovo in Central and Southeastern Europe, the Western Balkans Fund, modeled on the IVF, is operational.

Visegrad's cooperation has been held as a model further afield geographically. This includes the Eastern Partnership countries, quite separately from Visegrad's contribution to initiating and then contributing to this important flagship project of the EU's external relations. That the EaP has faltered is not Visegrad's fault but remains testimony to the value of its potential as a role model for cooperation, and that in regions where relations are conflictual.[41] A concluding statement marking Visegrad's thirtieth anniversary by the four Foreign Affairs parliamentary committees spoke well of how Visegrad appeared to outsiders: "We are able to organize ourselves in a way that still remains only a dream for many other countries."[42]

7. DON'T WORRY (TOO MUCH) ABOUT SOCIETAL NAME (NON-)RECOGNITION, BUT ALSO FOSTER AND REAP ITS BENEFITS

Public outreach is beneficial but not generally necessary for the success of regional state formations. If, however, forming or strengthening a regional identity is an important claim, then Visegrad sets a high standard. Visegrad seems disappointed when it receives only 50 percent name recognition in opinion polls. Previously, Visegrad had been mocked in often entirely unsystematized "polling."[43] It has improved its name recognition enormously and has done so also by engaging in societally focused, apolitical events such as the "Visegrad Marathon" and Visegrad bike rides. It also runs Visegrad summer schools and looks to have Visegrad included in curriculum inside and outside of the region.[44] That it bothers with societal name recognition speaks both to its importance to the diplomatic side of the Group and to further expectations for diplomatic-societal interaction.

An additional way to enhance name recognition, to develop greater legitimacy for the regional project, and, further still, to produce opportunities for idea generation and burden sharing, is to foster networks of think tanks and universities. Visegrad has become a frontrunner in this process.

8. COOPERATION WITH REGIONAL AND INTERNATIONAL THINK TANKS

V4 has been arguably an early promoter of think-tank activity. Its support for the Visegrad Think Tank Platform predates, for example, the OSCE Network, a group of now far more think tanks and universities, and in a much more formalized and funded intergovernmental organization, involving fifty-seven participating states.[45]

In turn, and perhaps as a statement of mutual appreciation, the Think Tank Platform writes that "the Visegrad Group can take pride in an excellent, unique and quite unmatched level of engagement with NGO institutions and think tanks; it achieved this level by continually contributing to an informal network of trust-based relationships between the various state administration branches and non-governmental sector."[46] Such a comment might be partisan: it is written by those receiving funds from Visegrad in order to write about the Group. Nevertheless, such activity intensifies name recognition and outreach, as well as generating new ideas.

9. HAVE REASONABLE EXPECTATIONS, AND DON'T PRESUME THAT ONE FAILURE IS A FINALITY

Visegrad may be the paragon of a cooperation format declared repeatedly dead, defunct, or superfluous. It has resumed in numerous circumstances, and it has also succeeded in continuing to function in other forms, and at other levels of cooperation, when presumed to have collapsed.

Visegrad is sensible in having what can be called tautological decision-making. Discussions with many national coordinators (and others) showed that officials of the Group engaged regularly with one another to determine the interest in and the viability of initial ideas. I have tried to determine examples of possible initiatives that were dropped, and we might also presume some. Russia as a whole, as mentioned elsewhere, tends to be a topic, well before the catastrophe of 2022, that Visegrad avoids—that is even "taboo." An example of a developing issue area where Visegrad did not take a position was on the EU's Permanent Structured Cooperation (PESCO), a defense cooperation initiative within the EU launched in 2018. While, as chapter 8 showed, Visegrad pursued military cooperation between the EU and NATO, no common Visegrad position emerged on PESCO and the countries joined separately. More important, the only Group statement that included mention of PESCO called it "historic," but immediately (and again in keeping with arguments from chapter 8) referred this EU defense initiative back to NATO, stating that what was needed were "concrete capabilities . . . that could meet NATO requirements as well." Visegrad had conducted informal discussions and decided not to take the matter further, attesting to a case, as Anna-Lena Kirch concluded, of "V4 self-understanding," to coordinate only when shared preferences were already determined.[47] Visegrad is often expected to tackle more and is judged, incorrectly, by what it does not address. It should be assessed instead by effectiveness on the issue areas and the techniques that it adopts.

Such self-managing processes are also a relative, though not absolute, safeguard against political influence. That tendency leads also to observations regarding the roles and impact of political, rather than diplomatic, leaderships in regional cooperation.

10. FEAR NOT THE POLITICIANS: DEVELOPING LONG-TERM COOPERATION INTERESTS AND MECHANISM AS A HEDGE AGAINST POLITICAL LEADERSHIPS

Visegrad has experienced enormous changes in the domestic leaderships of its member states and an extensive range of personalities. It has also been a victim of these fluctuations. The Group is a testament to interests in regional cooperation, ultimately being able to endure and even override idiosyncratic leadership preferences. Additionally, Visegrad shows how a regional format can serve the same politicians who were previously even associated with the termination of that cooperation.

The cooperation's initiation is generally, though hardly universally, credited to former dissident Václav Havel and to his appreciation of communist-era support among independent activists. His efforts to kick-start cooperation in 1990 faltered in part because neighboring countries still had some communists in power, and a fuller transition to non-communists was required. But once former dissidents were all at the helm, particularly Poland's Lech Wałęsa, interpersonal relations became *worse*. Hungary's reformist communist foreign minister Gyula Horn said nothing at the first regional cooperation meeting's press conference in April 1990; indeed, he even left before the summit concluded. Yet, when Horn returned four years later as prime minister he became a proponent of Visegrad. He would witness, with Havel, and Aleksander Kwaśniewski, the ex-communist presidential successor to Wałęsa, those countries were invited to join NATO.[48]

Visegrad collapsed in the middle 1990s largely because of the personalities and policies of Klaus and Mečiar. Ironically, a cooperation originally seemingly predicated on dissidents as individuals, on their common communist-era experiences, and the presumption of shared political values was not sustainable. The Visegrad cooperation was relaunched in 1998–99 substantially by a combination of former dissidents (Warsaw's Geremek; Prague's Šedivý) in foreign-ministerial leadership and another generation of politicians.

Moreover, the personalities either held responsible for or who even have declared themselves opposed to the cooperation have later emerged as Visegrad's promoters. Klaus, Visegrad's nemesis, reversed his position as EU accession approached in the early 2000s, pronouncing that he had been misunderstood regarding Visegrad. He would attend Visegrad summits, photographed in joyfully emphatic Group hand-clasping.

By contrast, Orbán simultaneously launched what became a paralyzing assault on Visegrad in 2002. He did this in advance of Hungarian elections. Addressing the European Parliament, Orbán demanded that Czechoslovakia's postwar Beneš Decrees, which legitimated the expulsion of Germans and Hungarians, be rescinded in advance of Slovak and Czech entry into the EU. Neither Austria nor Germany, to which many of the expellees went, supported Hungary's call. Nor did the EU accept Budapest's efforts to have this historical revision attached to the final accession conditions for Prague and Bratislava.

So bad was the reaction to Orbán's efforts that the Czech and Slovak prime ministers refused to attend the next Visegrad summit, which was to convene in Hungary. Poland also withdrew, although Polish motives were interpreted variously: as outright solidarity with the Czech Republic and Slovakia, to the nonpolitical, practical view that without those two countries attending, it was hardly worth Warsaw doing so. Irrespective of the cause, the Visegrad cooperation flamboyantly derailed.

Many analysts and practitioners consequently but erroneously proclaimed Visegrad's next death. Orbán's misuse of Visegrad even earned him criticism in Hungary, including that he had engaged in "blackmail," had "disregard for national sensitivities," and had caused "gross diplomatic offenses." The criticisms also suggested that Orbán had not merely used Visegrad to such ends; rather, "to grind the V4 down" was not collateral but intentional.[49] A major Hungarian daily called Orbán's actions a "scorched earth" attack on previously seemingly indestructible diplomacy. Rudolf Chmel, a Czechoslovak ambassador to Hungary and perennial V4 supporter, warned that the reelection of

Orbán's party could result in Visegrad's breakup.[50] Yet it was Orbán who successfully mobilized Visegrad to launch his effective campaign against the EU's plans for mandatory acceptance in 2015 by member states of "migrants." And even Orbán's critics recognize his "great victory" in maneuvering Visegrad to his position.[51]

None of this is to suggest that the cooperation should drive itself, exempt from political decision-making. Nor has Visegrad exceeded its agreed mandates. Visegrad history shows too well how idiosyncratic political leadership choices can derail the cooperation or even seize it as a tool to pressure partners.

11. KEEP TIGHT MEMBERSHIP BUT HAVE COALITION STRATEGIES

Regional formations may feel stronger and better by virtue of size. The OSCE is proud of being the world's largest regional security organization by membership. Yet precisely that varied membership, resting on consensus or consensus "minus one," hamstrings it.

Visegrad unique among the many Central, Southeast, and East European regional formations not to have expanded its membership beyond its original three, except the two as Czechoslovak successors. Many cases of interest have been rebuffed, as chapter 2 illustrated. Visegrad's exclusivity helped it early along to secure name recognition from and working relations with multilateral institutions in Brussels.

Exclusivity, however, bears costs. In its early and later years, Visegrad generated envy and resentment from those excluded.[52] It has surmounted such sentiments by including neighbors in policy advocacy, including as chapters 5 and 6 showed in the EU, making both the group and partners more successful.

The V4+ format is highly effective, allowing Visegrad itself to build coalitions and for others to approach the Group and to work with it on selective issues, another reason for Visegrad's own success and as a model for others is its engagement with major actors, frequently in Europe, and occasionally globally. The V4+ format, in some ways obvious, nevertheless functions optimally.

12. WELCOME CRITICISM; PUSH BACK AND MAKE A VIRTUE OF IT

Success can be receiving criticism from high levels. Institutional ingenuity, in turn, is transforming attacks into virtues. Visegrad has done both.

Visegrad countries have earned the ire of foreign leaders. Perhaps most notable was French president Jacques Chirac, who (albeit with contestation over the precise language) told the Central European governments to "shut up" for their support of Anglo-American bellicosity toward Iraq in 2003. Central European leaders acknowledged Chirac's right to speak but asserted, often in vivid language, their own right to expression and to policy alignment.[53]

The Group earned public chastisement by another French president in 2009, when Nicolas Sarkozy attacked it for convening in advance of European Council meetings. At that point the V4 had only met twice before Council sessions, but thereafter—instead of heeding Sarkozy—the V4 governments regularized the practice. And numerous Visegrad officials flipped Sarkozy's criticisms against him, remarking that France and Germany met before Council summits and that to prevent the V4 from doing the same was hypocritical. Better still, Visegrad spokespeople said that the Group's preparations benefited the EU, by offering ideas and saving time by arriving at these large multilateral forums with a coordinated position.[54] The month after accession, the Czech Foreign Ministry's section head for the EU explained: "Visegrad Group is an important platform where we can test our views before we go to an EU session and say this is how we think things should develop."[55]

Visegrad's biggest pushback came in 2015 in relation to the migrant crisis. As controversial as its actions became, Visegrad successfully resisted initiatives from other member states, which put forth a system of mandatory quotas of migrants accepted by each member state. The Visegrad countries certainly view their ability to arrest a major EU initiative as an outright success. Furthermore, the Group presented its actions in virtuous terms, including, if audaciously, that it was the voice of truth in the EU and the protector of what it framed as "European civilization." Through this new rhetoric it also challenged its many critics by asserting that it was Visegrad that acted responsibly.

These actions also secured Visegrad's greatest international name recognition to the point that major media used the group name in headlines and often without explanation or qualification.[56] Many disagree with Visegrad's position and its appropriation of European values, but the migrant crisis and the Group's handling of it were a leading case of reshaping the policy initiatives of much larger countries and to gain unprecedented if still controversial recognition. And certainly also, Visegrad flipped the criticism that it received over the migrant crisis to being the defenders of "European" values, even if few believed it.

Visegrad's use of "Europe" and European "values" provides a final lesson for regionalism: the appropriation and shaping of "history" for positive purposes.

13. GRAB—AND SCULPT—HISTORY

We have seen that the name Visegrad was a fortuitous one, practicable linguistically for all partners and with a history that could be built upon. Post-1991 analyses, especially in popular forums, almost unquestioningly accept that Visegrad today is a continuation of a history of earlier and positive "regional" cooperation.

True, the kings of the precursor nations of the Czechs, Poles, and Hungarians met in Visegrád in 1335. But the "history" ceases there. The following observations are not about historical disjunctures or continuities but instead the uses of history to make successful regional cooperation.

The year 1335 aside, the region boasts little common cooperation. Rather, millennia of this region's history can (generalizations being permitted for purposes of regarding how contemporary cooperation functions) be summarized as local powers siding unilaterally with larger, external ones against their neighbors or their common, often forced, submission to great powers. When regional powers should have joined against collective threats, they abandoned one another and even turned against each other militarily.

The formation of Visegrad was therefore essential to begin to counteract regional and external perceptions of a profoundly distrusting mutual history. To that end, Visegrad itself became a manipulation of history. We are told in what is now the "Visegrad Declaration of 1991"[57] that the countries were returning to the positive cooperation of 1335.

As chapter 2 indicated, the physical re-creations of 1335 are constructions. The official website shows the Castle atop Visegrád hill (see photograph in figure 2.1). The original application of "Visegrad" to a castle, however, was to *another* in the same area, one no longer even standing.[58] A purist point of historicism, perhaps, as are the medieval re-creations in the castle where the 1991 signing is presented as having occurred but did not. So too are the four flags in the revamped fourteenth-century banquet hall, including that of Slovakia.

But the constructive misuses of time and place continue. Where those historically anachronistic flags are hung is not the castle in which Visegrad began, even if it has featured as the cooperation website's lead image (as per chapter 2). Instead, the meeting occurred at a second castle, one not on the high hill over the Danube, and so often referred to, even poetically.

Chapter 2 included a photograph (figure 2.7) of commemorative national wreaths placed by each Visegrad foreign minister in 2008, marking the 1991 Visegrad Summit in the lower castle, a venue generally excluded from the official representation.

Inaccuracies of history and of location aside, far more important is that the cooperation was astute in its choice of its setting, name, and historical parallels of cooperation. That inventiveness may have aided securing some of Visegrad's early praise, with accounts of the 1991 version also harking back to 1335 as a case of regional leaders resolving matters "in a mature way." Rarely is it noted that the fourteenth-century agreements were short lived and were heavily concerned with strategic alliances and power politics, not the values-infused postmodern humanistic language in 1991.[59]

So be it, Visegrad has continued with commemorations of its anniversaries, with both societal outreach and diplomatic events. Other formations seeking the same could borrow from some of its activities.

A telling reference of Visegrad's positive, if misleading, use of history is of the two Visegrads 500 kilometers apart. The second, referred to in this volume only in its preface, spelled Višegrad and pronounced alike, lies in former Yugoslavia, in today's eastern Bosnia. That Višegrad was overrun in spring 1992 by Bosnian Serbs, where Bosnian-Muslim men, women, and children were killed in initial stages of wider ethnic cleansing.

The pseudojustification for what became Serbian atrocities was also the use, and misuse, of fourteenth-century history.[60] In contrast to the inaccurate yet positive interpretations of Visegrad's fourteenth-century cooperation, Serbian leadership references to Kosovo in the period preceding Visegrad's foundation stoked division, fear and terrorization, displacements and deaths. For all of Visegrad's economies with history, and with enduring contention surrounding Visegrad's positions on the migrant crisis, the identification and then the sustained exploitation of that history helped to create multilateralism that likely would not have existed, let alone endured.

Visegrad's use of history may seem sui generis and therefore not universalizable. Nevertheless, multilateral endeavors often seek commonalities to legitimate their activities. Other regional formations across the post-communist space sought to mobilize shared geographic features, particularly invoking common waterways or bodies of water (Baltic Sea, Black Sea, Three Seas) or mountains (Alpen-Adria) and using, if in a far more limited manner, seeming common histories that emerge. The Council of the Baltic Sea States, for example, sought to use the Hanseatic League to convey a shared history among its disparate members.[61] Regionalism and especially region-ness—the building of regional identity—need entrepreneurship. None of these initiatives identified or employed historical analogies as well as Visegrad. Visegrad had no identifiable geographic feature to seize but made its own reference point.

FINAL LESSONS OF SMALL(ER)-STATE MULTILATERALISM

Even before Visegrad became a familiar name from its contentious yet successful initiatives over the 2015 migrant crisis, the group was a leading foreign policy tool for its member states, and it had engaged in high-level diplomacy with actors across the globe.

Its experiences inform that unlikely countries, with limited resources and issues that still divide them, can produce an effective multilateral system. Part of Visegrad's teaching, one intrinsic to all political analysis but readily overlooked, is that actions should be judged in terms of aims and abilities and what convincing it needs to do or what resistance it may need to surmount. Visegrad has come, especially since 2015, to be expected to assume challenges that it cannot overcome or for which it is knowingly unsuited. Within those terms, Visegrad's experience can inform others to use history, engage with populations, employ separate but creative other parties like think tanks to stimulate both debate and further awareness, and retain cohesive membership over expansion; but to engage openly and decisively with others, as through its "+" format.

Visegrad also now has an extensive history of the effects of how domestic political and regional change can affect multilateralism and how to cope with them. Visegrad shows that cooperation can endure against political interference and indeed political manipulation. Cooperation even in those circumstances can productively continue whether channels are made, even if less visibly, between constituent actors, especially governmental, of the member states.

While short- and medium-term aims can be assessed—such as stopping selection of a European Commission president for the former, and Euro-Atlantic accession for the latter—multilateralism also needs to be judged over the longer term. Visegrad presents lessons also from defeat; this is a group that was repeatedly ruled defunct, and for reasons that extend from the negative and to even the positive. The former include the atypical challenges of the dissolution of a member state (and the predecessors to the Central European Initiative suffered badly from founding-member Yugoslavia's disintegration), to the hypernationalism of individual leaders who used the cooperation platform as a means to attack other members. Visegrad has also endured against, counterintuitively, too much success. Its members' accession to NATO and especially to the EU were seen as cause for the Group to desist. The Group endured and has been recognized by those very institutions as significant actors in Europe. And that was before its controversial yet successful actions against mandatory migrant relocation in 2015. Increasing after 2014,[62] then decidedly after February 24, 2022, Russian aggression against Ukraine also posed challenges, to the point that the Group again was considered thoroughly irrresuscitable. Thereafter Orbán, at times a derailer and at others a redirector of the Group, has faced severe criticism and has acted even more outside Visegrad, even turning to alternative platforms, for example, with Austria and Serbia, for migration controls. But those remain extreme political-security circumstances: Russia's war is the greatest challenge to the European post–Cold War order. No entity, let alone the smaller Visegrad, can be judged for effectiveness in the immediacy of an unprecedented, multifaceted challenge. Among Visegrad's many lessons are that single events, no matter how large, cannot serve as definitive testing grounds for long-haul success. Visegrad has disproved its skeptics too many times.

NOTES

1. See chapter 2.
2. Government of the Czech Republic, "V4 Prime Ministers Met in Bratislava with German Chancellor Merkel," February 7, 2019, including for photographs, https://www.vlada.cz/en/media-centrum/aktualne/v4-prime-ministers-met-in -bratislava-with-german-chancellor-merkel-172254/.
3. Kruk and Molo, 299.
4. See esp. Hettne and Söderbaum.
5. Pomorska and Vanhoonacker, 76.
6. Zielonka, 41.
7. See, e.g., "Several CEE [Central and East European] capitals have been reluctant if not resentful of Poland's attempt to position itself as a regional power or even a regional leader." Bugajski and Teleki, 99. Quotation from Cabada, 176.
8. Merheim-Eyre, 99.
9. Zięba, "Three Things," 264.
10. Collectively written and published as Valášek and Šuplata, 5.
11. Nič, "Visegrád Group," 284.
12. Le ministère de l'Europe et des Affaires étrangères, "The Weimar Triangle," n.d., accessed June 28, 2021, https://www.diplomatie.gouv.fr/en/country-files/poland /the-weimar-triangle.
13. "30 Jahre Weimarer Dreieck," accessed November 12, 2023, https://thueringen.de /30-jahre-weimarer-dreieck, printout retained.
14. "Foreword of Minister of Foreign Affairs of the Republic of Poland Radosław Sikorski," in *Polish Presidency Report, 2012–13*, 5, https://www.visegradgroup.eu /documents/presidency-programs/2012-2013-polish.
15. Świeboda, 68.
16. Giusti, 156.
17. "Address by the Minister of Foreign Affairs on the Goals of Polish Foreign Policy in 2013," https://www.msz.gov.pl/resource/b67d71b2-1537-4637-91d4-531b0e71 c023:JCR.
18. Czech President Miloš Zeman, was seen also as "building on" the "extreme" positions of his predecessor Václav Klaus, who inferred that Crimea should belong to Russia. Řiháčková, 25.
19. For other examples of international attention to Visegrad's divisions on responses to the Russian invasion, see Victor Jack, "Visegrad Defense Meeting Called Off over Russia Split," Politico, March 29, 2022, https://www.politico.eu/article /visegrad-group-ukraine-russia-war-orban-putin-war-zelenskyy/.
20. See comments in Jan Lopatka/Reuters, "Czechs, Poles Criticize Hungary's Orban amid Divisions over Ukraine War," November 24, 2022, https://nationalpost.com

/pmn/news-pmn/czechs-poles-criticize-hungarys-orban-amid-divisions-over
-ukraine-war-2.
21. The Visegrad website has run that strident statement for years, and it remained current in January 2023, https://www.visegradgroup.eu/about/aims-and-structure.
22. As additional reiteration, the IVF states it is the "only institution of the Visegrad cooperation," cited in "International Visegrad Fund Celebrates 20 Years Advancing Ideas for Regional Cooperation," https://www.visegradfund.org/news/international-visegrad-fund-celebrates-20-years-advancing-ideas-regional-cooperation/.
23. The distinction of "institution" rather than "organization" is used here because the former is generally taken to lack full international legal personality, and Visegrad does not claim such.
24. Further indicative perhaps of Visegrad's institutionalization, this is listed under "Mechanisms of Co-operation," in the Declaration of May 12, 2004, accessed December 17, 2023, https://www.visegradgroup.eu/cooperation/guidelines-on-the-future-110412.
25. Useful early comparative analyses include Cottey, *Subregional*; Bailes.
26. Gianni de Michelis, "Europe: A Golden Opportunity Not to Be Missed," *International Herald Tribune*, March 26, 1990, in Freedman (ed.), 514–16.
27. See Fawn, "Regional," and earlier comparisons, "International."
28. A CEI representative stressed to me that Italy was trying not to have such prominence. Nevertheless, the Italian involvement remains.
29. Bajda, "Visegrad Group," 29.
30. Incisive practitioner-analyst Jiří Schneider asked, "Was Visegrad Defeated in Slavkov?" *Visegrad Insight*, February 11, 2015, https://visegradinsight.eu/was-visegrad-defeated-in-slavkov11022015/. See also Dariusz Kałan, "The Slavkov Triangle: A Rival to the Visegrad Group?" Warsaw: PSIM Bulletin No. 19 (751), February 16, 2015, who wrote, "Its creation is troublesome for the Visegrad Group."
31. Szent-Iványi, 45.
32. "Slavkov Format," https://www.mzv.sk/en/web/en/diplomacy/slavkov-format.
33. "Slavkov Cooperation," accessed April 13, 2020, https://www.mzv.sk/web/en/slavkov-cooperation.
34. *Report on the Foreign Policy of the Czech Republic: Between January 2003 and December 2003*, 48, https://mzv.gov.cz/file/414924/Report_2003.pdf.
35. The proposals are given in the 160-page *The Three Seas Initiative: Priority Interconnection Projects*, from the Bucharest Summit of September 2018, http://three-seas.eu/wp-content/uploads/2018/09/LIST-OF-PRIORITY-INTERCONNECTION-PROJECTS-2018.pdf.
36. "Consulate General of the Republic of Poland in New York City Hosted Consuls General of the Visegrad Group and NYC's Commissioner for International Affairs," October 26, 2020, https://www.gov.pl/web/usa-en/consulate-general-of-the-republic-of-poland-in-new-york-city-hosted-consuls-general-of-the-visegrad-group-and-nycs-commissioner-for-international-affairs.
37. The most comprehensive assessment of CEFTA remains Dangerfield, *Subregional*, and updated with "CEFTA" and "Subregional Integration."
38. Divergent views on Poland's withdrawal are in Jolyon Naegele, "Central Europe: Is Summit Cancellation Another Nail in Visegrad Four Coffin?," RFE/RL, February 25, 2002, https://www.rferl.org/a/1098911.html.

39. V4 Statement on the Western Balkans, September 12, 2019, http://www.visegrad group.eu/documents/official-statements/v4-statement-on-the-190912.

40. When referring to Kosovo, Visegrad uses that spelling and explains that "this designation is without prejudice to positions on status, and is in line with UNSCR 1244/1999 and the ICJ Opinion on the Kosovo declaration of independence." "The Visegrad Group Joint Statement on the Western Balkans," November 29, 2016, https://www.visegradgroup.eu/calendar/2016/the-visegrad-group-joint.

41. That Visegrad states and the Group might no longer serve as role models to EaP states derives from domestic political changes in the former. A synopsis of Visegrad expert views is given in Lucia Yar and Radovan Geist, "V4 No Longer a Role Model for Eastern Partnership Countries," Euractiv, October 27, 2017, https://www.euractiv.com/section/europe-s-east/news/v4-no-longer-a-role-model-for-eastern-partnership-countries/. Domestic political priorities in Visegrad states may also change.

42. "Conclusions of the Video Conference of the Foreign Affairs Committees of V4 Parliaments," June 9, 2021, https://www.visegradgroup.eu/calendar/2021/conclusions-of-the-video.

43. See, e.g.: "If you don't know anything about the Visegrad Group and which countries it represents, you can be forgiven. When I asked people in the streets around the radio building here in Prague whether they had heard of Visegrad, almost all gave the same answer: a very firm 'No.' I asked around fifteen people."
"What is the future for regional cooperation in Central Europe?," Radio Prague International, September 10, 2002, https://english.radio.cz/what-future-regional-cooperation-central-europe-8065731.

44. The author declares an interest in and some possible impact on this, by having included Visegrad in successive comparative regionalism courses run as it happens by my now-colleague Matteo Fumagalli, then at the Central European University, and while it was still in Budapest. The Hungarian national coordinator Edit Szilágyiné Bátorfi graciously also engaged the groups each year, which was drawn from dozens of countries.

45. See the OSCE Network, https://osce-network.net/.

46. Kořan et al., 8.

47. Kirch, 260.

48. "Joint Press conference," July 8, 1997, https://www.nato.int/cps/en/natohq/opinions_25606.htm?selectedLocale=en.

49. Tibor Kiss, "Bankruptcy Procedure," *Népszabadság*, February 23, 2002, as "Hungarian Daily Calls PM Orban 'Gravedigger' of Visegrad Four," *FBIS*, February 26, 2002.

50. ČTK, March 28, 2002.

51. Szelényi, 342.

52. See chapter 2.

53. Sample Central European views (written as "East European") in Craig S. Smith, "Chirac Upsets East Europe by Telling It to 'Shut Up' on Iraq," *New York Times*, February 18, 2003, https://www.nytimes.com/2003/02/18/international/europe/chirac-upsets-east-europe-by-telling-it-to-shut-up-on.html.

54. Honor Mahony, "Sarkozy Warns Visegrad Countries Not to Make a Habit of Pre-summit meetings," EUobserver, November 4, 2009, https://euobserver.com/news/28928.

55. Cited in "The Future of the Visegrad Group within the EU," Radio Prague International, May 14, 2004, https://english.radio.cz/future-visegrad-group-within-eu-8086520.
56. See chapter 7.
57. As chapter 2 noted, the 1991 document has been referred to since as the "Visegrad Declaration," including in official pronouncements and publications, but the founding document did not include "Visegrad" in its title.
58. Rácz, "Congress," 262.
59. Such a correct assertion in post-1991 reference is in Spero, "Central," 141.
60. Literature on the Yugoslav wars of the 1990s is vast and contentious. A single study, analyzing 113 other major studies, remains: Ramet. That Serbian leaderships in both Bosnia and in Yugoslavia/Serbia invoked the memory of the Battle of Kosovo Polje is unquestionable. The interpretations of it and how it contributed specifically to violence can be debated.
61. Interview at the CBSS Secretariat, December 2013.
62. See chapter 8; and Fawn and Drobysh.

ACKNOWLEDGMENTS

Resuming from the introduction, and the mention of compensatory measures taken to address the absence of Hungarian language, acknowledgments are therefore especially due to many Hungarian diplomats and analysts, in Budapest, Brussels, and elsewhere, who generously gave time and insights and in several cases, repeatedly, over years. These especially including Hungarian Visegrad National Coordinators László Püspök and Edit Szilágyiné Bátorfi and their staff.

National Coordinators and their personnel in the other three ministries were also welcoming and helpful. The International Visegrad Fund, also a product of that relaunch, has similarly been very welcoming, including particularly Director Petr Vágner, who held that position during several years of earlier research, and then throughout that time and beyond, with Jiří Sýkora. Visegrad, and those interested in it, are fortunate to have people running it who have tremendous capacity, skill, and dedication.

To the many credits of Visegrad and its wide cadres of interested and talented people, I offer thanks for being awarded an International Visegrad Fellowship in 2013, a small example of Visegrad's outreach and interest in ideas and perspectives. The fellowship afforded extensive interviewing in the region, including with dozens of foreign diplomats on their perceptions of Visegrad. It also allowed me to work with and get to know the tremendous staff of the Europeum think tank, including its then director, and later diplomat David Král, and successor Director Vladimír Bartovic, as well as Ivo Šlosarčík and Zuzana Stuchlíková, and later, Michal Vít, who also kindly brought me into a sizeable and informative collection on Central European cooperation, with a contribution, perhaps illustratively, entitled "the historical difficulties of regional cooperation in a space where my hero is your enemy."

Special thanks are due to the Ústav mezinárodních vztahů / Institute of International Relations (IIR), which has extended research hospitality and assistance to me since my graduate studies in the early 1990s. A succession of directors were extremely welcoming and helpful, including in arranging further interviews and meetings, and access to materials that would have otherwise been difficult to obtain. These Institute directors include luminaries in the study of the region and in policymaking over decades: Jiří Valenta, Otto Pick, Jiří Šedivý, Petr Drulák, Ondřej Ditrych, and Mats Braun.

There I also met Vladimír Handl, whose many works are indispensable to understanding Central Europe. He additionally offered invaluable and kind help, from those early days and since. Alice Kizeková has been gracious and helpful in more recent years, as was Ben Tallis, and the publications overseen by each of them. Reference to the IIR would be incomplete without mention of Michal Kořan, who facilitated much more assistance, as well as convening events and writing contributions that have shaped Visegrad action and thinking. I appreciated the opportunity to work with and to receive comments from Tomáš Strážay, as well as to benefit from his many written analyses. Vladimír Handl and Nik Hynek provided another opportunity and feedback on what became "Visegrad: Fit for Purpose?"

Others go unacknowledged but appreciated nevertheless, from the many Visegrad-related meetings, sessions, and conferences in which I have had the privilege to participate. Those events, many with packed audiences, are also testimonials to the interest that Visegrad generates.

Several people gave feedback on written drafts and join all of those already named in being absolved of what follows. Jason Bruder, Martin Dangerfield, Tomasz Kamusella, Vítek Střítecký, and Martin Zubko kindly and astutely commented on extensive drafts, and other comments were received from Anna-Lena Kirch and Paolo Zucconi. Filippo Costa Buranelli, Anders Wivel, Revecca Pedi, and Tom Long provided comments on an earlier version of chapter 9.

Don Jacobs from Georgetown University Press has been a gracious and profoundly understanding and patient commissioning editor. My deepest gratitude really needs to be expressed. Georgetown University Press also arranged for reports from three anonymous reviewers, whose time and expertise are appreciated. Elizabeth Sheridan of Georgetown University Press provided kind assistance in seeing the typescript through production, and Sonya Manes gave invaluably meticulous and thoughtful suggestions throughout the final draft. Needless to say, but nevertheless: everyone mentioned is exempt from responsibility for errors, omissions, and otherwise in the preceding pages.

This a new work and not replication of publications, although research content, certain arguments, and categorizations have appeared previously. Permissions and assistance were received, with thanks. Tomáš Strážay deserves thanks again for his previous help and for permissions to draw from two articles in *International Issues & Slovak Foreign Policy Affairs*: "Visegrad's Place in the

EU since Accession in 2004: 'Western' Perceptions,'" 23:1–2 (2014): 3–24; and "External Assessments of Visegrad since Its International Recognition over the 'Migrant' Crisis," 27:1–2 (2018): 63–79. Parts are drawn also with thanks and permission from "Visegrad: Fit for Purpose," *Communist and Post-Communist Studies* 46:3 (September 2013): 339–49; "Visegrad: The Study and the Celebration," *Europe-Asia Studies* 60:4 (June 2008): 681–92; and "The Elusive Defined? Visegrád Cooperation as the Contemporary Contours of Central Europe," *Geopolitics* 6:1 (Summer 2001): 47–68.

Finally, friends and family are as essential to a book's emergence, and are invisible, unlike the personalities and processes that constitute its narrative. Especially in the times preceding what became a protracted completion of this book, and in which too many life matters forcibly inserted themselves, several people unconnected to this research ensured that it resumed. I remain confident that they do not know just how much, which is a testament to them, but I privately wish to express a modicum of that especially to Peter, Nicholas, and Katherine. My parents were a paragon of cooperation between themselves, and then toward me. They did not see this work appear but were unfailingly, selflessly supportive of my life overseas. It is to my thankfully living, and truly indispensable, Aunt Sue, who helped in times of deep loss and to whom in tiny measure this book is dedicated. Little could acknowledge that properly.

APPENDIX I:
VISEGRAD COOPERATION
PERSONALITIES

Antall, József (1932–93). Post-communist prime minister of Hungary, May 23, 1990, to December 12, 1993. Suggested the location of Visegrád and was a signatory of the February 1991 Declaration creating Visegrad cooperation.

Dienstbier, Jiří (1937–2011). Czechoslovak dissident; post-communist foreign minister, December 1989–92; and leading proponent of Visegrad.

Figeľ, Ján (1960–) Slovak politician, including as state secretary of the Ministry of Foreign Affairs between 1998 and 2002, when Slovakia rejoined Visegrad and pursued its "catchup" Euro-Atlantic accession.

Geremek, Bronisław (1932–2008). Post-communist Polish dissident; later post-communist foreign minister (1997–2000), chairman of Polish Parliament's Foreign Affairs Committee, and supporter of Visegrad, particularly for Slovakia's reintegration.

Göncz, Árpád (1922–2015). Former dissident writer/translator, jailed by communists. Elected first non-communist president of Hungary; served May 2, 1990, to August 4, 2000. Credited by Havel as having chosen Visegrád to be the location of the founding meeting.

Havel, Václav (1936–2011). Leading Czechoslovak communist-era dissident, also involved in cross-border dissident activities and whose seminal essay "Power of the Powerless"[1] was dedicated to Czechoslovak-Polish dissident solidarity. Post-communist Czechoslovak and Czech president. Can be considered a leading figure, even probably the parent of Visegrad. Signatory of the February 1991 Declaration creating the Visegrad cooperation.

Holáň, Vilém (1938–2021). Czech defense minister between 1994 and 1998 who in the Klaus government worked to lessen and spoke against Visegrad defense cooperation, including as preparation for NATO accession (despite his attendance at some meetings).

Horn, Gyula (1932–2013). Hungarian politician who, in 1956, fought for the regime against fellow Hungarians in the Uprising and who in 1989 as communist foreign minister cut open barbed wire along the Austro-Hungarian border. He attended Havel's 1990 Bratislava Summit and was Hungarian prime minister between 1994 and 1998, when he eased regional tensions and oversaw new treaties with Hungary's neighbors. He also signed Hungary's NATO accession document when President Göncz could not.

Jaruzelski, Wojciech (1923–2014). Polish Communist general and president, responsible for the imposition of martial law during the Solidarity crisis and imprisonment of dissidents. Arguably therefore an unlikely attendant at Havel's Bratislava meeting in April 1990, but each got on, and Jaruzelski uses language similar to Havel's, supportive of regional cooperation and a return to Europe.

Klaus, Václav (1941–). Post-communist Czechoslovak finance minister, then Czech premier. Made efforts to undermine Visegrad in the 1990s, acts that are formally recalled in V4 materials long after; he was, though, a later Visegrad supporter.

Kováč, Michal (1930–2016). First president of independent Slovakia, 1993–98, and maintained a cooperation foreign policy that helped keep aspects of Visegrad and Euro-Atlantic cooperation continuing despite the disruptions caused by Prime Minister Mečiar.

Kukan, Eduard (1939–2022). Czechoslovak diplomat and Slovak foreign minister in 1994 and again in 1998–2006, in both Dzurinda governments. Between those posts he was deeply critical of Klaus's anti-Visegrad policies and highly supportive of its 1998–99 relaunch and of Slovakia's reintegration into it.

Kundera, Milan (1929–2023). Czech/Czechoslovak/Moravian author who went into exile in France in 1975, from where in 1983 he wrote "Un Occident kidnappé ou la tragédie de l'Europe Centrale," published in English in 1984 as "The Tragedy of Central Europe." The essay sparked debates inside and outside the region on the cultural and the political meaning and the possible fates of "Central Europe." Never involved in Visegrad cooperation itself.

Kwaśniewski, Aleksander (1945–). Polish president, 1995–2005, during which time (in 2002) he spoke very supportively of Visegrad, including of its role in both NATO and the EU following accession and also as a problem-solving body for regional-specific issues. He did also briefly propose a larger format of EU accession candidate countries but stated that that would still draw on Visegrad.

Martonyi, János (1944–). FIDESZ (Hungarian Civic Alliance) member and longer-serving Hungarian minister of foreign affairs, 1998–2002 and 2010–14. Supporter of a Hungarian law that gave citizenship to coethnics abroad, and to which Slovakia objected.

Mazowiecki, Tadeusz (1927–2013). Solidarity activist who became Poland's first post-communist prime minister, in September 1989. In that post a supporter of what became regional cooperation and at the November 1990 CSCE he followed Antall's suggestion of a trilateral meeting with a further one, in Kraków, Poland.

Mečiar, Vladimír (1942–). Ex-communist and ex-boxer who became Slovak prime minister, 1990 to 1991, 1992 to 1994, and 1994 to 1998. Domestic and foreign policy priorities harmed Visegrad cooperation. Electoral defeat in 1998 paved the way for Visegrad's relaunch, in Bratislava.

Michnik, Adam (1946–). Leading communist-era Polish dissident who met with Czech counterparts and who partook in the "roundtable" talks in 1989 that ended total communist control. He was briefly in the parliament but otherwise not in public office and was surely one of the members of "civil society" to whom Havel referred who should be and was included in the early regional cooperation. He has been a Visegrad supporter. He remains editor of the influential *Gazeta Wyborcza*.

Orbán, Viktor (1963–). Hungarian student leader in 1989 during regime change and elected to Parliament in 1990. Prime minister 1998–2002 and again from 2010. He caused ruptures in Visegrad relations in 2002 by demanding revocation by Prague and Bratislava of the postwar Beneš Decrees. In 2015 he moved Visegrad into what was internationally seen as a hardline, illiberal but successful position in the EU, resisting forcible quota on accepting migrants.

Šedivý, Jaroslav (1929–). Czechoslovak dissident historian who became a diplomat after the 1989 revolution. As foreign minister in a caretaker government from late 1997 and 1998, his was an auspicious time appointment allowing for signature of the Czech Republic's accession to NATO and the resumption of Visegrad cooperation.

Skubiszewski, Krzysztof (1926–2010). Polish foreign minister (September 12, 1989–October 26, 1993), cofounding foreign minister of Visegrad, and also of the regional cooperation initiative the Council of the Baltic Sea States.

Wałęsa, Lech (1943–). Polish Solidarity leader and Nobel Laureate. Hoped for Polish presidency after collapse of communism and invited as "civil society" to the pre-Visegrad meeting in April 1990. Signatory of the February 1991 Declaration creating the Visegrad cooperation.

Zieleniec, Josef (1946–). Moscow-born first foreign minister of the Czech Republic who served under Klaus, from 1993 to 1997, and spoke of the new country as having moved away from the post-communist world and cooled Prague's previous support for Visegrad.

NOTE

1. Václav Havel, "Power of the Powerless."

APPENDIX II:
CHRONOLOGY

Bold indicates core Visegrad developments.

Events in italics affect Visegrad rather than being produced by it.

1989

June: Polish Roundtable talks lead to the first partially free elections in communist Eastern Europe. Former Polish dissidents gain some political positions.

November 9:   Berlin Wall and other border crossing points controlled by East Germany with West Germany are opened.

November 11:   Governments of Italy, Austria, Hungary, and Yugoslavia sign an agreement for the cooperation that will later become, with expanded membership, the Central European Initiative (CEI). Czechoslovakia and Hungary join the initial cooperation in 1990.

December 10:   The Czechoslovak Communist regime concedes to a majority non-communist cabinet. Dissident Jiří Dienstbier becomes Czechoslovak foreign minister.

December 29:   Havel becomes Czechoslovak president.

1990

January: Václav Havel travels as president, first regionally, to Germany, Hungary, and Poland, rather than to the Soviet Union or the United States, and in addresses to the Polish and Hungarian Parliaments calls for cooperation in their "return to Europe." He proposes and convenes a first meeting to develop those ideas. These speeches are the seeds of Visegrad.

April: Havel convenes an informal meeting of six foreign-ministerial delegations in Bratislava. While the meeting is criticized for amateurism and produces no declaration, it nevertheless should be credited with starting multilateral regional cooperation and is, especially by Slovaks, regarded as the start of Visegrad.

May 2:   Dissident historian Árpád Göncz is installed as Hungarian president.

June 7:   The Warsaw Treaty Organization (WTO) meets in Moscow. Hungary alone demands termination of the Alliance. For Hungarian foreign minister Géza Jeszenszky (and probably only for him) this meeting and action constitute a founding moment for Visegrad.

October 2:   German unification; former East Germany automatically becomes a member of the European Communities (EC) and North Atlantic Treaty Organization (NATO) and any possible inclusion of it in other regional formations becomes moot.

November 21:   Conference on Security and Co-operation in Europe (CSCE) Summit in Paris, culminating in the Paris Charter, which UK prime minister Margaret Thatcher calls a "magna carta" for Europe. At that summit, Hungary's Antall proposes a trilateral meeting (which grounds to later Hungarian claims of initiating Visegrad), and Poland's Tadeusz Mazowiecki suggests a further meeting in Poland. Some genesis of Visegrad dates from this time, with the three countries coordinating aspects of their foreign policy.

1991

January 11–13:   Fourteen unarmed civilians are killed and more injured in Lithuania by Soviet security forces.

January 21:   Czechoslovak, Hungarian, and Polish foreign ministers decide to seek "the speediest disbanding of the Warsaw Pact."[1] Some accounts also note intensive trilateral work on what becomes the Visegrad summit in February.

February 15:   "Visegrad Summit" and signing of the Declaration.

February 25:   Ending of Warsaw Pact is announced (and it is formally terminated on July 1).

July 1:   Already defunct in practice, the Warsaw Treaty Organization is formally disbanded at its final summit, in Prague. Visegrad supporters consider the end of the WTO a cooperation achievement.

November 7–8:   NATO's Rome Summit launches the North Atlantic Cooperation Council (NACC), which meets for the first time on December 20, 1991, as outreach to non-member states.

December 1991: EC Association Agreements are signed with each of and separately with Czechoslovakia, Hungary, and Poland.

1992

March 5–6: The Council of the Baltic Sea States is launched. Poland is a member, and landlocked Czechoslovakia is not, but Havel suggests, unsuccessfully, that his country become a member and thereby bridge the region's northern and southern parts.

May 6: The Prague Summit of Visegrad takes place. The Central European Free Trade Agreement (CEFTA) is launched and the first, clear declaration from the three countries seeking full membership of NATO is made.

June 5–6: Czechoslovak elections result in Václav Klaus becoming prime minister in the Czech Republic and Vladimír Mečiar in Slovakia; Dienstbier loses, removing a Visegrad supporter from office.

July 18: Havel resigns as Czechoslovak president, removing from office a key Visegrad supporter.

October 21, 1993: German defense minister Volker Rühe proposes Visegrad membership of NATO.

October 28: Using the name "Visegrad Summit," the prime ministers of Poland and Hungary and Klaus and Mečiar as premiers of the Czech Republic and Slovakia meet in London with European Commission president Jacques Delors and vice-president Henning Christophersen. Summit chair British prime minister John Major says that the Visegrad countries are making their case for early EC accession, and Delors says that he supports enlargement.

1993

January 1: The formal end of Czechoslovakia occurs; the Czech Republic and Slovakia come into existence.

March 1: CEFTA comes into effect.

April 22: The Holocaust Memorial in Washington, DC, has its official opening, attended by Central European leaders who also each press US president Bill Clinton to open NATO membership (and to confront increasing violence in Bosnia).

June 21–22: The Copenhagen European Council announces criteria for accession by associated countries of Central and Eastern Europe.

July 24: Havel participates in a first meeting of "Central European" presidents in Salzburg, Austria, with his counterparts from Austria, Germany, and

Hungary. This meeting becomes annual, with increased presidential participations and as a possible rival to Visegrad.

October 22:   Returning from a state visit to Poland, Havel says that unity within Visegrad is no longer necessary and that its objectives have either been achieved or have disappeared, particularly Soviet control over the region.

1994

January 10–11:   NATO's Brussels Summit launches Partnership for Peace (PfP) and the Combined Joint Task Force. These cooperation initiatives carry no specific indications of membership but signal nevertheless that it could occur.

January 12:   In a landmark statement, US president Clinton announces in the presence of the presidents of the Czech Republic, Hungary, Poland, and Slovakia, and referring to them as "Visegrad," that NATO enlargement is no longer a question of "whether" but "when."

April 15–16:   Havel convenes Central European presidents in Litomyšl, Czech Republic, a forum that his foreign policy adviser says demonstrates that Visegrad is "dead."

July 1:   As an indicator of support for CEFTA, the Amending Protocol to the CEFTA Agreement comes into effect, increasing trade liberalization of industrial products and expanding the framework of liberalization for agricultural products.

November 25:   CEFTA summit in Poznań, Poland, agrees to abolition of further agricultural trade barriers and to almost complete free trade in industrial products, a year earlier than previously agreed.

December 1:   The North Atlantic Council makes clear that some accession will occur.

December 5:   To the shock of the Clinton administration, Russian president Boris Yeltsin attacks the idea of NATO enlargement and says a "Cold Peace" now is a threat. NATO accession plans for Central Europe nevertheless continue.

1995

June 1:   Czech defense minister Vilém Holáň says that despite his attendance at a Visegrad meeting of his counterparts, no change in Czech policy toward Visegrad had occurred; Prague does not support that cooperation; and its approach to joining NATO remains different from the other three.

August 24:   As signs of further development and interest, CEFTA agrees to removal of tariffs on industrial products as of 1997 and admits Slovenia.

September 3:   NATO's Enlargement Study issues guidelines for accession.

1996

April 1–2:   Meeting of V4 supreme audit authorities is one of only three Visegrad meetings listed on Visegrad website for 1996 in a period when the cooperation is moribund or dead.

September 27–28:   V4 defense ministers meet, an indication of the continuity of military cooperation despite increasing absences of the same in other Visegrad sectors and despite Holáň's earlier comments.

1997

Visegrad records one activity in this year: that of the nongovernmental actor the Red Cross. Nevertheless, multilateral military cooperation continues.

January 1:   All industrial products traded among CETFA countries are now done entirely freely.

May 29:   The Euro-Atlantic Partnership Council is created as a successor to NACC as a more intensified form of cooperation between the Alliance and post-communist states and intended to coexist with PfP.

July 8–9:   At the Alliance's Madrid Summit, membership invitations are issued to the Czech Republic, Hungary, and Poland; even close to the summit date, which specific other countries will be invited remains unclear.

July 10:   Slovak president Kováč blames Mečiar for Slovakia not even receiving mention at NATO's summit as a possible future candidate country.

August 22:   Czech, Hungarian, and Polish prime ministers convene following NATO's accession statement. The meeting is not recorded on Visegrad's website, but attendee Hungarian ambassador Gábor Hárs refers to the meeting as "long overdue" and as a Visegrad meeting that, on that occasion, has occurred without Slovak representation.

1998

September 25–26:   Although unofficial initial results indicate that Mečiar will win, he is defeated in Slovak elections and a new government is formed under the government and the election of Mikuláš Dzurinda.

October 21:   Marking the resumption of Visegrad, the Czech, Hungarian, and Polish presidents meet in Budapest to announce commitments to revitalize cooperation, including in fields beyond the political.

1999

March 12:   Czech, Hungarian, and Polish foreign ministers sign the accession protocols at the Truman Library in Independence, Missouri, bringing their countries into NATO. For Visegrad supporters, NATO accession is an achievement of its cooperation.

April–June: NATO is at war against Yugoslavia over the treatment of Kosovo's Albanian population. The neighboring post-communist states, either joining NATO or intent on doing so, make contributions to facilitating the war effort.

April 24–25:   NATO's Washington Summit commemorates the Alliance's fiftieth anniversary and is the first in which new members of the Czech Republic, Hungary, and Poland participate. Among initiatives is the launch of Membership Action Plans, which establish specifics for Alliance membership of other countries.

December 3:   The V4 presidents issue the Tatras Declaration, reaffirming their cooperation and their resolve to gain EU membership; the meeting is also intended to signal that Slovakia is ready for EU accession talks.

2000

May 4:   In, arguably, an expansion of Visegrad's European recognition, V4 prime ministers meet with their French counterpart.

June 9:   V4 prime ministers create the International Visegrad Fund (IVF).

August 15–16:   Founding meeting takes place of interior ministers of Austria, the Czech Republic, Hungary, Poland, Slovakia, and Slovenia as well as the European commissioner for justice and home affairs in Fuschl am See, Austria. Sometimes called a competitor to Visegrad, the forum has always contained the V4 countries and has focused on specialized issues, including ones in the pre-accession period to the EU, in which existing EU members have aide interests, without distracting from Visegrad.

2001

January 1:   Although this is the intended date, from its 1993 inception, that CEFTA will achieve the elimination of all tariff and nontariff restrictions on industrial trade, these restrictions had been removed four years earlier.

January 19:   Marking Visegrad's tenth anniversary, the Declaration of the Presidents of the V4 States commends the past cooperation, salutes its expansion, and calls its cooperation a model for others.

June 1:   A summit of V4 prime ministers in Kraków gives particular attention to the Group's external relations, particularly with Benelux and Austria's
regional partnership, to EU accession, and for funding of the IVF.

**December 5:   A summit convenes in Luxembourg between Benelux and
Visegrad and issues a statement that affirms Visegrad's integrationist
behavior by confirming "this cooperation fits harmoniously into the historical progress of unification of the European continent, whose cornerstone is the enlargement of the European Union and NATO."[2]**

2002

**February 22:   With EU accession expected, Hungarian premier Viktor
Orbán tells the Foreign Affairs Committee of the European Parliament
that the Czech Republic and Slovakia should rescind the postwar Beneš
Decrees that allowed for the expulsion of Hungarians (and Germans) from
Czechoslovakia. The leaders of those states refuse in protest to attend a
Visegrad prime-ministerial summit in Budapest. Warsaw also withdraws.**

**September 5:   V4 prime ministers issue a statement supporting NATO
expansion, with the meeting's host Leszek Miller stating of Slovakia:
"Given its geographical position but also given its long-term partnership
within the V4 [it] has our special recommendation for entry to NATO."
In turn, Slovak premier Dzurinda says that he received "unambiguous
support."**

**All Visegrad leaders confirm the necessity of having the Visegrad cooper-
ation continue in the EU after their countries' anticipated entry in 2004.**

October 17:   V4 presidents write joint op-ed in the *Irish Times* encouraging
referendum voters to support the Nice Treaty.

*November 21–22:   NATO's Summit in Prague issues membership invitations to
Bulgaria, Estonia, Latvia, Lithuania, Romania, Slovakia, and Slovenia.*

December 12–13:   Copenhagen EU Summit takes place, including the final
decision on accession. Visegrad premiers agreed in advance to demand restoration of enlargement funds. The Danish premier says that the negotiations
were intense and difficult. Little mention of Visegrad occurs at the summit;
instead, there is wide media coverage of the concessions that Poland achieved,
including ones that assist other accession countries.

2003

**March 9:   In another move to increase societal involvement in Visegrad,
the Visegrad Youth Confederation is launched.**

April 16:   The Treaty of Accession to the European Union is signed individually by the V4 and other countries.

June 24–25:   A V4 meeting takes place in Tále, Slovakia, at which the Czech Visegrad presidency establishes the Group's cooperation on securing access to Schengen, arguably becoming one of Group's major achievements in its early years in the EU.

September 11:   Further V4 efforts to prepare for their entry into Schengen are represented in a Statement of the Ministers of the Interior of the Visegrad Group and in their Schengen Action Plan.

October 1:   V4 prime ministers convene a summit at Dobříš, Czech Republic, to coordinate in advance of the EU's Intergovernmental Conference, another significant example of the Group contributing to its advocacy of accession objectives.

2004

March 29:   In NATO's largest enlargement, seven post-communist states became NATO members, including Slovakia, thereby completing the NATO membership of the V4.

May 1:   EU enlargement extends to ten countries, including all four Visegrad states.

May 12:   Visegrad Four leaders issue the Kroměříž Declaration, reaffirming their countries' cooperation even and especially after their entry into the EU.

2005

June 5:   V4 prime ministers issue a joint declaration on the EU, including in favor of the ratification of the Constitutional Treaty.

June 5:   As a sign of ever-increasing Visegrad interest in Ukraine, especially after its "Orange Revolution" the year before, and in intensifying EU-Ukrainian relations, V4 prime ministers issue a Joint Declaration on Ukraine, both pledging Visegrad support to it and stating Visegrad desires for the new EU-Ukrainian Action Plan to succeed.

2006

October 10:   A meeting in Visegrád of V4 prime ministers marks the cooperation's fifteenth anniversary, calling it "a well-established and useful framework." They also warn that any delay to their countries' scheduled

accession to Schengen in October 2007 harm new-member populations' views of the EU.

December 19:   EU launches CEFTA-2006 among Western Balkan states; none of the original members, having attained EU membership, remain. Bulgaria and Romania will leave January 1, 2007, upon their entry into the EU.

2007

June 26:   Statement by the V4 and Bulgaria and Romania Regional Development ministers declaring the importance of common positions of the V4 and of it also coordinating and safeguarding the interests of the other two countries.

December 21:   After concerted efforts, Visegrad ensures that its populations gain access to the EU's borderless Schengen area.

2008

April 3:   Albania and Croatia receive invitations to join NATO at the Alliance's Bucharest Summit. Georgia and Ukraine are told that they will receive a Membership Action Plan but also that they have much to accomplish before that. The statement may alarm Russia into thinking that Alliance memberships for these post-Soviet states is imminent.

April 23:   The Joint Statement of Visegrad, Swedish, and Ukrainian foreign ministers pledges intensive support for Ukraine's European integration. The statement, which can be read as a precursor to the EU's Eastern Partnership advanced by Poland and Sweden and launched in Prague in 2009, also intensifies Moscow's alarm about the absorption of post-Soviet states into Western influence.

September 12–13:   The V4 Summit of Presidents acknowledges that the group has not secured all of its aims, such as the relocation of European institutions and the appointment of certain candidates but reaffirms the platform's utility and reiterates its support for further EU enlargement, starting with Croatia.

2009

April 22:   In Crimea, Ukraine, the IVF director announces, "We would like to foster a much closer cooperation between civil societies in Crimea and in the Visegrad Group."

May 7:   Stemming from a joint Polish-Swedish initiative in the EU, the Eastern Partnership is inaugurated in Prague.

October 6:   Visegrad foreign ministers convene a special summit to pronounce the Group's support for the integration of the Western Balkans into the EU.

2010

December 8–9:   V4 political directors in Washington, DC. US policymakers note that they have come as a group.

June: the Central European Defence Cooperation (CEDC) is launched by the defense ministers of seven states, potentially creating a military-security competitor to Visegrad.

2011

February 15:   Visegrad celebrates its twentieth anniversary; the Summit Declaration calls the V4 "a model for regional cooperation" and "constructive, responsible and respected partners" for advancing EU programs.

2013

March 6:   V4 defense ministers sign a letter of intent to form the Visegrad Battlegroup.

July 1:   Croatia joins the EU, having had support of its candidacy from Visegrad.

July 3:   In a retrospective harbinger of Ukrainian president Viktor Yanukovych's refusal to sign an Association Agreement with the EU, he discusses these prospects with his four Visegrad presidential counterparts.

2014

March 18:   Moscow incorporates Crimea and Sevastopol as federal subjects of the Russian Federation; no other country recognizes the border changes.

June 24:   A Budapest prime-ministerial declaration announces a "call for even closer regional defence cooperation and multinational programs deeply rooted in NATO and EU policies."[3]

November 16:   V4 presidents meet with new Ukrainian president Petro Poroshenko in Prague; V4 presidents call the Russian annexation of Crimea aggression.

December 9:   V4 prime ministers mark the twenty-fifth anniversary of the 1989 revolutions and also pledge greater military cooperation among themselves, as well as in and between the EU and NATO, and say that they will include Ukrainian participation in the V4 Battlegroup that is on operational standby in 2016.

2015

August: Some 200,000 refugees/migrants from Syria and elsewhere reach Hungary through Southeastern Europe.

September 4:   Anticipating an EU plan to force member states to resettle migrants, Visegrad convenes an "extraordinary summit," producing plans of its own.

September 15:   The EU agrees on a distribution plan for refugees/ migrants, but the Czech Republic, Slovakia, and Hungary refuse, soon joined by Poland. The V4 is outspoken on accepting migrants and create its own border protection force.

November 13:   V4 foreign ministers sign an agreement with six Western Balkan counterparts establishing the Western Balkans Fund to assist their regional cooperation. The fund is inspired by and models the IVF.

2016

February 15:   V4 prime ministers issue the Twenty-Fifth Anniversary Declaration, extolling cooperation, including that it does so without institutionalization.

September 16:   The EU meets in Bratislava and issues the "Bratislava Declaration," which effectively rescinds mandatory migrant settlement.

2017

February 2:   A joint communiqué of V4 defense ministers confirms continued positioning of personnel in the Baltic republics and the successor of the Visegrad Battlegroup in 2016. Ongoing preparations are pledged to ensure the ability to be on deployment standby again in 2019.

July 19:   After discovering that common-brand foods are sold in post-communist EU states with inferior ingredients to identical ones sold elsewhere, Visegrad governments issue a statement demanding equality of consumer goods and the upholding of internal market principles. The European Commission initially denies such is in its competence, but Visegrad continues to raise the matter; in April 2018 the commission does ban such "dual" practices.

2018

October 1:   In response to long-standing, well-known deficiencies in regional rail connections, V4 ministers announced a "Declaration of Intent" for cooperation to develop a high-speed railway network.

2019

February 7:   Visegrad prime ministers meet with German chancellor Angela Merkel and mark (in advance) the thirtieth anniversary of the anti-communist revolutions.

September 12:   Western Balkan–Central European summit convenes in Prague; V4 prime ministers call on the EU to accept these countries as members.

2020

April 8:   The V4 announces an extraordinary "V4 East Solidarity Program" for Eastern Partnership countries to assist in fighting Covid-19, pledging up to €250,000. South Korea also gives funds through this program.

September 24:   Visegrad prime ministers meet with European Commission president Ursula von der Leyen to object to German-led plans reattempting to tackle the migrant issue through relocation quotas.

2021

February 17:   V4 prime ministers meet in Wawel Castle, Kraków, with European Council president Charles Michel in attendance, to mark the cooperation's thirtieth anniversary. They call on the EU to expedite COVID vaccine deliveries to their countries

November 30:   V4 presidents issue a joint appeal to their populations calling for vaccination and acknowledging that "our region is facing a dire pandemic situation."[4]

December 13:   At Hungary's invitation, French president Emmanuel Macron attends a Visegrad Summit in advance of France assuming the presidency of the Council of the European Union to discuss its priorities.

2022

February 24:   After ever-increasing military buildups in Belarus and southwestern Russia, Moscow invades Ukraine. Ukrainians flee internally and externally, numbers quickly rising to millions.

March 8:   V4 and the UK issue a joint statement pledging their full support to Ukraine.

March 8:   Visegrad issues a "Joint Communiqué on Providing Joint V4 Assistance to Refugees from Ukraine," with additional funding for their bilateral efforts, to be administered through applications submitted to the IVF.

March 30–31:   A two-day V4 meeting of defense ministers scheduled for Budapest is "cancelled" by the Hungarian government, after others (including also the invited Austrian) withdraw in protest at Orbán's position on the Russian invasion of Ukraine. The Czech defense minister tweets that Orbán cares more for Russian oil than for Ukrainian lives.

November 9:   The V4's Military Planning Group pledges continued military cooperation and exploration of other collaboration, including in defense procurement.

NOTES

1. Dienstbier, "Visegrad" [1999], 16.
2. "Summit Meeting between Benelux and the Visegrad Group Luxembourg (5 December 2001)," https://www.visegradgroup.eu/2001/summit-meeting-between.
3. "Budapest Declaration of the Visegrad Group Heads of Government on the New Opening in V4 Defence Cooperation: June 24, 2014," https://www.visegradgroup .eu/calendar/2014/budapest-declaration-of.
4. "Joint Appeal of the Presidents of the Visegrad Countries Regarding the COVID-19 situation," https://www.visegradgroup.eu/documents/official-statements/joint -appeal-of-v4.

BIBLIOGRAPHY

Note: diacritics are retained or omitted as originally published. The same author may therefore appear both with and without diacritics in this bibliography. Authors are listed in alphabetical order in English, regardless of alternative wordings in the original language.

Ágh, Attila. "Processes of Democratization in the East Central European and Balkan States: Sovereignty-Related Conflicts in the Context of Europeanization." *Communist and Post-Communist Studies* 32:3 (September 1999): 263–79.

Alecu de Flers, Nicole, and Elfriede Regelsberger. "The EU and Inter-regional Cooperation." In Christopher Hill and Michael Smith (eds.), *International Relations and the European Union*. Oxford: Oxford University Press, 2005, 317–42.

Altshuler, David S. "Tunneling towards Capitalism in the Czech Republic." *Ethnography* 2:1 (March 2001): 115–38.

Andor, László. *Hungary on the Road to the European Union: Transition in Blue.* Westport, CT: Praeger, 2000.

Annuaire Européen 1992 / European Yearbook 1992, vol. 40, section 15. Leiden: Brill for the Council of Europe, 1993.

Antall, József. "Ties that Bind: The Visegrád Summit. Address Delivered by the Prime Minister of Hungary at the Prague Summit of the Visegrád Three (Prague, 6 May 1992)." In Jeszenszky (ed.), *József Antall*, 276–79.

Antohi, Sorin. "Habits of the Mind." In *Between Past and Future: The Revolutions of 1989 and Their Aftermath*. Budapest: Central European University Press, 2013, 61–77.

Appel, Hilary. "Corruption and the Collapse of the Czech Transition Miracle." *East European Politics and Societies* 15:3 (2001): 528–53.

Applebaum, Anne. *Twilight of Democracy.* London: Penguin, 2020.

Arató, Krisztina, and Boglarka Koller. "Hungary in the Visegrád Group: Introducing a Three-Level Game Approach." In Schweiger and Visvizi (eds.), 90–105.

Asmus, Ronald D. *Opening NATO's Door: How the Alliance Remade Itself for a New Era.* New York: Columbia University Press, 2002.

Baer, Josette. "Boxing and Politics in Slovakia: 'Meciarism' Roots, Theory, Practice." *Democratization* 8:2 (2001): 97–116.

Bailes, Alyson J. K. "Subregional Organizations: The Cinderellas of European Security." *NATO Review* 45:2 (March 1997): 27–31.

Bajda, Piotr. "The Visegrad Group between the Trade-Mark and the Political Organization of the Peripheral Countries." In Marušiak et al. (eds.), 28–41.

Bakos, Gabor. "After COMECON: A Free Trade Area in Central Europe?" *Europe-Asia Studies* 45:6 (November 1993): 1025–44.

Balcer, Adam. "A Wishful Thinking? Military Cooperation in the Visegrad Group." *V4 Revue*, 2013.

Baldock, David. "Retaining the Centre Stage." In Haigh (as overall author), *EU Environmental Policy: Its Journey to Centre Stage.* London: Routledge for Institute of Environmental Policy, 2016.

Bali, Zoltán, Jozef Bátora, István Gyarmati, Jan Havránek, Jan Jireš, Jan Wojciech Lorenz, Mário Nicolini, Milan Šuplata, and Marcin Terlikowski. *DAV4 II Expert Group Report on Visegrad Defence Collaboration.* Bratislava, Budapest, Prague, and Warsaw: Central European Policy Institute, 2013.

Balogh, Péter. "The Revival of 'Central European' among Hungarian Political Elites: Its Meaning and Geopolitical Implications." *Hungarian Geographical Bulletin* 66:3 (2017): 191–202.

Barany, Zoltan. "Hungary: An Outpost on the Troubled Periphery." In Michta (ed.), 74–111.

Barany, Zoltan. *The Future of NATO Expansion: Four Case Studies.* Cambridge: Cambridge University Press, 2012.

Barnes, Ian, and Pamela M. Barnes. *The Enlarged European Union.* Harlow: Longman, 1995.

Basora, Adrian A. *The Value of the Visegrad Four.* Washington: Atlantic Council, 2011.

Bátora, Jozef, and Janne Haaland Matlary. "Regional Security Integration: Nordic and Visegrad Approaches." In Jozef Bátora and Harald Baldersheim (eds.), *The Governance of Small States in Turbulent Times: The Exemplary Cases of Norway and Slovakia.* Opladen, Germany: Barbara Budrich Publishers, 2012, 19–37.

Batt, Judy. "The Political Transformation of East Central Europe." In Hugh Miall (ed.), *Redefining Europe: New Patterns of Conflict and Cooperation.* London: Pinter Publishers, 1994, 30–47.

Bauerová, Helena. "Migration Policy of the V4 in the Context of Migration Crisis." *Politics in Central Europe* 14:2 (2018): 99–120.

Bebler, Anton. "Slovenia and the Second Round of NATO Enlargement." *European Security* 9:1 (2000): 105–12.

Behr, Timo, and Albane Siwiecki. *EU-Enlargement and Armaments Defence Industries and Markets of the Visegrad Countries.* Paris: EU Institute for Security Studies, 2004.

Bell, Joseph P., and Ryan C. Hendrickson. "NATO's Visegrad Allies and the Bombing of Qaddafi: The Consequence of Alliance Free-Riders." *Journal of Slavic Military Studies* 25:2 (2012): 149–61.

Beneš, Vít, and Mats Braun, "The European Dimension of the Czech Foreign Policy." In Kořan (ed.), 59–92.

Black, James, Stephen Flanagan, Gene Germanovich, Ruth Harris, David Ochmanek, Marina Favaro, Katerina Galai, and Emily Ryen Gloinson. *Enhancing Deterrence and Defence on NATO's Northern Flank: Allied Perspectives on Strategic Options for Norway.* Santa Monica, CA, and Cambridge: RAND Corporation, 2020.

Blackwell, Stephen. "An Alliance within an Alliance?" In Roger E. Kanet (ed.), *The New Security Environment: The Impact on Russia, Central and Eastern Europe*. Aldershot, UK: Ashgate, 2005, 135–45.

Blinken, Donald. "How NATO Joined Hungary." *European Security* 8:4 (1999): 109–29.

Blinken, Vera, and Donald Blinken. *Vera and the Ambassador: Escape and Return*. Albany: State University of New York Press, 1999.

Bojkov, Victor D. "Neither Here, Not There: Bulgaria and Romania in Current European Politics." *Communist and Post-Communist Studies* 37:4 (December 2004): 509–22.

Bolton, Jonathan. *Worlds of Dissent: Charter 77, the Plastic People of the Universe, and Czech Culture Under Communism*. Cambridge: Harvard University Press, 2008.

Bombik, Svetoslav and Ivo Samson. "Slovakia." In Smoke (ed.), 146–63.

Boyes, Roger. *The Naked President: A Political Life of Lech Walesa*. London: Secker and Warburg, 1994.

Bozóki, András. "The Image of Europe: European Integration and the New Central Europe." In Sergio Ortino, Mitja Zagar, and Vojtech Mastny (eds.), *The Changing Faces of Federalism: Institutional Reconfiguration in Europe from East to West*. Manchester: Manchester University Press, 2005, 85–106.

Braun, Mats. *The Politics of Regional Cooperation and the Impact on the European Union*. Cheltenham, UK: Edward Elgar, 2021.

Brix, Emil, and Erhard Busek. *Central Europe Revisited: Why Europe's Future Will Be Decided in the Region*. London: Routledge, 2021.

Brown, J. F. *The Grooves of Change: Eastern Europe at the Turn of the Millennium*. Durham, NC: Duke University Press, 2001.

Brown, J. F. *Hopes and Shadows: Eastern Europe after Communism*. Durham, NC: Duke University Press, 1994.

Brown, J. F. "Introduction: A Year of Productive Discontent." In *Forging Ahead, Falling Behind: The OMRI Annual Survey of Eastern Europe and the Former Soviet Union 1996*. New York: M.E. Sharpe, 1997, 1–8.

Brown, J. F. *Surge to Freedom: The End of Communist Rule in Eastern Europe*. Durham, NC: Duke University Press, 1991.

Brusenbauch Meislova, Monika. "Great Expectations or Misplaced Hopes? The Role of the Visegrád Group in the Brexit Process." *Europe-Asia Studies* 71:8 (2018): 1261–84.

Brzezinski, Zbigniew. "Post-communist Nationalism." *Foreign Affairs* 68:5 (Winter 1989/90): 1–24.

Bugajski, Janusz. *Nations in Turmoil: Conflict and Cooperation in Eastern Europe*. 2nd ed. Boulder, CO: Westview Press, 1995.

Bugajski, Janusz. "Visegrad's Past, Present and Future." *Hungarian Review* 2:3 (April 2011). https://hungarianreview.com/article/visegrads-past-present-and-future/.

Bugajski, Janusz, and Ilona Teleki. *Atlantic Bridges: America's New European Allies*. Lanham, MD: Rowman and Littlefield, 2006.

Bukalska, Patrycja, and Mariusz Bocian. *A New Visegrad Group in the New European Union—Possibilities and Opportunities for Development*. Warsaw: Centre for Eastern Studies, 2003.

Bunce, Valerie. "The Visegrad Group: Regional Cooperation and European Integration in Post-Communist Europe." In Katzenstein (ed.), 240–84.

Burant, Stephen R. "After NATO Enlargement: Poland, the Czech Republic, and Hungary, and the Problem of Further European Integration." *Problems of Post-Communism* 48:2 (2001): 25–41.

Burant, Stephen R. "International Relations in a Regional Context: Poland and Its Eastern Neighbours—Lithuania, Belarus, Ukraine." *Europe-Asia Studies* 45:3 (1993): 395–418.

Burant, Stephen R. "Visegrad in All but Name." *Analysis of Current Events* 10:6 (June 1998): 6–11.

Busek, Erhard, and Emil Brix. *Mitteleuropa Revisited: Warum Europas Zukunft in Mitteleuropa entschieden wird.* Vienna: Verlag Kremayr and Scheriau, 2018.

Bútora, Martin. "The Spirit of Visegrad Was Revived in Washington." In Jagodziński (ed.), 90–93.

Bútora, Martin. "A Miracle Called Visegrad." In Jagodziński (ed.), 142–44.

Bútora, Martin, and Zora Bútorová. "Slovakia: The Identity Challenges of the Newly Born State." *Social Research* 60:4 (Winter 1993): 705–36.

Cabada, Ladislav. "The Visegrad Cooperation in the Context of Other Central European Cooperation Formats." *Politics in Central Europe* 14:2 (2018): 165–79.

Cabada, Ladislav, and Šárka Waisová. "The Visegrad Group as an Ambitious Actor of (Central-) European Foreign and Security Policy." *Politics in Central Europe* 14:2 (2018): 9–20.

Cabada, Ladislav, and Christopher Walsch. *Od Dunajské federace k Visegrádské skupině.... a zpět?* [From the Danube Federation to the Visegrad Group . . . . and back]. Prague: Metropolitan University Prague Press, 2017.

Cameron, Fraser. "The European Union, Enlargement and Regional Cooperation." NATO Economic Colloquium 1997. https://www.nato.int/docu/colloq/1997/97-4-5.htm.

Čarnogurský, Ján. "Visegrad Yesterday, Today and Tomorrow." In Jagodziński (ed.), 33–35.

Carr, Matthew. *Fortress Europe: Inside the War against Immigration.* London: Hurst, 2015.

Central European Policy Institute. *Report by the High Level Reflection Group. Central Europe Fit for the Future. Visegrad Group Ten Years after EU Accession.* Bratislava and Warsaw: Central European Policy Institute, 2014.

Cercel, Cristian. *Romania and the Quest for European Identity: Philo-Germanism without Germans.* London: Routledge, 2018.

Chenoweth, Eric. "Dancing with Dictators: General Jaruzelski's Revisionists." *World Affairs* 177:3 (September/October 2014): 57–67.

Chmel, Rudolf. *Moja maďarská otázka: Zo zápiskov posledného česko-slovenského veľvyslanca v Maďarsku* Bratislava: Vydavateľstvo Kalligram, 1996.

Chmel, Rudolf. "My Visegrad Question." In Jagodziński (ed.), 36–38.

Chmel, Rudolf. "Syndrome of Trianon in Hungarian Foreign Policy and Act on Hungarians Living in Neighboring Countries." *Slovak Foreign Policy Affairs* 1 (2002): 93–106.

Christopher, Warren. "Toward a More Integrated World," US Department of State Dispatch 393, vol. 5, pt. 1, no. 25 (June 1994): 393–95.

Cianciara, Agnieszka K. *"Eastern Partnership"—Opening a New Chapter of Polish Eastern Policy and the European Neighbourhood Policy?* Warsaw: Institute of Public Affairs, June 2008.

Clarke, Douglas L. "Central Europe: Military Cooperation in the Triangle." *RFE/RL Research Report* (10 January 1992): 42–45.

Copeland, Paul. "Central and Eastern Europe: Negotiating Influence in an Enlarged European Union." *Europe-Asia Studies* 66:3 (2014): 467–87.

Cottey, Andrew (ed.) *Subregional Cooperation in the New Europe*. London: Macmillan, 1999.

Cottey, Andrew. "The Visegrád Group and Beyond: Security Cooperation in Central Europe." In Cottey (ed.), 69–89.

Czech National Interests. Prague: Institute of International Relations, 1993.

Dangerfield, Martin. "Defence Policies of Small States in Central Europe: The Role of Visegrad Cooperation." Paper presented at "Small States and the New Security Environment," Reykjavik, Iceland, June 2018, https://www.researchgate.net /publication/328808078_Defence_Policies_of_Small_States_in_Central_Europe _The_Role_of_Visegrad_Cooperation.

Dangerfield, Martin. "CEFTA: Between the CMEA and the European Union." *Journal of European Integration* 26:3 (2004): 309–38.

Dangerfield, Martin. "Ideology and the Czech Transformation: Neoliberal Rhetoric or Neoliberal Reality?" *East European Politics and Societies* 11:3 (1997): 436–69.

Dangerfield, Martin. "Subregional Cooperation in Central and Eastern Europe: Support or Substitute for the 'Return to Europe'?" *Perspectives on European Politics and Society* 2:1 (2001): 55–77.

Dangerfield, Martin. *Subregional Economic Cooperation in Central and Eastern Europe: The Political Economy of CEFTA*. Cheltenham, UK: Edward Elgar, 2001.

Dangerfield, Martin. "Subregional Integration and EU Enlargement: Where Next for CEFTA?" *Journal of Common Market Studies* 44:2 (2006): 305–24.

Dangerfield, Martin. "Visegrad Group Co-operation and Russia." *Journal of Common Market Studies* 50:6 (November 2012): 958–74.

Dangerfield, Martin. "V4: A New Brand for Europe? Ten Years of Post-accession Regional Cooperation in Central Europe." *Poznań University Economics Review* 14:4 (2014): 71–90.

Dangerfield, Martin. "The Visegrád Group in the Expanded European Union: From Preaccession to Postaccession Cooperation." *European Politics and Societies* 22:3 (2008): 630–67.

Daniška, Jaroslav. "Visegrad: From Intellectual Idea to Political Reality." *International Issues & Slovak Foreign Policy Affairs* 1–2 (2018): 43–53.

Dauderstädt, Michael. *The EC and Eastern European: The Light Is Failing in the Lighthouse*. Bonn: Friedrich Ebert Stiftung, 1993.

Davies, Norman. *Europe: A History*. London: Bodley Head, 1996.

De Santis, Hugh. "Romancing NATO: Partnership for Peace and East European Stability." *Journal of Strategic Studies* 17:4 (1994): 61–81.

Dean, Ambassador Jonathan. "Expansion Now Is Unnecessary." In Kenneth W. Thompson (ed.), *NATO Expansion*. Lanham, MD: University Press of America, 1998, 109–12.

Dhand, Otilia. *The Idea of Central Europe: Geopolitics, Culture and Regional Identity*. London: I.B. Tauris, 2018.

Dick, C. J., J. F. Dunne, and J. B. K. Lough. "Potential Sources of Conflict in Post-communist Europe." *European Security* 2:3 (Autumn 1993): 386–406.

Dienstbier, Jiří. *Od snění k realitě: Vzpomínky z let 1989–1999* [From Dreaming to Reality: Memories from 1989–1999]. Prague: Nakladatelství Lidové Noviny, 1999.

Dienstbier, Jiří. *Snění o Evropě: Politický Esej*. [Dreaming of Europe: A Political Essay]. Prague: Lidové Noviny, 1990.

Dienstbier, Jiří. "Visegrad." *Perspectives* 12 (Summer 1999): 15–21.

Dienstbier, Jiří. "Visegrad—The First Phase." In Jagodziński (ed.), 41–45.

Dienstbier, Jiří. "Why We Need Visegrád." *New Presence* (Autumn 2001): 10–11.

Dingsdale, Alan. "Redefining 'Eastern Europe': A New Regional Geography of Post-Socialist Europe?" *Geography* 84:3 (July 1999): 204–21.

Dostál, Vít. "Czech-Polish Relations." *New Eastern Europe* 6 (2017): 180–83.

Druker, Jeremy. "Vestiges of Visegrad." *Transitions* 5:9 (1998): 47–53.

Drulák, Petr. "When Does Regional Cooperation Make Sense?" In Šťastný (ed.), 47–66.

Dubowski, Tomasz. "Visegrad Group: Common Goals and Potential at the Level of European Union Institutions." In Agnieszka Piekutowska and Iwona Wrońska (eds.), *Ten Years of the Visegrad Group Member States in the European Union.* Warsaw: Bialystok, 2015, 11–24.

Dubravčíková, Klára, Filip Šebok, Martin Šebeňa, Matej Šimalčík, and Richard Q. Turcsányi. *Prospects for Developing the V4+China Cooperation Platform.* Bratislava: Central European Institute of Asian Studies, 2019.

Duleba, Alexander. "Russia, Central Europe and NATO Enlargement." *Medzinárodné Otázky* 7:4 (1998): 15–46.

Duleba, Alexander. "The Slovak-Ukrainian-Russian Security Triangle." In Margarita Mercedes Balmaceda (ed.), *On the Edge: Ukrainian-Central European-Russian Security Triangle.* Budapest: Central European University Press, 2000, 69–126.

Dunay, Pál. "Hungary: Defining the Boundaries of Security." In Carp (ed.), 122–54.

Dunay, Pál. "Subregional Co-operation in East-Central Europe: The Visegrád Group and the Central European Free Trade Agreement." *ÖZP* 32 (2003): 45–56.

Dunay, Pál. "Security Cooperation in the Visegrád Quadrangle: Present and Future." In Andrew J. Williams (ed.), *Reorganizing Eastern Europe.* Aldershot, UK: Dartmouth, 1994, 121–44.

Dutkiewicz, Piotr, and Robert J. Jackson (eds.). *NATO Looks East.* New York: Praeger Publishers, 1998.

Ehl, Martin. "The Three Seas Initiative through Czech Eyes: Unconvinced by Their Neighbour's Plans." *Polish Quarterly of International Affairs* 26:2 (2017): 200–205.

Engelmayer, Ákos. "Fanfares and Frictions." In Jagodziński (ed.), 46–47.

Epstein, Rachel A. *In Pursuit of Liberalism: International Institutions in Postcommunist Europe.* Baltimore: Johns Hopkins University Press, 2008.

European Movement in Serbia. *Advocacy Strategy for the EU Integration of the Western Balkans: Guidelines.* Belgrade: European Movement in Serbia, 2016.

European Perspectives, special issue on Slovenia's Role in Visegrad Group 7:2 (October 2015).

EUROPEUM. *From Warsaw to Tirana: Overcoming the Past Together: Good Practices and Lessons Learned from the Visegrad Four and Western Balkans.* Prague: EUROPEUM, 2019.

Falk, Barabara. *The Dilemmas of Dissidence in East-Central Europe.* Budapest: Central European University Press, 2003.

Fałkowski, Mateusz, Patrycja Bukalska, and Grzegorz Gromadzki. *Yes to Visegrad.* Warsaw: Institute for Public Affairs, November 2003.

Fawn, Rick. "Alliance Behaviour: The Absentee Liberator, and the Influence of Soft Power." *Cambridge Review of International Affairs* 9:3 (September 2006): 465–80.

Fawn, Rick. "'Bashing about Rights': Russia and the 'New' EU States on Human Rights and Democracy Promotion." *Europe-Asia Studies* 61:10 (December 2009): 1777–1803.

Fawn, Rick. "The Elusive Defined? Visegrád Cooperation as the Contemporary Contours of Central Europe." *Geopolitics* 6:1 (Summer 2001): 47–68.

Fawn, Rick. "External Assessments of Visegrad since Its International Recognition over the 'Migrant' Crisis." *International Issues & Slovak Foreign Policy Affairs* 27:1–2 (2018): 63–79.

Fawn, Rick. "The Historical Difficulties of Regional Cooperation in a Space Where My Hero Is Your Enemy." In Michal Vit and Magdalena M. Baran (eds.), *Transregional versus National Perspectives on Contemporary Central European History: Studies on the Building of Nation-States and Their Cooperation in the 20th and 21st Century*. Stuttgart: Ibidem Press, 2017, 10–20.

Fawn, Rick. "The International Transformation and Re-regionalization of 'Eastern Europe'." In Stephen White, Judy Batt, and Paul G. Lewis (eds.), *Central and East European Politics 5*. Durham, NC: Duke University Press, and Basingstoke: Palgrave, 2013, 119–38.

Fawn, Rick. "Reconstituting a National Identity: Ideologies in Czech Foreign Policy after the Split." *Journal of Communist Studies and Transition Politics* 19:3 (2003): 204–28.

Fawn, Rick. "Regional Relations and Regional Security." In Sabrina P. Ramet and Christine M. Hassenstab (eds.), *Central and Southeast European Politics since 1989*. Cambridge University Press, 2019, 507–38.

Fawn, Rick, "'Regions' and Their Study: Where From, What For and Where To." *Review of International Studies* 35 (February 2009): 5–34.

Fawn, Rick. "Symbolism in the Diplomacy of Czech President Václav Havel." *East European Quarterly* 38:1 (March 1999): 1–19.

Fawn, Rick. "Visegrad: Fit for Purpose." *Communist and Post-Communist Studies* 46:3 (September 2013): 339–49.

Fawn, Rick. "Visegrad's Place in the EU since Accession in 2004: 'Western' Perceptions." *International Issues & Slovak Foreign Policy Affairs* 23:1–2 (2014): 3–24.

Fawn, Rick. "Visegrad: The Study and the Celebration." *Europe-Asia Studies* 60:4 (June 2008): 681–92.

Fawn, Rick, and Iuliia Drobysh. "Visegrad and Ukraine between Maidan, the Seizure of Crimea, the Conflict in Eastern Ukraine, and the 2022 Invasion." *Europe-Asia Studies*. 76:3 (April 2023): 314–38.

Figel', Ján. "Foreword: Visegrad: Not Only a Symbol, but a Challenge for the Future." In Šťastný (ed.), 7–10.

Fingerland, Jaroslav. "Central and Eastern European versus Soviet Economic Reforms." In Reiner Weichhardt (ed.), *The Soviet Economy under Gorbachev: Colloquium 20–22 March 1991*. Brussels: NATO, 1991, 204–11.

Fisher, Sharon, with Zsofia Szilagyi and Jiri Pehe. "Central Europe Rethinks Russian Ties." In *OMRI Annual Survey of Eastern Europe and the Former Soviet Union 1996*. Armonk, NY: M.E. Sharpe, 1996, 378–83.

Fitzmaurice, John. *Damming the Danube: Gabčikovo and Post-Communist Politics in Europe*. Boulder, CO: Westview, 1996.

Forsberg, Tuomas. "The Rise of Nordic Defence Cooperation: A Return to Regionalism?" *International Affairs* 89:5 (September 2013): 1161–81.

Freedman, Lawrence (ed.). *Europe Transformed: Documents on the End of the Cold War*. London: Tri-Service Press, 1990.

Gaddis, John Lewis. "History, Grand Strategy and NATO Enlargement." *Survival* 40:1 (Spring 1998): 145–51.

Gärtner, Heinz, and Allen G. Sens. "The Adaptation of Institutions and Small States." In Ingo Peters (ed.), *The New Security Challenges: The Adaptation of International Institutions: Reforming the UN, NATO, EU and CSCE*. Münster. Lit Verlag and New York: St. Martin's Press, 1996, 179–202.

Garton Ash, Timothy (ed). *Freedom for Publishing, Publishing for Freedom: The Central and East*. Budapest: CEU Press, 1995.

Garton Ash, Timothy. *The Uses of Adversity: Essays on the Fate of Central Europe*. New York: Random House, 1989.

Garton Ash, Timothy. *We the People*. London: Granta, 1990.

Gerasymchuk, Sergiy. "Visegrad Group's Solidarity in 2004–2014: Tested by Ukrainian Crisis." *International Issues & Slovak Foreign Policy Affairs* 23:1–2 (2014): 42–54.

Geremek, Bronislaw. "The Transformation of Central Europe." *Journal of Democracy* 10:3 (July 1999): 115–20.

Germuska, Pál, "Balancing between the COMECON and the EEC: Hungarian Elite Debates on European Integration during the Long 1970s." *Cold War History* 19:3 (2019): 401–20.

Germuska, Pál. *Unified Military Industries of the Soviet Bloc: Hungary and the Division of Labor in Military Production*. Lanham, MD: Lexington Books 2015.

Gerosa, Guido. "The North Atlantic Cooperation Council." *European Security* 1:3 (1992): 273–94.

Giegerich, Bastian. "NATO's Smart Defence: Who's Buying?" *Survival* 54:3 (June–July 2012): 69–77.

Giusti, Serena. "The Light and Ancillary Regionalism in Central Europe." In Carlo Frappi and Gulshan Pashayeva (eds.), *Cooperation in Eurasia: Linking Identity, Security, and Development*. Milan: Ledizioni, 2018.

Gniazdowski, Mateusz. "Poland's Policy in the Visegrad Group." *Yearbook of Polish Foreign Policy* 1 (2008): 162–94.

Gniazdowski, Mateusz. "Possibilities and Constrains of the Visegrád Countries Cooperation within the EU." *Foreign Policy Review* 1–2 (2005): 77–96.

Gniazdowski, Mateusz. "Comments on the Structure of the Three Seas Initiative and the Warsaw Summit." *Polish Quarterly of International Affairs* 26:2 (2017): 229–32.

Gniazdowski, Mateusz, and Tomáš Strážay. "Visegrad Cooperation on Bosnia and Herzegovina: Challenges and Opportunities." In Marta Szpala (ed.), *Paradoxes of Stabilisation: Bosnia and Herzegovina from the Perspective of Central Europe*. Warsaw: Centre of Eastern Studies, 2016, 139–57.

Goldgeier, James M. "NATO Expansion: The Anatomy of a Decision." *Washington Quarterly* 21:1 (1998): 83–102

Goldgeier, James M. *Not Whether But When: The US Decision to Enlarge NATO*. Washington: Brookings, 1999.

Gołembski, Franciszek. "The Visegrad Group: An Exercise in Multilateral Cooperation in Central Europe." *Polish Quarterly of International Affairs* 3:3 (Summer 1994): 55–68.

Göncz, Arpád. "Visegrad Three, Visegrad Four." In Jagodziński (ed.), 48–49.

Gordon, Philip H. "Does the WEU have a Role?" *Washington Quarterly* 20:1 (1997), 125-40.

Grabiński, Tomasz, in collaboration with Peter Morvay. "The Summit in the Frosty Ruins: The Background of the 1991 Visegrad Meeting." In Jagodziński (ed.), 86–87.

Graubard, Stephen R. (ed.) *Eastern Europe . . . Central Europe . . . Europe.* Boulder, CO: Westview Press, 1991.

Grayson, George W. *Strange Bedfellows: NATO Marches East.* Lanham, MD: University Press of America, 1999.

Groszkowski, Jakub. "The V4 and the EU." *International Issues & Slovak Foreign Policy Affairs* 37:1–2 (2018): 3–15.

Grúber, Károly, Barnabás Kovács, and Csaba Törő. "In Search of Better Coordination and Representation of Shared Interests: Visegrad Cooperation within the European Union." *Foreign Policy Review* (2010): 37–53.

Gubová, Olga. "Comparative Regionalism and the Concept of Cognitive Regioness: The Case of the Visegrad Group." *Annals of the Ovidius University of Constanta Political Science Series* 9 (2020): 107–30.

Gyárfášová, Oľga. "Visegrad as Viewed by Citizens of the Four Member Countries." In Jagodziński (ed.), 150–55.

Hacker, Paul. *Slovakia on the Road to Independence: An American Diplomat's Eyewitness Account.* University Park: Pennsylvania State University Press, 2010.

Had, Miloslav, and Vladimir Handl. "The Czech Republic." In Smoke (ed.), 129–45.

Handl, Vladimir. "Germany and Central Europe: A Differentiated Dynamic Instead of *Mitteleuropa.*" In Šabić and Drulák (eds.), 104–24.

Handl, Vladimir. *Germany and the Visegrad Countries between Dependence and Asymmetric Partnership?* Hamburg: Institut für Internationale Politik an der Universität der Bundeswehr, 2002.

Handl, Vladimír. "Politika Sousedství a Středoevropské Spolupráce." In Otto Pick and Vladimír Handl (eds.), *Zahraniční Politika České Republiky 1993–2004.* Prague: Ústav Mezinárodních Vztahů, 2004, 57–63.

Handl, Vladimir. "Visegrad—Chances for Recovery?" In Martin Dangerfield and Vladislav Goryunov (eds.), *Subregional Dimensions of European Union Enlargement.* Wolverhampton, UK: University of Wolverhampton, 2001, 7–23.

Handl, Vladimír, and Adrian Hyde-Price. "Germany and the Visegrad Countries." *Slovak Foreign Policy Affairs* 2:1 (Spring 2001): 56–74.

Handl, Vladimír, Kerry Longhurst, and Marcin Zaborowski. "Germany's Security Policy towards East Central Europe." *Perspectives* 14 (Summer 2000): 54–70.

Hanley, Seán. *The New Right in the New Europe: Czech Transformation and Right-Wing Politics, 1989–2006.* London: Routledge, 2008.

Hardt, John P., and Richard F. Kaufman (eds.), *East-Central European Economies in Transition.* Armonk, NY: M.E. Sharpe, 1994.

Hárs, Gábor. "Visegrad—A Personal Memoir of Cooperation." In Jagodziński (ed.), 50–53.

Haughton, Tim. "Vladimír Mečiar and His Role in the 1994–1998 Slovak Coalition Government." *Europe-Asia Studies* 54:8 (December 2002): 1319–38.

Haughton, Tim. "When Permissiveness Constrains: Money, Regulation and the Development of Party Politics in the Czech Republic (1989–2012)." *East European Politics* 30:3 (2014): 372–88.

Havel, Václav. "An Anatomy of Reticence." In Vladislav (ed.), 164–95.

Havel, Václav. "A Call for Sacrifice: The Co-responsibility of the West." *Foreign Affairs* 73:2 (March–April 1994): 2–7.

Havel, Václav. "Power of the Powerless." In Vladislav (ed.), 36–122.

Havel, Václav. *To the Castle and Back*. London: Granta Books, 2008.

Havlíček, Tomáš, Milan Jeřábek, and Jaroslav Dokoupil. "The Schengen Phenomenon: Fact or Fiction?" In Tomáš Havlíček, Milan Jeřábek, and Jaroslav Dokoupil (eds.), *Borders in Central Europe After the Schengen Agreement*. Cham, Switzerland: Springer, 2018, 49–68.

Havlík, Vratislav, and Ondřej Mocek. "Václav Klaus as a Driver of Czech Euroskepticism." In Tom Hashimoto and Michael Rhimes (eds.), *Reviewing European Union Accession: Unexpected Results, Spillover Effects, and Externalities*. Leiden, Netherlands: Brill, 2018, 96–112.

Hettne, Björn, and Fredrik Söderbaum. "Theorising the Rise of Regionness." *New Political Economy* 5:3 (2000): 457–72.

High Level Reflection Group. *Central Europe Fit for the Future: Visegrad Group Ten Years After EU Accession*. Bratislava and Warsaw: CEPI and emosEUROPA, 2014.

Hill, William H. *No Place for Russia: European Security Institutions since 1989*. Washington, DC: Woodrow Wilson Centre, 2018.

Hodža, Milan. *Federalism in Central Europe: Reflections and Reminiscences*. London: Jarrolds, 1942.

Holbrooke, Richard. *To End a War*. New York: Modern Library, 1999.

Hornat, Jan. *The Visegrad Group and Democracy Promotion: Transition Experience and Beyond*. Basingstoke: Palgrave Macmillan, 2021.

Horváth, Gábor. "Perceptions of ESDP/CSDP in the Visegrad Countries: Current and Future EU-NATO Relations." In Csaba Törő (ed.), *Visegrad Cooperation within NATO and CSDP*. Warsaw: Polski Instytut Spraw Międzynarodowych, 2011, 59–68.

Huňátová, Dana. *Sametová Diplomacie: Vzpomínky na výjimečné roky 1989–1992*. Prague: Kniha Zlín, 2019.

Hynek, Nik, Vit Stritecky, Vladimír V. Handl, and Michal Kořan. "The US-Russian Security 'Reset': Implications for Central-Eastern Europe and Germany." *European Security* 18:3 (2009): 263–85.

Inotai, András. "The Visegrad Four: More Competition than Regional Cooperation?" In Barbara Lippert and Heinrich Schneider (eds.), *Monitoring Association and Beyond: The European Union and the Visegrad States*. Bonn: Europa Union Verlag, 1995.

Inotai, András, and Magdolna Sass. "Economic Integration of the Visegrad Countries: Facts and Scenarios." *Eastern European Economics* 32:6 (1994): 6–28.

International Business Publications. *Slovak Republic: Country Study Guide*. Vol. 1, *Strategic Information and Developments*. Washington, DC: International Business Publications, 2013.

International Visegrad Fund. *Two Decades of Visegrad Cooperation*. Bratislava: International Visegrad Fund, 2011.

Jacoby, Wade. *The Enlargement of the European Union and NATO*. Cambridge: Cambridge University Press, 2004.

Jagodziński, Andrzej (ed.). *The Visegrad Group: A Central European Constellation*. Bratislava: International Visegrad Fund, 2006.

Janas, Zbigniew. "How I Started Visegrad in Mroziewicz's Kitchen." In Jagodziński (ed.), 58–59.

Jařab, Josef. "CEU—Three Letters Prompting Good Memories in and Firm Faith." In Jagodziński (ed.), 157–58.

Jeszenszky, Géza. "Hungary's Foreign Policy Dilemmas after Regaining Sovereignty." *Society and Economy* 29:1 (2007): 43–64.

Jeszenszky, Géza (ed.) *József Antall: Prime Minister of Hungary, Selected Speeches and Interviews*. Budapest: Antall József Alapítvány, 2008.

Jeszenszky, Géza. "The Origins and Enactment of the 'Visegrad Idea.'" In Jagodziński (ed.), 60–62.

Jeszenszky, Géza. "The Visegrád Countries and the Migrants." *Hungarian Review* 7:2 (2016): 10–13.

Jeszenszky, Géza. "Visegrád: Past and Future." *Hungarian Review* 2:4 (2011). https://hungarianreview.hu/article/visegrad.

Juzová, Jana, Anna Orosz, Andrzej Sadecki, and Tomáš Strážay. *Visegrad Group's Cooperation with the Western Balkans: Achievements and the Way Forward*. Skopje, North Macedonia: Institute for Democracy—Societas Civilis, 2019.

Kajánek, Tomáš. "The Power of Small EU Member States after Brexit: How Powerful Is the Visegrad Group?" *Journal of Liberty and International Affairs* 8:1 (2022): 170–91.

Kalmar, Ivan. *White but Not Quite: Central Europe's Illiberal Revolt*. Bristol, UK: Bristol University Press, 2022.

Kaminska, Joanna. *Poland and EU Enlargement: Foreign Policy in Transformation*. Basingstoke: Palgrave, 2014.

Kamusella, Tomasz. "Central Europe in the Distorting Mirror of Maps, Languages and Ideas." *Polish Review* 57:1 (2012): 33–94.

Karolewski, Ireneusz Pawel, and Roland Benedikter. "Europe's Migration Predicament: The European Unions' Refugees' Relocation Scheme versus the Defiant Central Eastern Europeans." *Visegrád Group.* *Journal of Inter-Regional Studies* 1 (2016): 40–52.

Katzenstein, Peter (ed.). *Mitteleuropa: Between Europe and Germany*. Oxford: Berghahn Books, 1997.

Kazharski, Aliaksei. "The End of 'Central Europe'? The Rise of the Radical Right and the Contestation of Identities in Slovakia and the Visegrad Four." *Geopolitics* 23:4 (2018): 754–80.

Kaźmierkiewicz, Piotr, Dóra Husz, Juraj Misina, and Ivo Slosarcik. *The Visegrad States on the EU's Eastern Frontier: Consular and Visa Cooperation in East Central Europe for Residents of Ukraine and Moldova*. Budapest: Centre for Policy Studies Central European University, 2006.

Keane, John. *Vaclav Havel: A Political Tragedy in Six Acts*. New York: Basic Books, 2000.

Kearns, Ian. "Subregionalism in Central Europe." In Glenn D. Hook and Ian Kearns (eds.), *Subregionalism and World Order*. Basingstoke, UK: Palgrave Macmillan, 1999, 21–40.

Khol, Radek. "The Changing Role and Position of Visegrad Four in the Area of Security and Defence." In Šťastný (ed.), 193–217.

Khol, Radek (ed.) *Perspektivy středoevropské vojenské spolupráce* [Perspectives on Central European Military Cooperation]. Prague: Ústav Medzinárodních Vzahů, 2003.

Khol, Radek. "Policies of the Visegrad Countries towards CFSP/ESDP." Working Paper 3/2003. Prague: Institute for International Relations, 2003.

Khúlová, Lucia, and Lenka Šprochová. "Importance of TEN-T Corridors in the Development of Infrastructure Example of Visegrad Group Countries." *Studia Commercialia Bratislavensia* 9:33 (August 2016): 49–57.

Kim, Dae Soon. *The Transition to Democracy in Hungary: Árpád Göncz and the Post-Communist Hungarian Presidency*. London: Routledge, 2013.

Kirch, Anna-Lena. *Sub-regionalisms in the European Union: Bridge-Builders or Spoilers?* Berlin: Logos Verlag, 2021.

Klaniczay, Gábor. "Medieval Central Europe: An Invention or a Discovery?" In Lord Dahrendorf, Yehuda Elkana, Aryeh Neier, William Newton-Smith, and István Rév (eds.), *The Paradoxes of Unintended Consequences*. Budapest: Central European University Press, 2000, 251–64.

Kolankiewicz, George. "Consensus and Competition in the Eastern Enlargement of the European Union." *International Affairs* 70:3 (July 1994): 477–95.

Kolossov, Vladimir. "Geopolitical Scenarios for Eastern and Central Europe in a Post-bipolar World." In Francis W. Carter, Peter Jordan, and Violette Ray (eds.), *Central Europe after the Fall of the Iron Curtain*. 2nd rev. ed. Frankfurt: Peter Lang, 1998, 63–72.

Kopecek, Michal. "Politics, Antipolitics, and Czechs in Central Europe: The Idea of 'Visegrád Cooperation' and Its Reflection in Czech Politics in the 1990s." In A. Bove (ed.), *Questionable Returns*. Vienna: IWM Junior Visiting Fellows Conferences, 2002, 1–13.

Kořan, Michal (ed.). *Czech Foreign Policy in 2007–2009: Analysis*. Prague: Institute of International Relations, 2010.

Kořan, Michal. "The Visegrad Cooperation, Poland, Slovakia and Austria in the Czech Foreign Policy." In Kořan (ed.), 115–47.

Kořan, Michal. "The Visegrad Group on the Threshold of Its Third Decade: A Central European Hub?" In Šabić and Drulák (eds.), 201–18.

Kořan, Michal. "Visegrad Group's Goals and Challenges in Recent Europe: Czech Reflections." *International Issues and Slovak Foreign Policy Affairs* 20:4 (2011): 66–84.

Kořan, Michal. "Visegrádská spolupráce na prahu třetí dekády" [Visegrad Cooperation on the Threshold of Its Third Decade]. *Mezinárodní politika* 3 (2011): 4–6.

Kořan, Michal, et al. *V4 Trust—The Czech Presidency of the Visegrad Group (2015–2016). Think Visegrad Mid-Term Review*. Bratislava: V4 Think Tank Platform, February 2016.

Korbonski, Andrzej. "Facing the Legacy of Post-Stalinist Regimes." *European Security* 1:4 (Winter 1992): 41–55.

Korbonski, Andrzej. "The Security of East Central Europe and the Visegrad Triangle." In Jane Shapiro Zacek and Ilpyong J. Kim (eds.), *The Legacy of the Soviet Bloc*. Gainesville: University Press of Florida, 1997.

Koubská, Libuše. "Looking for Visegrád." *New Presence* (June 1998): 8–9.

Kovác Michal. "Slovakia and the Partnership for Peace." *NATO Review* 42:1 (February 1994): 15–18.

Kowalczyk, Jan. "Broad Approach to Human Security in the Visegrad Group Countries." *Bezpieczeństwo Teoria I Praktyka* 38:1 (2020): 59–80.

Král, David. "The Czech Republic and the Eastern Partnership—From a By-product to a Beloved Child?" In I. Albrecht (ed.), *The Eastern Partnership in the Context of the European Neighbourhood Policy and V4 Agenda*. Kraków and Brussels: The Kosciuszko Institute, n.d.

Král, David. *Profil zemí Visegrádské skupiny v debatě o budoucnosti Evropy* [Positions of the Visegrad Group Countries in Debates about the Future of Europe]. Prague: Europeum, 1999.

Krastev, Ivan, and Stephen Holmes. *The Light That Failed: A Reckoning*. London: Allen Lane, 2019.

Krause, Stefan. "A Year of Consolidation." In Peter Rutland (ed.), *Holding the Course: Annual Survey of Eastern Europe and the Former Soviet Union 1998*. New York: M.E. Sharpe, 1998, 250–55.

Kříž, Zdeněk, and Jana Urbanovska. "The Visegrad Countries as an Example to Emulate? German Expectations within the Eastern Partnership." *Studia Politica* 19:1 (January 2019): 83–101.

Kruk, Aleksandra, and Beata Molo. "Central and Eastern Europe in Germany's Foreign Policy." In Zięba (ed.), 297–316.

Kucharczyk, Jacek, and Grigorij Mesežnikov (eds.). *Diverging Voices, Converging Policies: The Visegrad States' Reactions to the Russia-Ukraine Conflict*. Prague and Warsaw: Heinrich-Böll-Stiftung, 2015.

Kugiel, Patryk (ed.). *V4 Goes Global: Exploring Opportunities and Obstacles in the Visegrad Countries' Cooperation with Brazil, India, China and South Africa*. Warsaw: Polski Instytut Spraw Międzynarodowych, 2016.

Kundera, Milan. "The Tragedy of Central Europe." *New York Review of Books* (April 26, 1984): 33–38.

Kundera, Milan. "Un occident kidnappé, ou la tragédie de L'Europe Central." *Le Débat*, November 27, 1983, 2–24.

Kupich, Andrzej. "The Central European Free Trade Agreement: Problems, Experiences, Prospects." In Cottey (ed.), 90–112.

Kuus, Merje. "Europe's Eastern Expansion and the Reinscription of Otherness in East-Central Europe." *Progress in Human Geography* 28:4 (2004): 472–89.

Kusý, Miroslav. "We, Central-European East Europeans." In Schöpflin and Wood (eds.), 91–96.

Kwaśniewski, Aleksander. "A History of Common Success." In Jagodziński (ed.), 67–69.

Lašas, Ainius. *European Union and NATO Expansion: Central and Eastern Europe*. Basingstoke, UK: Palgrave Macmillan, 2010.

Latawski, Paul. "On Converging Paths? The Visegrad Group and the Atlantic Alliance." *Paradigms* 7:2 (1993): 78–93.

Lazar, Zsolt. "Success and Failures of the Gripen Offsets in the Visegrad Group Countries." *Defense and Security Analysis* 35:3 (2019): 283–307.

Lendvai, Paul. *Orbán: Europe's New Strongman*. London: Hurst, 2019.

Lengyel, László. "Europe through Hungarian Eyes." *International Affairs* 66:2 (April 1990): 291–97.

Leška, Vladimír. "The Future of Czech-Slovak Relations in the Light of European Integration." *Perspectives* 6/7 (1996): 75–87.

Luers, William H. "Harmonizing U.S. and European Interests." In Ivo J. Lederer (ed.), *Western Approaches to Eastern Europe*. New York: Council on Foreign Relations, 1992, 76–104.

Lord, Christopher (ed.). *Central Europe: Core or Periphery?* Copenhagen: Copenhagen Business School Press, 2000.

Lukáč, Pavol. "Visegrad Co-operation: Ideas, Developments and Prospects." *Slovak Foreign Policy Affairs* (Spring 2001): 6–23.

Lukášek, Libor. *Visegradská skupina a její vývoj very letech 1991–2004*. Prague: Nakladatelství Karolinum, 2013.

Madej, Marek (ed.). *Visegrad Group Defense Cooperation: What Added Value for the European Capabilities?* (note n°19/13 NORDIKA Programme). Warsaw: Institute of International Relations, University of Warsaw, 2013.

Mandelbaum, Michael. "Preserving the New Peace: The Case against NATO Expansion." *Foreign Affairs* 74:3 (May/June 1995): 9–13.

Marek, Dan, and Michael Baun. *The Czech Republic and the European Union*. London: Routledge, 2010.

Maresca, John. *Helsinki Revisited: A Key U.S. Negotiator's Memoirs on the Development of the CSCE into the OSCE*. Stuttgart: Ibidem, 2016.

Marušiak, Juraj. "Instead of Introduction—How Much Is Visegrad Present in Europe?" In Marušiak (ed.), *Is Visegrad Still*, 9–27.

Marušiak, Juraj. "Slovak Presidency: Second Breath of Visegrad?" In *Yearbook of Foreign Policy of the Slovak Republic 2006*. Bratislava: Research Center of the Slovak Foreign Policy Association, 2007, 97–108.

Marušiak, Juraj. "Slovensko vo Vyšehrade: perspektívy po vstupe do EU." *Medzinárodné otázky*, 2005, 4, 47–62.

Marušiak, Juraj, et al. (eds.), *Is Visegrad Still a Central European "Trade Mark"?* Bratislava: VEDA, 2013.

Matynia, Elzbieta. *The Uncanny Era: Conversations between Vaclav Havel and Adam Michnik*. New Haven, CT: Yale University Press, 2014.

Mayhew, Alan. *Recreating Europe: The European Union's Policy towards Central and Eastern Europe*. Cambridge: Cambridge University Press, 1998.

Mazowiecki, Tadeusz. "The Mutual Return to Europe." In Jagodziński (ed.), 70–71.

Meredith, Sebastian. "The EU, the Visegrád Group, and Southeast Europe: Conflicting Perspectives within an Enlarging 'European Identity,'" *East European Politics and Societies and Cultures*. 36:4 (November 2022): 1292–1314.

Merheim-Eyre, Igor. "The Visegrad Countries and Visa Liberalisation in the Eastern Neighbourhood: A Pan Tadeusz Syndrome?" *East European Politics and Societies and Cultures* 31:1 (February 2017): 93–114.

Meri, Lennart. "Estonia's Role in the New Europe." *International Affairs* 67:1 (January 1991): 107–10.

Michaud, Claude. "The Kingdoms of Central Europe in the Fourteenth Century." In Michael Jones (ed.), *The New Cambridge Medieval History*. Volume 6, *c. 1300–1415*. Cambridge: Cambridge University Press, 2000, 735–63.

Michta, Andrew A. (ed.). *NATO's New Allies: Poland, Hungary, and the Czech Republic in NATO*. Seattle: University of Washington Press, 2000.

Miheljak, Vlado. "Slovenia in Central Europe: Merely Meteorological or a Value Kinship." In Dieter Fuchs, Hans-Dieter Klingemann, and Jan Zielonka (eds.), *Democracy and Political Culture in Eastern Europe*. New York: Routledge, 2006, 119–47.

Mikulova, Kristina. "Central Europe's Velvet Power: Can It Reinvigorate EU Foreign Policy?" *World Affairs* 176:3 (September/October 2013): 64–72.

Miłosz, Czesław. "Central European Attitudes." *Cross Currents* 5 (1986): 101–8.

Minić, Jelica, Dragan Đukanović, Tomáš Strážay, Hana Semanić, Marta Szpala, and Michal Vít. *European Integration of the Western Balkans—Can the Visegrad Group Countries Serve as Role Models?* Belgrade: European Movement in Serbia, 2015.

Ministry of Defence of Ukraine. *White Paper 2015*. Kyiv: Ministry of Defence of Ukraine, 2016.

Ministry of Foreign Affairs of the Czech Republic. *Report on the Foreign Policy of the Czech Republic: Between January 2005 and December 2005*. Prague: Ministry of Foreign Affairs of the Czech Republic, 2006.

Mišík, Matúš. "Crisis as Remedy? The 2009 Gas Crisis and Its Influence on the Increase of Energy Security within Visegrad Group Countries." *International Issues & Slovak Foreign Policy Affairs* 21:1–2 (2012): 56–72.

Mišík, Matúš. "Energy Union and the Visegrad Four Countries Blurred Unity?" *International Issues & Slovak Foreign Policy Affairs* 25:1–2 (2016); 68–80.

Mišík, Matúš. *External Energy Security in the European Union: Small Member States' Perspective.* London: Routledge, 2019.

Molnár, Anna, and Zoltán Szenes. "Cooperation or Integration? The New Defence Initiatives in the Visegrád Group." In Schweiger and Visvizi (eds.), 190–207.

Molnár, Bálint. "Israel and the Visegrád (V4) Group: Challenges and Opportunities." *Israel Journal of Foreign Affairs* 13:1 (2019): 3–21.

Moskalewicz, Marcin, and Wojciech Przybylski (eds.). *Understanding Central Europe.* London and New York: Routledge, 2017.

Mroz, John Edwin. "Russia and Eastern Europe: Will the West Let Them Fail?" *Foreign Affairs* 72:1 (1993): 44–57.

Musil, Jiří, and Radko Kubička. "Visegrád—Wanted or Not?" *The New Presence* (Autumn 2001): 6–7.

Myant, Martin. *The Rise and Fall of Czech Capitalism: Economic Development in the Czech Republic since 1989.* Cheltenham: Edward Elgar, 2003.

Nagy, Laszlo. "Security Concepts of the Visegrad Countries." *Atlantisch Perspectief* 8 (1998): 9–14.

Németh, Bence, and Tamás Csiki. "Perspectives of Central European Multinational Defence Cooperation: A New Model?" In Marian Majer and Robert Ondrejcsák (eds.), *Panorama of Global Security Environment 2013.* Bratislava: Centre for European and North Atlantic Affairs, 2013, 11–24.

Neumann, Iver B. "Russia as Central Europe's Constituting Other." *East European Politics and Societies* 7:2 (1993): 349–69.

Nič, Milan. "The Visegrád Group in the EU: 2016 as a Turning-Point?" *European View* 15:2 (2016): 281–90.

Nicolini, Mário, Rudolf Žídek, and Ján Pšida. "Slovakia." In Heiko Biehl, Bastian Giegerich, and Alexandra Jonas (eds.), *Strategic Cultures in Europe: Security and Defence Policies Across the Continent.* Wiesbaden, Germany: Springer, 2013, 307–18.

Novotná, Tereza, and Zuzana Stuchlíková. "Czechia: From a V4-Enthusiast to a V4-Sceptic and Back Again." In Ania Skrzypek and Maria Skóra (eds.), *The Future of the Visegrad Group.* Brussels and Berlin: Foundation for European Progressive Studies, 2017, 6–12.

Nowak, Jan, and Josef Pöschl. "An Assessment of Progress in Transition, Economic Performance and Market Attractiveness." *Journal of East-West Business* 4:4 (1999): 27–48.

Offe, Claus. *Varieties of Transition: The East European and East German Experience.* Cambridge: Polity Press, 1996.

O'Hanlon, Michael. *Beyond NATO: A New Security Architecture for Eastern Europe.* Washington, DC: Brookings Institution Press, 2017.

Okolicsanyi, Karoly. "The Visegrad Triangle's Free Trade Zone." *RFE/RL Research Report* 2:3 (January 15, 1993): 19–22.

Okowa, Phoebe N., and Malcolm D. Evans. "Case Concerning the Gabcïkovo-Nagymaros Project (Hungary/Slovakia)." *International and Comparative Law Quarterly* 47:3 (July 1998): 688–97.

Open Media Research Institute. *The OMRI Annual Survey of Eastern Europe and the Former Soviet Union 1995: Building Democracy.* M.E. Sharpe for OMRI, 1996.

The OMRI Annual Survey 1996. Armonk, NY: M.E. Sharpe, 1997.

Onderco, Michal. "The Czech Republic, Hungary, Slovakia." In Marco Wyss and Hugo Meijer (eds.), *The Handbook of European Defence Policies and Armed Forces.* Oxford University Press, 2018, 279–96.

Oravcová, Veronika, and Matúš Mišík. "EU Funds and Limited Cooperation Energy Infrastructure Development in the Visegrad Group." *International Issues & Slovak Foreign Policy Affairs* 27:3–4 (2018): 11–26.

Orosz, Anna. "Relations of Slovenia and the V4 from Perspective of Changing Foreign Policy of Slovenia." *European Perspectives* 7:2 (2015): 37–52.

Osička, Jan, Lukáš Lehotský, Veronika Zapletalová, Filip Černoch, and Břetislav Dančák. "Natural Gas Market Integration in the Visegrad 4 Region: An Example to Follow or to Avoid?" *Energy Policy* 112 (January 2018): 184–97.

Pakulski, Jan (ed.). *The Visegrad Countries in Crisis.* Warsaw: Collegium Civitas, 2016.

Papadimitriou, Dimitris. "Negotiating When Others Are Watching: Explaining the Outcome of the Accession Negotiations between the European Community and the Countries of Central and Eastern Europe, 1990–1991." In Michèle Knodt and Sebastiaan Princen (eds.), *Understanding the European Union's External Relations.* London: Routledge, 2003, 106–22.

Paroubek, Jiří. "Visegrad Group Celebrates Its Fifteenth Anniversary." In Jagodziński (ed.), 15–16.

Paulech, Michal, and Jana Urbanovská. "Visegrad Four EU Battlegroup: Meaning and Progress." *Obrana a Strategie* 14:2 (2014): 49–60.

Pavliuk, Oleksandr. "Ukraine and Regional Cooperation in Central and Eastern Europe." *Security Dialogue* 28:3 (September 1997): 347–57.

Pehe, Jiri. "The Choice Between." http://www.pehe.cz/clanky/1995/1995-14July1995 -Transition.pdf, last accessed January 21, 2020.

Pehe, Jiří. "Pochybnosti o Visegrádu" [Doubts about Visegrad]. *Mezinárodní politika* 3 (2011): 18–19.

Pernal, Marek, Jan Tombinski, and Rafal Wisniewski. "Countries of the Visegrad Group Prior to Accession to the European Union—Together or Separately." *Polish Foreign Affairs Digest* 2:1 (2002): 99–138.

Petőcz, Kálmán. "Slovak-Hungarian Relations: What Next?" In *Yearbook of Foreign Policy of the Slovak Republic 2006.* Bratislava: Research Center of the Slovak Foreign Policy Association, 2007, 69–86.

Pick, Otto. "The Demise of the Warsaw Pact." *NATO Review* 39:2 (April 1991): 12–16.

Pithart, Petr. "The Division/Dissolution of Czechoslovakia: Old Sins and New Forms of Selfishness." In Michael Kraus and Allison Stanger (eds.), *Irreconcilable Differences? Explaining Czechoslovakia's Dissolution.* Lanham, MD: Rowman and Littlefield, 2000, 227–33.

Pithart, Petr. "European Values and Courage." In Rupnik and Seifter (eds.), 17–26.

Poláčková, Hana. "Regional Cooperation in Central Europe: Poland, Hungary, Czech Republic and Slovakia. From Visegrad to CEFTA." *Perspectives* 3 (Summer 1994): 117–29.

Polreich, Miroslav. "Central East European Security Perspectives (The Czech Republic, The Visegrad Group, the Security Problems in the Area, and the German Position in Europe)." *Perspectives* 2 (Winter 1993/94): 55–63.

Pomorska, Karolina, and Sophie Vanhoonacker. "Poland in the Driving Seat: A Mature Presidency in Turbulent Times." *Journal of Common Market Studies* 50 (2012): 76–84.

Pontuso, James F. "Transformation Politics: The Debate between Václav Havel and Václav Klaus on the Free Market and Civil Society." *Studies in East European Thought* 54:3 (September 2002): 153–77.

Prizel, Ilya. *National Identity and Foreign Policy: Nationalism and Leadership in Poland, Russia and Ukraine.* Cambridge: Cambridge University Press, 1998.

Przybylski, Wojciech, Vít Dostál, Pavlína Janebová, Tomáš Strážay, and Zsuzsanna Végh (eds.). *V4–25 Years: The Continuing Story of the Visegrád Group 1991–2006.* Warsaw: Fundacja Res Publica im. Henryka Krzeczkowskiego, 2016.

Pulišová, Veronika, and Tomáš Strážay (eds.). *Ukraine and the Visegrad Four: Towards a Mutually Beneficial Relationship.* Bratislava: Research Center of the Slovak Foreign Policy Association, 2010.

Rácz, György. "The Congress of Visegrád in 1335: Diplomacy and Representation." *Hungarian Historical Review* 2:2 (2013): 261–87.

Rácz, György (ed.) *Visegrád 1335.* Bratislava: International Visegrad Fund, 2009.

Racz, Andras. "The Visegrad Cooperation: Central Europe Divided over Russia." *L'Europe en Formation* 374 (2014): 61–76.

Ramet, Sabrina. *Thinking about Yugoslavia: Scholarly Debates about the Yugoslav Breakup and the Wars in Bosnia and Kosovo.* Cambridge: Cambridge University Press, 2005.

Rebane, Mikk, and Merle Pajula. "Nordic-Baltic Co-operation: Unity across Border." In *Estonian Ministry of Foreign Affairs Yearbook 2008/2009.* Tallinn: Eesti Välispoliitika Instituut, 2009, 46–47.

Reich, Alfred A. "Hungarian Foreign Policy and the Magyar Minorities: New Foreign Policy Priorities." *Nationalities Papers* 24:3 (1996): 447–65.

Rhodes, Matthew. "Post-Visegrad Cooperation in East Central Europe." *East European Quarterly* 33:1 (March 1999): 51–67.

Richter, Sándor. "The Visegrád Group Countries' Expectations Vis-à-Vis Western Europe." *Russian and East European Finance and Trade* 32:1 (1996): 6–41.

Richter, Sándor, and László G. Tóth. "After the Agreement on Free Trade among the Visegrád Group Countries: Prospects for Intraregional Trade in East-Central Europe." *Russian and East European Finance and Trade* 30:4 (July–August 1994): 23–69.

Rieker, Pernille, and Marcin Terlikowski. "The Limits and Achievements of Regional Governance in Security: NORDEFCO and the V4." Warsaw: Polish Institute of International Affairs, PISM Policy Papers No. 25, August 2015.

Riggirozzi, Pía, and Diana Tussie. "Rise of Post-hegemonic Regionalism in Latin America." In Pia Riggirozzi and Diana Tussie (eds.), *The Rise of Post-hegemonic Regionalism.* Dordrecht, Netherlands: Springer United Nations University Series on Regionalism, 2014, 1–16.

Řiháčková, Věra. "Foreign Policy and External Security: The Diverging Trajectories of Domestic Actors vis-à-vis the Russian-Ukrainian Conflict." In Kucharczyk and Mesežnikov (eds.), 25–36.

Robinson, William H. "Parliamentary Development in Central Europe and the U.S.S.R." *CRS Review* (March–April 1991).

Rodman, Peter W. "NATO's Role in a New European Security Order." Working Paper 95.2 (October 1995), https://www.nato.int/acad/conf/future95/rodman.htm.

Rowen Karp, Regina (ed.). *Central and Eastern Europe: The Challenge of Transition.* Oxford: Oxford University Press for SIPRI, 1993.

Rowen Karp, Regina (ed.). *Central and Eastern Europe: The Challenge of Transition.* Oxford: Oxford University Press for SIPRI, 1993.

Rouček, Libor. *After the Bloc.* London: Royal Institute of International Affairs, 1992.

Rupel, Dimitrij. "Slovenia's Shift from the Balkans to Central Europe." In Jill Benderly and Evan Kraft (eds.), *Independent Slovenia: Origins, Movements, Prospects.* New York: St Martin's Press, 1994, 183–200.

Rupnik, Jacques. "Joining Europe Together or Separately: The Implications of the Czecho-Slovak Divorce for EU Enlargement." In Jacques Rupnik and Jan Zielonka (eds.), *The Road to the European Union.* Vol. 1. Manchester: Manchester University Press, 2003, 16–50.

Rupnik, Jacques. "Migrants as a Mirror: European Divides and Central European Narratives." In Rupnik and Seifter (eds.), 125–34.

Rupnik, Jacques, and Pavel Seifter (eds.). *Europe at the Crossroad: Democracy, Neighbourhoods, Migrations.* Prague: Václav Havel Library, 2018.

Rusnák, Urban. "Future of Visegrad Co-operation." *Medzinárodné otázky* 11:4 (2002): 102–12.

Rusnak, Urban. "One Year Experience of the International Visegrád Fund Activities." *Central European Political Science Review* 2:5 (2001): 244–51.

Rusnák, Urban. "Renesancia visegrádskeho zoskupeni: Zamyslenie sa nad jej motívmi a cieľmi" [The Renaissance of the Visegrad Group: Reflections on its Motives and Goals]. *Medzinárodné otázky* 8:2 (1999): 66–71.

Růžička, Jan. "Forum on 'Central Europe': From Eastern Europe to Central Europe and Back? On Regions, Transatlantic Relations, and Central Europe." *Perspectives* 18:2 (2010): 63–78.

Šabić, Zlatko, and Petr Drulák (eds.). *Regional and International Relations of Central Europe.* Basingstoke: Palgrave, 2012.

Samson, Ivo. "Assessment of Visegrad Cooperation from a Security Perspective: Is the Visegrad Group Still Vital in the 'Zeros' of the 21st Century?" in Törő (ed.), 9–40.

Samson, Ivo. "Slovakia: Misreading the Western Message." In Alex Pravda and Jan Zielonka (eds.), *Democratic Consolidation in Eastern Europe.* Vol. 2, *International and Transnational Factors.* Oxford: Oxford University Press, 2001, 363–82.

Samson, Ivo. "The Visegrad Four: From Loose Geographic Group to Security Internationalization?" *International Issues & Slovak Foreign Policy Affairs* 18:4 (2009): 3–18.

Sarotte, M. E. "The Convincing Call from Central Europe: Let Us into NATO. NATO Enlargement Turns 20." *Foreign Affairs,* March 12, 2019. https://www.foreignaffairs .com/united-states/convincing-call-central-europe-let-us-nato.

Sarotte, Mary Elise. *1989: The Struggle to Create Post–Cold War Europe.* Princeton, NJ: Princeton University Press, 2009.

Savranskaya, Svetlana. "The Logic of 1989: The Soviet Peaceful Withdrawal from Eastern Europe." In Thomas Blanton, Svetlana Savranskaya, and Vladislav Zubok (eds.), *Masterpieces of History: The Peaceful End of the Cold War in Europe, 1989.* Budapest: Central European University Press, 2011, 1–47.

Saxonberg, Steven. "Václav Klaus: The Rise and Fall and Re-emergence of a Charismatic Leader." *East European Politics and Societies* 13:3 (Spring 1999): 391–418.

Schimmelfennig, Frank. "The Community Trap: Liberal Norms, Rhetorical Action, and the Eastern Enlargement of the European Union." *International Organization* 55:1 (Winter 2001): 47–80.

Schweiger, Christian, and Anna Visvizi (eds.). *Central and Eastern Europe in the EU: Challenges and Perspectives under Crisis Conditions.* London: Routledge, 2018.

Schöpflin, George. *Nations, Identity, Power.* London: Hurst, 2000.

Schöpflin, George, and Nancy Wood (eds.). *In Search of Central Europe.* Cambridge: Polity Press, 1989.

Šedivý, Jaroslav. *Černínský palác v roce nula* [The Czernin Palace in Year Zero]. Prague: Ivo Železný, 1997.

Šedivý, Jaroslav. *Diplomacie je uměním kompromisu* [Diplomacy is the Art of Compromise]. Prague: Mladá fronta, 2009.

Šedivý, Jiří. "The Pull-out of Soviet Troops from Czechoslovakia." *Perspectives* 2 (Winter 93/94): 21–37.

Seegel, Steven. *Map Men: Transnational Lives and Deaths of Geographers in the Making of East Central Europe.* Chicago and London: University of Chicago Press, 2018.

Shishelina, L. N. (ed.). *Russia and the Visegrad Group: The Ukrainian Challenge.* Moscow: Russian International Affairs Council, 2015.

Simmons, Michael. *The Reluctant President: A Political Life of Vaclav Havel.* London: Methuen, 1991.

Simon, Jeffrey. "Czechoslovakia's 'Velvet Divorce,' Visegrad Cohesion, and European Fault Lines." *European Security* 3:3 (Autumn 1994): 482–500.

Simon, Jeffrey. "Partnership for Peace: Stabilising the East." *JFQ Forum* 5 (Summer 1994): 36–45.

Simon, Jeffrey. *Slovakia and NATO: The Madrid Summit and After.* Washington, DC: National Defense University Strategic Forum, 1997.

Simonovits, Bori. "The Public Perception of the Migrant Crisis from the Hungarian Point of View: Evidence from the Field." In Birgit Glorius and Jeroen Doomernik (eds.), *Geographies of Asylum in Europe and the Role of European Localities.* Cham, Switzerland: Springer, 2020, 155–76.

Simonyi, András. "Visegrad Cooperation: A 15-Year-Old Success Story." In Jagodziński (ed.), 96–97.

Skalník, Petr. "Becoming a Non-career Ambassador after the Velvet Revolution." *Diplomatic Studies Programme Newsletter* 4 (May 1998): 29–32.

Skilling, H. Gordon. *Samizdat and an Independent Society in Central and Eastern Europe.* Basingstoke, UK: MacMillan, 1989.

Skrzypek, Ania, and Maria Skóra (eds.). *The Future of the Visegrad Group.* Brussels and Berlin: Foundation for European Progressive Studies, 2017.

Slapin, B. Jonathan, and Julia Gray. "Depth, Ambition and Width in Regional Economic Organizations." In R. Daniel Kelemen, Anand Menon, and Jonathan Slapin (eds.), *The European Union: Integration and Enlargement.* London: Routledge, 2014, 88–102.

Ślufińska, Monika, and Agnieszka Anna Nitszke. "Activities of the Visegrad Group in the Context of the CFSP of the EU." *Historia i Polityka* 29 (2017): 9–27.

Smith, Karen E. "Enlargement and European Order." In Christopher Hill and Michael Smith (eds.), *International Relations and the European Union.* Oxford: Oxford University Press, 2005, 270–91.

Smoke, Richard (ed.). *Perceptions of Security: Public Opinion and Expert Assessments in Europe's New Democracies*. Manchester: Manchester University Press, 1996.

Sperling, James, and Emil Kirchner. *Recasting the European Security Order: Security Architectures and Economic Cooperation*. Manchester: Manchester University Press, 1997.

Spero, Joshua B. *Bridging the Divide: Middle Power Politics and Regional Security Dilemmas*. Lanham, MD: Rowman and Littlefield, 2004.

Spero, Joshua B. "The Budapest-Prague-Warsaw Triangle." *European Security* 1:1 (Spring 1992): 58–83.

Spero, B. Joshua. "Central European Security." *Problems of Communism* 40:6 (November–December 1991): 141–51.

Šťastný, Marek (ed.). *Visegrad Countries in an Enlarged Trans-Atlantic Community*. Bratislava: Institute for Public Affairs, 2002.

Statement on behalf of the North Atlantic Council by the Secretary General, Mr. Manfred Wörner, on the occasion of the visit to NATO by Mr. Václav Havel, President of the Czech and Slovak Federal Republic 21 March 1991, NATO Review 38:1 (February 1990): 29–30.

Štěpánovský, Jiří. "Cooperation within the Central European Visegrád Group: A Czech Perspective." *Perspectives* 4 (Winter 1994/95): 91–97.

Steves, F. "Poland and the International System: External Influences on Democratic Consolidation." *Communist and Post-Communist Studies* 34:3 (2001): 339–52.

Strategic Survey. "Central European: Adjusting to Reality." London: IISS, 1991, 150–61.

Strážay, Tomáš. "Neither Beautiful nor Ugly, but Functional: A Pragmatic View on the Visegrad Group." *Contemporary European Studies* 2 (2014): 37–47.

Strážay, Tomáš. "Regionálne iniciatívy v strednej Európe roku 2005—Od tematickej profilácie ku komplementarite postojov?" [Regional Initiatives in Central Europe in the Year 2005—From Topical Specialization to Complementarity of Approaches?]. In *Ročenka zahraničnej politiky Slovenskej republiky*. Bratislava: Research Center of the Slovak Foreign Policy Association, 2005, 9–87.

Strážay, Tomáš. "Second Generation Visegrad." *Yearbook of Slovakia's Foreign Policy*. Bratislava: Research Center of the Slovak Foreign Policy Association, 2011, 111–23.

Strážay, Tomáš. "Visegrad and Its 'Soft Power': The V4 Developments of 2009 Reviewed and Priorities of the Upcoming Period Outlined." *Yearbook of Slovakia's Foreign Policy*. Bratislava: Research Center of the Slovak Foreign Policy Association, 2009, 121–32.

Strážay, Tomáš. "Visegrad Four in 2007: Revitalization after the Post–Enlargement Fatigue." *Yearbook of Slovakia's Foreign Policy*. Bratislava: Research Center of the Slovak Foreign Policy Association, 2007, 52–61.

Strážay, Tomáš. "Jewel or Thorn? V4 in 2017 from Slovakia's Perspective." *Yearbook of Slovakia's Foreign Policy 2017*. Bratislava: Research Center of the Slovak Foreign Policy Association, 2018, 59–69.

Strážay, Tomáš. "Vyšehrad 2008: Dynamická regionálna platforma s pridanou hodnotou pre EÚ" [A Dynamic Regional Platform with Added Value for the EU]. In *Ročenka zahraničnej politiky Slovenskej republiky*. Bratislava: Research Center of the Slovak Foreign Policy Association, 2008, 93–101.

Strážay, Tomáš. "Visegrad: Arrival, Survival, Renewal." In *International Visegrad Fund: Two Decades of Visegrad Cooperation*. Bratislava: International Visegrad Fund, 2011, 14–38.

Strážay, Tomáš. "Visegrad Four and the Western Balkans: A Group Perspective." *Polish Quarterly of International Affairs* 4 (2012): 52–64.

Střítecký, Vít. "Doing More for Less: V4 Defence Cooperation in a Time of Austerity." *Polish Quarterly of International Affairs* 4 (2012): 65–82.

Stubbs, Paul, and Siniša Zrinščak. "Croatian Social Policy: The Legacies of War, State-Building and Late Europeanization." *Social Policy and Administration* 43:2 (April 2009): 121–35.

Suppan, Arnold. "Austria and Eastern Europe in the Post-Cold War Context: Between the Opening of the Iron Curtain and a New Nation-Building Process in Eastern Europe." In Günter Bischof and Ferdinand Karlhofer (eds.), *Austria's International Position after the End of the Cold War*. New Orleans: University of New Orleans Press, 2013, 143–66.

Suwara, Ewa. "Poland and the Visegrád Group: An Effective Interest Coalition in the Enlarged Union?" *Polish Political Science* 34 (2005): 45–58.

Świeboda, Paweł. "An Unforeseen Brussels Takeover." *New Eastern Europe*, December 1, 2014. http://neweasterneurope.eu/old_site/articles-and-commentary/1407-an-unforeseen-brussels-takeover.

Szayna, Thomas S. "The Breakup of Czechoslovakia: Some Thoughts about Its Implications." *Polish Quarterly of International Affairs* 2:1 (1993): 55–72.

Szayna, Thomas S. "The Czech Republic: A Small Contributor or a 'Free Rider'?" In Michta (ed.), 122–47.

Szelényi, Zsuzsanna. *Tainted Democracy: Viktor Orbán and the Subversion of Hungary*. London: Tauris, 2022.

Szent-Iványi, István. "Metamorphosis Visegradiensis: The Transformations of the Visegrad Group." In Dániel Mikecz (ed.), *The Future of the Liberal Visegrad Project*. Budapest: ELF, 2020: 35–50.

Szitás, Péter. *The Military Cooperation of the V4*. Budapest: Danube Institute, 2021.

Szomolányi, Sonia. "Why Slovakia's Transition Has Been So Difficult." *Társadalom és gazdaság Közép- és Kelet-Európában / Society and Economy in Central and Eastern Europe* 22:1 (2000): 60–86.

Terry, Sarah Meiklejohn. "Beyond the Cold War: Prospects for Central European Security and Cooperation in a Post-Communist World." In Sanford R. Lieberman, David E Powell, Carol R. Saivetz, and Sarah M. Terry (eds.), *The Soviet Empire Reconsidered: Essays in Honor of Adam B. Ulam*. Boulder, CO: Westview Press, 1994, 229–62.

Terry, Sarah Meiklejohn. "Poland's Foreign Policy since 1989: The Challenges of Independence." *Communist and Post-Communist Studies* 33:1 (2000): 7–47.

Thomas, Timothy. "The Significance of the Cracow Summit." *European Security* 1:1 (1992): 101–8.

Tiersky, Ronald. *François Mitterrand: A Very French President*. New York: St. Martin's Press, 2000.

"Ties That Bind: The Visegrád Summit. Address delivered by the Prime Minister of Hungary at the Prague Summit of the Visegrád Three (Prague, 6 May 1992)," in Jeszenszky (ed.), *József Antall*, 279.

Todorova, Maria. *Imagining the Balkans*. New York: Oxford University Press, 1997.

Tőkés, Rudolf L. "From Visegrad to Krakow: Cooperation, Competition, and Coexistence in Central Europe." *Problems of Communism* 40:6 (November 1991): 100–114.

Törő, Csaba (ed.). *Visegrad Cooperation within NATO and CSDP*. Warsaw: Polski Instytut Spraw Międzynarodowych, 2011.

Törő, Csaba, Eamonn Butler, and Károly Grúber. "Visegrád: The Evolving Pattern of Coordination and Partnership after EU Enlargement." *Europe-Asia Studies* 66:3 (2014): 364–93.

Torreblanca, José I. *The Reuniting of Europe: Promises, Negotiations and Compromises.* Farnham: Ashgate, 2001.

Tóth, Bálint Lászlo. "Visegrád: A Tool That Supports the Implementation of EU Strategies to Enhance the Connectivity and Interoperability of the Central East European Railway Network." *Foreign Policy Review* (2018): 158–81.

Treverton, Geoffrey F. *America, Germany and the Future of Europe.* Princeton, NJ: Princeton University Press, 1992.

Trubalska, Justyna. "The Prospects for Energy Cooperation in the Visegrad Group." *Annales Universitatis Mariae Curie-Skłodowska* 4 (2019): 69–79.

Tudoroiu, Theodor, Peter Horváth, and Marek Hrušovský. "Ultra-nationalism and Geopolitical Exceptionalism in Mečiar's Slovakia." *Problems of Post-Communism* 56:4 (July/August 2009): 3–14.

Tulmets, Elsa. "The Countries of the Eastern Dimension of the European Neighbourhood Policy and Czech Foreign Policy." In Michal Kořan (ed.), *Czech Foreign Policy in 2007–2009: Analysis.* Prague: Institute of International Relations, 2010, 213–30.

Tulmets, Elsa. *East Central European Foreign Policy Identity in Perspective: Back to Europe and the EU's Neighbourhood.* London: Palgrave Macmillan, 2014.

United States International Trade Commission. *Effects of Greater Economic Integration within the European Community on the United States.* Fourth Followup Report Investigation No. 332–267. Washington, DC: United States International Trade Commission, 1992.

Urban, Jan. "The Czech and Slovak Republics: Security Consequences of the Breakup of the CSFR." In Karp (ed.), 100–121.

Vachudova, Milada Anna. *Europe Undivided: Democracy, Leverage, and Integration after Communism.* Oxford: Oxford University Press, 2005.

Vachudova, Milada Anna. "The Visegrad Four: No Alternative to Cooperation." *RFE/RL Research Report* 2:34 (August 27, 1993): 38–47.

Vágner, Petr. "Can the Visegrad Group Serve as a Model for the Development of Cooperation among Other Countries?" In Veronika Pulišová and Tomáš Strážay (eds.), *Ukraine and the Visegrad Four: Towards a Mutually Beneficial Relationship.* Bratislava: Bratislava Research Center of the Slovak Foreign Policy Association, 2010, 9–12.

Valasek, Tomas. *Surviving Austerity: The Case for a New Approach to EU Military Collaboration.* London: Centre for European Reform, 2011.

Valášek, Tomáš, and Milan Šuplata (eds.). *Towards a Deeper Visegrad Defence Partnership.* Bratislava: Central European Policy Institute, 2012.

Vargovčíková, Jana. "Le Groupe de Visegrad, 20 ans après" [The Visegrad Group after 20 Years]. *Politique étrangère* 77:1 (Printemps 2012): 147–59.

Vašáryová, Magda. "The Optimal Format for Regional Cooperation." In Jagodziński (ed.), 77–78.

Végh, Zsuzsannah. "The Power of the Visegrad Cooperation." In Moskalewicz and Przybylski (eds.), 441–49.

The Visegrad Group Countries. Bratislava: International Visegrad Fund, 2011.

Vladislav, Jan (ed.). *Living in Truth.* London: Faber and Faber, 1986.

Vondra, Alexandr. "Visegrad Cooperation: How Did It Start?" In Jagodziński (ed.), 79–80.

Wagrowska, Maria. "Visegrad Security Policy: How to Consolidate Its Own Identity." *International Issues & Slovak Foreign Policy Affairs* 18:4 (2009): 31–43.

Waisová, Šarka. "Regionální Integrace ve Střední Evropě" [Regional Integration in Central Europe]. In Ladislav Cabada (ed.), *Perspektivy Regionu Střední Evropy* [Perspectives of the Region of Central Europe]. Pilsen: Západočeská univerzita v Plzni, 2002, 48–68.

Wałęsa, Lech. "From Solidarność (Solidarity) to Cooperation and Integration." In Jagodziński (ed.), 81–83.

Walker, Jennone. "Regional Organizations and Ethnic Conflict." In Karp (ed.), 45–66.

Wallace, William. *The Transformation of Western Europe*. London: Chatham House, 1990.

Wedel, Janine R. *Collision and Collusion: The Strange Case of Western Aid to Eastern Europe 1989–1998*. Basingstoke: Macmillan, 1998.

Wettig, Gerhard. "Post-Soviet Central Europe in International Security." *European Security* 3:3 (1994): 463–81.

Whitehall Papers. "The Visegrad Group: Aims and Evolution." 28:1 (1994): 14–32.

Wiatr, Jerzy J. *Polish-German Relations: The Miracle of Reconciliation*. Opladen, Germany: Verlag Barbara Budrich, 2014.

Williams, Andrew J. (ed.). *Reorganizing Eastern Europe: European Institutions and the Refashioning of Europe's Security Architecture*. Aldershot, UK: Dartmouth, 1994.

Williams, Kieran. "National Myths in the New Czech Liberalism." In Geoffrey A. Hosking and George Schöpflin (eds.), *Myths and Nationhood*. London: Hurst, 1997, 132–40.

Williams, Kieran. *Václav Havel*. London: Reaktion, 2016.

Williams, Kieran, and Dennis Deletant. *Security Intelligence Services in New Democracies: The Czech Republic. Slovakia and Romania*. Basingstoke: Palgrave Macmillan, 2001.

Williams, Margit Bessenyey. "Exporting the Democratic Deficit: Hungary's Experience with EU Integration." *Problems of Post-Communism* 48:1 (2001): 7–38.

Wolchik, Sharon L., and Richard Zięba. "Ukraine's Relations with the Visegrád Countries." In Sharon. L. Wolchik and Volodymyr Zviglyanich (eds.), *Ukraine: The Search for National Identity*. Lanham: Rowman and Littlefield 2000, 133–64.

Wolczuk, Roman. *Ukraine's Foreign and Security Policy, 1991–2000*. Abingdon, UK: Routledge, 2002.

Wörner, Manfred. "The Atlantic Alliance and European Security in the 1990s." May 17, 1990, archived at https://www.nato.int/docu/speech/1990/s900517a_e.htm.

Wrona, Anna, Małgorzata Jankowska and Iwona Grudziąż. *Migration Trends in the Visegrad Group*. Warsaw: MCRC Office of Foreigners, 2020.

Wyzan, Michael. "Slovenia: An Economic Success Story." In *Forging Ahead, Falling Behind: The OMRI Annual Survey of Eastern Europe and the Former Soviet Union 1996*. New York: M.E. Sharpe, 1997, 102–3.

Zakaria, Fareed. "The Rise of Illiberal Democracy." *Foreign Affairs* 76:6 (November–December 1997): 22–43.

Zantovsky, Michael. *Havel: A Life*. New York: Atlantic Books, 2014.

Zantovsky, Michael. "In Search of Allies: Vaclav Havel and the Expansion of NATO." *World Affairs* 177:4 (November/December 2014): 47–58.

Žantovský, Michael. "Visegrad between the Past and the Future." In Jagodziński (ed.), 84–85.

Zenker, Petr, and Tatiana Wartuschová. "Kolik lidí zná Visegrád?" [How Many People Know Visegrad?"]. *Mezinárodní politika* 3 (2011): 16–17.

Zetocha, Karel. "Spolupráce Visegrádské čtyřky v oblasti vyzbrojování" ["Visegrad Four Cooperation in the Field of Armaments"] *Mezinárodní politika* 3 (2011), 14–16.

Zięba, Ryszard (ed.). *Politics and Security of Central and Eastern Europe.* Cham: Springer, 2023.

Zięba, Ryszard. "The Three Seas Initiative." In Ryszard Zięba (ed.), 261–75.

Zielonka, Jan. *Security in Central Europe.* London: IISS, Adelphi Paper No. 272, 1992.

Znoj, Milan. "Václav Havel, His Idea of Civil Society and the Czech Liberal Tradition." In Michal Kopeček and Piotr Wciślik (eds.), *Thinking through Transition: Liberal Democracy, Authoritarian Pasts, and Intellectual History in East Central Europe after 1989.* Budapest: Central European University Press, 2015, 109–38.

Żukrowska, Katarzyna. "CEFTA: Training for Integration." In Sheila Page (ed.), *Regions and Development: Politics, Security and Economics.* London: Routledge, 2000, 227–38.

Zuokui, Liu. "How the Chinese Perceive the Visegrad Group." *Polish Quarterly of International Affairs* 2 (2016): 56–67.

INDEX

Abe, Shinzo, 121. *See also* Japan
academies of science, of Visegrad countries, 115
Act of Accession (to NATO), 148
Adriatic Sea, 259
Aeroflot, 71
Afghanistan, 229, 240
Agenda 2000, 85
agriculture, 145, 146, 150, 153, 156n51, 162, 166, 167, 286; and EU, 56, 103, 135, 150; and subsidies, 56, 146
aircraft. *See* Aeroflot; BAE Systems; FA-50s; Gripen; L-159 training jets; Mi-24 helicopters; MiG-29s
Al Jazeera, 211
Albania, 20, 72, 82, 186; and NATO, 291
Albright, Madeleine, 133
Allied Intervention, against Bolshevik Russia, 24
Alpen-Adria, 268. *See also* Central European Initiative (CEI); Hexagonale; Pentagonale
Amending Protocol to the CEFTA Agreement, 286. *See also* Central European Free Trade Agreement (CEFTA)
American Bell, 227
Amsterdam European Council, 103

Amsterdam, Treaty of, 133
Andor, László, 52
Antal, Laszlo, 69
Antall, József, 16, 17, 23, 40, 43, 49, 53, 54, 57, 69, 78, 134, 279, 281, 284. *See also* Hungary
AP. *See* Associated Press (AP)
armaments. *See* aircraft; 3D radar; Tier 1 smart defense
Armenia, 183
Asia-Europe Meeting, 159n134
Associated Press (AP), 204, 208
Association Agreements of the EC/EU, 61n42; and Bulgaria, Romania, 155n43; and CEFTA, 259; and Kosovo/a, 261; and Ukraine and V4, 235, 292; and Visegrad states, 135, 149, 155n43, 259, 285
Atlantic Alliance. *See* NATO (North Atlantic Treaty Organization)
August Coup, in Moscow, 1991, 23, 24, 27, 137
Austria, 8, 19, 62n73, 75, 82, 85, 112, 115, 123, 142, 167, 173, 174, 179, 180, 181, 195n128, 206, 223, 258, 259, 264, 269, 285, 288, 289, 295; and Bratislava Summit (1990), 8, 9, 10; Central European Initiative, 99n119, 258, 283; and opposition to Central European

Jospin, Lionel, 112, 114, 121, 128n76. *See also* France
Jourová, Věra, 177
Juncker, Jean-Claude, 208, 259

Kaczyński, Jarosław, 161, 211, 238, 249n126
Kadlečíková, Mária, 150
Karácsony, Gergely, 213
Keane, John, 29n4
Keleti (Budapest train station), 199. *See also* "migrant crisis"
Kennan, George, 132
Kennedy, John F., 48
Kenny, Enda, 214n4
Kerch Strait, 236
King Jan of Luxembourg, 38
King Kazimierz, 38
King Robert of Anjou, 38
Kirch, Anna-Lena, 263
Kiska, Andrej, 177
Klaus, Václav, 125n15, 139, 280; and Central European Free Trade Agreement, 57, 74–75, 77, 145, 260; and Crimea, 270n18; as Czechoslovak finance minister, 280; as Czech president, 175; as Czech prime minister, 37, 65, 67, 99n111, 280, 282, 285; opposing Visegrad/unilateral advancement of Czech Republic, 57, 60n13, 68–69, 73–77, 106–7, 139, 142, 260, 280; and Slovakia/relations with Vladimír Mečiar, 69, 71, 75; as speaker, Czech parliament, 10; supporting Visegrad/common foreign policies, 37, 147, 153, 175, 264
Klímová, Rita, 61n38
Kocourek, Martin, 181
Kolossov, Vladimir, 136
Kořan, Michal, 79, 171
Korbonski, Andrzej, 25
Korea. *See* South Korea
Kosovo/a, 109, 187–88, 197n168, 197n173, 261, 268, 272n40, 288

Kostov, Ivan, 94
Kováč, Michal, 68, 73, 91, 92, 280, 287
Kraków, 168, 223, 281, 289, 294. *See also* Cracow
Kraków Summit (2021), 294
Kraków Visegrad Summit (1991), 46, 48, 72, 137
Kroměříž Declaration, 166, 168, 169, 191n42, 223, 253, 257, 290
Krugman, Paul, 210
Kuehnl, Karel, 244n31
Kukan, Eduard, 108, 110, 280
Kundera, Milan, 16, 26, 280
Kurdi, Alan. *See* "migrant crisis"
Kusý, Miroslav, 115
Kwaśniewski, Alexander, 56, 85, 89, 120, 127n67, 264, 281

L-159 training jets, 225
Lada, Josef, 133
Langoš, Ján, 72
Lantos, Tom, 82
Latin alphabet, 43
Latvia, 22, 33n78, 289
Lavrow, Sergei, 196n141
Lexa, Ivan, 68, 96n19
Libya, 207, 208–09, 229, 246n72. *See also* "migrant crisis"
Liehm, A. J., 118
Lithuania, 22, 33n78, 45, 120, 237, 240, 284, 289
Lithuanian Soviet Socialist Republic, 21
Litomyšl, Czech Republic, 82, 286
Los Angeles Times, 55
Lower or Royal Palace (of Visegrád), 36, 39, 40
Luxembourg, 48, 114, 139, 153, 173, 289

Macedonia, 186, 201
Macron, Emmanuel, 172, 207, 258, 294. *See also* France
MacShane, Denis, 211
"mad cow disease," 145

ABOUT THE AUTHOR

RICK FAWN is a professor of international relations at the University of St Andrews in the United Kingdom and a specialist on international security, with a geographic concentration on the former communist space. He has conducted research in almost all post-communist states, from the Baltic, through Central Europe to Southeastern Europe, and across Russia, the Caucasus, and Central Asia.

His publications include thirteen books, such as *International Organizations and Internal Conditionality: Making Norms Matters* (2013), and, as editor, *Globalising the Regional: Regionalising the Global* (2009). He has authored dozens of refereed book contributions and journal articles, such as in *Democratization, European Security, Europe-Asia Studies, Geopolitics, International Affairs,* and *Orbis.*

He has also made numerous invited contributions to governments, international nongovernmental organizations, international organizations, and media and has given many lectures and keynote addresses in the UK and overseas.

Fawn has served recurrent terms as director of interdisciplinary region-focused research centers. He has received many research grants and has run many large collaborative research and training grants, such as from Britain's Economic and Social Research Council/Arts and Humanities Research Council, and FP7 Marie Curie ITN and EU Horizon grants from the European Commission.

Milton Keynes UK
Ingram Content Group UK Ltd.
UKHW041510011124
450547UK00017B/189

9 781647 125066